Philosophy for Counselling and Psychotherapy

Also by Alex Howard and published by Palgrave

Challenges to Counselling and Psychotherapy

Philosophy for Counselling and Psychotherapy

Pythagoras to Postmodernism

ALEX HOWARD

Published by
PALGRAVE
Houndmills, Basingstoke, Hampshire RG21 6XS and
175 Fifth Avenue, New York, N.Y. 10010
Companies and representatives throughout the world

PALGRAVE is the new global academic imprint of
St. Martin's Press LLC Scholarly and Reference Division and
Palgrave Publishers Ltd (formerly Macmillan Press Ltd).

ISBN-13: 978-0-333-75098-8   paperback
ISBN-10: 0-333-75098-5   paperback
ISBN-13: 978-0-333-92624-6   hardcover
ISBN-10: 0-333-92624-2   hardcover

This book is printed on paper suitable for recycling and
made from fully managed and sustained forest sources.
Logging, pulping and manufacturing processes are
expected to conform to the environmental
regulations of the country of origin.

A catalogue record for this book is available
from the British Library.

Editing and origination by
Aardvark Editorial, Mendham, Suffolk

Typesetting by T&A Typesetting, Rochdale

Printed and bound in Great Britain by
CPI Antony Rowe, Chippenham and Eastbourne

Contents

Introduction   vii

Acknowledgements   xvi

1 Pythagoras (*c.* 580–500 BC)   1

2 Heraclitus (*c.* 540–480 BC)   10

3 Sophocles (*c.* 496–406 BC)   17

4 Socrates (*c.* 470–399 BC) and Plato (*c.* 427-347 BC)   24

5 Aristotle (384–322 BC)   39

6 Epicureanism   55

7 Stoicism   62

8 St Augustine (354–430 AD)   80

9 St Thomas Aquinas (1225–1274)   90

10 Niccolo Machiavelli (1462–1527)   98

11 Martin Luther (1483–1546)   106

12 Thomas Hobbes (1588–1679)   115

13 René Descartes (1596–1650)   126

14 Baruch de Spinoza (1632–1677)   138

15 John Locke (1632–1704)   148

16 Gottfried Wilhelm Leibniz (1646–1716)   158

17 George Berkeley (1685–1753)   165

18 David Hume (1711–1776)   172

19 Jean Jacques Rousseau (1712–1778)   182

20 Immanuel Kant (1724–1804)   197

21 Jeremy Bentham (1748–1832)   207

22 Georg Wilhelm Friedrich Hegel (1770–1831)   214

23 Arthur Schopenhauer (1788–1860)   225

24 John Stuart Mill (1806–1873)   238

25 Sören Aabye Kierkegaard (1813–1855)   249

26 Karl Marx (1818–1883)   262

27 Friedrich Wilhelm Nietzsche (1844–1900)   274

28 Sigmund Freud (1856–1939)   287

29 Carl Gustav Jung (1875–1961)   300

30 Ludwig Wittgenstein (1889–1951)   313

31 Martin Heidegger (1889–1976)   327

32 Jean-Paul Sartre (1905–1980)   341

33 What next?   356

    Conclusion   368

    Appendix   375

    Index   377

Introduction

I am relieved that the word 'philosophy' has not yet stopped you reading any further. Philosophers have a reputation for being incomprehensible, irrelevant and naïve. Yet the questions asked by philosophers are the same big questions we all ask from time to time: Questions about how we make sense of our existence; how we are to understand, and achieve, 'happiness'. We wonder whether trying too hard to be happy itself makes us miserable. Perhaps happiness is a by-product of other activity? If we chase it we lose it?

At the turn of a millennium, perhaps, we are more than ever inclined to take stock and ask what our lives amount to, who we are beneath pretences, where we are going, where we should be going?

For people in distress, questions like this can be charged with particular, practical urgency. Philosophers have been chewing on them for at least two and a half thousand years. Children occasionally nudge towards them, before their inherent curiosity is papered over by the certificates needed to take them to the more serious life of work, shopping and social status.

The big philosophical questions about life, and its meaning, are not medical matters. They are not solely, or even primarily, psychological questions. They cannot be squeezed into the narrower therapy agendas of contemporary psychology. Therefore, this book will try to show why care workers, and clients taking stock of their lives, could benefit by looking beyond the therapy literature of the last fifty or one hundred years.

When philosophers ask questions of interest only to other philosophers they do themselves, and philosophy as a whole, a grave disservice. The Greeks knew better. They knew that philosophy should be asking the questions that, self-evidently, mattered to all of us. They knew that the subject should interconnect with, and underpin, every other human study and that, if it were serious, it should have important, daily, practical consequences for the way all of us thought, felt, chose, acted and interacted with the people around us.

So what *is* philosophy? Here is a simple answer: *It is what you end up doing if you keep on asking questions about the basis of previous answers.* Inquisitive children keep on asking why. Eventually they may therefore ask philosophical questions without realising it. At this stage, they may well be advised to stop asking questions, just accept what they are told, and do what is required of them. I, certainly, learned at school that if you kept on questioning answers already given, teacher impatience could grow. I was told to accept a few assumptions or advised that 'not many people ask that'.

When I discovered that a few were actually allowed to go on asking awkward questions in higher education and that this was called philosophy I could not believe my good fortune. The psychology I studied with it seemed deeply disappointing in comparison.

Eventually, I came to the conclusion that the psychology that could not withstand the interrogation from philosophy did not deserve to survive. Little, therefore, was left of the psychology I had learned after the philosophy I had been taught had rolled over it. A great deal of contemporary psychology seemed alarmingly ignorant of social and cultural history. It made assumptions about identity, purpose and methodology without considering the basis of these assumptions and what alternatives existed. It begged too many questions. It presupposed a body of knowledge, skill and a capacity for objectivity that it did not possess. It *professed* to a range of professional services that it could not in fact provide.

Philosophical questioning does not demolish everything. But it clears the ground so that stronger varieties of ideas can grow and prosper. In the following pages, therefore, I shall gather together the voices of many philosophers who have something to say that, I believe, is of particular use to people trying to make sense of their lives or who are helping clients take stock. Readers will, of course, make their own individual judgements about who and what is most, and least, relevant. I will not hide my own views. But I do not imagine, or expect, that everyone will share them.

Counselling and other professional 'care packaging' have become one of the cultural phenomena of our time. Counsellors and professional carers have, for many, replaced priests; they follow accident and emergency services and are routinely included by the media within the journalist's bundle of expected (but often queried) remedies to many diverse problems. Many categories of staff in health and social care professions now find that 'counselling skills' are an important component of their work. They claim, or seek to acquire, skills in counselling. 'Counselling', once rare, now appears everywhere. Thousands call themselves counsellors, or practitioners of counselling skills. Counsellor training has grown correspondingly, with a maze of courses and an enormous choice of textbooks and journals. Before 1985 there was almost nothing published in the UK. It is tempting, then, to conclude that counselling is a recent activity and that it has only existed on any scale for a few decades.

A particular family of industries has grown and, along with it, a choice of vocabularies, libraries and halls of fame. Counsellors and psychotherapists[1] train within specific schools, adopting preferred models, according to the teachings of certain favourite counselling gurus, personalities and theoreticians. All this is well known and documented. So what is there new to be said? Do we need another theory of counselling or another school?

In my view it is time to take stock, and look at the ground and context within which all these schools operate. Counselling tends to focus on individuals, and what goes on within and between them. I want to examine the depth and strength of the cultural and philosophical roots of this activity. How do our own struggles to stay sane, disciplined, determined, motivated and inspired compare with the efforts of our ancestors? How much history is worth unearthing? How far back shall we go? Does a movement which seems so young have any history at all?

When people tell the story of counselling, they tend to begin their tale with Carl Rogers in the 1950s. Those who talk of psychotherapy more often start with Sigmund Freud from around 1900. More recently we have been offered 'counselling psychology', a term which appeared only a few years ago but is rapidly developing its own literature.

My own view, previously expressed,[2] is that talking treatments currently practice on inadequate foundations. Therefore I plan to work on an altogether larger canvas, going back not fifty or one hundred, but two and a half thousand years. My story of counselling will begin with the classical humanist culture of Ancient Greece. How so?

People were trying to make sense of their lives, and give and receive support, long before Rogers, Freud and his contemporaries. Is our current expertise really so great that we can afford to ignore these earlier efforts? Within the natural sciences, twentieth-century knowledge often makes earlier theorising obsolete. If our ancestors from two hundred, five hundred or two thousand years ago visited us they would

be overawed and overwhelmed by the scale of our technical competence and scientific understanding. We know so much more about how
bodies work and we can pamper, amuse and empower ourselves with
gadgetry that our ancestors could not have even imagined.

Our science and technology have undoubtedly advanced, and we
now know far more about the technology of, say, bridge building, than
our ancestors ever knew. Yet what about the building of the (metaphor-
ical yet even more vital) 'bridges' between ourselves and other people?
Would our great-grandparents be so impressed and overawed with our
moral sense? Our self-awareness? Our self-discipline? Our ability or
willingness to co-operate, communicate, give and receive support?
Here, we might admit, progress is far less spectacular, less obvious, altogether less likely to impress visitors from any time and place. We have
missile technology rather than wooden clubs but are we thereby less
likely to kill each other? The twentieth century saw more scientific
progress, *and* more human bestiality, than any previous generation of
(in)humanity. Our technology astounds, and we are in many ways
smarter and more knowledgeable. But it is not so certain that we are
more wise, compassionate or sensitive. Neither can we confidently
believe that we are more co-operative, communicative, supportive and
constructive with each other.

Consequently, I believe there are a wide range of thinkers, far
removed from here and now, who still have a great deal to offer on the
subjects of identity, co-operation, meaning, love and wisdom. In the
following pages I have selected several dozen of these, and I offer the
reader those observations that seem to me most relevant and helpful.
Professionals providing care to others, and clients in receipt of such
support, may equally be interested in exploring ways in which people
have sought to make sense of themselves and their options. How do
we help and hinder one another? It is a big enough question, and
people have been considering it for generations. It seems rather unwise
to imagine that all the interesting answers are confined to the last one
hundred years.

Some of the people I have selected wrote beautifully, simply and
clearly. These I have quoted extensively. They speak for themselves, and
I merely select what seems to me most relevant. With other writers,
their ideas are more impressive than their language and style. Here I
have felt the need to explain and summarise far more. I seek, thereby,
to attract and arouse both the general reader and would-be providers of
human care and support.

The relevance of some philosophers to daily life and practice will be obvious and easy to appreciate. Sometimes, however, we will explore ideas that seem strange, unreal and irrelevant to present-day concerns. There is an important reason for this: Staying with the familiar prevents us from escaping from current presuppositions, metaphors, mind-sets and habits. By escaping from them we start to *see* them for the first time and thereby gain perspective and a chance to choose and assess our assumptions.

Familiar looking individuals help us to go on thinking in our old, habitual, customary ways. Alien thinkers, with ideas that seem irrelevant to present-day life, are more difficult to understand. It is hard work to look *in* on what they thought and it is even more of a challenge to try to look *out* on the world in the way that they did. But if we persevere we really do start to see other worlds. We glimpse our own presuppositions which, until compared with very different alternatives, generally remain invisible. Awareness of our underlying philosophies allows a broader perspective and a more tentative, questioning approach to our lives. It may thereby be a little easier to understand and empathise with those who presume differently from us.

Finally, were we to restrict ourselves to the *familiar* we would miss out on much that is *important* in the history of ideas. Astronomers claim that invisible matter makes up more than 90 per cent of the material universe. Likewise, I would argue that the gravitational pull of 'invisible ideas' determines the movement of much of our own contemporary thinking. The familiar, we will learn, is shaped by the unfamiliar. Philosophy tests and extends mental maps. This is impossible if we only consider that which is habitual, homely, contemporary and immediate within our intellectual tool-kit.

History, when told without point or purpose, can be dull and lifeless. It can consist in dates and details that seem as dead as the people they describe. If it covers too much ground it can be superficial, providing only an illusion of insight about places and people long gone. Our ancestors thought and felt in words very different from ours, with different questions, assumptions and prejudices. We may think we know something about them, but what we learn is inevitably constructed and filtered through our own circumstances and understandings of what words mean and what matters. How, then, can we really make a coherent connection with someone who died hundreds of years ago?

History gets written and rewritten by each generation, from its own priorities and perspectives, for its own purposes. One person's or party's history may differ from another's. Given all these problems, and limitations, why bother with history? And what history? Of whom? Who selects? And why?

Authors, of course, have to be the arbiters of the choices they make. But, if they wish to interest an audience, their selection cannot be arbitrary. I have picked individuals whose ideas will help readers make sense of talking programmes and other forms of care here and now. The result, I hope, will be that care agendas will be observable from a broader perspective and readers will thereby be able to develop a wider and more profound sense of their identity, opportunities and limitations.

History matters insofar as what people once said, did and cared about is relevant to what we are doing and worrying about now. Events may not repeat themselves, but underlying principles of sanity and folly, truth and lies, love and indifference may not change so much. Hopefully we do not live in the past; but much of the past may live on in us whether we realise it or not. Not all the past is over and gone. It is alive, present, active and shaping the future right now. It can provide angles, ideas and insights about both an actual present and possible futures.

History is part of our story; part of the way in which we make sense of where we are. It helps us envision a future. Counsellors know this in relation to individual clients, and encourage them to explore those parts of their own past that are not at all over and gone. The counselling movement, equally, can take stock of itself and sharpen its practice by becoming more aware of its own historical influences.

The philosophy I am presenting is organised in strict chronological order. The time sequence is crucial. It is not arbitrary in the way that, for example, an alphabetical sequence would have been. First-rate philosophers cannot be moved backwards or forwards in time. What they say is informed by those who came before them. Their ideas instruct, inspire and incense those who come after. Locke could not possibly have come after Hume. Kant could not have come before. If they had been born in a different sequence, then, given their intelligence and ability, what they would have said would have been very different.

This survey does not, of course, require a comprehensive study of two and a half thousand years of history. I could not write it, and those with an interest in counselling and other care professions would have no reason, or wish, to read it. But the best of our ancestors, as we shall see, still have much to teach us. If we try to learn from them, we can develop a broader, deeper vision of therapeutic talk and action, its problems and its possibilities. At the end there will, of course, be no final answers and no end in sight. But insight there will be and a sharper, larger picture of where we are now and how we got here.

It has sometimes been claimed that counsellors and care workers do not have to be 'learned', or bother with philosophy or history or culture or models of the self or value systems. Why? Because the counsellor merely listens, facilitates, enables clients to discover for themselves their own values, priorities, direction, esteem, identity and reasons for living.

This notion that the counsellor is just a pair of ears and a warm heart is a dangerous illusion that has much more currency than it deserves. I shall show why as this book proceeds. For the present, let us just note that our ears are, in fact, a part of our brain and we hear nothing with them unless we already have some hardware and software between them. In other words, it is impossible in principle to just listen. Listening is a creative act that cannot take place without utilising the ideas, experiences and values that matter to us. Our verbal and non-verbal responses, likewise, can never just be driven by the client, but, most crucially are formed by our own constructions, values, priorities, ideas and history. This cannot but be influential. To imagine that I enable but do not influence is to show an alarming degree of ignorance and naïvety about the nature of human interaction. In any case, even when counsellors seek to avoid providing answers, they must surely be in the business of assisting clients to ask the right questions? Such facilitation requires considerable knowledge and skill. Socrates may well be a better role model for such activity than Sigmund Freud, Carl Rogers or any other contemporary therapist. More of this later.

Counsellors have been searching for status and respectability, and wish to be seen as professionals with a human face. Of course we already have Queen's Counsellors, counsels for the prosecution and the defence, and the legal profession was itself, once, supposed to help people settle their differences without fighting. Nowadays few can afford the lawyer's fees (but then, how many can afford those of a psychoanalyst?). Also the formality of the law is not seen as sufficient. We want to purchase a friendly human face and be 'enabled'. The priest, for many, is no longer the person to turn to. The counsellor promises to deliver. Is this viable?

Some of the more challenging questions about the nature of counselling were considered in my previous book.[3] I argued that there were too many unanswered questions and too many serious gaps in the way in which therapeutic talk is practised. Having said that there was a great deal missing, I myself felt driven to try to fill in some of the gaps that *Challenges to Counselling and Psychotherapy* identified. My last book raised more questions than answers. This current effort seeks to remedy that imbalance. It does not, of course, offer definitive answers (there are none, even in principle), but it will, I hope, provide material and stimulation of practical use to clients and 'care talkers' today.

Who am I? What do I really know? Where am I going? Where should I go? Here are four fundamental questions of concern to us all. And here, too, are more than thirty of the most important philosophers, from Pythagoras to the present, who have tried to tackle these questions. Many of the philosophers consider these four questions not so much in terms of 'I' but, more so, in relation to 'we'. What, they ask, is the identity of a *society*. What *collective* knowledge, direction and conscience is possible? This broader approach may seem irrelevant to carers who have habitually focussed their attention on particular individuals. We are living in a very 'me-centred' period of history and many counselling and care theorists attend to individual dilemmas and dynamics with scant attention to the society and culture of which we are a part. As you will see, such an individualistic perspective on healing and purpose has been heavily criticised, from the ancient Greeks onwards. Our contemporary individualism is almost an historical aberration and, in my view, a highly regrettable one. If personal and societal health and well-being really are inseparable then there can be no individual solutions that fail to address social, cultural and political concerns.

Philosophy underpins therapy as a means to healing, identity, direction and meaning. It deserves more attention. For that matter, many others have much to offer on the subjects of healing and meaning: poets, painters, essayists, novelists, players and composers. Healing and purpose are far too large and important to be the property of just one group of professionals or care specialists, be they doctors, psychologists, counsellors or whoever. The questions explored in these pages concern and belong to us all. We are the beneficiaries of a long tradition within western[4] philosophy. Its story is exciting, coherent and relevant. Philosophy, to repeat, is what you end up doing if you do not take the first, second or third answer as the 'final' answer. Here is a glimpse of what happened when some of our best western thinkers kept on asking questions. As a seeker, whoever, and wherever you are, you will make with it what you will.

Finally, readers cannot fail to notice that there is not a single female philosopher explored in these pages. I tried very hard to include one or two names but, in the end, I decided to resist tokenism and positive discrimination. Philosophy has always been an extremely male activity and any major female philosophers, if they existed, have been *very* effectively hidden from history. This will change now that women are appearing in strength within this as in other previously male bastions.

One problem for women may be that philosophy tends to attract those who go on asking questions even when the team would like to get on with the job. Women, as superior team players, may find this frustrating. Philosophy can be somewhat unworldly. Our culture encourages women to be down to earth, responsible doers. Philosophy questions, explores, tests, broadens and deepens the foundations of our thinking. Serious philosophy questions with a serious purpose. Decadent philosophy questions in order to undermine all activity without putting anything in its place. Philosophy, at its worst, is a kind of male intellectual vandalism that serves no positive purpose at all. A female intelligence, I believe, will be more inclined to resist this tendency and should be welcomed.

Alex Howard, February 2001
Email: consult@alexhoward.demon.co.uk

Notes

1. The words are often used interchangeably with uncertain clarity of definition.
2. Alex Howard, *Challenges to Counselling and Psychotherapy*, Macmillan, 1996.
3. Ibid.
4. Apart from the occasional pointer, I have confined myself to western philosophy, not just for reasons of space but, more honestly, because I am not personally equipped to give eastern philosophies the version of this book that, I am sure, they deserve.

Acknowledgements

The author and publishers wish to thank Blackwell Publishers and Dr Heidegger, son and heir of Martin Heidegger, for permission to quote from *Being and Time*. Thanks also to Max Niemeyer Verlag who retain copyright of the German original of *Sein und Zeit*; to Routledge for permission to quote extracts from C.G. Jung's *Modern Man in Search of a Soul* and J.P. Sartre's *Being and Nothingness*.

Every effort has been made to trace all the copyright holders but if any have been inadvertently overlooked the publishers will be pleased to make the necessary arrangements at the first opportunity.

Chapter 1

Pythagoras (*c.* 580–500 BC)

Key Points

▓ Pythagoras was convinced that fulfilment and peace of mind came from understanding the harmony of the universe. This was best achieved by music and mathematics

▓ We found ourselves only within the patterns, coherence and integrity of existence. The underlying design of life was unravelled, not just by words, but primarily by numbers. The language of the universe was mathematics

▓ Mathematics and meditation were seen as equally important as means of personal development and aesthetic understanding

▓ Pythagoras discovered simple numerical relationships between musical notes in harmony. Patterns of numbers and harmonies of sounds were as one. Mathematics became fused with the aesthetics of music and would one day unravel the 'music of the heavenly spheres'.

Application

● In a postmodern era, mathematicians and scientists explore 'theories of everything' just as (many) artists and writers abandon the humanist agenda and retreat into subjectivity and fragmentation. (See Chapter 33 and Conclusion)

● Machines simulate the activity of counsellors and the evolution of life forms

● Machines generate structures that appear organic rather than crudely geometric

● Mathematics is generally seen as disenchanting, alienating and irrelevant to our essential humanity. Pythagoras thought otherwise. Recently emerging evidence supports a Pythagorean vision of harmony

● Mathematical forecasts concerning risks and likely human choices are often more accurate than human 'intuitive' guesswork.

What can an ancient Greek, better known by schoolchildren for his right-angled triangles, add to our understanding of compassion and co-operation in the twenty first century? How can numbers help us understand other people? Pythagoras believed that, eventually, mathematics would help us gain insight into ourselves and others, not just into triangles and musical notes. Human geometry? This sounds utterly strange and ridiculous to modern ears. Mathematics (you will be pleased to know?) disappears again in almost all the chapters following this one. Pythagoras sits in a class by himself and my editor was, perhaps understandably, concerned that he would stop you reading any further (to more familiar territory). Yet contemporary mathematics does seem to be catching up on some of Pythagoras' predictions. So I have fought to keep a chapter for him.

Pythagoras lived on the island of Samos around 532 BC. He advised that we should abstain from beans, not pick up what was fallen, not touch a white cock, not break bread, and so on. The list is longer, but each item appears equally arbitrary and absurd to modern eyes. It did not appear so to the disciples who joined his religious order. So why go on with this? Many other lists of instructions, equally arbitrary, have been made in the subsequent two and a half thousand years. Each was dutifully and reverentially followed by those who wanted a set of rules to live by and who could not, or would not, think too hard for themselves. Needless to say, there are similar inventories and injunctions today. Which of our own will be an object of mirth and incredulity among the conventionally wise in two or three hundred years from now? The moral of the story is that, even among the biggest names, that tiniest minority who are remembered after many centuries, only a small part of what they believed is likely to gain much respect or interest today.

We, or mathematicians at least, are still impressed with Pythagoras' realisation that the square of the hypotenuse of a right-angled triangle is equal to the sum of the squares of the two adjacent sides. This kind of thing has also been sending most schoolchildren into a daze of indifference ever since Pythagoras hit upon it. It may not interest every counsellor or client either. So what other angles on Pythagoras are worth sharing?

Pythagoras and his colleagues became quite literally rapturous in their excitement about numbers when they began to discover numerical formulae that could be used to describe fundamental patterns and regularities. Triangles were exciting not because the world is full of right-angled triangles, but because via triangulation, computation within a triangular frame, calculations and measurements could be made that were impossible via any other method. Still more exciting were the relationships discovered between octaves and the lengths of the various musical strings that produced them.

To the Pythagoreans, all this suggested that, via numbers, we could determine the rules that governed the operations of, and the relations between, the phenomena of our lives. It was like breaking beneath the surface of appearances to discover the structures and principles that described and interlinked our experiences. Via mathematics, Pythagoras was convinced, we would discover the innermost workings of the universe. The language that gave access to the deep structure of the cosmos was not Greek, or Latin, or, as in our own day, English. It was mathematics. Its currency was not the letter, it was the numeral. For Pythagoras, in the beginning, was not so much the Word, his *logos* was Number. The Pythagoreans concluded that, if we sought to connect to the roots of reality, we needed to learn about mathematics. We would sing of the harmonies of existence, and mathematical equations would provide the score sheets. Music, mathematics, mysticism: the three Ms, the Three-in-One. This is hardly a fashionable road to personal development in a new millennium; but perhaps we should look again? Mastery of a musical instrument is considered to be highly therapeutic; instrumentalists routinely refer to the central place of their play as a source of meaning, inspiration and as a part of their identity. Musical and mathematical ability also appear to correlate positively. Perhaps we are just far too fragmented and blinkered in our views of what is relevant to personal development and well-being?

Certainly Pythagoras thought that the time would come when, in order to understand how we interconnected and related, we would not seek 'intuitive' answers 'inside' ourselves. Rather we would discover the true inner workings of the dance of life via mathematics.

Since Newton, as we shall see, the notion that maths is a royal road to understanding has been ever more borne out by evidence. To understand atoms, molecules, electrons, quarks, is not to get down to the basic 'grit' of their (would-be) 'substance'. It is not to give a visual verbal account as though we were looking through a microscope. It is to understand the equations that analyse their interrelationships. To see how these fundamental phenomena work is not to see them in the literal sense, but to 'see', as in to grasp intellectually, via mathematics, the equations that describe them. Objects 'are' insofar as they relate to other objects, and the relationships, described by number, are more fundamental, firm and long lasting than the objects which they interlink.

There is an important lesson here for those who wish to make better 'contact' with a basic fundamental 'core' self. Such psychological atomism may well be as misplaced as any other search for finally fundamental entities. Perhaps there is nothing finally fundamental, except for the (mathematical) principles that alone make sense of the emergence of patterned activity? 'Self', we imagine, is some sort of non-physical essence about which nothing whatsoever of interest and importance can be said by mathematicians whose methods apply only to inanimate, physical objects. But what if 'self' is an emergent property of the awesomely vast intricacy that is a body interacting with its environment? What if the patterns and processes and principles governing all this activity require, as they do, mathematics to describe them? Is maths then so mundane and so irrelevant to 'higher' phenomena? Perhaps not.

Numbers, and the formulae that organise them, are on the march in all the natural sciences. Progress is measured, just as Pythagoras predicted, according to the degree to which subjects can be not just quantified but also qualified, and thereby explained and understood, by mathematics. Social science, too, tries to emulate these natural sciences, and claims to be 'progressing' insofar as mathematical equations can be introduced into our ideas about social and human systems. People, too, are tagged by more and more numbers, but currently it is thought that to be human is to err, and to prefer words to numbers. Humanity, we believe, requires that we seek to avoid being boiled down to numbers and formulae. These, undeniably, comprise an ever-growing part of our lives, but it is generally thought that they kill life more often than adding any colour to it.

At present we still imagine that the best possible analysis of the 'psyche' (whatever that is) is to be done via words, talking treatments, introspection, and, best of all, within intensive therapy sessions using the skills of a qualified therapist. Yet numbers are creeping closer, numbers describe the double helix, determining our biological blueprint. Numbers, enough of them, construct the activity of everyone's word processor. Numbers run text to speech software, voice recognition software. Raw number crunching can defeat world chess champions.

Numbers count. Numbers even produce machines pretending to be counsellors. Numbers govern cyber-creatures that evolve, speak, interact and respond well to positive nurturing strategies. They operate according to hundreds of cyber-genes providing hundreds of trillions of genetic combinations. Numbers show that the pattern of growth of cities is similar to that of some bacterial colonies. This does not make us the same as bacteria; but it shows that we share similar opportunities and constraints within the deeper structures and essences of existence. Mathematical formulae can be better predictors of what a person might do, and what we ought to do next, than any imagined journey 'inside' to consult our own intuition. Is this person a suicide risk? A formula-driven evaluation of their (checklisted) past history may provide a more reliable assessment of the dangers than an intuitive judgement drawn from a more personal, individual yet incomplete discussion. How far am I at risk from whatever it may be that concerns me? An actuary will provide a more accurate answer than I can when I consult my own fantasies and the neuroses of my neighbour.

There are a growing number of examples of mathematical analysis providing better predictions of likely human choices than individual human judgement. Advertisers do not need to do therapy with you to find out what you are likely to buy. They will have analysed your position within the consumer marketplace and will be able to make frighteningly accurate assessments of your most likely 'profile' of opinions, values, possessions, pastimes and habits.

In more academic matters decisions are made according to numbers. You want to be accepted as an undergraduate at a prestigious university? A prose account of your abilities will be important, but unless your average exam results are higher than the threshold grade you will not even be considered.

Numbers, in enough quantity, offer qualities of their own. Formulae describe interrelationships with more subtlety, succinctness, sophistication and certainty than pages of verbal equivalents. Numbers do not, of course, substitute for words on all occasions. No one ever believed they would. Pythagoras was entirely happy with Greek as a language of everyday living. But when it came to the underlying principles of life, numbers, he thought, were needed. Numbers above all.

In this respect Pythagoras is far from being ancient and obsolete. His observations look increasingly potent and, to some, promising, while to others, highly threatening and alienating. He is one of the very earliest of the Greek philosophers, yet the vision of Pythagoras may, in its fullest expression and realisation, still await us in the future. His triangles may remind us of dull days divorced from play and life. Yet he glimpsed a time when human joy at the harmony of nature would become fused with intellectual analysis of numbers in nature. In recent years mathematics has actually begun to fulfill Pythagorean dreams. Mathematics can analyse forms and patterns in many kinds of object and organism. Formulae can 'generate' trees as easily as triangles. The

key is to find the rules that govern the construction of a particular form
or pattern. 'Soul', essence, is not thereby destroyed; it is revealed and
celebrated. The mathematician searches for the most 'beautiful', elegant
and powerful equations. Perhaps truth and beauty really are one?

One of the tragedies of contemporary life is that mathematics, our
most powerful language, tool and medium of thought and understanding, seems so remote, intimidating and irrelevant to so many
people. This is true even among those who, in every other respect,
may see themselves as cultivated, civilised and sophisticated. Yet to
understand maths is not simply to engage in a dry, arid and abstract
intellectual exercise. It is, in however small a way, to grasp, feel and
inhale some of the rhythms of existence. It is to see how phenomena
move and interact, not lie dead, dull and inert. Pythagoras discovered
simple numerical relationships between musical notes that were in
harmony. The aesthetics of numbers became fused with the aesthetics
of sound. It was, it is, beautiful, awesome in the simplicity underlying
such complexity, and the interconnection between seemingly quite
different phenomena.

As a result, Pythagoras became convinced that similar harmonies
would be discovered everywhere. Mathematics would be the means by
which these patterns and rhythms were uncovered and described. There
was, he felt sure, a 'music of the (heavenly) spheres' which we would
eventually be able to 'hear', not so much with our ears, but via our
intellect and heart. These would be fused together by the mathematics
that, for Pythagoras at least, was a source both of passion and analysis.
Each drove and, respectively, inspired and informed the other.

Via mathematics, we would ultimately get a bearing on the world
around us and, in so doing, arrive at a deeper understanding of
ourselves. We are an integral part of the harmony of the heavenly
spheres. We could not, therefore, expect to gain much insight into
ourselves or anything else if we turned away from the world around us
and merely looked at what we supposed to be 'within'. We would 'find'
ourselves in relationship, not in withdrawal, and therefore within
Orphic temples inspired by Pythagoras there would be study both of
singing and mathematics.

Numbers are generally thought to be too cold, lowly and impersonal
to be of relevance to personal development. Yet Bach put numerical
orderliness to music and we are transported to heaven. Mystics suggest
we stay with just one note in our meditation, one 'OM', in order to
find, by losing, 'ourselves'. So can such people claim to 'have our

number'? Or are such numerical explorations irrelevant to the understanding and development of identity?

Pythagoras' concern for mathematics was passed on among Greek philosophers who considered that a holistic approach to fundamental questions was essential if real wisdom were to be achieved. Hence, above the entrance to Plato's Academy, which operated for over 900 years in the gardens of Academe north west of Athens, was the inscription 'Let no one ignorant of mathematics enter here'.

Can such a statement be of relevance to talking treatments? Clients, surely, are often trying to find, or establish, an underlying coherence, direction, meaning (or *logos* as the Greeks called it) to their lives. The Pythagoreans claimed that such coherence was best revealed via mathematics and that numbers were a necessary, if not sufficient, means of uncovering the shapes of existence. Geometry held all of life together, and we would feel disintegrated and disorderly insofar as we failed to apprehend this underlying *logos*.

The long-lasting insights of Pythagoreans were, unavoidably, mixed in with a mish-mash of what we would now regard as ephemeral nonsense. He is so remote from us in time, his written work has not survived, and followers ascribed views to him that may or may not have been his own. Pythagoreans would study their maths; they would also take care not to stir the fire with an iron, not to eat from a whole loaf, not to pluck a garland, not to let swallows share their roof. And so on.

We need none of this. What we most desperately want are many more teachers of mathematics who can not only explain Pythagoras' theorem, but who can inspire twenty-first-century students so that they, too, feel the excitement, the sense of awe, wonder, reverence, the racing heartbeat, the sweaty palms, the music of existence. A mathematician can feel equations in the way that a musician can feel a symphony. The excitement, joy, appreciation, enrichment of life can be just as great in each case. Moreover the one may not be so very different from the other. But you have to hear it, to feel it, to know it. It is sad that so few can feel the dance of existence, which is to such a large degree the symphony of numbers. Via mathematics we could compete more effectively within the global marketplace. Much more crucially, we could develop a better grasp of the world of which we are a part and, in so doing, experience a deeper reverence and appreciation of the world and our place in it.

❓ Questions

1. When and why are numbers, equations and statistics helpful/a hindrance/ irrelevant, in helping you to understand another human being? Can you think of examples?

2. How far should psychologists, like physicists, use mathematics to express and explore psychological questions?

3. Music is often therapeutic. Faced with maths, most of us feel tense and inadequate. Numerical functions reveal worlds more fantastic than fairytale. How can we join the party?

4. Is it just a coincidence that the author of *Alice in Wonderland* (1865) was also the author of *A Syllabus of Plane Algebraical Geometry* (1860) and *Euclid and His Modern Rivals* (1879)?

EXERCISES

1. Try one or two of the growing library of mathematics and science books for non-mathematicians. Concepts including symmetry, chaos, complexity and n-dimensional space are proving to be fundamental as tools of thought.

2. Ants travel in columns along the shortest route to their food. It is all done by mathematics. Because the shortest route takes the least time, it carries the highest ant density and the strongest ant trail. It is then self-reinforcing. Try to find other examples of seemingly 'coherent', 'intelligent' behaviour governed by numbers. (There are many cases in nature of complex systems evolving according to relatively simple mathematical principles.)

3. Individuals wrongly estimate the dangers around them since they know so little about statistics and the analysis of risk. See if you can attach some numbers to the biggest risks faced by you and your clients.

4. Advertisers employ motivation research specialists who profile personality types and locate individuals within carefully analysed segments of the consumer marketplace. Discuss the strengths and weaknesses of statistical profiling of personality types and contrast with the insights obtainable via individual contact.

Conclusion

Pythagoras sits largely separate from, and outside, the thread of ideas explored in subsequent chapters. This may well change in future years.

Pythagoras would rejoice at the power of mathematics today. As he predicted, complex phenomena emerge from simple properties according to mathematical principles. He would be appalled that most of us still do not appreciate the aesthetic insights and harmonies of mathematics. He would insist that no personal development programme could be complete without mathematics. In this respect, he is ahead of most subsequent philosophers and belongs to the future more than to the past.

We tend to assume that numbers are soul*less* and therefore irrelevant to psychology and our personal lives. But what if soul is an 'emergent' property arising from a universe whose language is number? Pythagoras thought numbers were magical, enchanting and the root/route to the reality of existence of which we were an integral part. Perhaps the future will prove that, for all our current doubts, he was right.

Websites

http://members.aol.com/areoasis/Reviews/pythagoras.html

Bibliography

Christopher Bamford (ed.) *Rediscovering Sacred Science*, Lindisfarne Books, 1994

W.K.C. Guthrie, *A History of Greek Philosophy, Volume I: The Earlier PreSocratics and the Pythagoreans*, 1962 Cambridge University Press

Kenneth Sylvan, *Pythagorean Sourcebook and Library: An Anthology of Ancient Writings Which Relate to Pythagoras and Pythagorean Philosophy*, Guthrie, Phanes Press, 1991

Chapter 2

Heraclitus (*c.* 540–480 BC)

────────────────── **Key Points** ──────────────────

▓ Everything is flux, change, process, becoming something else

▓ It is not that we move through life; life flows through us

▓ We are not so much *in* the world, as *of* the world

▓ Boundaries between 'self' and 'world' are not absolute, but fluid within one interconnected process

▓ Permanence is an illusion; underlying it is... change.

─── *Application* ──────────────────────────

● Clients seek insight into their identity and their relationship with their environment
● Heraclitus offers a holistic vision of self and world that has been explored within a variety of spiritual traditions
● By embracing, rather than resisting, change we may best survive and find inspiration
● The movement and interconnection of existence may inspire awe, humility and reverence.

Pythagoras gives us an understanding of the profound importance of number. Heraclitus is to be remembered because of his appreciation of the significance of 'processes' as opposed to 'objects'. His most momentous idea is the notion that there is nothing at all permanent anywhere in the whole of existence. Everything is flux, change, process, becoming something else. Everything, therefore, is interconnected with everything else since there is no object or thing that has any permanent defined boundary keeping it separate, other and different from its surroundings.

10

Heraclitus observed that one could not step into the same river twice since it was always in process, in flow, always moving on. By implication, and this is what is of significance to contemporary counselling, one could not observe the same 'self' twice. The implication of the Heraclitean view is that 'I' am not some solid essence that can, as it were, be revealed like a glittering diamond. I cannot, via analysis and introspection, remove the mud of defensiveness and delusion that surrounds my 'essential' self. 'I', rather, am more like 'x' in algebra. I am a variable more than a constant. I change in meaning, direction, 'spin' and value according to the context, the circumstances. These, too, are ever changing. I am intimately intermixed with these surroundings. I am not just *in* them; I am *of* them.

The river cannot be extracted from its context since it is both the flow of the water and the context on which it sits and moves. Likewise, 'I' cannot be extracted from, analysed without, or understood independently of, my circumstances. They form and comprise me, and I form and comprise them, just as the soil on which the river flows shapes and is shaped by the movement of water.

Heraclitus offered this profound insight into our lives two and a half thousand years ago and Heidegger, above all, took it up in the twentieth century. Heraclitus' philosophy raises uncertainties concerning what a therapy agenda of finding 'oneself' can actually mean. The idea that we can discover a firm, fixed, authentically solid self becomes problematic. Moreover, can self best be explored, found and developed in a confidential meeting with a stranger? A fish loses its colour and life when taken out of water. Likewise, for Heraclitus, a person's true colours could not be known except within the stream of their own life, with their significant others, environments and routines. Knowledge of this context, by implication, becomes at least as important as information gained from private confessions concerning the client's inner stream of consciousness.

If you accept Heraclitus' philosophy, then the danger of exploring client agendas outside the actual stream of their life is that the activity of therapy can become somewhat 'dry'. The therapist certainly does not get scorched or soaked by the client's circumstance because the fire and flow of their life is described and analysed rather than actually entered and experienced. The therapist is a non-participant and thereby gains, and loses, all the insight and understanding that is available from the observer who does not directly observe anything. Many therapists claim that one of the most important ways in which they can assist is to 'be there' for the client. What they mean by this is that they are 'there' in imagination only, they seek to empathise with the client and feel with them. But they are never, *in fact*, there with the client, as an active participant in the client's daily circumstances. Therapy is, almost always, confined to the therapy room. It is a one-to-one encounter that remains both confidential and disconnected from the actual course, content and context of a person's life. This current and circumstance shapes and is shaped by the person yet the therapist never actually engages directly with it at all. The therapist, therefore, never allows himself or herself to be directly shaping of, and shaped by, the particulars of the client's existence.

There can be no denying that to be out of sight may allow some insight. We all need to withdraw at times in order to gain perspective. But how much is also lost? There is no independent 'self' that moves into, or out of, its life and its circumstances. Life flows through us. It scours, scores us and changes us continually. The river is the water, the riverbank, the rocks, sand and the contours that allow the river to be, at present, like 'this' rather than like 'that'. How can a river be just the water? It cannot. Similarly, how can a 'self' be just this body or this 'awareness'? All the surrounding paraphernalia of self does not merely surround self; they are, in part, a part of self, part of what we are, at present. Thus, when key people and circumstances of our lives change or disappear, we may sense a loss of self.

And here is the paradox: to be alive, to be aware and awake, is to be conscious not of a fixed and unchanging 'me' at all. Rather it is to inhale, in each moment, something new and mysterious, and to exhale and lose something old, familiar, precious and a part of what I had thought was 'me'. If Heraclitus is right, then it is not enough to say that I am *in* a process of change and movement; I *am* a process of change and movement. Therefore there can be no final 'finding' of myself, no certainty of self-awareness and insight. Instead there is just a continual loss of what we might have hoped we could keep as us and ours. A continual gaining of what we do not understand; what disturbs; mystifies and seems to undermine the self we thought we were.

If Heraclitus is right, we are events more than objects. We are flames that burn, throw light, take in, give out and expire. We move and change, we become attached to what seems fixed and final, only to see it move on. We may build up a mountainous, and momentous, 'self-awareness' of who and what we are. We may sit astride our 'mountain' with pride, or feel weighed down and crushed by it. Either way, mountains, too, move up and move on as they are eroded away. From our perspective they may look permanent. From the context of geological time, mountains rise up and blow away pretty much as the water in the sea does.

Heraclitus' views are unorthodox from a western perspective yet within eastern traditions the view of life as flow, process, a 'dance of Shiva', is the conventional wisdom. As our understanding deepens of the processes of existence, we see that all that we thought to be permanent and unchanging is not. Atoms do not exist as independent, 'gritty', fundamental entities. They are in continual relationship, 'wavy' rather than 'stuffy'. Their 'edges' are 'smeared' across space. Stars do not blaze indefinitely. They coalesce, burn, expire or explode, and coalesce again. Most of the elements exist only as debris from the explosion of stars. We are stardust, not just metaphorically, but literally. The science of all this is more fantastic than fairytale, and more beautiful.

Heraclitus' science, of course, did not have the benefits of the two and a half thousand years of hard labour that has gone on since his death. His *principle* of change and flux holds well; but the *details*,[1] as he understood them, have not all worn so successfully with the passing of the years. He was influenced by ideas of earth, air, fire and water as fundamental phenomena, and seemed to imagine that there is a hierarchy between them:

36. To souls, it is death to become water; to water, it is death to become earth. From earth comes water, and from water soul.

Hence there are various observations made about the 'wet' or 'dry' state of souls that, after so many centuries are curious and amusing rather than informative:

117. A man, when he gets drunk, is led stumbling along by an immature boy, not knowing where he is going, having his soul wet.

118. A dry (desiccated) soul is the wisest and best

The notion that the basic elements consisted of earth, air, fire and water was further developed by Empedocles (*c.* 490–430 BC) and Democritus (*c.* 460–370 BC). It became the 'common sense' of many (western and oriental) thinkers right through to the seventeenth century (AD!). These four elements were seen to be basic to the make up of the natural world and also to the physical and psychological components of human beings. For the doctor, from Hippocrates onwards, the elements manifested as four bodily 'humours': blood, phlegm, choler (yellow bile) and melancholy (black bile). Physical and psychological health depended on these humours operating in harmony.

Different personalities were formed according to which of these elements most predominated. Hence the phlegmatic personality, stolid, undemonstrative and apathetic, was overendowed with phlegm. Excess blood produced an optimistic, excitable, enthusiastic temperament. Dark blood gave rise to melancholy. Too much yellow bile produced an irritable and jaundiced personality. `

Heraclitus' principle of underlying unity was of more value than the four elements, but he had very little useful detail with which to furnish any of these ideas. He was one of many who have, over the centuries, thought that change within an underlying unity is more fundamental than solidity in diversity:

> 50. When you have listened, not to me but to the Law (*logos*), it is wise to agree that all things are one.

In the nineteenth century the philosopher Hegel was the most important and most influential supporter of this view. Hegel, as we shall see later, explored the notion that this overall unity existed in a state of dynamic tension, and Heraclitus, too, anticipated this:

> 51. That which differs with itself is in agreement: harmony consists of opposing tension, like that of the bow and the lyre.

We may look around and see a world of divergence, opposites, conflict, fragmentation, polarity. But beneath these surfaces were principles that brought the fragments and polarities together or, rather, revealed that everything was already an interconnected and harmonious unity. Versions of Hegelian integration provided the dominant way of looking at self and world in the nineteenth century; they then fell from prominence and we became, once again, more atomistic and mechanistic in our conception of how the fundamentals of existence were organised. The pendulum is moving once again, but, wherever its swing, time moves on, and overall, we may hope, the sophistication of the philosophy improves as well.

❓ Questions

1. What metaphors and images do you have of 'yourself'? Does anything come to mind or does this strike you as a 'strange' question?
2. What can you think of that is fixed and unchanging about 'yourself'?
3. What can you think of about yourself that has changed and/or will change? Because of you? Because of changing circumstances?
4. When is it worth asking 'who am I?' When is it best just to get on with the next task in hand? Can you think of a few examples of each?

EXERCISES

1. You, and/or a client, might like to assemble a list of what is important, and *unchanged* in yourself and your circumstances. How do you feel about each item?
2. Compare this with a list of what is important and *different* within and about you compared with five, ten years ago.
3. Make a list of the important items that will be the same and different in five, ten years' time.
4. 'If only...' If only... *what*, yesterday, would have made you a different person? *What*, tomorrow, would make you a different person? Different in what way? What thoughts come to mind? What feelings about the thoughts? Record and share your responses as appropriate.

Conclusion

Change does not imply chaos. Heraclitus thought he could see coherent principles, an underlying *logos*, governing an interconnected movement of existence. His views find important echoes within many Buddhist and Hindu teachings which have explored ways of coping with change more systematically than many western philosophies. Christian teaching has tended to strive for an 'anchor' of permanence via a patriarchal deity. Heraclitus and many oriental philosophers encourage us to swim in a river of change. Deeper still: you are 'dissolved' in the river. You are not *in* the river; you are *of* the river.

Note

1. The extracts that follow are taken from Heraclitus' *Fragments*.

Websites

http://home.fia.net/~n4bz/gsr/gsr7.htm

Bibliography

R.D. McKirahan, *Philosophy Before Socrates: An Introduction With Text and Commentary*, Hackett Publishing Company, 1994

M. Ring, *Beginning with the Pre-Socratics*, Mayfield, US, 1987

T.M. Robinson, (tr.) *Heraclitus*, University of Toronto Press, 1991

D. Sweet, *Heraclitus: Translation and Analysis by Heraclitus*, University Press of America, 1995

C.C.W. Taylor (ed.) *From the Beginning to Plato* (*History of Philosophy*, Vol. 1), Routledge, 1997

Chapter 3

Sophocles (*c.* 496–406 BC)

_____ **Key Points** _____

▦ Greek tragedy can show a more sophisticated understanding of the human predicament than can contemporary psychology

▦ Storytelling is a valuable medium for exploring psyche and circumstance

▦ Freud was significantly in error in his account of Oedipus. Freud's 'Oedipus Complex' lacks the complex subtlety of the Sophoclean Oedipus

▦ Greek tragedy did not blink before, yet was unbowed by, the harsh reality of human circumstances.

Application

● Contemporary psychology might benefit if it incorporated more of the insights of philosophers and dramatists
● Counselling focuses on the 'internal dynamics' of individuals. It might broaden its scope by exploring more thoroughly the dynamics of human circumstance
● The lessons of the Greek tragedians have been valued for centuries. Perhaps they deserve more attention?

he hath witnessed to mankind that, of all curses which cleave to man, ill counsel is the sovereign curse. (From *Antigone*)

No, for nothing is more hateful than bad counsel. (From *Electra*)

How precious, above all wealth, is good counsel. (From *Antigone*)

How and why shall we live? What is important? What might we die for, and why? It is easier to look more deeply at these perennial questions in times of modest comfort and security. Perhaps there is less room for philosophy and artistry when everyone is farming and fighting? Athens in *c.* 500 BC, with its plentiful slaves, provided some of its elite with time off to reflect.

Both philosophy and drama consider human meaning and purpose. Philosophers question and analyse. Dramatists tell tales. Stories, not theses, have more universal appeal. We engage with flesh and blood characters, not abstract concepts.

Yet, when confronted with a character, real or imagined, how committed shall we be? Shall we just fill in time? May we indulge in dreams and illusions or pander to our prejudices? Or shall we be more serious? Do we want a story that challenges, unsettles, inspires, uplifts, deflates, informs, humours or terrifies? It may do all this to one person within the same play. Messages may assault, emerge, creep up; on audience and author alike. We may sway together in our response, or occupy different worlds of experience. Audience and author may, or not, know if, or where, they are being taken.

One Greek tragedy passed into psychotherapy via Sigmund Freud. It is the story of Oedipus. The 'Oedipus Complex', as described by Freud, has disconnected us from the complexity of Oedipus, as told by Sophocles. This matters a great deal because Freud's version does not match, in either scale or sophistication, the Oedipus of Sophocles. Therapy thereby lacks a sense of history and is the poorer for making so little use of our rich cultural heritage.

According to Freud, Oedipus sought to kill his father and have sex with his mother. According to Freud, all men are like this. Sexually jealous of their fathers, they 'unconsciously', seek to murder them and make sexual conquest of their mothers.

For several decades, intelligent, sophisticated opinion assumed that this view of males was right, since Freud had said so. With hindsight, the Oedipus Complex looks as simple and as silly as, for example, Pythagoras' notions that we should abstain from beans, not pick up what was fallen and not touch a white cock. Very few of us want to kill our fathers or have sex with our mothers. We have sexual feelings and we feel angry, murderously so, at times. But we do not seriously, or slightly, plan to murder our parents, for all that we may fantasise the effect on us of their non-existence.

The fact that we did not think as Freud claimed did not greatly matter to Freud. His answer was that we *did* think this way, but *unconsciously*. The difference between thinking something 'unconsciously' and not thinking it at all was never made clear. But Freud presented us with an invisible inner world which made us both 'deep' and 'mysterious'. This was attractive to those who feared that in reality, and not just in appearance, they were shallow and dull. Consequently, awkward questions about Freud were postponed for several decades. The Freudian narrative, combining depth, drama and detached, impartial, 'science' captured the imagination (and cash) of sections of the western intelligentsia for several decades. More of this later.

Freud's version of the Sophoclean Oedipus is fundamentally and profoundly wrong and misses the whole point of the narrative. In the original story, Oedipus does not know that the person he kills is his father and has no idea that the woman he marries is his mother. He evidently has no intention of harming the one or marrying the other. Yet this is what happens. Why?:

> What is revealed to Oedipus by the Oracle at the end is not his forbidden sexual and aggressive longings, but the fact that he has been unable to escape his predicted fate.
> What is overwhelmingly tragic, is not that he desires his mother and wants to kill his father, but that he has committed all these ignominies while believing himself to be doing all the right things. (van Deurzen-Smith, 1997)[1]

So, a 'good enough' man, tries 'hard enough', or very hard indeed. But the outcome is not planned, desired or good. Where is justice? Answer? Life is unjust; not always, but often. The singer Leonard Cohen observed: 'Everybody knows that the dice are loaded... everybody knows that the good guys lost.' But this is too simple as well. The fight is never over, as Sophocles knew. We struggle on, but only sometimes do we win; and only sometimes, if ever, do we even know what winning consists of.

Sophocles saw, more than most contemporary therapists, that you might never 'find yourself' and that, if you did, you might not like what you found. You might just find fragments, ruins, debris. Some selves, like some trees, reach full stature and maturity. Many, however, are stunted, uprooted, malnourished, overshadowed, drowned, burned, blown down. There is not enough, or too much, water; too much sand; too many stones. To reach the full potential of our dreams is, in effect, to be *very* lucky.

The moral, I suggest, is that we need radically to change our conception of what comprises growth and maturity. Maturity recognises the reality not just of opportunity, but also of limitation, setbacks, frustration. Good luck, by definition, is relatively unusual. Average luck is the norm and bad luck is common.

This was profoundly understood by Greek tragedians. We could look within; but we should also move on, through the squalls and opportunities of our circumstances.

The heroes of Greek tragedy struggled on. Rarely did they achieve all they sought; rarely, indeed never, did events end happily ever after. Circumstance ruled, but psyche struggled on anyway. Oedipus tried, but ended up killing his father and marrying his mother. Circumstance appeared to make a mockery of him, but this was not really so. He proved himself merely to be a man, no less and no more, a plaything of the Gods, or an irrelevance to them. And is this not really what heroism consists in? Heroism requires struggling in the knowledge that one may very well lose. The evidence of the very real possibility of loss is overwhelming. All around us are littered the casualties of life. Ahead of us? Who knows?

Oedipus was a strong man, a good man, a success, a king, a hero, admired and followed. Then he was almost annihilated. For no particular reason. It transpired that he had been annihilated all along but had imagined otherwise. Circumstances, the whim of the Gods, chance, fortune, whatever, picked him up and hurled him to pieces. He was torn inside out, overwhelmed, flattened. It was not fair. He did what he could. There was no simple happy ending. There was a living human spirit amid a great deal of wreckage. Courage and wisdom were not always equal to the circumstances they faced.

So is this message of the Greek tragedians relevant to contemporary struggles with living? I think it is. Never mind the Oedipus Complex. Get back to Oedipus himself. Get back to Sophocles and others. The teaching of Sophocles is as alive now as ever. Matthew Arnold reflected on the message as he witnessed the sights and sounds of Dover Beach at night and the mood that it stimulated. He placed it into a poem of the same name. I believe it goes deeper into the human condition than too much that is on offer within contemporary care 'packages'. Here is a part. First, the sound:

> Sophocles long ago
> Heard it on the Aegean, and it brought
> Into his mind the turbid ebb and flow
> Of human misery; we
> Find also in the sound a thought,
> Hearing it by this distant northern sea.

Second, the message:

> Ah, love, let us be true
> To one another! For the world, which seems
> To lie before us like a land of dreams,
> So various, so beautiful, so new,
> Hath really neither joy, nor love, nor light,
> Nor certitude, nor peace, nor help for pain;
> And we are here as on a darkling plain
> Swept with confused alarms of struggle and flight,
> Where ignorant armies clash by night.
> (From Matthew Arnold, 'Dover Beach')[2]

Here is a dark vision. Shall we run from it? Shall we wallow in it? How can we use it? The contemporary dream, that sits within the heart of so much counselling, is the hope and belief that we can, and should, achieve happiness, completeness and fulfilment. Yet this is a relatively novel and rather silly expectation. It may well create more misery than joy. What if, instead, we learned to expect frustration as the very warp and weft of life rather than an obstacle to living? Paradoxically, but, on reflection, unsurprisingly, we might be happier more, and more often, if we reduced our expectations of happiness.

We have no entitlement to happiness, although we naturally prefer it, whatever form it may take. Few of us achieve much of our potential; circumstances and our own mistakes make sure of that. With luck and courage we carry our wounds with dignity. We may hope to remain relatively unbowed. But even the heroic among us may easily be flattened. Honour and heroism do not guarantee success but they are admirable anyway. Virtue, knowledge and wisdom promote, but do not ensure, fulfilment. Thus the complexity of the ancient Oedipus. In comparison with the simplistic inanity of the more contemporary Oedipus Complex, it still has much to offer.

❓ Questions

1. Can you think of particular fictional stories that would be helpful if told to particular clients?

2. What examples of contemporary dramatic art can you think of that deal effectively with human tragedy? Would they be worth recommending to particular clients and what might be the benefit?

3. How does/did your training as counsellor or care worker explore the tragic dimensions of human existence? What did you learn?

4. When is preoccupation with tragedy indulgent? When is comedy an avoidance? (Awareness of the questions may be more important than attachment to particular answers.)

EXERCISES

1. (During the rest of your career as a care worker!) Gradually assemble a list of plays, novels, paintings, poems and pieces of music that would be useful to clients. Build an index of themes so that you can match fact and art appropriately.

2. If these are unfamiliar, try Greek tragedy, try Shakespeare. Consider the multiplicity of ways in which we attempt to heal, stay sane, survive, thrive. Medicine and psychotherapy are a relatively small part of the picture. Culture, ('high' and 'low'), nature, other people, projects, a minimal degree of prosperity; all these are crucial.

Conclusion

We shall return to Freud much later. This chapter points to a vast agenda that lies beyond the scope of this book. What is healing and helpful? Counsellors and psychologists consider the question. I am offering philosophers who do, and many who should, contribute. But beyond all this is art, nature, culture, society (or the lack of it). Many more useful links could, and should, be made when examining the subject of healing.

Notes

1. Emmy van Deurzen-Smith, *Everyday Mysteries*, Routledge, 1997.
2. Matthew Arnold, *Poems*, Oxford University Press, 1913.

Websites

gopher://gopher.vt.edu:10010/02/142/4
http://www.perseus.tufts.edu/cgi-bin/encyclopedia?entry=Sophocles
http://www.watson.org/rivendell/dramagreeksophocles.html

Bibliography

Focus Multimedia, CD Rom: over nine hundred and fifty novels, plays and works of philosophy, including seven plays of Aeschylus, seven of Sophocles and nineteen of Euripides

D. Grene, *Sophocles* in R. Lattimore (ed.) *The Complete Greek Tragedies*, University of Chicago Press, 1992

Sophocles, *Oedipus the King, Oedipus at Colonus, Antigone (The Complete Greek Tragedies*, Vol. 1) R. Lattimore and David Grene (eds) University of Chicago Press, 1992

Chapter 4

Socrates (*c.* 470–399 BC) **and** Plato (*c.* 427–347 BC)

Key Points

- Socrates left no written record, we know him mostly via Plato

- Socrates kept on asking questions about the alleged knowledge of others. This is not always a recipe for popularity

- For Plato, self-expression was inseparable from self-control

- Self-discipline, reason and reflection distinguished us from other forms of life and allowed us to be self-aware

- Personal development could not take place without the development of the society of which we were a part.

Application

- The British philosopher, A.N. Whitehead (1861–1947), claimed that western philosophy has been a series of footnotes to Plato. The range of his work is enormous
- Plato shows that what we would call personal development is simply a component in the development of politics, education, art, religion, the body, nature and culture generally
- Plato's philosophy is more holistic than many more contemporary efforts at integration
- Plato has been valued within liberal education for centuries. He still has much to offer.

All good counsel begins in the same way; a man should know what he is advising about, or his counsel will all come to nought. (Plato, *Phaedrus*)

And good counsel is clearly a kind of knowledge, for not by ignorance, but by knowledge, do men counsel well? (Plato, *Republic*)

Wherefore my counsel is that we hold fast ever to the heavenly way and follow after justice and virtue always, considering that the soul is immortal and able to endure every sort of good and every sort of evil. (Plato, *Republic*)

Socrates (*c.* 470–399 BC) was proclaimed by the Oracle at Delphi to be the wisest person in the world. He was wise enough to be highly sceptical both of this claim and of other belief in 'oracles'. He thought he was guided by a divine voice and was reported to be capable of going into long, contemplative (cataleptic?) trances.

Socrates did not wish to be placed on a pedestal, and his scepticism led him to question anyone else who laid a claim to being wise and insightful. He accepted that he might well know more than others since others thought they knew quite a lot and Socrates sensed that he knew nothing. He did, nevertheless, believe that knowledge was ultimately attainable if only we were sufficiently sceptical, questioning and honest about how little we knew:

Why is it then that some people like to spend much of their time in my company? You have heard the reason, gentlemen; I have told you the whole truth. It is because they enjoy listening to the examination of those who believe themselves wise but are not; the experience is not devoid of entertainment. (Plato, *The Apology of Socrates*, p. 52)

Systematic questioning of the claims made by others to knowledge and wisdom became a way of life for Socrates. The 'Socratic method' did not depend on a particular theory or body of ideas that Socrates sought to sell to others. It was, rather, a disposition of mind wherein nothing was taken on trust, nothing was simply assumed to be so just because others assumed that it was so. Socrates would question, question and question again, not in order to demolish everything and everyone around him, but in order to test their foundations, their connections, and their coherence.

Socrates, as he has come down to us, was awake, penetrating, restless, and curious. What needed no explaining to others required plenty of explanation once Socrates had dug out all those awkward questions that others had been too sleepy, slow or self-interested to notice. Such an energetic, probing mind can produce admirers who like to see the mighty fall and who like to have their eyes opened. Such scepticism can also make enemies. Not everyone, first and foremost, is a seeker after truth. Most of us are most of the time seeking to make a living and secure a reputation. If truth and honesty help, then so much the better. Radical questioning may be less welcome if we have secured more power, status, income and advantage than we can actually justify. We may not then wish others to questions our effectiveness, insight or integrity. You can be as smart and as right as you like, but I may be less than pleased if this is at my expense. I will find it hard to be dispassionate when my very livelihood is threatened and the ground on which I stand starts to crumble away under the pressure of Socratic enquiry. We do not want the clothes and trappings by which we claim social status to be seen as illusory. We may not wish to follow the questions and arguments to wherever they may lead. We may, rather, seek to silence the questioner and the questions or, at the very least, attack and undermine the questioner's own credibility, motivations and competence. It is not very surprising, then, that Socrates ultimately was tried and put to death. He was charged with corrupting young people and not believing in the Gods of the city.

The wise seek truth, but if you want to live a long life and/or preserve the status and esteem of powerful contemporaries, you might sometimes be wise to postpone your search for truth.

Socrates left no writings and he seems to have been less in the business of providing answers than finding the right questions to ask. With skill like this, perhaps he was indeed one of the wisest of his time. Perhaps this is still the knowledge that matters most today; knowing what to ask, and persisting with the questions without being fobbed off with shallow answers that presuppose too much. But the question then arises: at what stage is it time to *stop* asking questions? At what stage is it time to act, to choose, to decide, even though the answers available to us are anything but adequate? If we were to wait until we were entirely clear about the assumptions underlying all our assumptions, if we demanded full and complete knowledge, evidence and coherence before taking action, then we would never act at all. The Latin root of the word 'philosophy' is 'lover of knowledge and wisdom'. But a government would not be wise that taught everyone to do nothing but question and philosophise. Someone has to sweep the streets. Someone must plough the fields and carry out policies most of which might be less than capable of surviving the rigours of a Socratic enquiry. There is a time for questioning and a time for doing. Each, at best, forms, informs and is informed by the other.

During the trial of Socrates, as described in detail by Plato, (c. 427–348 BC) there were many times when he could have preserved his life relatively easily if he had chosen to substitute tact, flattery and empathy for concern for truth:

> My offence is that I have not kept silent upon the lessons I have learned from life; I have scorned what most men cherish – money-making and the administration of their property, military command and mob-leadership, and all the various political offices, cabals and backstairs intrigue. (ibid. p. 56)

When judged guilty, he could have proposed a reduced sentence which, almost certainly, would have been accepted, thereby avoiding the death penalty. But to do so would have required admitting a plea of guilty when Socrates was convinced of his innocence:

> Since I am myself convinced that I have wronged no one, I am certainly not going to wrong myself by admitting that I deserve to suffer harm and proposing to myself any such penalty. Why should I? To escape the penalty proposed by Miletus? (ibid. p. 57)

Socrates opted to stand in support of truth even when this could not support his own life. Like many a martyr after him, his life was consequently shortened. He was well aware that this would be the consequence, and so his refusal to bend was conscious and courageous rather than merely naïve and ignorant. Whether it was necessarily wise is a question that Socrates might have considered more carefully. Perhaps he should have done? Contrariwise, one of the best ways of ensuring that your ideas outlive you is to die for them. Socrates was already seventy one. His choice of death has no doubt assisted in keeping his name alive for nearly two and a half thousand years! Perhaps he was right to observe that worthwhile options were running out on him? In any case, he seemed to believe in a world after life on earth and thought it to be a happy one:

> A fine life I should lead if I went into exile at my age, wandering from one city to another and always being driven out! For I know full well that, no matter where I go, young men will listen to my talk as they have done here. If I repel them, they will themselves persuade their elders to banish me; and if I do not, their fathers and other relations will oust me for their sakes. (ibid. p. 58)

What do we really know about Socrates? Did he know that he knew nothing? Or that he was guided by divine authority and would live an eternal life after death? Most of what is known comes to us through the writings of his pupil Plato, who discusses many philosophical issues in the form of dialogues between the ever-questioning Socrates on the one hand, and others who are invariably shown to be far more sure of themselves than they have any right to be on the other. How far is Socrates an imaginary, idealised figure in these dialogues? How many of them actually took place? How far is their 'flavour' influenced by Plato's own ideas and interpretations? How far is the Socrates described by Plato historically accurate? How far is it a projection, idealisation or convenient construction of Plato? We shall, of course, never know the answers to these questions. As ever, questions can be found more quickly and more easily than answers.

The only Socrates available to us is the one described to us by others, most of all by Plato himself, but also by Xenophon, another pupil, whose account is sometimes very different from that of Plato.

How far the Socrates we know is the same as the Socrates who actually existed remains uncertain. The questioning and the powers of perception of Socrates, as presented by Plato, are as much a tonic now as they ever were. He is like a blast of fresh air or cold water thrown over a slumbering intellect. His questioning spirit deserves to live on. Questions can be awkward and inconvenient. Sometimes they are unanswerable. But Socrates also appears to have had a knack of finding profoundly important questions rather than trivial, pedantic, irrelevant questions. This is probably what crucially distinguishes major from minor philosophers. The one gets to the root of the ways in which we make sense of our lives, the other indulges in pedantry without much point or purpose. There are never too many people around with the Socratic spirit, courage and skill. A Socrates living now would be as invaluable and as inconvenient as he was in his own day.

I have combined Plato and Socrates in one chapter since it is profoundly difficult to distinguish between their ideas. The pupil Plato uses the character of Socrates as a mouthpiece for his own ideas as well as those of his master who himself left no written records. Plato, by the same token, wrote extensively on a vast sweep of topics and not even the briefest account of the full range of his ideas could be given in these pages. As ever, I wish only to touch upon just a few samples of Platonic ideas that are of interest and relevance to contemporary counsellors or other carers.

In *Republic*, Plato carries out a wide-ranging survey of how individuals and societies need to organise themselves if they are to live well. This, additionally, involves examining what a fulfilling life might consist in. For Plato, mental health and happiness went together, tyrants were intrinsically sick and injustice caused harm to the doer even more than to the victim, even though the tyrant was probably not aware of this.

The 'good life' today often tends to be understood in consumerist terms; what we are consists in what we have bought and can sell. Good living involves being wealthy, powerful, vivacious, dynamic, confident, interesting and active – as seen on television. We become trained and educated so that we can qualify for further training in order to get certificates that will give us good jobs that are secure and well paid so that we can shop and assemble a designer lifestyle of success, achievement and fulfilment.

For Plato, however, the good life was less about consumption and expression and more about 'temperance':

> Temperance surely means a kind of orderliness, a control of certain pleasures and appetites. People use the expression, 'master of oneself', whatever that means, and other phrases point the same way. (Plato, *Republic*, p. 121)

Whereas today we tend to talk mostly about the need to *find* oneself and *express* oneself in order to live the good life, for Plato the agenda was more about the need to *master* oneself. What did this mean?:

> Is not 'master of oneself' an absurd expression? A man who was master of himself would presumably be also subject to himself, and the subject would be master; for all these terms apply to the same person. (ibid. p. 121)

So if in order to achieve mastery we also had to learn to submit, who was to be master of who or what? And on what basis? And who had the right to decide?:

> The phrase means that within the man himself, in his soul, there is a better part and a worse; and that he is his own master when the part which is better by nature has the worse under its control. It is certainly a term of praise; whereas it is considered a disgrace, when, through bad breeding or bad company, the better part is overwhelmed by the worse, like a small force outnumbered by a multitude. A man in that condition is called a slave to himself and intemperate. (ibid. p. 122)

Self-control, then, was given higher priority than our contemporary concern for self-discovery and self-expression. Indeed, Plato took the view that neither of these was possible unless and until self-mastery was achieved.

Plato/Socrates considered that people could be best understood by distinguishing three elements of the soul, or personality as we would now describe it. These three elements were appetite, reason and 'spirit'. They became evident when we suffered a conflict of motives. For example, we could be both pushed towards taking another drink and pulled away from this option, just as we could both push on a bow and pull on its string. Two elements within the self were evidently in opposition to each other:

> What, then, can one say of them, if not that their soul contains something which urges them to drink and something which holds them back, and that this latter is a distinct thing and overpowers the other?
>
> And is it not true that the intervention of this inhibiting principle in such cases always has its origin in reflection; whereas the impulses driving and dragging the soul are engendered by external influences and abnormal conditions?
>
> We shall have good reason, then, to assert that they are two distinct principles. We may call that part of the soul whereby it reflects, rational; and the other, with which it feels hunger and thirst and is distracted by sexual passion and all the other desires, we will call irrational appetite, associated with pleasure in the replenishment of certain wants. (ibid. p. 133)

Desire we shared with other animals; reflection was what made us special. Through our powers of reflection we could, with self-mastery, impose a check between the desire and the action desired. We could examine causes, consider consequences, explore competing desires and contrary and contradictory thoughts and opinions. We could, in short, behave like responsible human agencies rather than bodies of uncontrolled urgencies. This was not to say that there was anything inherently wrong with appetite. It was just that it needed to be steered, controlled, placed into perspective, within an order of priority.

Were emotions inevitably to be associated with appetites? Was the reasoning element always seeking to keep the emotions in check? Interestingly, Plato thought otherwise. Reason was not necessarily dry and arid. It could be passionate, and our feelings could be allied with, rather than in opposition to, our reason. We could, for example, feel positively angry when we found ourselves unable to keep our appetites in check:

> Anger is sometimes in conflict with appetite, as if they were two distinct principles. Do we not often find a man whose desires would force him

to go against his reason, reviling himself and indignant with this part of his nature which is trying to put constraint on him? It is like a struggle between two factions, in which indignation takes the side of reason. (ibid. p. 134)

Additionally, Plato suggested that:

I believe you have never observed, in yourself or anyone else, indignation make common cause with appetite in behaviour which reason decides to be wrong. (ibid. p. 134)

We *can*, however, be angry with ourselves for being 'too much' in control of our desires, thereby living a dull life. There may be anger for giving in too easily, or for being too controlled and inhibited. Reason can be at war with itself. We are not always sure if a desire is, or is not, reasonable. When does 'self-discipline' become conformity and cowardice? Is my desire a healthy appetite or a base distraction? Will it lead to fulfilment or failure? Will it strengthen or weaken our self-esteem? Will it assist or damage our reputation? And strengthen our identity? And purpose? The answers may be anything but clear. We may change our mind more than once and still be unsure of what is right, healthy and appropriate.

Plato took the view that:

When the soul is divided into factions, it is far more ready to be up in arms on the side of reason. (ibid. p. 135)

But after a highly destructive, bestial, progressive, civilised twentieth century, this seems to be true only sometimes.

For Plato, reason and reflection distinguished us from other forms of life. Our inner lives could be turbulent but, through self-mastery, we achieved overall balance, harmony, purpose, perspective, identity:

The just man does not allow the several elements of his soul to usurp one another's functions; he is indeed one who sets his house in order, by self-mastery and discipline coming to be at peace with himself, and bringing into tune those three parts, like the terms in the proportion of a musical scale, the highest and lowest notes and the mean between them, with all the intermediate intervals. (ibid. p. 139)

Plato would have recognised contemporary talk of 'sub-personalities', but far from encouraging clients to express all their various appetites and warring selves, he would have warned of the need to bring all these into some kind of overriding order. Indeed, Plato argued that only by, as it were, getting our act together in this way could we develop an adult identity at all. Self was developed not via immediate expression, gratification and indulgence, but through discipline, maturity, consideration:

> Only when he has linked these parts together in well-tempered harmony and has made himself one man instead of many, will he be ready to go about whatever he may have to do, whether it be making money and satisfying bodily wants, or business transactions or affairs of state. (ibid. p. 139)

The good life was not one of mere consumption, assertion, production; all these were part of a larger picture that could only make sense within a framework of justice and honour:

> In all these fields when he speaks of just and honourable conduct, he will mean the behaviour that helps to produce and preserve this habit of mind; (one self-disciplined mind rather than many contrary and mindless appetites)... and by wisdom he will mean the knowledge which presides over such conduct. (ibid. p. 139)

Interestingly, 'honour' is almost never discussed within contemporary therapy, yet for Plato it was the key to sanity, sense, coherence, identity and community. It is more than mere 'pride' since it places self-regard more clearly into a social context. I feel *proud* when I think I have done right and well for *myself.* I feel a sense of *honour,* and I am honoured by others, when I, and they, consider that I have done right for *us all.* Plato believed that the third component of self, 'spirit' as he called it, was an embodiment of our sense of honour. A person was poor in spirit who had no self-respect. A person was also poor in spirit whose self-respect was so self-focused that it did not interconnect with and embody the mutual respect for persons. Mutual respect was the glue that formed and held society together. Respect for me and respect for you, each was inseparable from the other. Hence the interconnections between individual spirit and collective spirit, as embodied above all by the auxiliaries, military classes, who defended, stood within and for, the values, honour, culture and shared purpose of their city-state.

For Plato, therefore, justice, balance, health, healing, self-discipline were all essentially different terms for the same reality, looked upon from different perspectives. Whereas now so much time and attention goes into the fulfilment of appetite, for Plato the problem was that of ensuring that we were not mere slaves of appetite. Without self-discipline such slavery would be unavoidable and with it a life of chaos, disintegrating identity, injustice and misery as we allowed short term preferences to ride roughshod over our longer term well-being, aims, purposes and obligations:

> This must surely be a sort of civil strife among the three elements, whereby they usurp and encroach upon one another's functions and some one part of the soul rises up in rebellion against the whole, claiming a supremacy to which it has no right because its nature fits it only to be the servant of the ruling principle (ibid. p. 139)

The solution, for Plato, was clear:

> It will be the business of reason to rule with wisdom and forethought on behalf of the entire soul; while the spirited element ought to act as its subordinate and ally. The two will be brought into accord, as we said earlier, by that combination of mental and bodily training which will tune up one string of the instrument and relax the other, nourishing the reasoning part on the study of noble literature and allying the other's wildness by harmony and rhythm. When both have been thus nurtured and trained to know their own true functions, they must be set in common over the appetites, which form the greater part of each man's soul and are by nature insatiably covetous. They must keep watch lest this part, by battening on the pleasures that are called bodily, should grow so great and powerful that it will no longer be able to keep to its own work, but will try to enslave the others and usurp a dominion to which it has no right, thus turning the whole of life upside down. At the same time, those two together will be the best guardians for the entire soul and for the body against all enemies from without: the one will take counsel, while the other will do battle, following its ruler's commands and by its own bravery giving effect to the ruler's designs (ibid. p. 137)

Reason would take counsel, a process that, far from being non-judgemental, would to its core involve judgement, weighing and assessing of options:

> It appears, then, that virtue is as it were the health and comeliness and well-being of the soul, as wickedness is disease, deformity, and weakness. And also that virtue and wickedness are brought about by one's way of life, honourable or disgraceful. (ibid. p. 140)

In many respects this analysis of Plato became a part of conventional wisdom. Adulthood required that we get a grip on our warring appetites, understand our interconnections with the society of which we were a part, and become masters of our own soul. Only in relatively recent times has this traditional agenda been replaced, in some circles, with a search for the 'inner child', and with it the childish view that expression of any and every emotion is necessarily more authentic and actualising than keeping emotions and appetites under control.

Only recently, too, has the search for personal fulfilment been so comprehensively split off from our need of, and responsibilities towards, the culture of which we are a part. For Plato, such a separation of personal and political agendas would have been inconceivable, incomprehensible and insane. Plato's view was that there were many kinds of fascinating parallels and interconnections between shared cities and individual souls:

> We shall conclude that a man is just in the same way that a state was just. And we have surely not forgotten that justice in the state meant that each of the three orders in it was doing its own proper work. So we may henceforth bear in mind that each one of us likewise will be a just person, fulfilling his proper function, only if the several parts of our nature fulfil theirs. (ibid. p. 136)

In a just individual the three components of the self, reason, appetite and spirit, worked in harmony under the government of reason. Plato considered that these individual components were quite possibly mirrored within society:

> Is the soul like the state, which had three orders to hold it together, traders, Auxiliaries, and counsellors? (ibid. p. 135)

The individual was governed by reason, the state by counsellors: guardians/philosophers, who, unlike contemporary non-judgmental, individualistic variants, would weigh, judge and exercise power and leadership while showing due respect for the talents of the people:

> When each order – tradesmen, Auxiliary, guardian – keeps to its own proper business in the commonwealth and does its own work, that is justice and what makes a just society. (ibid. p. 126)

The tradesmen dealt in appetite but acknowledged the leadership of the guardians. The auxiliaries, dealing in spirit, defended the state from internal and external threat. The guardians (always a small minority) recognised the important role played by the other two and brought their actions and interactions together within a framework of justice and harmony:

> A society is just... when each of the three types of human character it contained performed its own function; and again, it was temperate and brave and wise by virtue of certain other affections and states of mind of those same types. (ibid. p. 128)

A society would be unjust, therefore, if either of the more lowly components moved outside its proper station, displaced the guardians, and ruled in their place. For example, a tyranny might be a state governed by auxiliaries, governing with spirit but without a capacity for reason and justice. A market economy would be a state governed by tradesmen, driven by appetite but incapable of weighing and assessing the interests of society as a whole, therefore acting without reason or justice.

Such states were most unusual since, until very recently, tradesmen did not wield anything like as much power as the military aristocracy, the king or clergy. Now, of course, almost the entire world is governed by what Plato would have regarded as tradesmen and his picture of the state looks very quaint. And yet, his analysis offers considerable food for thought. If tradesmen rule the earth, is it realistic to expect them to maximise justice and well-being in the state rather than merely within their own businesses? And, if they are not willing or able to seek the good of society as a whole, can the best of all possible worlds really result from every businessman pursuing his own appetites without restraint? Will tradesmen make laws for the benefit of all and, if not, who will? We have suffered the rule of tradesmen for several decades now. Not everyone appears to have benefited. Perhaps Plato does, after all, deserve residual attention? I find that his analysis is less than adequate but far ahead of, and much more sophisticated than, some of the contemporary banality that is offered, within therapy and else-where, as the road to a full life.

Plato is quite unlike contemporary thinkers in the broad sweep of his ideas, linking the personal, the state, ethics, politics, education, health, all within one interconnected analysis. A healthy individual required a healthy society; each depended on the other, as did each of the elements within and between individuals and societies.

To achieve such ends, a broad and integrated physical, intellectual, musical and artistic education was essential. This was particularly true for the counsellors/guardians but everyone should have a chance to show their worth since Plato believed in meritocracy: the child of a lowly farmer might have all the qualities needed to become a counsellor and, if so, should be educated accordingly.

Plato is hence a source of inspiration for the liberal educational tradition which, until recently, was seen as lying at the heart of western culture. In the eighteenth and nineteenth century, both Europe and America built in the style of ancient Greece and Rome, via their buildings and, even more significantly, in the blueprint they used to build the 'inner man'. These Greeks are, still, the counsellors who have had the longest and more profound influence on western culture. The more recent segmented vision of 'counselling'; individualistic, fragmented, narcissistic, hedonistic, focusing on self and health at the expense of broader and deeper components of existence – all this is recent and, on balance, regrettable, as I shall be attempting to show in subsequent chapters.

Interestingly, Plato was also one of the first Communists, at least as regards the life he proposed for his guardians. These, he argued, should not own private property at all since their attention should be continuously directed towards the well-being of the state as a whole:

> If ever they should come to possess land of their own and houses and money, they will give up their guardianship for the management of their farms and households and become tyrants at enmity with their fellow citizens instead of allies. And so they will pass their lives in hating and being hated, plotting and being plotted against, in much greater fear of their enemies at home than of any foreign foe, and fast heading for the destruction that will soon overwhelm their country with themselves. (ibid. p. 106)

In this Plato was greatly criticised, not least by Aristotle. But he did, indeed, highlight a problem perennial within all government: When governors have great power, who or what is to prevent them from using that power in order to benefit themselves and their families first and foremost? How is kleptocracy to be avoided? The problem is every bit as real and pressing today as it was during Plato's life, nearly two and a half thousand years ago.

❓ Questions

1. Do you think counsellor training gives adequate attention to the topic of self-discipline? And honour? What other Platonic concerns ought to be added to the curriculum?

2. Are the concepts of 'appetite', 'reason' and 'spirit' still useful? What, if any, model of personal identity do you prefer and why?

3. Is a broad liberal humanist education achievable any more? Who should benefit? How?

4. Do we, like the ancient Greeks, feel an integral part of our own wider society? Does it matter if we do not? What is to be done?

5. Should counsellors govern the country? If so, should they be of the contemporary or the Platonic variety?

EXERCISES

1. List five important ways in which the development of society *helps* the development of the individual, and five important societal *hindrances* to the individual.

2. Consider what would be involved in taking a more 'Socratic' approach to your own learning.

3. Examine and assess the views you and your clients have of the 'good life'. Compare them with Plato's analysis.

4. Discuss instances where your responsibilities towards your client might clash with your wider duties as a citizen.

Conclusion

Socrates 'facilitated' others by, above all, knowing what questions needed to be put to them. Plato saw personal development as inseparable from the evolution of the city-state. Expression and insight required discipline and compromise. Unchecked growth and assertion of any one sentiment would destabilise the personality and the community as a whole. Passions needed to be put into perspective. Personal preferences had to compromise with community priorities. Wisdom was needed to achieve a balance between so many competing impulses and individuals. These perennial questions were subsequently explored by generations of philosophers and statesmen. The contemporary individualisation and 'psychologising' of human development would have been seen by Plato as decadent and immature.

Websites

http://www.unex.ucla.edu/plato/
http://www.geocities.com/Athens/Academy/3963/main.htm

Bibliography

Plato, *The Apology of Socrates*, Dent, 1963
Plato, *Republic*, Oxford University Press, 1970
Plato, *Trial and Death of Socrates*, Dover, 1992
Plato, *Defence of Socrates, Euthyphro, Crito*, Oxford University Press, 1997

Chapter 5

Aristotle (384–322 BC)

Key Points

- Understanding was built *up* from action and observation rather than *down* from Platonic (or any other kind of) abstraction

- Choice was only possible and meaningful in those who could exert control over their passions

- We are social creatures, therefore we learn with and in relation to others more than via introspection and isolation

- Detachment can be taken so far that it can dry up the person – Aristotle may have been a living embodiment of the problem!

Application

- Aristotle would have had a great deal of sympathy with cognitive behaviourist attention to observation and action
- He stressed our rootedness in biology as embodied organisms
- For Aristotle, as with Plato, a healthy individual lived in a healthy city and each required and supported the health of the other
- Life was a balancing act: a compromise with conflicting internal appetites and higher principles, self-centred concerns and shared responsibilities, moral ideals against flesh and blood limitations.

Aristotle's influence on his contemporaries was considerable. Indeed, one of his pupils was Alexander the Great. His work was then lost after the fall of Rome, at least in the west, in spite of being nurtured by an appreciative and highly sophisticated Islamic culture for a thousand years. Aristotle was then rediscovered in Europe as his works were translated into Latin. The result was so profound that he did not so much influence western scholastic thinking, he embodied it, providing the frame, the foundations, the questions and most of the answers. This was itself a recipe for ossification but Aristotle is not to be blamed for that.

Aristotle was a biologist above all, but the corpus of his work ranges everywhere. The subject boundaries we take for granted were not recognised by the Greeks. Once again, just a few fragments will be taken, insofar as these can stimulate, inspire, and provide pause for thought to contemporary carers.

Let us begin with 'happiness', a subject as topical now as it was then. What observations can Aristotle provide that might be of interest to readers at the end of a millennium?:

> When it comes to saying in what happiness consists, opinions differ, and the account given by the generality of mankind is not at all like that given by the philosophers. The masses take it to be something plain and tangible, like pleasure or money or social standing. Some maintain that it is one of these, some that it is another, and the same man will change his opinion about it more than once. When he has caught an illness he will say that it is health, and when he is hard up he will say that it is money. (Aristotle, *The Nicomachean Ethics*, p. 29)

This sounds as true now as ever it was. Aristotle offers a warning equally relevant:

> Conscious that they are out of their depths in such discussions, most people are impressed by anyone who pontificates and says something that is over their heads. (ibid. p. 29)

Certainly there are enough foolish followers to keep in business a great Babel and babble of pontificating. So let us try to beware of the danger and keep to the relatively plain and direct style of Aristotle (although I will try to be less dry and dull).

Aristotle was no democrat as we would understand the term. He did not believe that everyone had the potential to 'actualise' themselves as fully and finely as everyone else. His was a patrician view, and elites and hierarchies seemed so obviously part of his life that descriptions of happiness had to take such social differences into account:

> Persons of low tastes (always in the majority) hold that happiness is pleasure. Accordingly they ask for nothing better than the sort of life which consists in having a good time. The utter vulgarity of the herd of men comes out in their preference for the sort of existence a cow leads. (ibid. p. 30)

Development was possible within all of us, but talk was not enough. Actions spoke louder than words and actions needed to be practised again and again if real change was to occur. Aristotle would have had a great deal of sympathy with cognitive behavioural approaches to change:

> The moral virtues we do acquire by first exercising them. The same is true of the arts and crafts in general. The craftsman has to learn how to make things, but he learns in the process of making them. So men become builders by building, harp players by playing the harp. By similar process we become just by performing just actions, temperate by performing temperate actions, brave by performing brave actions. (ibid. p. 56)

> Men will become good builders by building well, and bad builders as a result of building badly. It is in the course of our dealings with our fellow men that we become just or unjust. Like activities produce like dispositions. This makes it our duty to see that our activities have the right character... So it is a matter of real importance whether our early education confirms us in one set of habits or another. (ibid. p. 56)

The road to happiness for Aristotle, therefore, was not so much via therapy or talk, but by education and action. The priority of education was shared with Plato; the concern for action was particularly Aristotelian. Plato believed that the world of abstraction was more real than day-to-day existence. The 'form', principle, or concept, of a cat was more essential, real and significant than the individual cat. In Plato's view, such abstract, underlying structural essentials were engaged with via the detached, contemplative mind. Active daily dealing with actual cats was a more lowly component of existence of lesser concern to philosophers.

For Aristotle this was emphatically not the case. We learned about universals only by dealing actively in particulars. Therefore a great deal of knowing required doing. We would then have a real experienced empirical basis on which to draw conclusions, make generalisations, infer principles. Without real cats we could envisage no 'form' of 'cathood' at all. Aristotle was, therefore, one of the first advocates of empirical research and, as a biologist, he tried to practice what he preached by categorising and describing living organisms on the basis of what he actually observed.

So an Aristotelian counsellor would have counselled for action and active engagement. Clients would need to do far more than talk or speculate. They would need to explore, observe, test, try out alternatives, carry out homework assignments. But how was progress to be made and measured?:

> It is in the nature of moral qualities that they can be destroyed by deficiencies on the one hand and excesses on the other. Physical strength is destroyed by too much and also by too little exercise. Similarly health is ruined by eating and drinking either too much or too little. It is the same with temperance, courage, and the other virtues. The man who shuns and fears everything and can stand up to nothing becomes a coward. The man who is afraid of nothing at all, but marches up to every danger, becomes foolhardy. In the same way the man who indulges in every pleasure without refraining from a single one becomes incontinent. If, on the other hand, a man behaves like the Boor in comedy and turns his back on every pleasure, he will find his sensibilities becoming blunted. (ibid. p. 58)

A middle way needed to be found, although this did not always necessarily lie in the middle; to assume such would itself be an extreme position. Balance, principle, discrimination, judgement and more judgement, an active, tentative, exploratory approach was needed. Needless to say, not even Aristotle could always get it right, as some of his own errors make clear:

> Again, it is the man who encounters danger gladly, or at least without painful sensations, who is brave; the man who has these sensations is a coward. (ibid. p. 59)

This, surely, is overstated and less than balanced. Courage and bravery require that we feel fear; otherwise what is it that the courage is needed to overcome? If we are not scared of danger, we are stupid; with courage we do not abolish our fear but we act in spite of it, knowing that action is needed. Medals should not be given to those who, for whatever reason, did not appreciate and fear the dangers.

Aristotle's notion of balance and of steering between opposite extremes may now seem a commonplace and can itself be overstated. But it is still ignored often enough:

> In agreeableness in social amusement the man who hits the mean is 'witty'... The excess is 'buffoonery'... At the other extreme is 'boorishness'. (ibid. p. 70)

He gives a similar example of needing to find a balance on the continuum of 'peevish–friendly–obsequious'. The aim, as with Plato, was to become a master of ourselves for, without this, happiness could only take the forms shared with cattle:

> The man who lacks self-control feels desire when he acts but does not exercise choice, while the exact opposite is true of the man who is master of his passions... Still less is choice to be identified with passion. Acts which are the effects of passion are surely the very last that can be called acts of deliberate choice. (ibid. p. 83)

Again, Aristotle overstates his case in his overearnest quest for symmetries. Without self-control we cannot exercise choice. But control does not abolish desire, it merely contains it. Moreover, when we act from passion we might still have made a choice. It is not acceptable always to claim that 'it was an act of passion therefore I had no choice'. If you had no choice you were not responsible. But we are, surely, responsible, to some degree at least, when we let passion overpower our better judgement and thereby overwhelm our efforts to control ourselves?

Aristotle warns us not to be overimpressed or overawed by the pontificating of 'great philosophers', and we would be wise to apply this principle to Aristotle himself. Bertrand Russell is, I think, right to observe that:

> There is an emotional poverty in the '*Ethics*', which is not to be found in the earlier philosophers. There is something unduly smug and comfortable about Aristotle's speculations on human affairs; everything that makes men feel a passionate interest in each other seems to be forgotten. Even his account of friendship is tepid. What he has to say is what will be useful to comfortable men of weak passions; but he has nothing to say to those who are possessed by a god or a devil, or whom outward misfortune drives to despair. (Russell, *History of Western Philosophy*)

But let us not generalise without evidence. Aristotle's own words certainly do damn him at times. For example:

> Another mark of the superior man is his refusal or reluctance to ask anyone to help him, while always ready to bring help himself. (ibid. p. 124)

It is not 'superior' to refuse to ask for help, it is foolish pride. Only those who have lived quietly and have never been struck down by a tough world can imagine themselves 'superior' enough to be able to manage without the help of others. The corollary is even more common; we may assume that those who need more help than we do must be inferior to us. In fact, it is more likely that they are facing tougher circumstances. How many counsellors might imagine, deep down, that they have got their lives more sorted out than their clients? But, in fact, the client might well already be coping more effectively than the counsellor could faced with the same situation and legacy from the past.

The danger of this foolish belief in independence and self-reliance is as great now as ever. Who does the 'great healer' turn to when they need help? Doctors, for example, have been notorious in their reluctance to lean on others, and high-status therapists are likely to be the same.

Aristotle's description of the 'superior man' is not so much wisdom as a warning of a real danger that needs to be avoided. To the extent that readers took his views on superiority seriously, Aristotle has had a destructive effect on human development. For example, of him that is 'superior':

> He is not a gushing person, because nothing strikes him as a subject of mighty admiration. (ibid. p. 121)

The 'big' person, never gets excited, we are to believe. He never gets thrown, never 'gushes', never admires mightily because nothing is so very awesome when compared with his own awesome magnificence. It is a pathetic and pernicious analysis. Compare it with, for example, the Japanese poet and sage, Basho (1967):

> Look, children, hailstones.
> Let's rush out!

This two-line poem, I believe, demolishes Aristotle's position, in observing that the truly wise person can share childish enthusiasm and wonder, without fearing the loss of an adult perspective:

> He does not nurse resentment, for it is not like a superior man to remember things against people, especially the mischief they have tried to do him – he tends to overlook all that. He does not care for personal talk, being indisposed to speak either about himself or anyone else. Add that he never hurries (or so people think) and has a deep voice, and a deliberate way of speaking. (ibid. p. 125)

All this is laughable. We can try not to nurse resentment but we are fools if we think we can always succeed. We are boorish if we think we are always above 'personal talk'. We are preposterous if we affect and cultivate a deep voice in order to carry authority (yet how many fall for the deep gravelly tone that so frequently advertises next week's film?).

> The man who believes there is little or nothing worth getting excited about will not be prone to hurry or be high-strung and as a result shrill in his tones and bustling in his movements. (ibid. p. 125)

The person who believes that there is little or nothing worth getting excited about will indeed cope well with most of life's challenges – simply because he or she will not experience, rise or commit to them. They will deal with life by not actually living a great deal of it. They will resist passion by living without passion. They will therefore be incapable of showing empathy with those who actually know passion that goes *through* you rather than *past* you.

Having acknowledged serious weaknesses in Aristotle's ethics, shall we go to the other extreme and dismiss his observations about psychology and morals as irrelevant to contemporary readers? I hope not. He had both great insights and great blindspots, like all of us no doubt. Moderation has its place, in moderation, and balance, too, deserves attention, except when it makes us unwilling to jump or tip ourselves into something new. The following, for example, is less easily dismissed:

> In social intercourse, when people live together and there is interchange of talk and business, we find a set of men who are thought to carry politeness too far. Everything according to them is splendid and delightful; they offer no criticism and suppose it is their duty to avoid giving distress to anyone they meet. But there is another set, just the opposite of these, who raise objections to everything and are totally regardless of any pain they may inflict – they are the people we call surly or quarrelsome. (ibid. p 130)

Counsellors, like everyone else, are prone to either kind of error. Some may be bullying and invasive. Other may avoid confronting clients for fear of losing their weekly fee. How many fail to criticise for fear of being seen as 'judgemental'? How many staff trained in 'customer care' mouth insincere words of 'genuine support'? How many talk about 'non-directive prizing' and 'unconditional positive regard' without considering whether these are possible or desirable?

Aristotle could be cool, dry and too detached to be human. But his careful analysis of options deserves attention and he, like Plato, had a

concern and understanding for the concept of 'honour' that we have
forgotten to our cost:

> Honour is the greatest of external goods. The superior man, then, has the
> right attitude to honours and dishonours. (ibid. p. 121)

Talk of 'superior men' quite rightly grates on contemporary ears, but
notions of honour should not. Like Plato, Aristotle saw that honour
was much more, and much more important, than mere pride. Honour
was about seeking to do what was right because it was right, not
because it made you an honourable person. By doing what was right,
we promoted meaning, coherence and connection within ourselves,
with others, and in the world of which we were a part. Doing wrong,
letting ourselves and others down, created disconnection, disintegration, incoherence, chaos and meaninglessness. So we sought virtue not
in order to be virtuous or to live a good life after death but in order
thereby to stay connected to the underlying *logos*, or coherence, of existence. In so doing we really would be living the 'good life' rather than
that contemporary illusion of consumerism, ostentation, entertainment
and distraction. Aristotle was well aware of these shallow diversions and
warned against them:

> To make a serious business of amusement and spend laborious days upon it
> is the height of folly and childishness. (ibid. p. 302)

To be happy was to be virtuous, to be committed, to be active:

> Happiness is an *activity*. (ibid. p. 278)

It was also a *by-product*; we would be happy if we did what was right,
but we should do what was right not *in order to be* happy, but because it
was right. Moreover, we should not do so alone:

> Nobody would deliberately choose to have all the good things of the world,
> if there was a condition that he was to have them all by himself. Man is a
> social animal, and the need for company is in his blood. (ibid. p. 277)

Aristotle shifts around in his views about how far people actually
achieve such ideals. He proposes that:

> (The honourable man)... would prefer one crowded hour of glorious life to
> a protracted period of quiet existence and mild enjoyment spent as an ordi-

nary man would spend it – one great and dazzling achievement to many small successes. And surely this may be said of those who lay down their lives for others; they choose for themselves a crown of glory. (ibid. p. 276)

Which raises the question: how many such 'honourable men' are there? Might they not also be prigs and should they not be focusing on others rather than on their own 'glory'? Presumably the truly honourable spend none of their time assessing just how honourable they are? Elsewhere, however, Aristotle is much more circumspect about how honourable real people actually manage to be in real life:

> The world blames those whose first thoughts are always for themselves and stigmatise them as self-centred. It is also generally believed that a bad man does everything from a selfish motive, and does this the more, the worse he is. On the other hand the good man is supposed never to act except on some lofty principle, the better the man – and to neglect his own interest in order to promote that of his friend. It is a view which is not borne out by the facts. Nor need this surprise us. (ibid. p. 274)

Even assuming that we can achieve an honourable existence on a regular basis, what actually constitutes honourable behaviour? How do we know if we are achieving it? Can we always tell when we are behaving justly or unjustly?:

> To do injustice is to have more than one ought, and to suffer it is to have less than one ought. (ibid. p. 154)

But, even if this is true, it just shifts the question. We are then forced to ask when are we getting more or less than we ought? In the real world people really do disagree about such a question, as Aristotle himself observes in his *Politics*. On the one hand:

> Those who are bent on equality start a revolution if they believe that they, having less, are yet the equals of those who have more. (Aristotle, *The Politics*, p. 193)

Yet on the other:

> And so too do those who aim at inequality and superiority, if they think that they, being unequal, are not getting more, but equal or less. The lesser rebel in order to be equal, the equal in order to be greater. These then are conditions predisposing to revolution. Now as to motives: we find these to

be profit and dignity, also their opposites; for in striving to avoid loss of money and loss of status, whither for their friend's sake or for their own, men often bring about revolutions in their states. (ibid. p. 193)

Some believe that they should have more than others and that it is an unjust world that gives everyone an equal stall. Contrariwise, the tendency to equate justice with equality is a strong one:

Inequality is generally at the bottom of internal warfare in states, for it is in their striving for what is fair and equal that men become divided. (ibid. p. 191)

Aristotle does not get to the bottom of the problem of how to relate justice and inequality but it would unfair to criticise him for this. The problem remains as unresolved today as ever. From a global perspective, inequality of power and material prosperity is arguably greater today than it has ever been. The liberal element in western societies lament this and send their worn-out goods and loose change to charity shops. But few of us seem prepared to do, or support, anything that would substantially change our existing lifestyle. We try as hard to keep our money as Aristotle observed among his fellow Greeks.

As a biologist, many of Aristotle's explanations within ethics, psychology and physics took a biological, organic perspective. We do what we do, he argued, because it is in our nature as organisms to strive towards certain ends. He thought it was the same with inanimate matter. Objects moved downwards not because of an external force of gravity, as Newton postulated much later, but because such motion was part of their character and nature. Movement and change was not inflicted upon passive objects, it unfolded from them. Objects acted according to their constitution rather than reacting to stimuli. For example, a ball comes back to earth because that is its nature. This may seem strange. But, for many years, action at a distance, where balls respond to a 'gravitational force', seemed far more occult. Newton himself was uneasy with the idea. Perhaps he would have preferred Einstein's theory that the ball travels on a straight line in curved space. This is now the 'common sense' of theoretical physicists but not yet of the general population.

Aristotle's ideas about biology and physics are not of pressing concern to contemporary carers. However, his views on ethics and psychology deserve attention if, as he suggest, happiness, fulfilment and maturity really do depend on virtue. If Aristotle is right, the first agenda of counsellors needs to be the client's moral qualities, sense of dignity, understanding of honour. Such an Aristotelian approach to counselling may seem eccentric now, but it is just the way in which, for example, countless priestly confidantes supported their flock over many centuries. Many still do today. Are we right to dismiss them? Only in recent times has personal development become disconnected from self-discipline and self-restraint.

For centuries it has been taken for granted that development is essentially and precisely about achieving discipline. This has been the case not just in the west, but also within oriental philosophical, ethical and spiritual traditions. Yoga, or union with God, in all its various forms has, above all, taught self-control, in its many varieties. You 'found yourself' by, for example, learning to sit upright on a stiff mat or a hard floor. Only in recent years have so many within counselling imagined that introspection was best achieved by sprawling across large cushions or lying flat on a chaise longue.

It is not at all obvious to me, and furthermore there is no good evidence to suggest, that people are 'finding themselves' via current psycho-technology any more regularly and reliably than in the past. On the contrary, many contemporary counselling agendas, far from providing any real healing, appear to be more a *symptom* of social dislocation and loss of collective meaning and identity than a *solution* to these social and spiritual problems.

Most of those providing counsel in earlier centuries have attended to the ethical and community development of clients and have been prepared to provide social education and moral guidance whenever they judged this to be necessary. Within some forms of contemporary counselling, in particular cognitive behavioural versions, such guidance is still important. But the moral dimensions tend to be played down as everyone leans over backwards in the view that no one should ever dare to judge anyone else.

This contemporary *laissez-faire* approach would have baffled healers throughout most of history. Few believed that clients were best assisted by being entirely non-judgemental. The 'Solomons' of previous centuries were considered wise, or not, according to the quality of their judgements. A failure to make judgements would have been seen as weak and irresponsible.

Can we really afford to avoid standing in, and for, a coherent system of values? If we do not, how do we avoid further fragmentation, self-obsession and amorality? If counselling is to move forward, therefore, I think it should look around more widely than it does at present, and draw systematically from the rich cultural traditions that have formed and informed us. This will involve moving beyond twentieth-century western culture. The twentieth century, for all its technical and scientific progress, has been far less successful in its moral, spiritual and humane achievements.

We would have much to teach Aristotle and other ancients concerning our enormous scientific and technological progress. We have not progressed so well in our understanding of ethics, psychology and counselling. On the contrary, we seem to be suffering from a Tower of Babel of simplistic homilies each rising and falling in fashion in short order, and each trying to outbid the other for status and a secure income.

Some of Aristotle's political observations have also worn well with the passing of the years. For example, he is highly critical of Plato's proposals that property should be commonly owned by the guardians/counsellors/rulers of a city-state:

> There is a further drawback to common ownership: the greater the number of owners, the less the respect for the property. People are much more careful of their own possessions than of those communally owned; they exercise care over public property only insofar as they are personally affected. Other reasons apart, the thought that someone else is looking after it tends to make them careless of it. (Aristotle, *The Politics*, p. 58)

Aristotle mixes realism with idealism. Ideally, the rulers should look after shared property as well as their own. But in practice? How far will rulers exploit their subjects? Will they be statesmen or kleptocrats? Will rulers prefer a free citizenry because this is the noble path? At times Aristotle is optimistic:

> They are also wrong in supposing that a lawgiver ought openly to approve the acquisition of mastery; for rule over free men is nobler than despotic rule and more in keeping with virtue. (ibid. p. 289)

On other occasions he is more pragmatic:

> The longest tyranny was the Sicyonian, that of Orthagoras and his sons; it lasted a hundred years. These monarchs owed their long innings to the fact that they treated their subjects with moderation and in many matters subjected themselves to the rule of law. Also Cleisthenes was a warlike person and therefore not one to be trifled with. In general they drew the people towards them by repeated acts of care for them. (ibid. p. 231)

In Aristotle a preference for ideal moral principle is often tempered with realistic perception that real human beings do not always live up to such high standards. Again, perhaps, it is a question of balance. If we are entirely selfish, and ignore the importance of principle, then we will create chaos and find no happiness. But if we are so perfectionistic that we cannot face up to and deal with unprincipled selfishness in fellow humanity, how will we survive:

> As for walls, it is quite out of date to say, as some do, that cities that lay claim to valour have no need of walls; we have only to look at what in fact has happened to cities that made that boast. (ibid. p. 279)

For Aristotle, life was a balancing act: finding a compromise with conflicting internal appetites and higher principles; self-centred concerns against shared responsibilities; moral ideals with real flesh and blood limitations. He observed many political difficulties that are still a problem today and showed their interconnection with personal dilemmas. For Aristotle, personal and political development were seamless; the one inseparable from the other. He supported democratic citizenship but was wary of its dangers:

> In democracies the most potent cause of revolution is the unprincipled character of popular leaders. Sometimes they bring malicious prosecutions against the property-owners one by one, and so cause them to join forces; common fear makes the bitterest of foes cooperate. At other times they openly egg on the multitude against them. (ibid. p. 200)

He supported a growing and successful city-state, but growth could not go on forever and remain healthy:

> Experience has shown that it is difficult, if not impossible, for an over-large population to be well and lawfully governed; at any rate I know of no well-constituted city that does not restrict its numbers. (ibid. p. 265)

He described sections of a middle class recognisable to this day, with its comforts, convenience, complacency, conservatism and lack of awareness of the naked power struggles going on elsewhere:

> The middle class is also the steadiest element, the least eager for change. They neither covet, like the poor, the possessions of others, nor do others covet theirs, as the poor covet those of the rich. So they live less risky lives, not scheming and not being schemed against. (ibid. p. 172)

He recognised that coherent societies required rules and that, as citizens we needed to play a part in shaping them, obeying them, criticising them and protecting them, each as and when required:

> But it is surely a good thing to know how to obey as well as how to command, and I think we might say that the goodness of the citizen is just this – to know well how to rule and be ruled. (ibid. p. 109)

We had to be willing both to judge and be judged, with a mixture of determination and humility. We had to learn that autonomy and authenticity existed only in our interconnectedness with fellow citizens. We 'found ourselves', not in the wilderness, not alone, not in isolation, not just by looking within, not in confidential communication in pairs, but in our society, in our city and our family. This was where we belonged, this was both what we were and where we were:

> I suggest that what effectively distinguishes the citizen from all others is his participation in Judgement and Authority, that is, holding office, legal, political, administrative. (ibid. p. 102)

Citizenship, then, was not just a spectator activity or one wherein rights were assumed but no responsibilities were accepted. Citizenship was an active process and individual citizens found their identity within their active participation in the city-state of which they were a part. It was this active involvement in politics and city affairs that, in the view of the Greeks, made them special, civilised, cultured and essentially different from their 'barbarian' neighbours. Through citizenship we discovered, and fostered, our humanity.

Personal development, from the Aristotelian perspective, required one to be a citizen, and every true citizen was an active citizen. This involved taking up responsibilities, making judgements, following rules, giving and receiving orders, living within a framework of law, sharing collective concerns, purposes, celebrations and cultural activities. A healthy individual lived in a healthy city and each required and supported the health of the other. Personal growth was impossible except from within the 'soil' of the city of which each citizen was an integral part.

All this, I believe, comprises an important lesson which we have largely forgotten. We cannot cultivate individual development without paying attention to cities and societies. They are inseparable.

For Aristotle the individual was a living organism and so was the city-state of which he was a part. Aristotle was concerned to explore the principles of healthy development in both. Cities could not be considered in isolation from citizens. Yet now it is a commonplace for psychologists to ignore politics and politicians and economists to pay little heed to personal needs and perceptions. In our 'advance' into specialist knowledge, we have become fragmented and isolated. The broad integrated liberal humanist tradition of Plato and Aristotle has become lost and forgotten. However, it is not too late to reclaim our identity as whole human citizens, and I do not believe that the perennial problems we face can be tackled effectively until this broader vision is regained.

❓ Questions

1. How far is education an important component of healing and maturity? What, if anything, do your clients need to know that they cannot discover for themselves? Which individuals and problems come to mind?

2. What actions do you think your clients should take to deal with their problems? How far is it your job to educate them? Who and what comes to mind?

3. Do you agree with Aristotle that virtue is an important means to happiness? Can you, should you challenge clients who you think lack virtue and self-discipline?

4. Should 'honour' be part of the curriculum of counsellor training? If so, what should be included and explored?

5. How do your own ethical principles impact upon your clients? What specific examples come to mind?

EXERCISES

1. List the kinds of practical exercises you set for your own clients. Do you invite/require them to participate? How important are practical tasks in your counselling?

2. Consider those ethical principles that you consider to be essential for the development of insight, self-esteem and maturity.

3. Explore ways in which developing citizenship develops the person and vice versa.

4. Discuss political changes which could assist the development of individuals.

Conclusion

Aristotle related personal development to biology, society, history, moral obligations, duties, a sense of honour. Like Plato, he argued for a rounded liberal education. He set up a school at the Lyceum in Athens rivalling Plato's Academy. He saw individuals and the cities of which they were a part as living organisms. Like Plato he was an 'all rounder' who thereby was able to see that the most important questions could not be confined within one academic discipline. Yet, given the growth in knowledge, how can anyone now achieve an overall grasp of the significance of what we know?

Websites

http://www.fortunecity.com/victorian/durer/192/
http://webatomics.com/Classics/Aristotle/metaphysics.html
http://webatomics.com/Classics/Aristotle/nicomachaen.html
http://webatomics.com/Classics/Aristotle/poetics.html
http://webatomics.com/Classics/Aristotle/soul.html
http://webatomics.com/Classics/Aristotle/youth_old.html
http://www.ucmp.berkeley.edu/history/aristotle.html
http://www.yale.edu/lawweb/avalon/athemain.htm

Bibliography

Aristotle, *The Nicomachean Ethics*, Penguin, 1963
Aristotle, *The Politics*, Penguin, 1967
Aristotle, *Poetics*, Penguin, 1997
Matsuo Basho, *Narrow Road to the Deep North and Other Travel Sketches*, trans. Nobuyuki Yuasa, Penguin, 1967
Bertrand Russell, *History of Western Philosophy*, Allen & Unwin, 1961

Chapter 6

Epicureanism

■ Short- and longer-term gratification often conflict. Immediate pleasure may be regretted at leisure

■ Present distraction blocks future distinction. Self-discipline shapes our identity and our future. A dissolute self is a disintegrated self

■ Wisdom brings true happiness. We must study how to live fully and fairly

■ We do not 'grow' naturally and automatically; maturity requires work, self-control, reflection and insight.

Application

● Clients seek to learn 'how to live'. Epicurus did not believe that they would find out without instruction
● Our contemporary culture focuses on self-*assertion*; Epicurus provides an antidote in stressing the need for self-*control*
● Counselling tends to look for the good in clients, but how are we to relate to, and deal with, 'evil'?
● Cultivation and renunciation do not play much part in contemporary healing programmes. Perhaps they deserve some attention?

But chief and regnant through the frame entire
Is still that counsel which we call the mind.
(Lucretius, *On the Nature of Things*, 1995)

Epicurus originally operated on the east Aegean coast but founded a school in Athens in 307 BC. Like Carl Rogers, although perhaps with more justification, Epicurus asserted the importance and the originality of his ideas. His was one of the earliest forms of secular hedonism. There were many gods, according to the Epicureans, but theirs was a

person-centred humanist philosophy because it argued that the
gods did not intervene in this world. Deities would neither help nor
hinder humanity.

Epicurus concentrated on personal morality, and paid little attention
to the social or political dimensions of ethical questions. He considered
this world of material flesh and blood humanity rather than speculating
about life after death or godly existences. Epicurus saw no cause for easy
optimism. Unconditional positive regard would not inevitably wash
away all our cares and tension. There was a problem of evil that had to
be confronted.

Is God willing to prevent evil, but not able? Then he is not all
powerful. Is he able but not willing? Then he is not all good. Why,
then, is there evil? Many have addressed the problem. One solution,
not accepted by Epicurus, is to assert that evil is just an illusion or
misunderstanding. If only we were warm, positive, empathic and
genuine, would evil vanish? If we communicated more clearly, would
we then naturally co-operate? Are wars and power politics simply the
result of misunderstanding and insecurity? If we forgave ourselves and
listened to others, could we all learn to dance and sing together? Could
there be an end to the manoeuvring, rape, pillage, exploitation,
banditry, hangings, drawings and quarterings that have so much and so
regularly accompanied the journey of humanity through the centuries?

We do co-operate, sometimes. Of course we do. We can dance, swim,
sing, listen and help each other grow – but not always. Sometimes we
have felt the need for a suit of armour, a castle, a body of men at arms.
Since most of us cannot afford the expense of all this ourselves, we have
been pleased to belong to, or find, a tribe led by some suitably powerful
and protective chieftain. We have knelt, paid tithes and taxes, and
hoped thereby to survive to reasonable old age. That, certainly, is how it
has been for most of human history.

Peace and power go hand in hand. Pax Romana, Britannia, Americana. Romano-British society could deliver jewels, costumes, conversation, culture, central heating not because the Romans showed
unconditional positive regard to others.

Unconditional positive power, used wisely and, when necessary, with
utter ruthlessness, was the more usual remedy. The Roman wall could
utterly overawe Pictish observers and Roman legions could crush the
opposition quickly, thoroughly, efficiently, even when hugely outnum-
bered.[1] Are we more civilised now? People are desperate and starving in
many parts of the world. The west is rich, fat, disproportionally inap-

propriate in its appropriation of the earth's resources. How do we maintain this inequality?

We no longer use castles. We have aircraft carriers, closed-circuit television, police, coastguards, gun boats. Do we really need this hardware? Is there anything that needs defending? Anyone who is a threat? Perhaps cushions, warmth and advanced empathy would serve us better? Should we learn to turn the other cheek? If we did, might we not be crucified? Good can triumph over evil, and can be infectious. But history provides many illustrations of evil triumphing over good. The meek and weak may eventually inherit the earth but, so far, they have more usually been trampled on. Love can be powerful – but so can power. And the love of power can be stronger than the power of love.

Epicurus addressed these problems of love and power and managed to avoid facile optimism and cynical despair. His *Principal Doctrines* is a collection of forty of the most important articles of his teaching which, it is assumed, were brought together by one of his students. It was preserved by Diogenes Laertius (third century AD) in his *Lives and Opinions of Eminent Philosophers* and, along with the *Letter to Menoeceus*, makes up the only first-hand body of Epicurus' ethical teaching.

For Epicurus, the good life did not come merely from trusting to nature. Virtue had to be cultivated, and ethical philosophies studied. 'The man who does not possess the virtuous life cannot possibly live pleasantly.' Short- and long-term options and consequences needed to be carefully weighed. If we slavishly avoided present discomfort, and sought immediate gratification, we might well damage our interests in the longer term. Desire could itself become a tyrant since it could lead to indulgence and excess followed by a much longer process of regret. Desire could also make you hostage to good fortune. Easy circumstances might not be permanent.

A plain and simple life was therefore recommended since it led to health, fitness, humility and real, more secure, happiness. The finer luxuries were to be only occasionally enjoyed. They were thereby more appreciated. Habitual and continual consumption merely dulled the senses.

Epicurus believed in the virtues of a quiet life consisting in a relative withdrawal from the world. Such a life should not be idle. 'Let no one when young', he wrote to Menoeceus, 'delay to study philosophy, nor when he is old grow weary of his study.' By philosophy, he did not mean academic pedantry or empty speculation. It should be an active study of principles by which we could live with coherence, purpose, equanimity, and genuine self-regard. We must study the patterns and consequences of action and interaction between people and weigh our own interests against those of others. We must, above all, be willing to face up to, and come to terms with, death. 'So death, the most terrifying of ills, is nothing to us, since so long as we exist death is not with us; but when death comes, then we do not exist. It does not then concern either the living or the dead, since for the former it is not, and the latter are no more' (Letter to Menoeceus).

Epicurus does not, of course, provide the last word on the subject of death or on anything else. If everyone were to act as he suggests and withdraw from affairs of state and its temptations, how then could a society form, function or continue? Epicurus did, however, make a serious effort to provide counsel on how to live and how to assist others in the process of living. In many ways this early humanist vision is more sophisticated and realistic than some of our contemporary humanistic variants.

Epicurus spoke in favour of virtue, but was not so naïve as to believe that it could always combat vice. Being genuine, liking people, understanding them could be infectiously helpful. It could reduce evil but was unable to remove it. History makes this pretty clear, but our contemporary utopians, like those who went before them, tend not to trouble themselves with history. Hence so many present-day therapists recycle a variety of earlier ideas without realising that they are doing any such thing. Therefore they tend not to anticipate the problems they are likely to encounter and which themselves have been addressed, thoroughly, in earlier centuries.

For example, we may not easily know what our 'genuine' thoughts may be. Today's apparent authenticity may prove to be tomorrow's folly. We misconceive and misunderstand. An idea or emotion that was profound and moving yesterday may seem trite and facile by today. It is unwise to 'prize' every opinion and emotion that swarms into our head or heart. Judgements change but judgement is needed. Our opinions may be contrary and contradictory. Where will they be tomorrow? What bad and unforeseeable consequences will result from today's good intentions?

Understanding is difficult to achieve. How will you show you understand if you do not understand? How do you know that you do understand? Understanding may change over time. Contemporary advice that we be genuine and prize others too often ignores the difficulties and paradoxes recognised and explored by our ancestors. Epicurus, in comparison, comes across as more aware of the complexities of a person-centred vision than twentieth-century teachers of this philosophy.

Who was the 'real' Epicurus? How can we ever know? What does the question even mean? If we went back in a time machine to sit at his feet, we might each come away with a different experience and interpretation. Most of his writings, apparently, have not survived; he seems to have suffered a great deal of criticism from his rivals and contemporaries, the Stoics, and translations can never be freed of the interpretations and very different cultural circumstances of the translator.

Epicureanism did not move on from the views of its founder. Epicurus, it seems, had to be learned rather than questioned and explored. In this respect, he was neither the first nor the last of a long tradition of gurus who, free thinkers themselves, seek to ensure that their disciples merely rehearse, repeat, respect and regurgitate the Great Works, on and on down to children, grandchildren and beyond. As it was then, so it is now. So, too, the tendency of rival schools of thought to overestimate the uniqueness and value of their own vision and distort the views of competitors.

For example, Epictetus, the (rival) Stoic guru, said of Epicurus; 'This is the life of which you pronounce yourself worthy: eating, drinking, copulation, evacuation and snoring.'[2] This was scarcely fair to someone who said 'I am thrilled with the pleasure in the body when I live on bread and water, and I spit on luxurious pleasures, not for their own sake, but because of the inconveniences that follow them.' Epicurean pleasures were static, modest and centred around equilibrium. Gluttony was to be avoided because it produced a stomach ache. Drink led to a hangover. Wealth and honour led to restlessness. Sexual intercourse was monstrously destabilising. Friendship of a quiet and reflective kind, was best, lived via a life withdrawn from public attention so as to ensure that no dangerous, disrupting enemies or rivalries were made. Bacchanalian carnival and licence would upset one's digestion, equilibrium and tranquillity. Epicurus may have been a young fogey!

Epicurus' teaching proposed that, via a study of how to live, we can attain wisdom and achieve *ataraxia*, or freedom from care. There are many inadequacies in this programme but at least Epicurus advocated and understood the need for hard work to establish the nature of understanding and friendship. We do not grow naturally like oak trees. Unlike trees, we have some responsibility to examine, to weigh, to assess and to make difficult choices each of which may raise its own questions, doubts, dangers and uncertainties.

For that matter, acorns do not grow naturally and inevitably into fine oak trees. Only a minority actually achieves this. Most find that the soil and circumstances within which they are thrown do not allow full 'actualisation' into our idealised conception of what real oak trees actually look like. As for the rest, even when the environment is benign, the genetic blueprint may be flawed in a variety of ways or, if not actually damaged, the seed may only be capable of producing a tree that is merely adequate, modest, moderate and mediocre rather than wonderful. As it is with trees, so it is with human beings. We do not all excel, we do not all win prizes, we do not always behave, think or feel in ways that are at all prizeworthy. We do not help ourselves or anyone else by pretending otherwise.

? Questions

1. Can you think of occasions where your clients suffer because of a lack of self-discipline? What do you do to help them tackle this problem?

2. Should the counsellor/care worker ever be in the role of providing 'instruction' to the client? Is so, why? If not, why not? What specific examples come to mind?

3. Have you ever come across morally repugnant behaviour in a client? What did you do? How far were you happy/unhappy about your response? What specific examples come to mind?

4. How far do you encourage clients to weigh short- against long-term consequences? What specific examples come to mind?

EXERCISES

1. See if you can begin to 'map' your own system of values in relation to the philosophers described in this and subsequent chapters. How similar, different, are your beliefs to Rogers? Epicurus?

2. Keep a journal on those writers who have had most influence so far on your values, ideas and methods of practising counselling/professional care.

3. Include in your journal notes on the ways in which, you imagine, your own values and counselling methods influence your clients. What is it that they are likely to think and do as a result of spending time with you?

Conclusion

We talk of an 'Epicurean' as a person of refined and fastidious taste, especially in food, wine, and, less so, as devoted to sensual enjoyment. In fact this seems to be the reputation more than the reality of Epicurean philosophy. Epicureans were similar to the Stoics in their attention to simple living and avoidance of short-term sensuous distraction. They stressed the importance of coping with adversity. A study of philosophy was seen as essential to living fully and fairly. Through such study we would learn those attitudes and beliefs that would help us utilise opportunity and survive adversity. Without it we would be undisciplined, easily distracted, unaware, immature and irresponsible.

Notes

1. Eight thousand Roman legionaries destroyed, in one battle, over one hundred thousand Britons under Boadicea, almost without loss to themselves. The conquest of Britain did not greatly ravage and ruin the country because of superior tactics and the overwhelming weight of, for example, eight hundred Roman galleys hovering off the Kent coast.
2. Epictetus, *Discourses*, Book II, Chapter xx.

Websites

http://www.creative.net/~epicurus/

Bibliography

Epicurus, *The Essential Epicurus; Letters, Principal Doctrines, Vatican Sayings, and Fragments*, Prometheus, 1993
Epicurus, *The Epicurius Reader: Selected Writings & Testimonia*, trans (ed.) L.P. Gerson, Brad Inwood. Hackett Publishing Company, US, 1994
Epicurus, *Guide to Happiness*, Phoenix, 1995
Lucretius, *On the Nature of Things*, Johns Hopkins University Press, 1995

Chapter 7

Stoicism

_____ **Key Points** _____

- Virtue consists in living in harmony with nature
- We are disturbed more by our reactions and expectations than by events themselves
- Mastering desire, thinking accurately, performing duties are all essential to maturity and personal well-being
- It is fallacious to imagine, and unwise to expect, that the world will fit in with our preferences.

_____ *Application* _____

- Stoic principles are used, but not sufficiently acknowledged, within cognitive therapy/rational emotive therapy
- Stoic principles add wisdom, maturity, self-discipline, morality and duty to the agendas of talking treatments
- Stoic principles are particularly helpful when coping with adversity and when client expectations are unrealistically high.

The soul of man does violence to itself, first of all, when it becomes an abscess and, as it were, a tumour on the universe, so far as it can. For to be vexed at anything which happens is a separation of ourselves from nature, in some part of which the natures of all other things are contained. In the next place, the soul does violence to itself when it turns away from any man, or even moves towards him with the intention of injuring, such as are the souls of those who are angry. In the third place, the soul does violence to itself when it is overpowered by pleasure or by pain. Fourthly, when it plays a part, and does or says anything insincerely and untruly. Fifthly, when it allows any act of its own and any movement to be without an aim, and does anything thoughtlessly and without considering what it is, it being right that even the smallest things be done with reference to an end;

and the end of rational animals is to follow the reason and the law of the most ancient city and polity. (Marcus Aurelius, *Meditations*, Book 2)

When anything shall be reported to you which is of a nature to disturb, have this principle in readiness, that the news is about nothing which is within the power of your will. Can any man report to you that you have formed a bad opinion, or had a bad desire? By no means. But perhaps he will report that some person is dead. What then is that to you? He may report that some person speaks ill of you. What then is that to you? Or that your father is planning something or other. Against whom? Against your will? How can he? But is it against your poor body, against your little property? You are quite safe: it is not against you. (Epictetus, *Discourses*)

Stoic philosophy deserves serious attention. It is still operative today, albeit under different names. We talk about taking a stoical attitude towards life and this word is part of our everyday vocabulary. Zeno, the founder of the Stoic school in the early third century BC, believed that, in the beginning, there was only fire. Air, water and earth then emerged in that order. Eventually, Zeno held, all will again revert to its original fieriness. Such speculation provides a (very) crude version of contemporary 'Big Bang' and 'Big Crunch' models of the evolution of the universe.

How, within a world destined to return eventually to undifferentiated fieriness, are we to make sense of our existence? The Stoic view was that we should avoid becoming mere pleasure seekers and use virtue as our loadstone and guide. The virtuous life was one lived in harmony with nature. For Stoics, this meant living according to reason. Nature had endowed us with reason and this is what made humanity special in comparison with other animals. The Stoic's emotional and moral attraction to reason is in sharp contrast with the contemporary romanticism within the 'human potential' movement, which tends to see reason as cold, unnatural and alien to nature. Reason, for many of the personal growth aficionados who emerged from the 1960s, was likely to cut you off from your authentic self, your natural emotions, your intuitive knowledge of your inner and outer worlds.

The Stoic view, on the contrary, was that we were beset with mundane, short-term desires. These could corrupt our perceptions and judgement. Will power was needed to see beyond our baser instincts and to develop self-discipline. Maturity of perception and self-control were in our best longer-term interests. They were also best for the society to which we belonged as active citizens.

Everyone, according to Stoic philosophy, could therefore live the 'good life' since its achievement consisted in our finding not so much the 'inner child', as in contemporary parlance, but in developing, cultivating and committing to the 'inner adult'[1] Currently the good life, as seen on television and as underlying our entire consumerist culture, consists in material status and comfort, celebrity, excitement, eternal youth. The easiest passions to arouse when selling goods and services are those that represent the lowest common denominator within human motivation. Such an agenda is emphatically not the Stoic road to virtue. It is the childish route to distraction, superficiality, false idols and idolatry. So have we moved on from Stoic philosophy? Or have we degenerated behind and beneath it? Are contemporary preoccupations with 'personal growth' an improvement on this early Greek analysis? Or are they altogether inferior, since they provide no central place for, and analysis of, virtue?

Stoic principles can keep people intact, coherent, proud and at peace with themselves in the toughest circumstances. They may be poor, imprisoned, unjustly treated, physically vulnerable to oppressive and tyrannical authority. But if they can have appropriate control over their thoughts, feelings and actions, if they can know what it is to respect themselves and others, then there is a precious central sense of their own identity and direction that cannot be stolen or manipulated. They may not be aristocrats or media celebrities, but they can be 'nobles' in the best and truest sense of the word. And if they achieve this prize, they will know it to be far more priceless than a fleet of luxury cars and castles in the air or on the ground. They will have found themselves, but not easily and effortlessly; not by prizing and cherishing every wandering, rambling demanding and demeaning whim and bleating protest of our monkey minds and hearts.

The Stoic road, then, can be a stony road. But it can, and it has over many centuries, provided a means by which people prevent themselves from disintegrating when the circumstances around them might crush a weaker spirit.

The Stoic view, however, like all the rest, is not free of problems, dangerous tendencies and limitations. For example, it sounds impressive to talk about living 'in harmony with nature' and this is a song that has been repeated endlessly over the centuries and is still sung today. But what does it actually mean? There are, seemingly quite 'naturally', contrary, contradictory and downright destructive feelings, thoughts, intentions and tendencies at work within us all. Can we say that some are natural and some are not? Nature, naturally, produces plagues and disasters as well as harvests and happiness. Can we reliably consult 'nature' to tell us which options to select and which to discard? Perhaps we should, together, take responsibility for ourselves, construct our own principles and live up to these within our own practice.

Technology was once seen as a 'natural' part of human activity and human superiority. Our nests were as natural as the bird's but better because of our bigger brains. Now we tend to see nuclear, chemical and genetic industries as 'unnatural' and as 'against nature'. What does this mean? Harmonies there may be, but there is nothing easy or straightforward about finding these and living by them. Geneticists must discover deep structured harmonies within DNA if they are to produce any kind of genetic technology. Does that mean that all such technology is inharmonious? If we reverted to earlier, supposedly more 'natural' forms of agriculture most of us would die. Does that mean that it is unnatural for most of us to be alive? Innovation produces seemingly 'unnatural' results until we get used to it. Surely 'natural' cannot be allowed to mean 'familiar'?

It could be said that cruelty and injustice are 'natural'. Certainly they provide an opportunity for Stoics to develop their powers of endurance, inner peace and self-control. But it is doubtful that self-discipline can always triumph over adversity, and there is little virtue in seeking virtue as an end in itself. Virtue surely provides a means to other ends, which themselves deserve scrutiny.

The danger of the Stoic mentality is that it produces a survivalist mind set, albeit without the bitterness and pessimism of other forms of survivalism. The Stoic seeks peace, insight, restraint, but if this search is carried too far the disciple opts out of life. To live is to risk getting dirty, confused, damaged, to commit oneself, to role up one's sleeves and to act, to make mistakes and to suffer the consequences. Within Stoicism lies the tendency to quietism, to withdrawal, to a kind of tranquillity and cosmic perspective that leaves the observer cold and indifferent to individual success and suffering. A similar danger has been recognised in most other monastic traditions. We look for insight so much that we move out of sight of the day-to-day world. We see ourselves as 'above' and 'beyond' daily routines, struggles and confusions.

The seeker after truth, the spiritual disciple, imagines that theirs is the higher path compared with that of the householder with the screaming kids, the daily compromises, responsibilities and constraints. The householder mops up the mess of day-to-day existence in a daily cycle that goes round and round without end. The truth seeker tries to attain something more 'ultimate', but the mopping up is what is needed if any kind of life is to go on at all. No wonder, then, that wiser commentators have often suggested that the highest road is in fact the lowest, where you are up to your neck in the daily chores of uncertainty, frustration, passion, confusion, limitation. These sometimes, it is hoped, produce real practical achievement and they are the cake upon which the 'cherry' of higher consciousness may sometimes sit.

Stoicism, unlike Epicureanism, did not stay fixated around the thoughts and writings of its founder, but moved on and developed under the inspiration of a variety of names. Chrysippus (280–207 BC) argued that virtue would always lead to happiness and that wickedness brought its own misery and dissatisfaction here on earth. He has been followed by multitudes, from Stoic and other traditions, taking a similar view. Here is another version of our need to believe in justice on earth: good people will be happy, bad people will not. Here is a good enough incentive for people to practice virtue. Many who lie, cheat, steal and distract themselves are, beneath surface appearances, miserable, insecure, ridden with guilt. Warm, helpful, generous, co-operative people may indeed be happy, respected, loved and loving, at peace with themselves.

But are these 'just' outcomes guaranteed? Is every member of the Mafia miserable? Does every loving child find a place in the sun? Do all those who are struck down, damaged, demoralised, destroyed as human beings deserve this fate? Do they all discover ways of coming to terms with it and finding peace? It seems self-evident that they do not and, if we are to take a mature view of the human predicament, this is a truth that we must face and with which we must be reconciled. It is not a just world. The good people do not always win and are not always, in any sense, happy or 'self-actualised'. The bad people, however we may want to define good and bad, do not always lose. They do not necessarily feel miserable, guilty or uncomfortable in any way. They may live happily ever after, contrary to the scripts we see in the stories we like to tell and hear.

Good does not necessarily triumph over evil. Misfortune and injustice are real and long lived. Sophocles showed their power, as we saw in Chapter 3. This reality has often been thought to be unbearable. Consequently, many theologies propose that justice will be restored, if not in this world, then in the next. The gods, we are advised, are keen observers and accountants. After we have died, all worldly accounts will be settled. Those who have been cheated will be restored and rewarded. Those who were themselves cheats will be disqualified and punished. There will, in short, be pie in the sky when you die and it will taste better than all those earthly pies currently being enjoyed by the thugs and hooligans holding sway in many corners of a continuously troubled and troubling world.

Stoics disagreed about whether or not the essence of our personalities lived on after the body had rotted away. Even if there was survival after death, it was not clear that there was heavenly compensation or punishment for wrongs suffered or committed on earth.

Three Roman Stoics of note were Seneca, Epictetus and Marcus Aurelius. Seneca (3 BC to 65 AD) was unlucky to be banished from politics, lucky to get a job later as a tutor, but unlucky to have the Emperor Nero as his pupil. Seneca, as a Stoic, was 'above' the grubby business of amassing money, yet still managed to amass an enormous fortune. Much of this was gained by loaning money to Britain, at a huge rate of interest. Queen Boadicea objected, but Roman arms had their way of settling this problem (as described in Chapter 6). The money was not loaned without conditions, Boadicea's regard was neither unconditional nor positive and the Roman response was not empathic. Although not empowering to the Britons, it was certainly powerful. All this seemed 'natural' enough behaviour to contemporaries; natural human behaviour, red in tooth and claw.

Seneca's powerful pupil eventually accused him of plotting against him. Whether this was true or not is unclear. Either way, Nero decided to be generous. Rather than torturing and killing his tutor, Seneca was allowed to commit suicide. He did not even have time to make a will but, turning to his family, said 'Never mind, I leave what is of far more value than earthly riches, the example of a virtuous life.'[2] Or so, at least, it is claimed. He cut himself open and his words continued to flow as well as his blood, says Tacitus.

Epictetus (60 to 100 AD), of Greek origin, was a Roman slave. Marcus Aurelius (121 to 180 AD) was an emperor. Despite such huge differences in background, their Stoic philosophy was very much the same. They really were capable of addressing general questions without the intrusions or distortions of slavish or royal circumstances. Aurelius, something of a liberal by the standards of the time, allowed gladiators to fight with blunted swords. It was hard for him to be optimistic, since the Roman Empire's fortunes were going very much from bad to worse. Thus both he and Epictetus found that Stoic philosophy suited their circumstances. It provided consolation, inner resourcefulness and a means of enduring with a sense of pride and purpose when their surroundings were becoming a chaotic, dangerous wasteland of decay and decline.

Epictetus said: 'Men are troubled not so much by circumstances, as by their reactions to circumstances.' This is often true, and some reactions can be controlled more easily than some circumstances. Both expectations and environment, however, can often be very difficult, and sometimes impossible, to control. Epictetus went so far as to suggest that the good man could find fulfilment even on the rack. It has been observed that this would require a very good man on a very bad rack.

The racks are often better than the men, and Stoicism sometimes portrays us as too good to be true. In truth we are not always able to be either so good or so strong as Stoics would hope. Heroism is admired, not just because it is virtuous, but because it is rare.

Nonetheless, heroic fortitude can, and does, take people through some very rough circumstances. It deserves more attention than it currently receives within many parts of the counselling community. Contemporary counselling often seeks to improve the well-being of those who, from a historical perspective, have comparatively few problems. Clients who can afford the high cost of intensive psychological attention are generally far wealthier than that great mass of the people, past and present, who are just hoping to get through the day in one piece.

When your material needs are being met more completely than even those of a medieval king, you certainly can find the time to cultivate, explore and decorate whatever you imagine to be your 'inner life' (of which more later). When your daily circumstances appear to be disintegrating at least as fast as they are developing, you need a philosophy of life that has more grit in it than most of that available within the contemporary humanist*ic* movement.

Since the humanist movement has passed through two and a half thousand years of greatly varied circumstances, it must be expected that it has developed versions, like Stoicism, that provide combat fatigues rather than party clothes. When there is a war on, a search for your 'inner child', whatever that may be, can be an indulgent and dangerous luxury you cannot afford. You might be wiser to look for your 'inner soldier'. This may sound overly grim if you are sitting in a hot tub in California, but it may be just what is needed if you are living off rats and trying to survive yet another German bombardment during the Siege of Leningrad. It may be just as useful in contemporary St. Petersburg, when negotiating with starvation and threats from the Russian Mafia.

A whole vision of the human predicament must certainly embrace love and sunshine. But it must not close its eyes to the hell that has been, and is, the daily experience of so many people.

So, if your life is hellish, why not try to be a hero? Here is a script:

> I must die. But must I die groaning? I must be imprisoned. But must I whine as well? I must suffer exile. Can any one then hinder me from going with a smile, and a good courage, and at peace?[3]

Inner child? Why not find the 'inner hero'? You may need it. It may help you survive. It is the stuff of adventure stories, westerns, historical dramas and science fiction novels. It is John Wayne, Mother Courage, 'When the going gets tough, the tough get going' (and so on). It is easy to sneer and laugh at its more simplistic versions. But it is no laughing matter when this is the kind of spirit you need to cope with your circumstances. You may not, of course, succeed. You may go down a hero or broken entirely. Either way you may go down, crushed, ground, worn, torn. Not everyone grows and actualises.

Epictetus taught that, in order to transcend tough times, we needed to conquer not just fear but also hatred of our enemies. Loving our enemies was not about trying to be too good to be true. It was about seeing our whole drama of love and hate from a larger perspective. In that way we could avoid being helpless victims. By taking the perspective of the gods we could, in a sense, participate in the divine taste of life's possibilities. However, we are not gods and we are not always, or often, able to achieve superhuman abilities to rise above our daily pride, complacency, shame and suffering. Christ, too, taught that we should love our enemies. The number of ordinary or extraordinary human beings who have achieved this is not, I suspect, very great. Nietzsche commented that he could believe that Christ was a redeemer if Christians looked more redeemed.

Stoic survivalism works well if your circumstances provide more adversity than opportunity. If we cannot be happy let us at least try to be good. Maybe that will deliver the deepest, most worthwhile and robust form of happiness. It is wise to see earthly pleasures as distractions from higher goals when you are deprived of earthly enjoyment. I do not want the finest wines, I say to myself; and this is sensible because I cannot afford them. This may also be sour grapes within both me and my second-rate wine.

Monks avoid temptation by ensuring that there is none to avoid. Kings, aristocrats, plutocrats may fall deeply into debauchery and bacchanalia because power provides exceptional opportunities. The army remains disciplined, but when conquest is complete and the conquered nation's womenfolk are unprotected, then what? Read your history to find out. Or use your imagination. Self-discipline is real enough, but often we are good, or harmless, simply because we do not find much opportunity to be bad. Temptation can be a relatively rare. Perhaps that is just as well.

Stoicism can look forbidding, pessimistic and irrelevant among the comfortably situated. But just how typical are the circumstances of the western middle classes? The security and comfort enjoyed by many of counselling's clients is most extraordinary when compared with the lack of opportunity and abundance of threat endured by most people, in most places and at most times. Even at the height of Roman prosperity, for example, the fragility of the peace, the danger from the poor and the slaves, the poverty in the countryside, the risk of a bad harvest, the possible civil dislocation, rural banditry, civil war, local crime and exploitation, ordinary brutality, all this was normal and natural however much it was not desired or desirable.

We do not have to go back so far in time. The twentieth century has witnessed two World Wars that have torn the hearts and lives out of tens of millions. Scores of wars have occurred in the 'peace' that has followed. Western (so-called) 'civilisation' is a thin veneer that hovers, delicately, around a few airports, suburbs and supervised shopping malls. A third world war has been avoided so far but the future, we hope, is much longer than the fifty odd years during which we have managed to possess, but not use, nuclear weapons. Even as I write, some impoverished Russian officer could be selling nuclear arms to terrorists. The threat of social and civic disintegration is very real for more than half of the world's population. So do not forget your Stoic philosophy. You may need it. And sooner than you think.

One concept, not yet mentioned, that is central to Stoicism, yet too often absent from contemporary healing programmes, is the notion of 'duty'. The true Stoic would do the right thing in the knowledge that peace of mind came from living in harmony with fundamental moral principles. Stoics felt a sense of oneness with their society and environment (look again at the quotations at the beginning of this chapter). To do wrong to other people and objects damaged the very ground on which you stood. If you let 'us' down, you thereby let yourself down. You could not possibly 'find yourself' in a social or moral vacuum. We found and expressed ourselves by finding what was fitting for us to do. We developed and expressed ourselves by recognising and undertaking duties, by shouldering our obligations, not with reluctance, but freely, actively and responsibly.

This integration of civic and ethical values with personal fulfilment and maturity has been the vision of the good life among the best governing circles from the Stoics on. It is what Roman generals and administrators, in the best times, were brought up to believe. It is what medieval knights were taught. It is what the English Victorian squire learned. Duty. Honour. To yourself, to your country, to your people. Each inseparable from the other. Each the means by which you could live with yourself and others in peace and goodwill.

Needless to say, people fell short of these ideals far more often than they achieved them. Ideals, by their nature, provide a beacon to aim for more than a destination at which we arrive. Cynics, confidence tricksters and criminals down the centuries have scorned anyone 'foolish' enough to try to live by such goals. In an unjust world why live a just life? The Stoic view, at its best, was that we do right because it is right, not because it is necessarily rewarding. Societies are more or less 'civilised' precisely insofar as these virtues are practised.

The British civil service, for example, may not always have been efficient, but it really did, and hopefully still does, live according to a tradition of public service and takes pride in upholding such a tradition. It thereby disproves the cynical view that everyone has a price and everyone can be bought. Corruption never disappears entirely. The amount of corrupt practice among the powerful worldwide is, as ever, almost too terrible to contemplate. But there are times and places when it is not endemic; sometimes it is relatively rare. These are the 'good times'. This is the 'good life'. Those living in such societies are fortunate indeed. We may take notions and traditions of public space and public service for granted. They may be easier to destroy than to rebuild. We may miss them only when they are gone.

For Epictetus, mastering desires, performing duties and thinking accurately about yourself and your place in the world were essential and interrelated. Healing programmes lacking this agenda hastened social fragmentation, self-obsession, indiscipline and naïve notions of identity, independence and authenticity.

In Epictetus' view we became upset when we had not found an accurate balance between what we wanted and what the world made available to us. There was no reason to expect circumstance to accommodate the desires of even the most comfortably situated. Rather than try to reconcile the world with our plans, we needed to trim our plans so that they fitted our circumstances. Desire, Epictetus argued, can be brought under control with self-discipline, much more easily than our entire environment and circumstances. Absurd expectations that we had a right to be happy about, and in control over, all our circumstances could only lead to misery.

The Stoic message was easy enough to assert and to understand, but how could it be achieved? Epictetus argued that the necessary virtue needed to be put into practice by practice and meditation on the nature of right action. We needed to imagine tough situations and how we would respond in order to cope with them. Our good and bad times should be placed within a broader perspective. Were we ready to respond if tomorrow was worse than today? Could we remind ourselves that bad times came to an end as well, even though they might seem to fill a lifetime?

Could we whisper to ourselves 'Tomorrow you may die' without terror or despair? Could we stay comfortable with the fragility and fleeting uncertainty of our lives? Moments could be savoured that we knew would end. Our ignorance and uncertainty could point to awe and mystery not just frustration and fear. We could prioritise, be realistic and courageous. We could weigh, balance, judge, contextualise, analyse and explore. We could thereby live productively within uncertainty, limitation and injustice. We could avoid destructive and self-defeating emotion. Epictetus enjoined us to: 'Study not to die only, but also to endure torture, and exile, and scourging, and, in a word, to give up all which is not your own.' We could learn to be responsible, and come to see how 'Everything has two handles, the one by which it may be borne, the other by which it may not.'

Contemporary 'how to' writers tend to address individual readers struggling alone. Epictetus and other Stoics stressed that we were social beings: 'Duties are universally measured by relations.' 'Do you know that as a foot is no longer a foot if it is detached from the body, so you are no longer a man if you are separated from other men? For what is a man? A part of a state, of that which first consists in gods and men; then of that which is called next to it, which is a small image of the universal state.' We were citizens of the world, not gods, but more than mere animals. 'For you are capable of comprehending the divine administration and of considering the connection of things.'

As social beings, our development was primarily a public process: 'Engaging in public business, marrying, begetting children, venerating God, taking care of parents, and generally having desires, aversions, pursuits of things and avoidances, in the way in which we ought to do things, and according to our nature.' We could only find ourselves with others, by shouldering obligations, making choices, weighing, assessing, prioritising, putting thoughts and feelings into wider perspective. We would need to judge and judge again, not in order to condemn or moralise in a negative hostile way, but in order to understand, so as to be able to see and act with wisdom. Marcus Aurelius' advice was to spend each moment as though it were your last. We could thereby savour moments and confront the awesome mystery of existence. We were a product and component of a society, therefore: 'That which is not good for the beehive cannot be good for the bee.' Bees that sat alone in their cells could be of no use to themselves or their hives. The world was coherent, rather than chaotic, and our lives could be so, too, if we learned to discover congruent and principled relationships within ourselves and our society: 'Herein doth consist happiness of life, for a man to know thoroughly the true nature of everything; what is the matter, and what is the form of it: with all his heart and soul, ever to do that which is just, and to speak the truth.'

In more recent years, others have taken up the Stoic message, but called it something else. For example:

> Cognitive-behaviour therapy (CBT) is one of the youngest of today's popular psychotherapies, and I think I can immodestly say that I seem to have originated it in January 1955, under the name of rational therapy (RT) and rational emotive (RET). (Ellis, 1957, 1958, 1962)[4]

RET and CBT attempt to show that 'people largely needlessly disturb themselves by, first, self-downing (SD) and, second, indulging in low frustration tolerance (LFT) or by demanding that their life absolutely must be easier and more gratifying than it is and by awfulizing and whining when it is not' (Ellis, 1957, 1962, 1979, 1980, 1985, 1988, 1994, 1996).[5]

Albert Ellis, one of the biggest names in cognitive therapy, is clear about his own contribution as it stretches back all the way to 1955. Ellis explains that REBT:

> Hypothesizes that a prime factor in disturbance is cognitive-emotional musturbation – the dogmatic, rigid, and forceful holding of absolutistic shoulds, oughts, and demands on oneself, on others, and on external conditions; and it focuses on showing people how to become aware of and change their core dysfunctional philosophies, including their innate tendencies to overgeneralize, reify, and absolutize, which Korzybski (1933) and others have pointed out. (Ellis quoted in Palmer and Valma)[6]

Ellis writes clearly and with a punch. His style obviously belongs to twentieth-century America rather than to Greece or Rome BC. I prefer

Ellis' North American style to the jaded view that 'we've tried everything, and it does not work'. But tentative and reflective qualities are sometimes lacking. Ellis' terminology is catchy and memorable, but encumbered by abbreviation and jargon. His confidence can be infectious, yet also seductive and naïve. He speaks of 'dysfunctional philosophy' and philosophy is certainly part of his agenda. But Ellis' claim to have originated REBT in January 1955 does less than justice to the many earlier western and oriental efforts to develop this philosophy, from the Stoics onwards.

Ellis coins various terms such as 'unconditional self-acceptance' which became memorable acronyms (USA). Perhaps this is both the strength and weakness of some of its citizens, yet Ellis sees no irony.

The trouble with unconditional self-acceptance is that it pays no attention to the role of guilt. Shame, remorse, contrition can all be disabling and masochistic. But sometimes we feel guilty for good reason. If we never feel shame and regret, how can we ever learn? Ellis advises: 'Don't rate, measure, or evaluate your highly complex self, essence, or being at all. Only rate your thoughts, feelings, and actions. No self-rating!' (Ellis, 1973, 1994, 1996). Yet our thoughts, feelings and actions are *ours* even if not *us*. We feel proud when we do well. By what right, therefore, should we avoid shame when we do badly?

Ellis is proud enough to have 'originated' CBT in 1955, but perhaps a little remorse is also due for suggesting that he originated it at all. Certainly he developed it, but it had been developing for centuries prior to our own. Ellis originated a suitably contemporary *presentation* of Stoic principles, but current versions tend to be overly individualistic, and shorn of the Greek apprehension of the tragic dimensions of human existence.

Even the earlier, more sophisticated, versions of Stoicism run into problems: I agree to *prefer* justice and fairness rather than *insisting* on them. What am I to do, however, when not even my mildest and most modest preferences are met? What if I get no share at all of good luck and experience? Am I to be allowed to feel no emotion at all? Is every feeling of disappointment, sadness and irritation illegitimate and self-defeating? Am I never to feel anger? Or hurt? Or in despair?

If we always put Stoic principles into practice we would never disturb our underlying 'tranquillity' because of mere circumstance, however disastrous. We would be like Dr Spock, in the TV soap opera *Star Trek*. We would always be saying 'It is irrational to fret and fuss about what has happened to us. Why make our experience worse by feeling sad about our misfortune? Isn't the misfortune itself sufficient?' This kind of attitude, whereby Stoic 'reasonableness' is taken to 'unreasonable' (and inhuman) extremes, would make us cold and indifferent to ourselves and to others.

How could you relate at all to a partner who never felt elated and enraged, regardless of what you did or did not do in relation to them? In some couples one person may indeed try to emulate Ellis's teaching and say: 'Now dear, there is no use worrying about it, it won't help. It just makes you disturbed and agitated.' This may be good advice if we have missed a television programme or suffered some other trivial disappointment. But what if our child has just been killed? Or we have been assaulted in the street, or dismissed from work, or our house has burned down? Who is going to say: 'There is no point in getting disturbed; people die, houses burn, crimes take place every single day, why should it not happen to us?'

If our friends or partners behaved in this way we would leave them in disgust, or we would wonder if they had gone mad, or were suffering such trauma that they were denying their circumstances. In less extreme instances of partners attempting to stay overly tranquil, our usual strategy is to goad them so much that they can no longer maintain their serenity. We then give a sigh of relief that they are human after all, score ourselves as 'one up' on our partner, friend or colleague, and try to console them about their loveable limitations and ordinary humanity.

When struck by a long sequence of what everyone agrees are unlucky misfortunes, it is only human to raise our fists to the sky and cry 'Why me?' The Stoics are right in suggesting 'Why *not* you?' The misfortune of strangers requires no explanation. In the lottery of circumstance, we know that some are winners, with or without good reason, most are somewhere in between, and some just keep on getting hit over the head, whatever they do. When we step back, we can see all this; but if we were always stepping back and looking down, we would never be down on the ground as active participants. The footballer scores a goal. He, the team, and the fans all race and jump and cheer. They do not say: 'Why get excited; sometimes you score and sometimes you miss.' In the long run we are all dead. But should we, therefore, become emotionally dead, right here and now?

The Stoics observed the ephemeral nature of human emotions. If we took the longer view we would be more detached both from our joys and woes. But can we, and should we, always adopt an Olympian perspective? Can we witness, rather than ride, the rollercoaster of our emotions? It cannot be done, and why should we even try?

Stoicism is relevant if you tend to overreact to misfortune; but it is less helpful for those who prefer to be spectators on their lives rather than active participants. Stoicism can assist the overly emotional; but some are already dumb to their feelings and perhaps too reluctant to suffer.

Stoicism, like Buddhism, teaches that suffering can be avoided via detachment. Yet why should we always seek to avoid suffering? To do so can be cowardly, irresponsible, inhuman. Christian teaching, on the contrary, enjoins us to 'pick up thy cross and walk'. This can be masochistic, but suffering is not always an avoidable obstacle to life. It often seems to be welded in as an inevitable component of existence.

Ellis and earlier Stoical approaches can help in adversity. They can also be relevant for those (not you and me, of course!) who really are whining, lazy and undisciplined and whose relatively comfortable circumstances ought not to give rise to very much complaint. Since many clients of counselling in western societies are indeed in the most comfortably situated corners of the most congenial parcels of planet earth, Stoic therapy undoubtedly has a place. Ellis' contemporary interpretations of Stoicism are much more problematic, however, when applied to those who have behaved really badly or who face, not merely tough, but truly overwhelming circumstances.

For example, it is absurd to say: 'I'm OK as a person, although my action of killing my children is bad.' Common sense and common traditional wisdom would suggest that a person cannot be 'OK' when their behaviour is atrocious.

The sinner, within every religious tradition, is generally forgiven if they repent. But not if they brush away culpability with banalities such as: I will not rate myself, only my actions. Only those who have been deeply immersed in psycho-babble can imagine that: 'I am angry with your actions but not with you.' The rest of us would hold that: 'I am angry with you because of your actions, and you should take responsibility for them.' We do not say: 'I am ashamed of my actions but I am proud of me.' Real pride finds the courage to admit to serious mistakes and can even confess that: 'I am ashamed of myself.'

There are some whose pride and self-esteem is too low when compared with their behaviour. But pride can run ahead of achievement just as confidence can outrun competence. It is easy for a counsellor to say: 'You need to take pride, think well of yourself and thereby be at peace.' Clients will readily pay to hear this and our me-centred society is full of programmes designed to raise confidence and self-esteem. But can a counsellor, who is financially dependent on the client, afford to say: 'You are too proud, your confidence outreaches your competence, you are smug, self-satisfied, amoral'?

'Prizing' and praising people is called 'support' and 'empowerment'. It prizes money from clients. Priestly challenges of immoral or amoral behaviour are now called 'judgements'. Within many schools of counselling, judgement now carries negative connotations. It is considered unprofessional, arrogant and unhelpful.

From a historical perspective, such unconditional prizing is something of an abberation. Cleric, confessor, counsellor, shaman, witch-doctor, wise person, philosopher – all were prepared to judge and be judged. All would encourage the seeker after truth to judge themselves. Repentance was a crucial component of maturity and insight. Regret, guilt, remorse, wailing and gnashing of teeth, sackcloth and ashes, weeping, mourning, for months, even years; all this was common currency within healing in most traditions, cultures and centuries. Doing penance can become masochistic, and self-loathing can turn into a bad habit that feeds off itself. But we currently seem overly focused on joy and woefully ignorant of the place of woe as a means to healing.

Everywhere there are confidence-building programmes, assertiveness-training courses, interventions designed to raise self-esteem and remove guilt and self-doubt. *The Story of Myself* is running everywhere and achieving high audience ratings. Yet what if we are overconfident, insensitive, overblown, self-preoccupied? What if we have behaved destructively and selfishly, yet feel no guilt, regret or remorse?

When injured we suffer. Were we not to feel them, the injuries we never noticed could kill us. If we injure others, perhaps we *should* suffer at the thought of their pain. Otherwise, the body politic may die of its injuries from amoral individuals. Pain can be a teacher of last resort. We learn and change both from satisfaction and dissatisfaction, rewards and punishments. Life is a dynamic between balance and imbalance. If we were too balanced and satisfied we would still be balancing somewhere in a tree.

So where is the optimum to be found between these contrary and contradictory principles? There may be no single or easy answer. That is why the art of living is just that, an art, and therefore not confinable within a computer program and advanced counselling training or any other kind of professional care package.

In physics and other sciences we are undoubtedly ahead of our ancestors in the breadth and depth of our understanding. In psychology and the (so-called) social sciences, progress is much less certain. Is this a particularly successful era in human understanding? Are we more civilised than our ancestors? For example, Amnesty International claims that state authorities in one hundred and seventeen countries routinely torture and abuse prisoners (*Time*, 6 July 1998). Individuals are studied in isolation from their communities. Our soul-destroying consumerist philosophy regards people as commodities and objects of manipulation.

At its worst, contemporary counselling and unconditional self-acceptance seeks to abolish the 'shoulds' of existence. We judge that we should not judge. This judgement, it seems to me, is most unwise.[7]

❓ Questions

1. What, if anything, could Stoicism add to contemporary care worker training?

2. Do you think that virtue, duty, self-discipline are appropriate agendas within the practice of care? Are they adequately addressed within your own training?

3. Cognitive-behaviour therapy (CBT) is one of the youngest of today's popular psychotherapies. Do you agree?

4. What do you see as the principle strengths and weaknesses of Stoicism as a philosophy that you could offer to your clients?

EXERCISES

1. Compare CBT texts with some of those listed in the bibliography in this chapter and note major similarities and differences.

2. Make notes on the kinds of client problems where Stoic principles would be most/least beneficial.

3. Consider how far the notion of 'living in harmony with nature' is of practical relevance and use within your own practice as a care worker.

4. Stoicism, and contemporary versions like cognitive-behaviour therapy, stress the importance of challenging and exploring the judgements we make. Other therapists argue that we should not be 'judgemental'. Consider your own opinions on the importance of making, or avoiding, judgements.

Conclusion

Stoic principles have been a major part of the survival strategy of many people for centuries, regardless of whether or not they have ever been familiar with Stoic philosophy as such. Stoicism explores ways in which we can discipline ourselves to cope and come to terms with adversity and limitation. It is a strategy for survival rather than celebration but it ought to be part of every counsellor's basic tool-kit. Stoicism, in more up-beat forms, has been adapted and incorporated within cognitive-behavioural and rational-emotive therapy. The original versions are sometimes more sophisticated, mature and realistic than contemporary modifications.

Notes

1. The notion of an 'inner adult' is not part of Stoic vocabulary but it describes Stoic principles so exactly, and provides such a stark contrast to contemporary narcissism, infantilism and hedonism, that it is worth highlighting.

2. Bertrand Russell, *History of Western Philosophy*, Allen & Unwin, 1961, p. 267.

3. From W.J. Oates, *The Stoic and Epicurean Philosophers*, in Russell, p. 270.

4. Albert Ellis in *The Future of Counselling and Psychotherapy*, S. Palmer and V. Varma (eds) Sage, 1997, p. 1.

5. Ibid. p. 7.

6. Ibid. p. 6.

7. Indeed, it is impossible, even in principle, to avoid making judgements, all the time, about everything and everyone.

Websites

http://www.eb.com:180/cgi-bin/g?DocF=macro/5004/99/91.html

Bibliography

Marcus Aurelius, *Meditations*, Penguin Classics, 1969

A. Ellis in S. Palmer and V. Valma (eds) *The Future of Counselling and Psychotherapy*, Ch. 1, Sage, 1997

Epictetus, *A Manual for Living*, HarperCollins, San Francisco, 1994

Epictetus, *That We Ought not To Be Disturbed by any News* in C. Gill (ed.) *Discourses of Epictetus*, Everyman, 1995

F. and H. Hazlitt (eds) *Wisdom of the Stoics: Selections from Seneca, Epictetus and Marcus Aurelius*, University Press of America, 1984

B. Inwood, *Ethics and Human Action in Early Stoicism*, Oxford University Press, 1987

S. Lebell, *Epictetus; The Art of Living*, Audio Literature, 1997

A.A. Long (ed.) *Problems in Stoicism*, Athlone Press, 1996

L.A. Seneca, *Letters from a Stoic*, Penguin Classics, 1969

Chapter 8

St Augustine (354–430 AD)

Application

- Augustinian teaching reveals, via stark contrast, the highly secular nature of our contemporary society
- How far have I made a god of 'Myself'? What are the effects on personal, social and spiritual well-being?
- How far is contemporary life the living hell Augustine described in *City of God*?
- Augustine's felt sense of spiritual connection is palpable in his *Confessions*. Is this of any relevance today?
- The spiritual dimensions within all forms of care deserve attention.

Augustine converted to Christianity in 386 AD. What could it offer him? His *Confessions* (*c.* 397) describe his own spiritual development. His *City of God* (*c.* 413–426) provides an account of history in terms of two forms of love. We can, Augustine asserts, inhabit one of two cities: an earthly city, which is driven and organised by a love for and preoccupation with self; and a heavenly city, whose focus of meaning and concern is around the love of God.

Augustine uses the notion of the 'city' as a metaphor to denote a universe of concern, the focus of attention, an organising principle around which we seek to make sense of our lives. For Augustine there are two major options. It will not be difficult to guess which of the two he preferred.

For Augustine, the essence of sin was the secular belief that we create ourselves, sustain ourselves and can depend on ourselves. In other words, the agenda of contemporary counselling would have been, for Augustine, a fall from grace, a move into chaos, a disconnection from our roots, a fragmentation, a dislocation, a lost cause, a false consciousness, an aridity, an illusion:

> The weakness of his soul was in relying upon itself instead of trusting in you.

> You taught him to trust in you, not in himself. (*Confessions*, p. 122, p. 123)

Self-esteem, that commodity so much in demand nowadays, was, for Augustine, a temptation to be avoided:

> I was inflated with self-esteem, which made me think myself a great man. (ibid. p. 60)

This kind of talk is in such stark contrast to what we now see as contemporary wisdom that it is interesting and useful to introduce Augustine to present-day counsellors, carers and clients, albeit briefly. To modern eyes he may seem obscure, distant, irrelevant. But he is considered to be one of the two most important and influential Christian philosophers/theologians of *all* time (the other being St Thomas Aquinas).

Augustine's ideas did not pass away when he died. They became central pillars of the Christian tradition and their influence is traceable right through to the nineteenth century. It is only in the last one hundred years that they have become alien, strange, unusual and unfamiliar in what is now, finally and undeniably, a secular society.

Evil, for Augustine, is the result of directing our love away from God and towards ourselves. It is not so much that we plunge wilfully into darkness; rather that we lose the Divine light, the only light. Darkness is the only alternative. Introspection is impossible. There is no light within. I can only gain insight, or any other sight, via God, via prayer. By focusing on me instead of on God, I lose you and I lose us. Since 'we' are part of the ground from which 'I' am formed, I also lose myself. Instead, I chase after illusions. I become ever more dissatisfied, ever more shallow, ever more disconnected, disconcerted, distressed, distracted. Only in God can I find the ground of all life, of us, of you, of me. To go inside myself, without God, is to go nowhere at all:

> The soul of man, although it bears witness of the Light, is not the Light. (ibid. p. 144)

Augustine's *Confessions* are not an introspective monologue wherein he considers his past actions, since he did not believe that introspection was possible. His *Confessions* are, rather, a *dialogue* between himself and his maker. God, for Augustine, is evidently a real, revealed and continued presence. The saint does not so much *believe* in God, rather he experiences himself as being in *contact* with Him.

> You commanded me not to commit fornication, and although you did not forbid me to marry, you counselled me to take a better course. (ibid. p. 233)

Who needs an earthly counsellor when they have the Divine original continuously available? This does not mean that Augustine thereby feels able to understand, comprehend, describe and in any way find words adequate to embrace God. He does not believe that, via human intellect, we can shine any light on the mystery of God. All we can do is make ourselves available for God to shine His light upon and within us. We are not stars. We can only reflect. We give out no light at all. We cannot unravel the mysteries of existence; we can only stand within them, with receptivity, awe, patience, humility, reverence.

Divine encounter, therefore, is not a process by which we are active, assertive, probing and comprehending. To suppose any such thing would have been, for Augustine, an act of blasphemy and absurdity. In God's light we do not so much gain insight and comprehension; rather we are lifted, thrown, scattered, flattened in ecstasy, awe, wonder, worshipful prostration. The power of God's presence for Augustine can be felt by the reader in virtually every line of his *Confessions*:

> Listen to my soul as it cries from the depths. For if you are not there to hear us even in our deepest plight, what is to become of us? To whom shall we cry? (ibid. p. 254)

For Augustine, the earthly city, with every self preoccupied with self, could provide no one with fulfilment or empowerment, and no means by which anyone could become 'self-actualised'. The message is clear within Augustine's teaching.

If self, personal development, and all the other narcissistic paraphernalia of modern living, were to become the object of my attention, concern and love, then how could I seriously, rather than superficially, be bound together with anyone else? How could I belong anywhere, except on my own, with my introspection and self-concern? What of the world would I ever see if I spent so long at the looking glass of introspection and self-consciousness? And if I hold up a mirror in darkness what do I think I will learn? If we were each to become preoccupied with ourselves then in truth we would not be bound together at all. We would be alone, in a vacuum. Such an existence would be meaningless, purposeless, pointless.

If we all became isolated and self-preoccupied, then why would anyone want to listen to us? Why would anyone be concerned for us? For any interest to be taken there would have to be some pay-off for the other person. But such 'relationships' would become conditional, fragile and ultimately illusory. What if one partner gave more than the other? One would be in debt and would be a loser. The other person would want to withdraw and might do so as soon as possible. When mutual self-preoccupation was the ultimate god, there would be no real giving and receiving at all. To give in the expectation of getting is not to give at all. To receive in the belief that one is now in debt is not to receive. It is investment. It is buying and selling. It is all calculated around an earthly city where self-promotion, self-cultivation, self-concern, self-defence, lie at the heart of life.

In such a city, the safest, easiest, way of being heard would be to hire someone to listen to you. You would then receive professional attention, as long as the care person was paid, either by you, or an insurance company or the taxpayer. That way the contract would be clear and clean because commercial. We would all understand such a contractual relationship. In an earthly city it would be all we were capable of understanding since our god would be self, and the commercial transactions of autonomous selves.

Is such an 'earthly city' the current reality of our down to earth existence? Without doubt, Augustine would have thought so. He would have seen our contemporary life as the hell on earth that is the inevitable consequence of there being no effort to be receptive to his heaven on earth. He would have seen our current predicament as obviously and evidently riven with pain, distraction and illusion. Having abandoned our Divine counsellor, our secular alternative of 'person-centred' counselling would have been seen by Augustine as a glowing, growing, bursting boil that merely illustrated the true extent of our underlying sickness.

For Augustine, salvation was not to be found in futile excavations into individual interiors. We would find peace and fulfilment only by attention to others and, above all, in God who was the ground of our being both individually and collectively:

> Sell what you have. Win a full harvest by giving to the poor, and the treasure you have shall be in heaven. (ibid. p. 327)

> Let us share our bread with the hungry, give the poor and the vagrant a welcome to our houses, meet the naked, clothe him, and from our own flesh and blood not turn away. (ibid. p. 325)

> We see the things which you have made, because they exist. But they only exist because you see them. (ibid. p. 346)

Individual assertion and self-preoccupation was a journey after 'fools' gold'. It involved illusions of individual autonomy and competence. It showed a failure to understand how much we depended on God for everything we saw, said, did and thought:

> But we, O Lord, are your 'little flock'. Keep us as your own. Spread your wings and let us shelter beneath them. Let us glory in you alone. (ibid. p. 245)

It was arrogant for humankind to imagine that it could function without God even for a moment. Our powers of reasoning were, admittedly, greater than those of 'lower' animals; but they were pitiful in relation to the Divine power and of little use when employed independently of Divine support:

> We are too weak to discover the truth by reason alone and for this reason need the authority of sacred books. (ibid. p. 117)

Human pride in human intellect, virtue and insight were forms of arrogance and ignorance of our true weakness and dependence on Divine support. We could not, via our own curiosity and intellect, shine any kind of light on the mysteries and uncertainties of existence:

This futile curiosity masquerades under the name of science and learning, and since it derives from our thirst for knowledge and sight is the principle sense which knowledge is acquired, in the Scriptures it is called 'gratification of the eye'. (ibid. p. 241)

Going it alone, exploring where no man has been before, trusting one's own judgement, relying on one's own intuition or systematic observation: all these humanist agendas were seen as hubris and folly. We might pretend that we could employ our critical intelligence to the sacred texts and argue how best to interpret them. We might believe that we could speculate on philosophical questions about the nature of life. And yet, ultimately:

I listen to all these arguments and give them thought, but I will not engage in wordy disputes, such as can only unsettle the minds of those who are listening. (ibid. p. 295)

The resolution of our questions, conflicts, uncertainties could only come ultimately from God:

If any other than you were to inspire me, I do not believe that my words would be true, for you are the Truth, whereas every man is a liar, and for this reason he who utters falsehood is only uttering what is natural to him, what is his alone. If, then, I am to speak the truth, let men utter not what is mine, but what is yours. (ibid. p. 337)

Augustine would have denied that he was a great man. If he were a saint (as indeed he was declared by the Catholic Church), this was not because of anything that he did, or said or was. Rather, it was because he allowed himself to become a vehicle through which God could move and speak. Augustine was merely a receiver, and transmitter, of Divine love and insight. This is all we ever could be that was of real value to ourselves and others:

I speak in your presence, O Lord, and therefore I shall say what is true. (ibid. p. 340)

Even when we sought to make contact with God, we should not imagine that we were thereby seeking to attract the attention of our maker. Since He was omnipotent, omniscient and omnipresent, He was perfectly well aware of who, where and what we were, what we wanted and what we needed:

Your heavenly Father knows well what your needs are before you ask him. So by confessing our own miserable state and acknowledging your mercy towards us we open our hearts to you, so that you may free us wholly, as you have already begun to do. Then we shall no longer be miserable in ourselves, but will find our true happiness in you. (ibid. p. 253)

In other words, in the process of prayer we were not making ourselves known to God, who already knew us. We were, in fact, making ourselves known to ourselves, through the process of seeking to connect to Him. You want to 'discover yourself'? Then you must come closer to God. For Augustine there was no other way; anything else was distraction and illusion. Know thyself. Know thy God, as far as God makes Himself known to you through His Divine Grace. These were one and the same thing. Know God and everything else falls naturally into its place in the great scheme of things.

Within this agenda humility, virtue and self-abnegation stand high as topics of concern. Self-preoccupation, self-esteem, the direct pursuit of satisfaction were pitfalls to be avoided. Yet some of Augustine's observations have an ominous ring to them. The metaphor of a flock of sheep is not always empowering. Sometimes it is merely pathetic. Nietzsche found it obscene. But Christian lambs sometimes carried quite a bite. If you assume that God is the only salvation, that God is speaking through you, that without this God others are inevitably damned, then how will you feel if you interpret others as speaking and acting in (wilful or ignorant) opposition to the teachings of our Maker? Augustine was clear enough:

How hateful to me are the enemies of your Scripture! How I wish that you would slay them with your two-edged sword, so that there should be none to oppose your word! Gladly would I have them die to themselves and live to you. (ibid. p. 290)

With fighting talk like this from the mild-mannered saint, it is not surprising that over the centuries so many have been interrogated, tortured, hung, drawn, quartered and burned in order to be saved from their sins and thus increase their chances of finding 'eternal life'. While some Christian teaching has preached the virtues of tolerance and acceptance, it is hard to stay inactive if you are convinced that the Divine voice is using you as a vehicle, and that someone else is getting in the way of Divine destiny.

It is easy to look down on others when you believe that your intellect is more powerful than theirs. But how much more will you look down on the opposition if you assume that your own voice is not being driven by mere intellect, but by God Himself? Your conviction that this is happening will be stronger than a mere 'belief' and it will not be open to intellectual discussion and analysis since revelation is altogether stronger stuff than intellect. When God reveals Himself through me, I am just an empty vehicle. But in such circumstances, woe betide anyone who tries to argue. They cannot be arguing with me since it is not my will but Thine that is at work. I am a vessel. I will not argue. They are arguing with God. I do not merely believe this. I know this. Therefore I do not need evidence or argument. If God moves through me then I have spiritual gifts from God. They are not of my doing but they are not to be treated lightly since this would be blasphemy against God. If the Lord moves through me then I will have to face up to awesome responsibilities:

> The man who has spiritual gifts also judges the faithful, approving what he finds to be right and blaming what he finds to be wrong in their deeds and their morals. He judges them by their almsgiving, which is like the earth bearing fruit, and by their passions, which, in the living soul, are tamed into submission by the practice of chastity, by fasting, and by the soul's regard for its duty to God when it reflects upon the sensations of which it is conscious through the body. For he judges only those things which he also has the power to correct. (ibid. p. 334)

As the Christian Church grew in power, its power to 'correct' grew accordingly, along with its wish, willingness and 'duty' to judge. The result, you might believe, was that countless souls were thereby saved. And/or that countless bodies were killed!

At least, though, some responsibility was taken:

> I still thought that it is not we who sin but some other nature that sins within us. It flattered my pride to think that I incurred no guilt and, when I did wrong, not to confess it so that you might bring healing to a soul that had sinned against you. I preferred to excuse myself and blame this unknown thing which was in me but was not part of me. The truth, of course, was that it was all my own self, and my own impiety had divided me against myself. My sin was all the more incurable because I did not think myself a sinner. It was abominable wickedness to prefer to defeat your ends and lose my soul rather than submit to you and gain salvation. (ibid. p. 103)

For Augustine, God was not a concept to be derived and proved from philosophical principles or processes of reasoning. Neither was He an abstraction to be inferred from systematic observation of daily life. For

Augustine, God was a continuous real lived presence that required no proof once His reality and divinity was revealed. You just needed to know where to look and to look. And then God was simply obvious and everywhere. Indeed the power of God was overwhelmingly strong and bright. Did we need to prove that the sun shone down on us? Look at it, if you dare. Feel it. See its effects and its strong reflections all around you. And how much brighter is the Light of God?

Augustine converses mainly with God in his *Confessions*. He takes it for granted that when he moves, decides, feels, thinks, searches, hides, he does it all in relation to God. It is not even that God is an external agency to Augustine, prodding, pushing, probing him. God is 'outside' but God is also within him. Freud found an 'id' deep inside us, driven by a pleasure principle. Many Christians would have called this the Devil but for Augustine the deepest principle at work within was God. The Kingdom of God was within.

This way of experiencing ourselves is increasingly alien to modern and postmodern secular societies. Our ultimate sovereign, our God, indeed, in contemporary western cultures, is 'Me'. Self becomes its own deity. I come to my counsellor to help me find Myself. I am the last word on every dilemma I face. To be authentic and 'real' is to be driven by and in continuous contact with Myself.

Yet Augustine was by no means unusual in feeling himself to be driven by an agency that was much more than the self he might imagine he knew. Who or what are we? What drives, what opposes us? What is within, what is at peace and at war within? None of these is an easy question. All kinds of fascinating answers have been proposed and experiences reported, as we shall see in subsequent chapters. It is not at all certain that our most recent metaphors for self and agency are either the most sophisticated, the most comprehensive, or the most healing.

❓ Questions

1. What do you mean by, and how important is, a 'spiritual' dimension in the practice of care?

2. Is there any use for the notion of 'God' in the practice of care?

3. What do you do if God is, or is not, a central component in the experience of your client?

4. What, if any, role and meaning does 'prayer' have for you?

EXERCISES

1. Consider and discuss what it might mean to 'feel', 'experience' and 'know' God rather than merely to 'believe' in Him.

2. Share your ideas about what is meant by 'spirituality'.

3. Discuss why there should, or should not, be a role for 'spirituality' within the practice of care.

4. Discuss what clients may gain and lose from relating to their God as intimately as does Augustine.

5. Compare Augustine's account of spirituality with that of Nietzsche (Chapter 27).

Conclusion

St Augustine did not merely believe in God, he was in continuous dialogue with Him. Personal development was only possible within God. If we made a deity of Myself and thereby lived on an earthly city without God, we would be in Hell. Our lives would be fragmented and isolated. We would be at odds with each other, lost in illusion, living in fruitless irrelevance. God was our counsellor. We could counsel only before God; with God as our witness; supported by God. Without God we were nothing; counselling was nothing; our projects, our values, our lives were of no consequence.

Websites

http://ccat.sas.upenn.edu/jod/augustine.html

Bibliography

St Augustine, *City of God*, Doubleday, 1958
St Augustine, *Confessions*, Penguin, 1977
B. Stock, *Augustine the Reader: Meditation, Self-Knowledge, and the Ethics of Interpretation*, Harvard University Press, 1998

Chapter 9

St Thomas Aquinas (1225–1274)

Application

• Religious belief has declined but not disappeared; care workers need to determine how they relate to clients for whom God is a major component in their lives

• Religious belief provides a framework of values and purposes. Carers need to consider on what basis, and by what means, clients are to find secular purpose and direction. Alone? From the carer? From whom?

• Aquinas was, for centuries, a towering authority, vastly more significant than contemporary gurus of psychotherapy. Yet now he is largely ignored. This should give us pause for thought and engender suitable humility about our own current 'certainties'

• Aquinas put his life into exploring the intellect but, ultimately, his belief in God was immune to intellectual debate. What contemporary deities are similarly immune?

Aquinas' ideas, like those of St Augustine, grew after his death. Even as late as 1879, Pope Leo XIII determined[1] that, whenever philosophy was discussed, Aquinas' philosophy had to be taught as the only correct version of the truth in all Catholic educational institutions. In Aquinas' own time he was a more controversial figure, but he is now regarded as the greatest of the scholastic philosophers. This is less of an honour than it was, however, given that the standing of scholastic philosophy is no longer very great.

Scholasticism was the medieval Christian philosophical effort to reconcile Christian teaching with classical Greek texts. These had been translated into Latin and rediscovered in medieval Europe, having been preserved for a thousand years within Islamic teaching. Islamic scholars had particular respect for Aristotle, and Aquinas was the prime vehicle by which Aristotelian ideas became dominant once again within medieval Europe. It was Aquinas above all who did most to convince Catholics that Aristotelian ideas were consistent with Christian teaching.

Aquinas was more concerned than Augustine to provide rational foundations and 'proofs' of the existence of God. His proofs are elaborate but unconvincing to present-day philosophers. It may be asked why he felt the need to take so much trouble given that Christianity, for Aquinas and his contemporaries, was ultimately built upon Divine revelation. If you 'know' that you have directly encountered God, you will not feel much need to find proofs of His existence. Kierkegaard argued this point forcefully in more recent times (see Chapter 25). Aquinas was convinced that his intellectual reasons were adequate and that his intellect could find arguments to support Divine existence. Ultimately, however, he believed that his intellect depended on God infinitely more than God had any need of his intellect. Therefore, if his arguments fell down, this would be no real threat to his faith in God, which transcended all intellect.

This is mere background for carers who may decide that they have little reason to study scholastic philosophy. I have no intention of exploring Thomist thought in any detail, merely those components which provide useful insights and approaches to more contemporary concerns.

As philosophers often do, Aquinas saw wisdom and truth as the most important goals in life. These were much more significant than animal superficialities such as fulfilment, personal development or satisfaction.[2] But truth for Aquinas came from God, who was revealed directly to us and needed no analysis or justification via our powers of reason. As a result of this, discussion with a Thomist philosopher is a bit like playing chess with someone who you find to be playing by two sets of rules. For as long as he is convincing his audience, he will operate those principles of intellectual coherence and evidence recognised in secular intellectual society. But if he loses ground in the discussion such that you are, as it were, near to removing his king from the board (or his god from the planet), then he will invariably revert to the view that intellect, argument and analysis are trivial human preoccupations that cannot really grapple with cosmic consciousness. His lord and king, you will be told, is still alive and on the board because God's existence does not depend on mere rules and reason at all.

When faced with this kind of player, it is useful to ask them, not just what would have to happen for them to win the argument, but, even more important, what might count for them to be wrong and to change their minds? Aquinas could under no circumstances ever feel obliged to concede that: 'My arguments for God have proved to be false. I will have to abandon Christianity.' Consequently, discussing God with a Thomist philosopher can become an exercise in futility. Thomists, for all their interest in intellectual discussion, are not dependent on the truth or validity of their arguments and ideas. Therefore proving their adequacy or otherwise does not ultimately make any difference to the conclusions they will draw. The conclusion is determined in advance, God exists.

Why is this intellectual sleight of hand still relevant? You are unlikely to become a Thomist philosopher and neither am I. Thomist ideas no longer have much appeal but their imperviousness to argument deserves attention since many contemporary ideas are similarly protected. We have no right to imagine that Aquinas was any more prejudiced in his thinking than we are ourselves. The difference, essentially, is that Thomist prejudice is far more readily apparent to us than the biases of a new millennium. For example, how many contemporary schools of counselling have themselves been embraced in an act of faith? How far does the dearth of evidence, and the shallowness of much underlying thinking, impact upon counsellors or their clients? Counsellors often claim just to 'know' that counselling is a good thing. Their confidence rarely seems to relate to any evidence worthy of the name. They cite their own contentment and that of their clients as though this were evidence. Yet history shows that, as might be expected, people are generally contented with whatever dominant ideas and institutions hold sway over, and thereby make sense of, their lives. For centuries, priests and congregation were deeply 'contented' by St Thomas Aquinas and his methods for providing support to an ever-struggling humanity. Now contemporary, secular carers may be so dissatisfied with, and bemused by, Aquinas that they may wonder why this chapter exists at all. With a sense of history, however, we come to see that much of what we think is new is a recycled permutation of often repeated principle, practice – and prejudice.

We will, of course, welcome whatever positive evidence can be found for our own one-sidedness. But if evidence is unsupportive, then there is something wrong with the evidence, not the revered product. Counselling is good, we know this intuitively. In Aquinas' day people were at least as happy with Catholicism. Aquinas explored the arguments and evidence, but with hindsight it is clear that these were not of central importance to him, and certainly not to Catholic congregations. However, neither teachers nor disciples wish to consider that their beliefs are based more on prejudice and habit than on reason and evidence. Each generation likes to imagine that it is more reasonable and open-minded than older generations. But this itself is a prejudice based on no reason and no evidence. Evidence to the contrary will no doubt occur to our own children.

If we reflect on the matter it is clear that *feeling* good about something does not mean that it is necessarily *doing* us much good. This does not prevent us from feeling good about all kinds of products and services whose value is in no way supported by evidence of any kind. As it was then, so it is today.

In Aquinas' day there was concern about whether or not the priesthood were always the good people we hoped and expected them to be. This parallels contemporary concerns about whether counsellors and carers can ever be as skilled and as virtuous as they need to be. Aquinas 'solved' the problem by arguing that the sacraments, and the Church as a whole, carried their own power, and were therefore effective even when sacred services were dispensed by wicked clergy. This brought great relief to congregations for many centuries, since they could see with their own eyes that the clergy were sometimes very far from saintly in their daily practice. Aquinas' strategy preserved the Church as an institution even when so much of its priesthood descended into serious depths of depravity, corruption, cynicism and selfishness. Of course, there were limits to how much people would tolerate. They did not call for revolution, but eventually some called for a reformation.

Aquinas insisted that priests could do good even if they were not themselves much good. The virtue of the institution, as an expression of the will of God, overcame individual human failings. Can counselling find a similar solution given that it, too, seems to require an exceptional degree of human virtue in its practitioners? For example, if the counsellor is 'registered', will that make up for their technical and ethical shortcomings? Counselling cannot call upon a superhuman deity to bolster human limitation, but if we make a deity of 'procedures' and 'mechanisms', however ineffectual, perhaps that will solve the problem?

Aquinas sought to prove that God existed, but he also 'knew' Divine reality and claimed that he had experienced the being of God, within the considerable limits of human comprehension. But only in the life after this one would we really meet our maker and achieve the fullest vision, humanly possible, of Divine essence. Such vision would be so vast, brilliant, awesome and wondrous that everything we ever experienced on this earth could only be a pale shadow of, and patient preparation for, this cataclysmic encounter; the real life to come when our present life had ended. We would really start to live only after we had died!

Life on earth was nonetheless important. Our conduct here determined our place in the hereafter. Our behaviour should be of concern to ourselves and was certainly of interest to our maker. What were our aims, intentions and purposes? Did we seek wealth, fame, honour, power? Aquinas, and God, saw these as earthly distractions, superficialities, illusions taking us ever further from our only real source of happiness, which was to be touched by the grace of God. We could be more or less receptive to Divine contact, but Aquinas agreed with Augustine that such communion was not something that we could control. God could not be summoned at will. But if we acted basely, outside the Divine law, we took ourselves further from Him. God was omnipotent, but we had free will since God had willed it to be so. Salvation was more likely if what we willed was consistent with Divine intentions. It was nonetheless a gift of the Holy Ghost, and we had no right to imagine that we could entirely predict and control our fortunes either in this life or in the life to come.

Aquinas analysed sin in its various categories: mortal, venial, original. He related individual action to collective law making but all these earthly agendas were, of course, subordinated to his largest spiritual concern, the reunion of mankind with God. His *Summa Theologica* is a vast encyclopaedia. He was at the heart of a vast Catholic institution, teaching, supporting, comforting, explaining, governing and offering compassion and consolation. Like Augustine, he was convinced that any efforts at personal development were of no account without God. Even more than Augustine, Aquinas was certain that the living embodiment of God's teaching on earth was the Church. The Kingdom of God was 'within' (ourselves) but, above all, it was to be found within the process of our following the sacred teachings of Catholicism.

Just as contemporary counsellors may carry Rogers or Egan on their shelves, traditional Catholic teachers, priests and counsellors (these were traditionally 'three in one') would have Aquinas occupying a central part of their libraries. For centuries, throughout Europe, Aquinas was discussed, analysed, quoted, annotated, written about and presented. Students were trained in Thomist principles and practice and passed on what they had learned both to their own disciples and to the ever needy laity. Aquinas was like a vast intellectual cathedral beneath whose cognitive columns, canopies, arches and spires millions sheltered from the storms of existence for over six centuries. He provided meaning, purpose, a framework of coherence within which people could identity themselves and from which they could gain inspiration, support, faith, consolation. His ideas were not, as in our own time, just material for a debating society. They were the glue that held societies together; the vision that gave people reason to begin each new day; the authority that protected us from chaos; compassion and support in the face of doubt and disillusion. For the believer, and for Aquinas, his teaching was a manifestation of the will of God, and the saint was merely God's mouthpiece. From our own, much more secular perspective, however, it is easier to believe that God came to the people care of Aquinas, rather than the other way round. Aquinas, therefore, was an enormously powerful and significant human being. There is no one in our own time who comes, or will come, anywhere near to achieving the comprehensive, all embracing and long-lasting influence of these two hugely important saints, Augustine and Aquinas.

Yet nowadays, Thomism has virtually disappeared. Are any traces worth keeping? How much speaks to our own preoccupations? Will contemporary gurus be as long lived as Aquinas by remaining active and significant for another six hundred years? I rather doubt that Carl Rogers, or any other contemporary teachers, will be compulsory reading in whatever 'encyclicals' may be published in the year 2600.

? Questions

1. How important to you is evidence and reasoning in defining and supporting your practice of care and support?

2. To what extent is your own belief in counselling an act of faith?

3. Who are your important counselling teachers? Will their influence survive another century? Does it matter?

4. Do you need a system of values and purposes to offer clients, or is it enough, or preferable, to let clients find their own way?
5. Can you counsel without a system of values, meanings and priorities? If not, what is the basis of yours?

EXERCISES

1. Discuss the most important cultural influences currently operating upon counselling and the practice of professional care. How far are they adequate? How do you decide?
2. Consider how you would like counselling and care practice to develop and change over the next fifty years. What would have to happen for you to say that your practice has grown, developed, matured?
3. Discuss how far you think it is relevant that a client does or does not believe in God. In what way could this affect the practice of care?

Conclusion

St Augustine's God was so evident to him that reasoning was irrelevant. St Aquinas felt the need to 'prove' his God. But reason was an optional extra, rather than an essential support, to Divine existence. Aquinas was concerned to rehabilitate Aristotle and other Greeks who had been preserved within Islam for a millennium. We owe a debt of thanks to eastern 'infidels' for preserving the ancient Greek roots of western civilisation. Aquinas laboured under the shadow of Aristotle but Aquinas himself became an intellectual giant who comprised most of the ground and perimeter of western thinking for six hundred years. If we are to locate our own contemporary thinkers in a proper historical context, we need to paint them into this larger cultural canvas. Humility might be a desirable consequence.

Notes

1. Encyclical letter '*On the Restoration of Christian Philosophy*'.
2. Augustine observed that the Greek for 'philosophy' *means* 'love of wisdom'.

Websites

http://www.home.duq.edu/~bonin/thomasbibliography.html
http://members.aol.com/jmageema/index.html
http://www.nd.edu/Departments/Maritain/etext
http://www.knight.org/advent/summa/summa.html

Bibliography

St Thomas Aquinas, *God's Greatest Gifts*, Sophia Institute Press, 1996
F. Copleston, *Aquinas*, Penguin, 1991
B. Davies, *The Thought of Thomas Aquinas*, Oxford University Press, 1993
A. Kenny, *Aquinas on Mind*, Routledge, 1994
R. McInerny (ed.) *Selected Writings: St Thomas Aquinas*, Penguin Classics, 1998
L.H. Yearley, *Mencius and Aquinas: Theories of Virtue and Conceptions of Courage*, State University Press, New York, 1990

Chapter 10

Niccolo Machiavelli (1462–1527)

─────────────── **Key Points** ───────────────

■ The love and realities of power are more significant than the power and reality of love

■ The illusion of honour and love may produce results more effectively than the reality

■ No leader who is not prepared to be ruthless can hold a society together

■ Good behaviour is desirable when it is possible, but it is not always possible if we are to survive.

── *Application* ──

● Machiavelli challenges carer assumptions that people are basically trustworthy, honourable and loving
● He made a major contribution to the study of power, a subject too often neglected within counselling
● He challenges simplistic accounts of honesty and authenticity
● He argues that self-awareness requires us to be awake to the personal and national power that supports us
● He shows that humans do not just try to get *through*; they also attempt to get *the better of* each other. They sometimes need to get *away from* each other!

Counsellors tend to take a relatively optimistic view of humanity. People, they assume, are generally redeemable, loving and loveable if only misunderstandings and frustrations can be clarified, expressed and resolved. Individuals are blocked and stuck rather than boorish and bullying. Anger, when expressed, will dissipate rather than destroy. If we wish to make a better world, and, it is assumed, we surely all do, then we need to focus on the healing power of love. We must open lines of communication and show mutual empathy and understanding.

Machiavelli is therefore worth examining by counsellors since he, more than virtually any other philosopher, challenges the very foundations of such an optimistic vision of society. Machiavelli, I hope, paints too dark a picture of human potential and actuality. Contemporary counselling, I fear, tends to be naïve about the more malevolent and selfish components of human existence, not least its own. We must surely engage with and understand, without succumbing to, the wickedness of the world. We must, therefore, come to grips with the Machiavellian dimensions of (in)humanity. What better way than via consideration of the work of Machiavelli himself?

Machiavelli's most celebrated work is *The Prince* (1513). This is a kind of DIY guide for anyone who seeks to rule over others and has been studied as such by many in authority ever since. It is practical, down to earth, and considers human failings in a direct, blunt, ruthless fashion devoid of any tactful, or elliptical phraseology. Machiavelli's style of writing is so honest, direct and clear that it requires no summary or explanation. Unlike many philosophers, whose prose can be painful and almost incomprehensible, the simplicity and succinctness of Machiavelli cannot be improved upon.

For example:

> A prince ought to have no other aim or thought, nor select anything else for his study, than war and its rules and discipline; for this is the sole art that belongs to him who rules, and it is of such force that it not only upholds those who are born princes, but it often enables men to rise from a private station to that rank. And, on the contrary, it is seen that when princes have thought more of ease than of arms they have lost their states. (*The Prince*, Chapter XIV)

This is, surely, an overstatement of the case, and, Machiavelli must have known so himself since he goes on to consider other core skills to be included in the kit of every ruler. But Machiavelli seems to enjoy having a shock effect on his reader. He uses forceful, painful, language devoid of flattery and manipulation. In this he rather goes against his own advice. Perhaps that is why he was not as successful as he wished to be in courting the approval of the powerful. Only after his death did his book really become alive and influential. Does it live on today? Should it?:

For among other evils which being unarmed brings you, it causes you to be despised... it is not reasonable that he who is armed should yield obedience willingly to him who is unarmed... He ought never, therefore, to have out of his thoughts this subject of war, and in peace he should addict himself more to its exercise than in war; this he can do in two ways, the one by action, the other by study. (ibid.)

Machiavelli was nothing like as crude as some of his language. He was subtle and sophisticated and consequently realised that brute force alone, if used without wisdom, could create enemies faster than it could subdue them. He focused both on the love of power and the power of love. Power, it has to be said, was the key for Machiavelli, but diplomacy and manipulation was often the route rather than just brute force:

Coming now to the other qualities mentioned above, I say that every prince ought to desire to be considered clement and not cruel.

Upon this a question arises: whether it be better to be loved than feared or feared than loved? It may be answered that one should wish to be both, but, because it is difficult to unite them in one person, is much safer to be feared than loved, when, of the two, either must be dispensed with. Because this is to be asserted in general of men, that they are ungrateful, fickle, false, cowardly, covetous, and as long as you succeed they are yours entirely; they will offer you their blood, property, life and children, as is said above, when the need is far distant; but when it approaches they turn against you. And that prince who, relying entirely on their promises, has neglected other precautions, is ruined; because friendships that are obtained by payments, and not by greatness or nobility of mind, may indeed be earned, but they are not secured, and in time of need cannot be relied upon; and men have less scruple in offending one who is beloved than one who is feared, for love is preserved by the link of obligation which, owing to the baseness of men, is broken at every opportunity for their advantage; but fear preserves you by a dread of punishment which never fails.

Nevertheless a prince ought to inspire fear in such a way that, if he does not win love, he avoids hatred...

Returning to the question of being feared or loved, I come to the conclusion that, men loving according to their own will and fearing according to that of the prince, a wise prince should establish himself on that which is in his own control and not in that of others; he must endeavour only to avoid hatred, as is noted. (ibid. Chapter XVII)

This overt acknowledgement of the power of power is highly unfashionable. It is not 'politically correct'. Moreover, Machiavelli is surely wrong to suggest that punishment never fails. We are all democrats now, or claim to be. Fascism was a great celebration of power and ruthlessness, and Hitler lost. He also lacked strategy and subtlety. So does democratic rhetoric actually describe democratic reality? The west lives well compared with others, takes and keeps a disproportionate share of goods and resources. How do we manage to keep them? Because others know we work harder and smarter than they do, and seek only to emulate us? Because our planes, tanks, missiles, warships can entirely outperform anything the dispossessed might try to throw at us?

International power may seem less important when wealthy nations are no longer at odds with each other. There is no significant power struggle with poor nations. Why is that? Because we have gone beyond the resolution of issues by force of arms? More likely it is because we are so much more powerful than the poor that it feels, to us at least, that power is simply not a part of the story.

And what about integrity? Have we gone beyond craftiness and manipulation? During the Gulf War, the west claimed that it was defending democracy and national autonomy. We all, surely, know, that in fact we were defending western oil supplies and, as Machiavelli would say, why not? Even Pentagon officials were honest enough to admit that they would not have been much exercised by Kuwait if its main export were cucumbers. So what did Machiavelli offer as comment on the place of principle, ethics, integrity?:

> Everyone admits how praiseworthy it is in a prince to keep faith, and to live with integrity and not with craft. Nevertheless our experience has been that those princes who have done great things have held good faith of little account, and have known how to circumvent the intellect of men by craft, and in the end have overcome those who have relied on their word. You must know there are two ways of contesting, the one by the law, the other by force; the first method is proper to men, the second to beasts; but because the first is frequently not sufficient, it is necessary to have recourse to the second. Therefore it is necessary for a prince to understand how to avail himself of the beast and the man... Therefore, it is necessary to be a fox to discover the snares and a lion to terrify the wolves. (ibid. Chapter XVIII)

So, Machiavelli does not dismiss law. He acknowledges that the rule book is what distinguishes humans from animals who rely on claws and speed. But he suggests that there is still a great beastliness to contend with in all of us, and that we must all therefore know how to fight and flee as necessary and all the more so if we wish to be boss in our own barnyard. Books and rules do not always work. We must also know how to duck and weave and, on occasion threaten others so successfully that they will back down without a fight. Lions fight rarely with jackals. This is not because of the power of laws but of jaws and claws. So what then of goodness and principle?:

> If men were entirely good this precept would not hold, but because they are bad, and will not keep faith with you, you too are not bound to observe it with them. (ibid.)

Shall we be honest about our basic beastliness? Will that make friends and influence people? Machiavelli thinks not. We need to pretend, deceive, posture, convince via our own public relations efforts that we are more principled and honourable than is really the case. Of beastliness:

> It is necessary to know well how to disguise this characteristic, and to be a great pretender and dissembler; and men are so simple, and so subject to present necessities, that he who seeks to deceive will always find someone who will allow himself to be deceived.
> Therefore it is unnecessary for a prince to have all the good qualities I have enumerated, but it is very necessary to appear to have them.
> And you have to understand this, that a prince, especially a new one, cannot observe all those things for which men are esteemed, being often forced, in order to maintain the state, to act contrary to faith, friendship, humanity, and religion. Therefore it is necessary for him to have a mind ready to turn itself accordingly as the winds and variations of fortune force it, yet, as I have said above, not to diverge from the good if he can avoid doing so, but, if compelled, then to know how to set about it. (ibid.)

So, Machiavelli suggests, we must not diverge from good behaviour if that is at all possible. But we must recognise that, in real life, good behaviour is not always possible if we are to survive and that, in any case, one good goal often conflicts with another. This means that, to be successful in everyday affairs, a willingness to compromise is essential, and this includes compromising virtue. Goodness can be a winning quality, but if you want to go on winning you may sometimes need to jettison goodness in order to avoid martyrdom. If you want to be respected, be virtuous by all means, but ensure also that you are tough, flexible, fast, ruthless. Ensure, too, that you do not have too much of a reputation for ruthlessness. You must be smart enough to *appear* good more often than you *are* good:

For this reason a prince ought to take care that he never lets anything slip from his lips that is not replete with the above-named five qualities, that he may appear to him who sees and hears him altogether merciful, faithful, humane, upright, and religious. There is nothing more necessary to appear to have than this last quality, inasmuch as men judge generally more by the eye than by the hand, because it belongs to everybody to see you, to few to come in touch with you. (ibid)

Appearances matter, they form their own reality and it is a reality that counts for much. Of this, Machiavelli was convinced. It is a view shared by marketeers and do not forget that, in western countries today, more is spent on marketing, public relations and advertising, the promotion of appearances, than on education, the understanding of reality:

Every one sees what you appear to be, few really know what you are, and those few dare not oppose themselves to the opinion of the many, who have the majesty of the state to defend them; and in the actions of all men, and especially of princes, which it is not prudent to challenge, one judges by the result. (ibid)

History, it has often been said, is the story of the victorious. The good guys generally win if only because the winners always describe themselves as the good guys:

For that reason, let a prince have the credit of conquering and holding his state, the means will always be considered honest, and he will be praised by everybody because the vulgar are always taken by what a thing seems to be and by what comes of it; and in the world there are only the vulgar, for the few find a place there only when the many have no ground to rest on. (ibid.)

Is there no hope, then, for honourable and honest behaviour? Of course there is, says Machiavelli:

Nothing makes a prince so much esteemed as great enterprises and setting a fine example. (ibid. Chapter XXI)

Good and honourable behaviour creates a good impression. The trouble is that, for Machiavelli, the injunction seems to be that we must do good because it is often good for us, it is in our interests, it promotes our power and reputation. We do not, and we should not, he suggests, do good just because it *is* good. Goodness is often in our interests but when it is not, then too bad for good. Interests come first, middle and last. Goodness comes and goes according to what is necessary and manageable. As Disraeli explained to Queen Victoria, our alliances change, our interests remain much the same. And, if we do not protect them, who will?

So now we have international corporations with more power than ever before, leaning over backwards to show how concerned they are about the planet, about principle, honour, equity, democracy, stewardship. Do they claim to be honourable because they believe in honour and justice? Or because they believe in power and act, always, to protect and promote their interests? Are they as good as they claim? Could they ever be as good as they claim? Would it be in their interests to be as honest as they pretend?

Is it any different for the rest of us? Let us not indulge in beastliness but how beastly are we really? If we are to be wise and helpful, to ourselves and others, how much of the beast are we to recognise in all of us? How are we to come to terms with it? How honest can we afford to be about it?

These questions, I am sure, are every bit as important now as they were in 1513. There is a Machiavelli in all of us. If counsellors are, as they claim, to concern themselves with internal and social realities, let them watch out for him, within and around us all.

? Questions

1. Are your clients seeking, only and always, to get through to other people? What do you do when their agenda is about getting the better of others? What examples come to mind?

2. Should your clients always be honest and real and open? What do you do when they seek to manipulate appearances? What examples come to mind?

3. What is your response to client behaviour that you find morally repugnant? What examples come to mind?

4. What can we learn from Machiavelli without becoming cynical?

5. How honest can you afford to be with your clients? When did you last put your own interests before those of your client? What examples come to mind?

EXERCISES

1. Explore in your own counsellor or care worker training the place that has been given to honour, ethics, honesty, power. Should more attention be given to these topics?

2. Consider the various schools of counselling and professional care with which you are familiar and examine the view they tend to take of the *competence, honesty, integrity* and *courage* of human beings.

Conclusion

Machiavelli explored the dark underside of the human soul. We cannot escape it yet we should not embrace it. Can we learn from these shadows without being entirely overshadowed by them? Can we cope with inhumanity without becoming inhumane? Can we be realists without becoming cynics? Ethics, for Machiavelli, is subservient to power and self-interest. We do good if it secures our reputation. Yet people are most admired who do good because it *is* good, not because it will do *them* good. How are we to steer a middle way between naïve utopianism and amoral cynicism? There are no easy answers, but Machiavelli makes an important contribution by clarifying the questions.

Website

www.sas.upenn.edu/~pgrose/machi/index.html

Bibliography

N. Machiavelli, *The Prince*, W.W. Norton, 1992

Chapter 11

Martin Luther (1483–1546)

―――――――――――――― **Key Points** ――――――――――――――

■ Individuals could, with the help of the Holy Spirit, find God directly via scripture

■ The Church assisted, but was not essential to, mankind's communion with God

■ Individual conscience, aided by the Holy Spirit, could interpret and form an understanding of scriptural teaching

■ Clerical authority could therefore be challenged by one's own felt sense of inspiration from Scripture and the Holy Spirit.

―― *Application* ―――――――――――――――――――――――――――

• The parallels between 'high' and 'low', in both churches and schools of therapy, are worthy of attention
• Luther's was a more 'person-centred' route to salvation than that offered by Catholicism
• Luther believed that persons were, nonetheless, entirely dependent on support from the Holy Spirit when interpreting scriptural authority and were lost and damned without it
• How are we to assess contemporary acts of conscience and interpretations of experience that do not invoke any particular external authority?

Aquinas was a man of God *and* of the Church. For him the two were inseparable. The Church was the route that all must take to find God. The Church was the institution that would interpret God to mankind. There was no way to God except via the Church, which was organised within a strict hierarchy. The clergy would supervise the spiritual development of the laity. Their own spiritual life was itself supervised by more senior clergy. This line management went all the way to the top, to the pontiff himself whose supervision was directly in the hands of God and whose act of worship was the closest that mankind could come to God, at least on earth.

The Pope, supported by his scholarly, wise and learned counsel, was therefore the supreme authority on all matters of biblical interpretation, moral exhortation, liturgical development and ecclesiastical law. He consequently had a right to concern himself with the moral and spiritual development of every member of the catholic clergy and laity, and this included, not least, every European king, baron, soldier, merchant and statesman.

In practice, of course, he had to develop a working alliance or accommodation with a wide variety of fallible, energetic, superstitious and aggressive elites whose daily practice did not always live up to the high principles described in sacred Christian texts. For that matter, Catholicism's own clergy were not always as pious, holy, honourable, honest, or even half decent as the laity might have preferred and expected.

Many people have suffered and died in the name of God. Many God-fearing individuals have killed, robbed and raped each other in the name of God. Just suppose Christianity had not risen to predominance. What if one of its many competitor religions, or a secular humanist alternative, had succeeded at the expense of Christianity? Would Europe have been a more or less moral place to live? Would more or fewer people have died? Would more or less scientific, artistic, cultural and philosophical development have taken place? The question is almost undoubtedly unanswerable, certainly within the confines of these pages. Speculation soon becomes too broad and empty to have any real meaningful content. But it is not self-evident that 'heathen' nations were in fact more destructive, cruel or backward than medieval Europe. Indeed, it is worth remembering that the overwhelming dominance of Christianity within early and medieval Europe corresponds precisely with that 'dark age' of one thousand years that was so much feared as Rome fell around 400 AD and confirmed by contemporaries as Renaissance Italy was born after 1400.

Of course the Catholic Church also had its saints and these were always liable to short-circuit the hierarchy by going directly into an ecstatic communion with their maker without any assistance from the local priest, monk or other accredited guide to God. God could be known by revelation and He did not always confine His infrequent earthly visits to the Pope or other senior Catholic authorities. Individuals might appear at any time claiming miracles, ecstasy, union, communion and other tidings of great joy. Their claims would, of course, need to be investigated by church officials and not all would be accepted. Some claimants risked extreme condemnation for daring to make blasphemous assertions of non-ordinary religious experience. These would not always meet with the approval of accredited and registered external validators and quality assurance managers. Most mystical and miraculous claims of Divine light or voice would be rejected. Some claimants might need to be burnt at the stake. Others would be hung, drawn and quartered for their sins. Harsh treatment might be the only way of saving them from the devil. A forced confession of the error of their ways might provide one final chance of redemption in the life to come. In the process of saving the souls of the blasphemous, their earthly body functioning might need to be brought to an abrupt and painful end.

It was dangerous to claim you had met God, arrogant to imagine that you could interpret the experience and folly to dispute with the clergy, especially when they were the only people in the entire society who actually knew how to read the Bible (or anything else). But when printing presses made books available, and other technical advances required a different kind of readership, then the sales of Bibles could begin to outpace the numbers of priests. In these circumstances, a corrupt church, a southern church, a church that taxed too heavily and which interfered with northern mercantile and princely preference, was at risk.

Luther, then, was not the first 'person-centred' (as opposed to Church-centred) Christian; but the circumstances within which he claimed freedom from papal intrusion were powerfully supportive of him and, this time, too strong to be overcome by Catholicism.

Luther was an Augustinian friar, ordained in 1507, who became a professor in 1511 at the University of Wittenberg in Saxony. In the following years he developed the belief that personal salvation could be found through faith alone – without the intercession of the Church. We could read the scriptures for ourselves and, with God's help, we could understand them and be inspired and supported by them. Luther's was the first 'DIY approach' to the Christian deity, cutting out the 'middleman' retailer of the Catholic Church.

Luther was unimpressed with the low moral state into which he believed the Catholic Church and its clergy had sunk. For example, Catholicism was making a fortune selling 'indulgences' to the laity. This was a system whereby, if you had sinned, you need only pay a suitable fine to church funds and you would be automatically 'forgiven'. This, it seemed to Luther, made a mockery of notions of repentance, but it was certainly highly profitable for Church and clergy. Luther began his own independent study of the Bible and concluded on the basis of the evidence, in 'Romans' for example, that righteousness was a gift of God, not of the clergy. Authenticity of repentance was important, an empty ceremony or payment was not enough, and ultimately it was for God to decide how repentant we really were, not we ourselves or our priest.

Needless to say, the clergy did not approve of this sort of radicalism and the conflict came to a head when, on 31 October 1517, Luther nailed his famous 'Ninety-five Theses' to the door of the church in Wittenberg to protest the practice of selling indulgences.

In the next few years Luther's criticism grew both broad and deep. In his *Address to the German Nobility*, he challenged papal authority and invited Germans to unite against Catholic abuse and to reform the Church. In *On Christian Liberty*, he explored his radical 'person-centred' perspective on Christian faith. In *On the Babylonish Captivity of the Church*, he rejected most of the sacraments and other doctrine. He was called to defend himself and was excommunicated. Charles V, Holy Roman Emperor, observed at the Diet of Worms in 1521 that:

A single friar who goes counter to all Christianity for a thousand years must be wrong.

But the German aristocracy, including his own Duke Frederick of Saxony, supported him. Catholicism was not strong enough to crush this rebellion (although it certainly tried hard enough and, in subsequent struggles, much of Germany was laid waste).

The Protestant principle was that humanity would relate to God not just via the Church but also through each individual conscience and earnest effort to study and understand Christian teaching, directly, from one's own Bible. Hence the many various sects within Protestantism which allowed more or less autonomy to individuals and congregations to find their own way of sensing and praising God. At one extreme, within 'High' Protestant teaching, the power and control of the Church and its clergy would be much the same as within Catholicism. At the other, 'lower' end of the spectrum, members of the congregation were almost without any clerical leadership at all, merely electing one of their own to make arrangements for worship, or waiting for anyone who might find themselves possessed by the voice of the Lord, who could be relied upon to make Himself known as required.

In these ways psychodynamic therapy is the secular equivalent of Catholicism. It is hierarchical, requires long training, the interpretations of its priesthood are to be accepted by an ignorant laity, there can be no discussion among equals since the laity are not equal either in knowledge or insight and there is no way of progressing far without expert assistance. Just as you could not find God without the Catholic Church, so you could not find 'yourself' without psychoanalysis.

Client-centred approaches, in contrast, constitute the Protestant version of the faith. The therapist is thought to carry varying degrees of insight and authority but the last word must lie with the laity who must interpret, experience, develop and judge for themselves. You can certainly find yourself for yourself and you must find your own interpretations, understandings, narratives and make your own judgements. It is not the task of the therapist to do this for you; indeed, the largest judgement they may decide to make is the judgement that they should not judge at all. In therapy, just as within Christianity, there is a continuum of practice ranging from complete client self-determination at one extreme and total professional control of all interpretations at the other.

A citizenry wherein individuals trust more in their own conscience and less in the authority of the priest may be attractive to barons seeking to break the power of the church. The danger is, however, that citizens will get into the habit of trusting their own judgement and break free of the direction not just of the priest but also of the king and his aristocrats. 'Extremists' will even challenge the wisdom and authority of middle-class employers and professionals. Thus the tendency of Protestantism to produce sects seen as extreme, anarchical and unacceptable to existing national authority. Hence the need of a working alliance to be formed between church and state authorities so that priest and prince can stay in business and, working together, ensure that the people were kept in their place.

This pattern of power relations soon emerged around Luther himself. As an academic, he made his own study of the Bible, produced the first translation into German, and drew his own conclusions. But there were plenty of other academics around able to make their own studies. Once the authority of the Pope had been successfully questioned by one critic, a free for all from others was possible. Would these academics come to the same conclusions and form a consensus? Of course not. Very soon, Luther was in heated controversy with, for example, Zwingli and Calvin. Printing presses were increasingly available. Printing presses became increasingly necessary.

An ally of Luther,[1] the Dutch humanist, Erasmus, observed that:

> Luther was guilty of two great crimes – he struck the Pope in his crown and the monks in their bellies.

Luther could be sharp in his criticism:

> So our Lord God commonly gives riches to those gross asses to whom he vouchsafes nothing else. (*Colloquia* Chapter XX)

News of 'blasphemous' argumentation of this sort spread rapidly. What were the peasantry to make of it? They had plenty of material grievances of their own. If their own princes were questioning the authority of the Pope, could they not join in with their own criticisms of princes? Could they, too, argue for their own preferred forms of emancipation? They soon found out. It was one thing for Luther and the German aristocracy to criticise Catholicism, but this did not mean that everyone, from every station in society, was going to be allowed to join in with free-thinking contributions of their own. When the German peasantry, inspired in part by Luther's writings, rose up in 1524–25, Luther observed that:

> Anyone who can be proved to be a seditious person is an outlaw before God and the emperor; and whoever is the first to put him to death does right and well. (*Against the Robbing and Murdering Hordes of Peasants* Broadsheet, May 1525)

In the same month, Luther confided in a letter:

> In my opinion it is better that all of these peasants should be killed rather than that the sovereigns and magistrates should be destroyed, because the peasants take up the sword without God's authorization. (Letter to Nicholas von Ansdorf, 30 May 1525)

Notice Luther's matter-of-fact view that the peasants were acting without Divine authorisation. Yet who is Luther to say what God does and does not authorise? If he disqualifies the Pope as arbiter and interpreter of God's Word, on what basis can he say that any particular academic carries the necessary authority? Once the process of Socratic questioning begins, where does it end? When Pandora's box is opened, how and why should it ever be closed? What is to prevent representatives of the peasantry, of lower social standing, but with closer concern for, and understanding of, the plight of the poor, from usurping Luther, just he usurped the authority of the Pope? Hence the Methodist tradition and, behind that, still more radical, the Primitive Methodists. Hence, much later, the close relationship between Methodism and the rise of the British Labour Party.

The questioning process, once reawakened by the Reformation, could not easily be gagged. Scholarly study of the Bible could be used to support one of other of many Protestant versions of Christianity. Renaissance questioning could take scepticism and criticism further still and, ultimately, could result in an agnostic or atheist humanist vision that altogether rejected any notion of God.

Jesus was seen as a rebel, a puritan, or a supporter of the status quo, depending on the temperament of the scholar more than the reality of the texts. Luther himself was not so fierce about the need to control human sin as, for example, Calvin:

> Who loves not wine, woman and song,
> Remains a fool his whole life long.

That is attributed to Luther and certainly not to Calvin. How far he shared Protestant discomfort with sexuality is unclear. Hopefully he was being ironical in the following:

> The reproduction of mankind is a great marvel and mystery. Had God consulted me in the matter, I should have advised him to continue the generation of the species by fashioning them of clay.

Yet Luther could hardly avoid being a product of his own time:

> Men have broad and large chests, and small narrow hips, and more understanding than women, who have but small and narrow breasts, and broad hips, to the end they should remain at home, sit still, keep house, and bear and bring up children. (*Table-Talk*, 'Of Marriage and Celibacy')

Luther's Protestantism was not quite so strongly of the 'fire and brimstone' variety found in other Protestant sects, but neither was he a New Age, New Dawn, 'Born Again' optimist:

> The world degenerates and grows worse every day... The calamities inflicted on Adam... were light in comparison with those inflicted on us. (Commentary on the Book of Genesis)

Luther began a whole tradition of scholars taking from the Bible what they projected in to it. Optimists saw hope in scripture. Pessimists saw prophets of doom. Lovers of humanity believed that the Bible 'proved' that we should forgive and be forgiven. Those in despair about human beings read their Bible and, for them, it showed that we were, most of us, damnable and damned.

Now that psychotherapy has in many respects become our substitute religion, we find, inevitably, the same range of messages within the various 'schools' of therapy. Once again the underlying therapeutic message is determined, above all, by the personality of the guru. Each psychotherapist celebrity unfailingly finds the evidence that best suits their own temperament. There are 'high churches' and 'low churches'. There are optimists and pessimists, radicals and conservatives, puritans and libertarians, anarchists and authoritarians, and everything in between on these, and other, polarities.

The radicals see therapy as a means of challenging the wider social status quo. The conservatives see it as a way of reinforcing the status quo. The conservatives are generally better funded, now as ever, by that very status quo. So, for example, we may expect that counsellors who wish to be employed by commercial organisations will not find it in their interests to encourage a clientele that does not function effectively in the labour market.

❓ Questions

1. The Protestant Reformation gave greater autonomy of thought and action to individuals. Secularism gave still more. But how autonomous can your clients be? Is there ever a higher authority than 'individual conscience'?

2. If so, what is it and how do you ensure that you and your clients abide by it? What examples come to mind?

3. Who is best placed to interpret the experience of your clients? You? The client? Some other authority? Who decides and on what basis?

4. Is your style of counselling 'high' or 'low' church? Explain your answer.

5. If no single authority can be the arbiter of authenticity, who is to judge and how?

EXERCISES

1. Compare the schools of counselling with which you are familiar according to the authority each gives to counsellors and clients to interpret human experience.

2. Consider what authority, if any, other agencies could and should have over the interpretations made by counsellors and other care workers.

3. Counselling places great importance on the authenticity of individual experience. Consider what systems for determining authenticity are available within your own approach to counselling.

Conclusion

Luther matters more for the enormous influence he had on European history than for the stature of his ideas in themselves. Luther was in the right place and at the right time and consequently he was taken up by northern merchants and aristocracy who might well have selected another Christian rebel had Luther himself not been available. The status quo could not continue because of decadent Catholicism and Northern European pressures for independence. There are high and low churches both in Christianity and psychotherapy. How are we to reconcile principles of autonomy and authority within both theological and secular societies? The many parallel problems and opportunities deserve careful attention.

Notes

1. When he was not an enemy.

Websites

http://members.aol.com/umartyl/index.htm
http://members.aol.com/xrysostom/index.html
http://www.golden.net/worship/index.html

Bibliography

J. Atkinson (ed.) *Daily Readings with Martin Luther: M. Luther,* Templegate Publishers, US, 1987
H.P. Grosshans, *Luther,* Fount, 1997
M. Luther, *Basic Luther: Four of His Fundamental Works,* Templegate Publishers, US, 1994
M. Luther, *Colloquia,* trans. J. Aurifaber, Bloomsbury, 1994
H. Marcuse, *From Luther to Popper: Studies in Critical Philosophy,* Verso, 1983

Chapter 12

Thomas Hobbes (1588–1679)

Key Points

- ▓ Hobbes asked how we could live together constructively and co-operatively within societies

- ▓ He believed that a central royal authority was essential. Without such authority our lives were 'nasty, brutish and short'

- ▓ For Hobbes social values shaped individual consciences more than vice versa

- ▓ Therefore society was the bedrock of individual identity, development and well-being. We ignored it at our peril.

Application

- Counsellors see personal development, authenticity and integrity from an individualistic perspective. Hobbes argues that these all have social roots
- If Hobbes is right then counsellors and other care workers might need to pay more attention to the social components of individual health and well-being
- We tend to be fragmented in our specialisms; focusing on individuals or societies. A truly holistic vision would seek a broad integration that was more commonplace historically than it is today
- Hobbes challenges the notion that identity and conscience can be analysed merely by 'going within'. Perhaps we need to get 'out' more to understand how individuals succeed, or fail, to 'grow'.

Hobbes, like Machiavelli before him, explored the vicious underside of the human spirit. Machiavelli's _Prince_ provides practical advice to those who would seek to rule over others; Hobbes' _Leviathan_ (1651) offers reasons why it is in the interests of citizens to obey their ruler.

Hobbes was a Royalist during the Civil War in England. He wished to provide a justification for royal authority but he could see that, in a more questioning society, it was not enough merely to claim to rule by 'divine right'. So why should we take orders from kings if we no longer accepted that their particular authority was sanctioned directly by God? To answer this question Hobbes considered the alternative. What happens to us if we try to live without any central overriding sovereign authority? Hobbes accepted that individuals were indeed born essentially equal:

> Nature hath made men so equal in the faculties of body and mind as that, though there be found one man sometimes manifestly stronger in body or of quicker mind than another, yet when all is reckoned together the difference between man and man is not so considerable as that one man can thereupon claim to himself any benefit to which another may not pretend as well as he. For as to the strength of body, the weakest has strength enough to kill the strongest, either by secret machination or by confederacy with others that are in the same danger with himself. (*Leviathan*, Chapter XIII)

Lions and jackals might live in relative peace since jackals would always back away from conflict. Any human had sufficient strength or cunning to be able to kill any other human, relatively easily. What was to stop them? Hobbes believed that a central authority was essential:

> Men have no pleasure (but on the contrary a great deal of grief) in keeping company where there is no power able to overawe them all. (ibid.)

Is this pessimism? Surely we are more innately decent that that? Yet it is easy to underestimate the importance of central authority when that authority is strong, stable and has been in place for many generations. Citizens living within strong and stable states may well not appreciate what they have got until it has gone. Look at the Balkans in the 1990s. Look at many other imploding countries throughout the Third World and the ex-communist world. Then ask if it is enough just to focus on individual determination, conscience, ethic and honour.

We can afford to be so preoccupied with individualism in western societies precisely because the states of which we are a part are, relatively, strong, stable and powerful. We can talk about supposedly 'free' markets of supposedly individual buyers and sellers precisely because the states and the laws that construct and constrain these markets are so strong and stable. Take away a strong state and what becomes of the market? Look at Russia and you will find your answer. You have a battleground.

Without state authority, Hobbes argued, quarrel was inevitable:

> In the nature of man, we find three principal causes of quarrel. First, competition; secondly, diffidence; thirdly, glory. The first maketh men invade for gain; the second, for safety; and the third, for reputation. The first use violence, to make themselves masters of other men's persons, wives, children, and cattle; the second, to defend them; the third, for trifles, as a word, a smile, a different opinion, and any other sign of undervalue, either direct in their persons or by reflection in their kindred, their friends, their nation, their profession, or their name. (ibid.)

So, what becomes of people who seek to live without central authority?:

> Hereby it is manifest that during the time men live without a common power to keep them all in awe, they are in that condition which is called war; and such a war as is of every man against every man. (ibid.)

Surely this is an exaggeration? Or is it? Hobbes does not say that a state of war consists in continual fighting:

> For war consisteth not in battle only, or the act of fighting, but in a tract of time, wherein the will to contend by battle is sufficiently known: and therefore the notion of time is to be considered in the nature of war, as it is in the nature of weather. For as the nature of foul weather lieth not in a shower or two of rain, but in an inclination thereto of many days together: so the nature of war consisteth not in actual fighting, but in the known disposition thereto during all the time there is no assurance to the contrary. All other time is peace. Whatsoever therefore is consequent to a time of war, where every man is enemy to every man, the same consequent to the time wherein men live without other security than what their own strength and their own invention shall furnish them withal. (ibid.)

In other words, without a central state, Hobbes believed that we were condemned to live continually in a state of chronic mistrust, unease and insecurity. We might not be actually fighting, but we would be in continual fear of robbery and violence. What would be the consequences?:

> In such condition there is no place for industry, because the fruit thereof is uncertain: and consequently no culture of the earth; no navigation, nor use of the commodities that may be imported by sea; no commodious building; no instruments of moving and removing such things as require

much force; no knowledge of the face of the earth; no account of time; no arts; no letters; no society; and which is worst of all, continual fear, and danger of violent death; and the life of man, solitary, poor, nasty, brutish, and short. (ibid.)

Is this another exaggeration? Consider a contemporary example: Since the collapse of organised government in Russia the life expectancy of males has collapsed with it. In 1965 a Russian male could expect to live 64 years. In 1997 male life expectancy had fallen to 59, below that of Europe, the US and all of Asia, except Afghanistan and Cambodia.[1]

For Hobbes an absence of central authority creates a state of war. Fighting is by no means continuous but everyone is on a 'war footing'; wary, defensive, defended, insecure. Similarly, between nation-states:

> In all times kings and persons of sovereign authority, because of their inde-
> pendency, are in continual jealousies, and in the state and posture of glad-
> iators, having their weapons pointing, and their eyes fixed on one another;
> that is, their forts, garrisons, and guns upon the frontiers of their king-
> doms, and continual spies upon their neighbours, which is a posture of
> war. But because they uphold thereby the industry of their subjects, there
> does not follow from it that misery which accompanies the liberty of
> particular men. (ibid.)

Again, this does not mean that warfare between nations is contin-uous, only that no nation could afford to avoid spending considerable sums of money on guns, spies, propaganda departments, navies and (now) aircraft and missiles. For Hobbes, international tensions were unavoidable; talk of international justice was a mere propaganda exer-cise; self-interest predominated above any other principle. International peace was most likely when power between opposed alliances was evenly balanced or when one regional power so overwhelmed its rivals that it could impose, by force, peace on the rest.

Was this thesis true in seventeenth-century Europe? Will it be any less true in the twenty first century? At the end of the 'high civilisation' that comprised the twentieth century, we have just come out of a period of balanced terror between two superpowers. This did perhaps ensure that the war remained 'cold' at least in the central areas of each Empire. We are now in a period where there is just one global power, the United States. If any two countries go to war with each other they had better ensure that they have US indifference or support. Pax Americana does not create a perfectly peaceful world. It certainly does not produce a just world. But how many wars simply do not develop as possibilities because the US would not approve of them? Is American military power irrelevant and unnecessary? Or is its relevance affirmed by the fact that, being so overwhelming, it needs to be used so little? Does history suggest that peacekeeping is best achieved by persuasion or by the threat of force?

For Hobbes, issues were settled by force far more profoundly and regularly than by reason or moral sensitivity. What, then, was the place of 'justice' in a world where might determined what was right? Did this mean that might and right were essentially the same thing? Or was there no such thing as right?:

> To this war of every man against every man, this also is consequent; that nothing can be unjust. The notions of right and wrong, justice and injustice, have there no place. Where there is no common power, there is no law; where no law, no injustice. Force and fraud are in war the two cardinal virtues. Justice and injustice are none of the faculties neither of the body nor mind. If they were, they might be in a man that were alone in the world, as well as his senses and passions. They are qualities that relate to men in society, not in solitude. It is consequent also to the same condition that there be no propriety, no dominion, no mine and thine distinct; but only that to be every man's that he can get, and for so long as he can keep it. And thus much for the ill condition which man by mere nature is actually placed in; though with a possibility to come out of it, consisting partly in the passions, partly in his reason. (ibid.)

This is not to say that Hobbes was a cynic. He was not saying that 'justice' did not exist at all. His point, rather, is that concepts of justice are cradled, defined, developed and defended by the state and not by the individual conscience. This is directly contrary to what most people imagine they experience. In determining what is right or wrong, we suppose that we must each consult our own conscience. Ethics, we imagine, are an individual matter and nation-states emerge as a result of collaboration between individual consciences. Hobbes turns this round the other way. Ethics are produced via a central power determining, by defining, what is right and wrong, acceptable and unacceptable. The rules are made by the state, we learn the rules and we internalise them. We then consult what we have internalised and call it our individual conscience. Freud, much later, as we shall see, similarly took the view that conscience arose as a result of our internalising external authority.

For liberal individualists (and this includes almost everyone in the counselling movement), the sequence is individual conscience–ethics–laws–state. For Hobbes it was the other way round: state–ethics–

laws–individual conscience. Consciences do not create states; rather they emerge from the context of individuals being nurtured within a coherent and organised society.

We are, if we are lucky, born within a reasonably stable state whose sovereign power determines rules embodied in laws and ethical principles. These we learn, accept and incorporate. We incorporate them so well that, instead of going to the law book, we go 'inside' to (what we call) our conscience.

If we are unlucky, we are born in an anarchic territory devoid of any central authority. The result will be that our 'conscience' will remain undeveloped or underdeveloped. We will be riven with fear, aggression, self-centredness. Our lives and souls will be, in Hobbes' memorable words: 'Nasty, brutish, and short'!

The moral of all this, for contemporary counselling is that it is quite impossible to talk about individual and personal development separate from the development of the state. Hobbes failed entirely, I think, to show that the powerful sovereign authority should be a royal authority. Thus it was that subsequent political philosophers, such as Locke and Mill, could show that sovereign central state power could, and should, be more democratic and collective, via parliaments, pressure groups, elections, constitutions and so on. But Hobbes certainly did show how central authority, seemingly separate from the process of personal development, was in fact the very ground, circumference and ceiling comprising the public space within which personal development took place. Without it, such development was impossible. When central authority is strong and stable it may be invisible to us. But it is as important as ever to our very identity. Furthermore, it is not so stable and secure that we can afford to forget it or ever take it for granted.

Individualists argue: 'Let the person develop and society will gradually improve.' Hobbes' view was that there needs to be a strong stable society, held in place by central authority, and then and only then, does it even make sense to talk about justice, conscience and individual development.

State power, then, was Hobbes' central concern, a state embodied in the central sovereign power of the king. For Hobbes we did not require Divine justification for kings. We could calculate their importance and value for ourselves and we could freely give ourselves over as citizens of our sovereign authority. Having done so, though, we had no right to withdraw our consent. But personal powers and perspectives and personal development were also of some interest to Hobbes. He even had a chapter on the nature of 'counselling' (as understood within a

seventeenth-century context). Some of his comments on this subject
are worth recording:

> Between counsel and command, one great difference is that command is
> directed to a man's own benefit, and counsel to the benefit of another man.
> And from this ariseth another difference, that a man may be obliged to do
> what he is commanded; as when he hath covenanted to obey: but he
> cannot be obliged to do as he is counselled, because the hurt of not
> following it is his own; or if he should covenant to follow it, then is the
> counsel turned into the nature of a command. (*Leviathan*, Chapter XXV)

This is not so different as might be observed today except for Hobbes it
is impossible to separate 'counsel' from 'advice'. Today we imagine that
such a separation is possible, but I remain unconvinced. The counsellor's advice may not be overt, explicit, or commanding; but it is
impossible for anyone to give even the tiniest non-verbal reaction
except from a particular perspective; with all the values, beliefs, ideas
and experiences that this presupposes. The 'advice' from counsellors
may not be overtly asserted; it is, rather, implicit in shaping the counsellor's response. It is still, all the same, advice, and it is surely disingen-
uous and irresponsible to pretend otherwise?

Hobbes has some interesting observations to make about the necessary qualifications of counsellors:

> Because the ability of counselling proceedeth from experience and long
> study, and no man is presumed to have experience in all those things that
> to the administration of a great Commonwealth are necessary to be
> known, no man is presumed to be a good counsellor but in such business
> as he hath not only been much versed in, but hath also much meditated on
> and considered. (ibid.)

This suggests that Hobbes had little time for generic counselling. You
could not possibly be a counsellor in relation to 'how to live your life'.
You could be a counsellor in relation to specific areas, issues and problems that you had taken some trouble to study and reflect upon.
Neither could you be a counsellor who was just trained to 'listen'. You
had to know something about the problem of concern, otherwise what
was the point of listening and how would you even be able to listen?
You would 'hear' what the person was saying but you would not
understand much of what they were saying because you would not
have enough knowledge or experience to be able to follow what was
being said.

So, if I want someone to provide 'counsel' on possible reasons why my car is not working I will want to talk to someone who knows about cars. Conversely, if I want to listen in on conversations about cars I will have to study car mechanics. A study of 'listening skills' alone will not get me very far at all since it will not be sufficient for me to understand what is being said.

Of course, therapeutic counsellors do not provide counsel on faulty cars. But, Hobbes would have argued, the principle is the same in relation to any problem a client brings to a counsellor. The client talks about debt, or depression, or crime, or step parents. Can the counsellor be any help if they just make do with 'listening skills'? Or ought they not to learn something about debt, depression, crime, step-parenting, or whatever? And, realistically, how much, and how many, of the myriad dilemmas, concerns and problems that a client might present can any one counsellor expect to know about?

Too many contemporary counsellors seem to imagine that they can learn a 'process' – counselling – quite independently of a knowledge base: debt, depression, divorce. Too often, contemporary discussions of counselling veer between focusing on either human qualities or practical skills. A third dimension often gets missed altogether, namely *knowledge* (both theory and practice) of possible solutions to the problem(s) that concern the client. The excuse offered for this omission is that counsellors do not need to know about solutions because it is the client's job to determine which option to try. Hobbes would have agreed with that but would have been scornful of the idea that a counsellor could help a client move towards a solution if the counsellor was no kind of expert on solutions to the problem at hand.

In seeking counsel, Hobbes recommended that we make use of as much expertise as possible. It was unwise to rely on just one counsellor, however experienced and learned. We should weigh and judge the views of a variety of third-party outsiders. We should also ensure that each was kept each out of earshot of the others:

> Supposing the number of counsellors equal, a man is better counselled by hearing them apart than in an assembly; and that for many causes. First, in hearing them apart, you have the advice of every man; but in an assembly many of them deliver their advice with aye or no, or with their hands or feet, not moved by their own sense, but by the eloquence of another, or for fear of displeasing some that have spoken, or the whole by contradiction, or for fear of appearing duller in apprehension than those that have applauded the contrary opinion.

> A man that doth his business by the help of many prudent counsellors, with every one consulting apart in his proper element, does it best. (ibid.)

I could not agree more, and I only wish that this was the way in which counselling was practised now. Yet we imagine that we are ahead of previous practice. So much for our sense of history:

> Another business of the sovereign is to choose good counsellors; I mean such whose advice he is to take in the government of the Commonwealth. For this word counsel (consilium, corrupted from considium) is of a large signification, and comprehendeth all assemblies of men that sit together, not only to deliberate what is to be done hereafter, but also to judge of facts past, and of law for the present... The most able counsellors are they that have least hope of benefit by giving evil counsel, and most knowledge of those things that conduce to the peace and defence of the Commonwealth. (*Leviathan*, Chapter XXX)

This is consistent with Hobbes' views of the prime importance of a stable state. For Hobbes, the 'outcomes' of counselling were not to be defined in terms of the personal development of particular individuals. The peace of mind of the individual was of lesser importance than the peace, strength and security of the society as a whole. This was not because Hobbes was indifferent to individual peace and well-being but because he believed that individual development was only possible within the continued defence and development of the state as a whole. We were, as it were, passengers on the ship of state and we only really moved anywhere when the ship moved. We could only stay standing if the ship stayed afloat. The larger that vessel was, the more easy it was for us to imagine that it did not exist at all since its boundaries were invisible to us. Those on the *Titanic* could imagine that they were not on a liner at all but part of a comfortable world in itself. But break the skin that made the boundary of that boat intact, let the ice of alien intrusion pour cold water into the bowels of your world, wait awhile. Then see how far you go with your individual autonomy and personal development.

Hobbes wrote in 1651. Will his views be any less relevant in 2051?

❓ Questions

1. Can you think of occasions where the 'sovereign' independence of a client clashed with their and/or your wider social obligations? What was your role and response? What examples come to mind?

2. What do you think of Hobbes' views about the way to choose good counsellors?

3. How far do you agree with Hobbes that, without central authority, our lives would be 'nasty, brutish, and short'?

4. How far do you agree that the counselling movement pays insufficient attention to the social roots of (so-called) individual autonomy?

EXERCISES

1. Examine how far your own training details the knowledge and skills that clients need to acquire.

2. Consider how far your own training required you to develop specialised knowledge of the particular problems faced by categories of clients.

3. Discuss how far counselling is a generic activity as opposed to a collection of problem-focused specialisms.

Conclusion

For Hobbes, personal development could not be understood except within the context of social development. The social was more fundamental, more important and more influential. If we could produce a healthy society we would have healthy individuals. Hobbes' argument that central authority needed to be of royal blood did not stand the test of time. However, counsellors need to realise that clients are not sovereign judges of their destiny, even within the confines of the counselling contract. Counsellors and clients are themselves subject to a wider social contract of duties, rights, obligations, and are not free to ignore this larger association and fellowship.

Note

1. *Time* Magazine, 11 August 1997

Website

http://www.arrowweb.com/philo/Pers/HobbPers.htm
http://www.rjgeib.com/thoughts/nature/hobbes-bio.html

Bibliography

G.B. Herbert, *Thomas Hobbes: The Unity of Scientific and Moral Wisdom*, University of British Columbia Press, 1989

T. Hobbes, *Human Nature*, Oxford University Press, 1994

T. Hobbes, *Leviathan*, Oxford University Press, 1998

G.A. Rogers, *Perspectives on Thomas Hobbes*, Oxford University Press, 1991

Chapter 13

René Descartes (1596–1650)

--------- Key Points ---------

■ To establish knowledge we need to strip away all that is uncertain

■ We then find that our indubitable starting point is the non-material thinking 'self'

■ 'I think, therefore I exist.' From this starting point we can derive God, the material world and other minds

■ There are three kinds of basic 'stuff': the first two, matter and mind, were created by the third, God

■ The essential 'self' is a non-corporeal mind inhabiting a physical body.

--- *Application*

● People are often Cartesians without realising it. Like Descartes, they imagine 'self' to be a non-physical mind inhabiting a material body

● The connections between mind and body are mysterious. The nature of 'mind' remains unclear

● Descartes begins an era of self-centredness. Starting with 'me', I derive God and then everything else

● We look out so much from this dualistic paradigm of mind and matter that it is hard to look in on it

● Descartes' dualism may have raised more problems than solutions to the riddle of personal identity.

Descartes proposed three basic kinds of 'stuff', or substance: God, mind and matter.[1] Mind and matter were creations of God. Some matter took the form of living bodies and these were all machines. The matter of which they were comprised was matter just like that of any inanimate material. Bodies were alive/animate, however, because within them (in some sense), was a 'mind'. The mind was what 'I' really was. I occupied, but did not consist of, my body. The inanimate universe was like a vast clockwork mechanism and minds, if large enough, could understand it through processes of reasoning.

Other minds were more difficult to understand given that all we could witness were the words and actions of other bodies. The interconnection of mind and body was a vexed problem not settled adequately by Descartes or by anyone adopting mind and body as distinct and basic categories.

Ask most people which philosopher has had most influence on them and they would think you were trying to be funny. Most people have read no philosophy, could name no or few philosophers, and might thereby assume that philosophy and philosophers have had nothing whatever to do with their lives, thoughts, hopes or fears.

In this they would be quite wrong. Philosophers elaborate basic assumptions, key ideas and priorities about self and world, and these comprise the framework within which others think, feel, plan, hope and speculate. Philosophers clarify and construct conceptual building blocks from which others try to make shapes in their lives. Given that we are most preoccupied with the structure of our own ideas, we tend not to notice the blocks from which they are constructed unless we have been encouraged to think about the foundations of our thoughts or are temperamentally inclined to ponder such abstractions.

Descartes died well over three hundred years ago, yet it may well be that most westerners are still Cartesians, with all the insights and blindspots that this conceptual framework provides. The fact that they are unaware of their Cartesian tendencies makes them all the less able to reflect upon, challenge and move on from the basis of thinking which Descartes developed. Certainly whenever the counselling movement refers to finding 'myself' it seems to be presupposing very much a Cartesian view of personal identity. This is important and unfortunate because, as I will try to show later, the Cartesian model of personal identity has almost certainly overrun its 'sell-by' date. It is time to move on, but how are people to do so if they do not know what assumptions they are making or what other options are available?

Descartes found a very useful way of expressing geometric forms algebraically, and children still learn about Cartesian co-ordinates today. His algebra also allowed us to analyse geometries in n dimensions rather than just three. Of more relevance to counselling, Descartes was keen to try to produce, as it were, an adequate system of co-ordinates to describe and locate both the self and the basis of our knowledge of the world. He wanted to cut away all that was uncertain and unclear in our knowledge of self and world and, with all the system and rigour of a mathematician, he set about the task. The results he describes in his *Discourse on Method* (1637).

He begins by listing the procedures he would follow when setting about his work:

> The first was never to accept anything for true which I did not clearly know to be such; that is to say, carefully to avoid precipitancy and prejudice, and to comprise nothing more in my judgement than what was presented to my mind so clearly and distinctly as to exclude all ground of doubt.
>
> The second, to divide each of the difficulties under examination into as many parts as possible, and as might be necessary for its adequate solution.
>
> The third, to conduct my thoughts in such order that, by commencing with objects the simplest and easiest to know, I might ascend by little and little, and, as it were, step by step, to the knowledge of the more complex; assigning in thought a certain order even to those objects which in their own nature do not stand in a relation of antecedence and sequence.
>
> And the last, in every case to make enumerations so complete, and reviews so general, that I might be assured that nothing was omitted. (*Discourse on Method*, p. 15)

Additionally, Descartes drew together the moral principles which would themselves shape the way in which he would proceed, these would provide him with a guidepost as he set to work to cut away most of the other conceptual baggage that could not survive his systematic and sceptical critique:

> The first was to obey the laws and customs of my country, adhering firmly to the faith in which, by the grace of God, I had been educated from my childhood and regulating my conduct in every other matter according to the most moderate opinions, and the farthest removed from extremes, which should happen to be adopted in practice with general consent of the most judicious of those among whom I might be living. (ibid. p. 19)
>
> My second maxim was to be as firm and resolute in my actions as I was able, and not to adhere less steadfastly to the most doubtful opinions, when once adopted, than if they had been highly certain; imitating in this the example of travelers who, when they have lost their way in a forest, ought not to wander from side to side, far less remain in one place, but proceed constantly towards the same side in as straight a line as possible, without changing their direction for slight reasons, although perhaps it might be chance alone which at first determined the selection; for in this way, if they do not exactly reach the point they desire, they will come at

least in the end to some place that will probably be preferable to the middle of a forest. (ibid p. 20)

My third maxim was to endeavour always to conquer myself rather than fortune, and change my desires rather than the order of the world, and in general, accustom myself to the persuasion that, except our own thoughts, there is nothing absolutely in our power; so that when we have done our best in things external to us, all wherein we fail of success is to be held, as regards us, absolutely impossible: and this single principle seemed to me sufficient to prevent me from desiring.

Having thus provided myself with these maxims, and having placed them in reserve along with the truths of faith, which have ever occupied the first place in my belief, I came to the conclusion that I might with freedom set about ridding myself of what remained of my opinions. (ibid. p. 23)

Descartes was looking for a firm foundation of knowledge from which he could build his understanding. He decided to take no chances, to reject anything and everything about which there was room for uncertainty:

To reject as absolutely false all opinions in regard to which I could suppose the least ground for doubt, in order to ascertain whether after that there remained aught in my belief that was wholly indubitable. (ibid. p. 24)

Descartes observed that our sense observations could sometimes deceive us, and that, additionally, we could sometimes make errors in our reasoning. But if we threw all this away as uncertain, subject to suspicion, then what, if anything, was left?:

I observed that, whilst I thus wished to think that all was false, it was absolutely necessary that I, who thus thought, should be somewhat; and as I observed that this truth, I think, therefore I am (*COGITO ERGO SUM*), was so certain and of such evidence that no ground of doubt, however extravagant, could be alleged by the sceptics capable of shaking it, I concluded that I might, without scruple, accept it as the first principle of the philosophy of which I was in search. (ibid. p. 27)

So there it is, the philosophical basis of the 'me'-centred cosmos. Everything else, apparently, is open to doubt, but here am I, doubting this, doubting that. Whatever else gets torn away, *I* remain, questioning, tearing, thinking, thinking, thinking. Even my body is less substantial than 'me':

> I attentively examined what I was and as I observed that I could suppose that I had no body, and that there was no world nor any place in which I might be; but that I could not therefore suppose that I was not; and that, on the contrary, from the very circumstance that I thought to doubt of the truth of other things, it most clearly and certainly followed that I was. (ibid. p. 27)

The body could be made to vanish in our imagination, but still we could go on imagining. What was left?:

> I thence concluded that I was a substance whose whole essence or nature consists only in thinking, and which, that it may exist, has need of no place, nor is dependent on any material thing; so that 'I,' that is to say, the mind by which I am what I am, is wholly distinct from the body, and is even more easily known than the latter, and is such, that although the latter were not, it would still continue to be all that it is. (ibid. p. 27)

Here, then, the jewel of certainty in a potentially non-existent crown: 'ME', the thinker, and the foundation from which all other knowledge might be built. And here is the basis from which so much of our current thinking and liberal tradition is built. 'Selves' are real and certain. Bodies are less real. Societies are even less actual. It is a quick jump to presuming that what is most indisputable is also what is most important.

In some ways Descartes' suggestion is not new. Others, from Plato onwards, had explored versions of the view that the non-material 'soul' was more real than the material body. How else could we justify personal immortality given the evident fact that bodies invariably rotted away after three score years and ten? Plato, however, had a whole cast of 'forms' that were the ultimately real. He was not just left with the lone 'self'.

Of course, even as Descartes is sceptically vanishing his world out of the status of indubitable existence, he specifically reminds us that he is going to stay a law-abiding and God-fearing citizen. Indeed Descartes does not manage to pull very far alone on the bootstrap of self. When alone he finds he is not always happy. So is he really alone?:

> I perceived that doubt, inconstancy, sadness, and such like, could not be found in God, since I myself would have been happy to be free from them.
>
> In the next place, from reflecting on the circumstance that I doubted, and that consequently my being was not wholly perfect (for I clearly saw that it was a greater perfection to know than to doubt), I was led to inquire whence I had learned to think of something more perfect than myself; and

I clearly recognised that I must hold this notion from some nature which in reality was more perfect... a nature which was in reality more perfect than mine, and which even possessed within itself all the perfections of which I could form any idea; that is to say, in a single word, which was God. (ibid. p. 28)

For Descartes, God is safely in place, and he explores and accepts a variety of arguments for God's existence. Of course, the fact that he feels the need to 'prove' Divine existence suggests that God is less indubitably a part of his felt experience than it was for, say, St Augustine. Remember that Augustine's *Confessions* consists in a dialogue with God who is far more present to Augustine even than Augustine is to himself. Descartes' *Discourse* is much more of a monologue. God gets pulled in only after 'self' has reasoned Him back into the frame. The door is thereby wide open for other selves to question Descartes' arguments for Divine existence. In subsequent centuries they did just that. So now we have many more people than ever who take either the agnostic view that the arguments are uncertain, or the atheist belief that there is clearly no meaningful concept of Divine reality at all.

When God is discarded, what is left that is real? Well, 'me', of course, as Descartes would have it. 'Me' then takes the place of God since nothing else so 'tangible' and 'authentic' remains. Traditionally, it was the Church that provided sanctuary, meaning, consolation, comfort, a confessional. With the decline of the Church, a religion of 'self' comes in to replace it. If 'self' is most central, most real, most important then we must organise our lives to satisfy this 'self'. We must 'consume' in order to be more of a 'somebody'. And, if embodied objects are less real than disembodied selves yet we are feeling unsure about ourselves, we must find someone who can help us 'explore' ourselves, 'develop' ourselves, 'express' ourselves, provide a language by which we can furnish, discuss, and present our psychic 'interior'.

There are now scores of such languages to choose from. Do you have an id, ego and superego? Are you looking for your 'inner child'? A 'subpersonality'? The marketplace is now full of different languages by which people can explore, describe, develop and express aspects of 'themselves'. Above all, there are armies of specialists who will help you find your 'true' self because, after all, you do not want to settle for one of the many varieties of false self, do you?

The fact that there are so many different ways in which I can 'find myself' is thought, by some, to be a sign of all the supposedly enormous progress that our *ologies* of the psyche have been making in the past hundred years or so. It may, though, signify that the entire exercise is, in some way, fundamentally flawed. Are we just creating and chasing more and more fictions of what we imagine to be 'myself'? Is this really getting us anywhere?

It is one thing for a counsellor to offer to help you with a specific problem, for instance debt or timidity. But what about the more generic agenda of 'finding' and 'developing' 'myself'? What does this mean? If Descartes is to be believed, then 'myself' is that which is most certain, most fundamental, most indubitable. But is Descartes right? I think not, and we shall explore more useful observations about self later. For example, Heidegger, more than anyone else in the twentieth century, utterly demolished Cartesianism. But few read Heidegger. His abstruse language, and questionable politics, do not encourage a popular following.

The modern agenda, following from Descartes, has been very much one about 'self'. Liberal democracies were to assist selves to explore and express themselves in a 'free' market. However, self-preoccupation proves to be sterile and unfulfilling. We 'find ourselves', whatever that will prove to mean, more by commitment to others, people and principles, than to whatever we may imagine to be ourselves. Moreover, we may apply Cartesian scepticism to 'self' and find that self, too, is something of a fiction, a construction. This becomes more and more likely as we observe how many constructions of self are now available in the cultural marketplace. Hence the *post*modern agenda which no longer worships at the alter of 'self' but which 'deconstructs' self, along with everything else. And leaves? Nothing? More of this later.

Descartes distinguished between a physical world (within which machines were to him, and others, of great fascination) and a mental world of selves, each of which was the essence of the unique individual human personality. It takes a philosopher, of course, to be able to keep a straight face while concluding that we are not really in the physical world at all. Philosophers, after all, tend to be less physically connected to day-to-day existence than most, as their wives might wryly agree.[2]

This means that, when we observe other people, we are not observing them at all. We are merely observing the bodies that, somehow or another, 'contain' the non-material soul/mind/self that is the essence of identity. I 'know' that I (non-corporeal) am looking out through my (physical) eyes from somewhere 'inside' my physical head. At least, I imagine I know this if I subscribe, as most people inadvertently do, to the Cartesian world view. Correspondingly, I imagine that I can 'look in' on the (non-corporeal) you by, for example, making 'meaningful' eye contact with you. But all I see are the whites and darks of your eyes. If I shine a light into those eyes I can light up the blood vessels through which you see the world. I cannot throw any light onto you. Of course I cannot if, as Descartes believed, your essential, real, authentic self is an incorporeal 'ghost in the machine'.

This raises the question of whether I am the only real person around! Maybe you are all cleverly constructed robots? Or, if real robots can be so cleverly constructed, ought we to assume that they, too, have souls, minds, selves and personalities? These questions are currently being actively considered and have been the stuff of a huge number of science fiction dramas. Descartes was one of the first to spot the problem (not surprisingly, perhaps, since it is an inevitable consequence of his own model):

> Were there such machines exactly resembling organs and outward form an ape or any other irrational animal, we could have no means of knowing that they were in any respect of a different nature from these animals. (ibid. p. 44)

But what if a machine was made to look and act like a man? Could we tell the difference? Descartes thinks we could:

> If there were machines bearing the image of our bodies, and capable of imitating our actions as far as it is morally possible, there would still remain two most certain tests whereby to know that they were not therefore really men. Of these the first is that they could never use words or other signs arranged in such a manner as is competent to us in order to declare our thoughts to others: for we may easily conceive a machine to be so constructed that it emits vocables, and even that it emits some correspondent to the action upon it of external objects which cause a change in its organs; for example, if touched in a particular place it may demand what we wish to say to it; if in another it may cry out that it is hurt, and such like; but not that it should arrange them variously so as appositely to reply to what is said in its presence, as men of the lowest grade of intellect can do. (ibid. p. 44)

This was true enough in 1637, but who can be sure that it will remain true for much longer? Computer scientists are now working flat out to produce conversation and counselling programmes precisely designed to mimic human conversation so well that, when you talk to them, you cannot tell from their answers whether they are human or not. Alan Turing proposed his 'Turing Test' just after World War Two. The challenge – can we produce a computer which we cannot identify as non-human even after a half-hour conversation? (You are to assume that it is behind a wall, the test is of the conversation not the physical embodiment.) No machine has passed this test yet, but some are getting *much* closer![3]

So, on to Descartes' second test:

> The second test is, that although such machines might execute many things with equal or perhaps greater perfection than any of us, they would, without doubt, fail in certain others from which it could be discovered that they did not act from knowledge, but solely from the disposition of their organs: for while reason is an universal instrument that is alike available on every occasion, these organs, on the contrary, need a particular arrange-ment for each particular action; whence it must be morally impossible that there should exist in any machine a diversity of organs sufficient to enable it to act in all the occurrences of life, in the way in which our reason enables us to act. Again, by means of these two tests we may likewise know the difference between men and brutes. (ibid. p. 45)

This, too, is less obviously true than it used to be. Robots do not, of course, offer anything like the range of behaviours and 'conversations' that humans can manage. But they are improving steadily. Different components can be put together so that, it is hoped, we will have robot butlers able to walk, talk, welcome us in the morning, fetch breakfast. Science fiction writers explore the possibility of their 'making love' to us as well. I would not be surprised if serious efforts along these lines are already being made.

The interesting point about Descartes' discussion of robots, that no one else, to my knowledge, has noticed, is that he uses *behavioural* criteria to determine whether or not you are a person or a robot. In (Cartesian) reality, you are a person because you have (and are) an incorporeal soul. But none of us can observe *other* souls at all. Therefore I decide if you are a person or a robot by observing the quality and variety of your conversations and actions. Folk wisdom proposes that, if it walks and sounds like a duck, it *is* a duck. Likewise, if you talk and behave personably enough, you *are* a 'person'. If not, you are a machine. I suspect Descartes would be extremely concerned about his tests if he could come alive in our own time and observe just how close machines are getting to passing them!

For Descartes, the incorporeal soul is apparently what is most real, most important and which most quintessentially comprises who we are.

Yet although we are, as it were, rubbing (non-materially) against our own soul on a continuous basis, we have no access to the soul of other people at all. In determining who they are and what makes them unique, and on what basis we like or dislike, engage or disengage with them, we use bodily and verbal criteria. We observe what people say and what they do, and this is what really matters to us. Yet what really matters to them, if Descartes is to be believed, is their non-physical soul, or 'self'.

It might be asked, if we engage with words and actions, day to day, in every way; and if it is these that determine whether we are happy or sad, inspired or depressed, then do we need a concept of a 'soul' at all? Is the physical world we have not good and complete enough? If we assume that it is devoid of 'souls' in the metaphysical sense, does that mean that it is in any way deprived of excitements, experiences, hopes, fear, achievements, connections, intentions and all the rest?

As machines become more competent, will we discover those special (small) territories that make us truly human and which only we humans can achieve? Robots and humans may each throw light on the other. Work and play with some clever machines and perhaps, before long, it may be easy to imagine that they have 'personal' characteristics. Work and play with some sleepy humans, and it is already easy to imagine that they are existing, rather than living, in a robotic fashion. For example, when listening to some of the psycho-babble offered about one's 'real self' among counselling students, even at postgraduate level, I have not always found it easy to assume that here is a unique soul grappling individually with human problems. On the contrary, it can sound like an automatic algorithm that has adopted, and is mindlessly reciting, off-the-shelf platitudes about authentic self-hood.[4]

Horror stories about 'people' proving themselves to be androids have their power precisely because we *can* imagine that perhaps after all, the people around us are not people at all. If not robotic, maybe they have been taken over by alien life? (Another science fiction favourite.) In any case, if personhood requires that we must keep on managing to say something unique, then perhaps all our 'personhoods' are under threat? How often do *any* of us think truly original thoughts? How many go to their graves without ever having thought anything uniquely new or interesting at all?

? Questions

1. What picture do you have of the 'real you'? Does it make sense to imagine that there is a real, ultimate, essential self? Is it non-physical?

2. If we lose an arm have we lost ourself? But if we lose our mind? What then?

3. Is it useful/meaningful to go 'inside' in order to find ourselves? Or might it be better to look at our actions? Give examples to illustrate your answers.

4. Could there be a self without a body? Could a well-crafted machine deceive you into believing it had a mind?

5. Are the many languages of 'self' a sign of progress in our understanding of identity, or regress in our grasp of community?

EXERCISES

1. Share views about the location, if any, of the 'real me'? Is it behind the eyes more so than under the toe nails?

2. Discuss your experiences of 'discovering myself' and the language and metaphors you use to describe this.

3. Consider, compare and discuss your experience with, and interventions towards, clients concerning their views of their own identity.

Conclusion

Descartes considered questions of personal identity more than his predecessors. He gave us a model of mind and matter that people passively adopt today who have never heard of Descartes. In so doing, he displaced God somewhat, and raised questions about the relation between minds and bodies that continue to perplex us to this day. It is possible that Descartes' mind–matter dualism has created more confusion for us than insight. But it is difficult to escape a dualistic analysis since it provides so much of the framework within which we continue to construct our thoughts about 'self' and 'world'. For alternatives, compare Descartes with, in particular, Spinoza, Leibniz, Berkeley, Hegel, Heidegger and Sartre.

Notes

1. The notion of a basic 'substance' may itself need some basic questioning, but this will come out later.
2. I fear that I am still fairly safe with this generalisation. Philosophers have, overwhelmingly, been men although I am sure that the subject could achieve more if feminine perspectives on it were more in evidence.
3. A conversation I had with my counselling robot, Dr Sbaitso, about the robotisation of counselling is recorded in my last book, *Challenges to Counselling and Psychotherapy*, Macmillan, 1996.
4. On some of the juvenile 'chatlines' that I have witnessed through my daughter's early encounters on the internet, it really is impossible to know if the voice is a human or a conversation programme behind all the fantasy and disconnected time filling.

Websites

http://www.geocities.com/Athens/Forum/5507/descartes.html
http://philos.wright.edu/DesCartes/Meditations.html

Bibliography

K.F. Barber, J.E. Gracia (eds) *Individuation and Identity in Early Modern Philosophy: Descartes to Kant*, State University of New York Press, 1994
R. Descartes, *Discourse on Method*, Everyman, 1965
R. Descartes, *Meditations*, Cambridge University Press, 1998

Chapter 14

Baruch de Spinoza (1632–1677)

─────────────────────── **Key Points** ───────────────────────

▓ God *is* the whole of existence in its vast, mysterious and indivisible totality

▓ We see the universe in fragments merely because our minds are too small to grasp it as a single unity

▓ We fragment experience into past, present and future because our minds cannot grasp its timeless singularity

▓ Components do not interconnect because they are not in any way separate

▓ We neither control nor are we determined by our circumstances, since the separation of self and surroundings is itself an illusion.

Application

• Spinoza's vision is similar to Buddhist and Hindu teachings that dissolve the distinction between self and world

• Yoga ('union with God', however practised) is seen by many to be the royal road via which we escape the tortuous delusion of a separate self

• Spiritual teaching, concerning the union of self and world, is thought to be crucial in finding meaning, strength and purpose

• Within such holistic, integrationist, pantheistic teaching, self is found in communion with, rather than in distinction from, the 'rest' of existence

• In feeling 'at one' with the world and other people, our mutual obligations become more evident. The ethical imperative can be felt from within rather than argued and enforced from without.

Descartes, as we saw in the previous chapter, proposed three kinds of basic 'stuff': matter, mind and God. Spinoza argued that there was only one kind, God. For Spinoza God was not some force, person or principle that set the universe of matter and mind into existence. God *was* the whole of existence in its vast, mysterious and interconnected totality.[1] (All quotations from Spinoza are taken from his *Ethics*, 1677).

Spinoza sought to prove this pantheism, and all his other notions, from first principles and by a process of reasoning that modelled itself on geometry. For example, God being perfect, He could not be any *less* than the universe as a whole. Mind and matter, therefore, are aspects of the universe. They have no independent existence. We may see them as separate, we may ask questions about their interconnections, but these questions have more to do with our inevitable human ignorance, fallibility and limited perception, than to the inherent nature of the universe.[2] Spinoza thereby swept away at a stroke all the insoluble questions about how bodies and minds interacted and the role of a transcendental God. There was no interaction since there was no separation. God was immanent; the universe could not exist separately from God since it *was* God.

For Spinoza, the universe/God was one totality, and any kind of separation and conceptualisation within it was the product of small minds being able to apprehend only small parts at a time.[3] We broke the universe into parts, tables, chairs, atoms, molecules and then asked inappropriate questions about how the parts interrelated. What we forgot was that there were 'parts' to the universe only because in our minds it was chopped into parts.[4] The universe was, as it were, one vast whole seamless picture. It is too big for us to comprehend, so we turn it into a jigsaw of trillions of pieces, each piece being small and simple enough for our minds to grasp. We then ask, how do the pieces of the jigsaw interconnect? How can we put them together?

What we forget is that really they do not interconnect; they do not fit together because in reality there are no pieces at all. Interconnections are what we make in our minds, not realities to be found in the world. Minds can only get to grips with the universe by chopping it up into small bits. It could be apprehended as one whole totality but only by an infinite power to apprehend an infinite reality. This is God, that is the universe as a whole.[5]

Mystics in many places and times have claimed to glimpse the universe as one interconnected totality. This vision, and way of being, has been offered as a source of healing, strength, inspiration and understanding. Spinoza does not claim the unity of existence as a result of mystical experience, more from mathematical analysis and deduction. His prose to modern eyes (mine at any rate) is truly dreadful. As a rationalist he seeks to unfold consequences from ideas, words, the relations between words and concepts. Empirical observation and test does not seem to figure in his work at all.

This rationalist approach is alien to modern ways of proceeding and is now so discredited that it is no wonder that few are prepared to bother to 'check' whether his ethical and metaphysical 'axioms' are solid, consistent and adequately 'unpack' to his endless ethical and metaphysical 'consequences'. Spinoza tries to show that what he is saying is true in exactly the same way that Euclid deduced rules of geometry from basic axioms, with propositions, postulates, proofs, definitions, lemmas, corollaries and notes all laid out systematically, the one proceeding logically, we are to believe, from the other. The process seems contrived, tortuous and is entirely unconvincing.[6] It is interesting for a historian of ideas. It is not of much interest if you only wish to retain those ideas that still look alive and relevant for today.

With hindsight, the rationalist project might look as though it was always destined to be doomed. But, when it is remembered how successful mathematics has been as a process of abstract rationality, it is less surprising that, for many years, there were high hopes that the natural sciences might similarly advance without the need for empirical observation.

Descartes, likewise, believed that his ideas were derivable from a process of reasoning. His conclusions were different from Spinoza's. Leibniz, a third major contemporary rationalist, produced a system of ideas that was different again. They would have each agreed that not all of them could be right. Only later was this method of deriving truth independent of observation defeated by philosophical empiricism.

Spinoza believed that the unity of existence was not just of abstract interest to philosophers. It was, he thought, of practical value to ordinary people in their daily lives because our happiness and misery were so much bound by the narrow view that we took of everything. Misfortune came our way, we felt low. Tomorrow was more kind, our mood rose again. Up and down, up and down, or down and lower. We rode on a rollercoaster of emotion, thinking that life really was good or bad or worse. We failed to see that, from a broader perspective, all these seemingly weighty matters were tiny specks of colour within a vast kaleidoscope.

We hung on to, or regretted, the past; we fretted about the future. All the time we forgot that time itself was just a fiction of the mind. Minds experienced time, past, present, future, because minds could not apprehend the whole of the universe. For an infinite mind, God, past, present, future were all one. Yesterday was not 'gone'; tomorrow was not 'yet to arrive'. Everything, here, far, past, future was all *here together* if your mind was large enough to hold it all together. Only God could do this, and get to all the parts, places and times and hold them all as one. But, if we could achieve just a glimpse of true cosmic communion, we could put some of our 'highs' and 'lows' into a larger perspective and thereby feel less like victims on a rack or ants on a leaf in the sea. Moreover, we would also, thereby, develop a suitable sense of awe, reverence, humility, wonder, even sheer delight at the vast interconnected mystery of existence.

This vision would itself provide sustenance for the soul, and a means of finding tranquillity and peace within ourselves, almost regardless of what life appeared to throw at us. In this sense it could be argued that Spinoza had a deeply religious mentality, but this was not recognised by the bureaucrats, administrators and gatekeepers of the time who saw him as a heretic for daring to think outside the official party line.

So Spinoza has his place on these pages. He like every counsellor and care worker, wanted to believe that he could offer something of relevance to the perennial phenomenon of human misery.

There is no doubt that people have found, and will find, a way of coping with distress by putting their individual concerns into a larger perspective. The Stoics tackled this, as we have seen, via self-discipline and control of self-defeating attitudes. Spinoza's thought was less a matter of 'getting tougher' with ourselves and more a process of broadening our grasp (or gasp) of our communion within existence. We need not look out from the perception of an ant-like human adrift on its floating leaf. We could apprehend a whole flooded landscape of dry, drowned, determined and drifting ants. This larger setting would be a tiny step closer to Divine experience. It would allow us to collect ourselves, calm ourselves, cope, if coping was available, as best we may with whatever powers and opportunities were at our disposal.

Spinoza, by all accounts, did actually seek to live according to these principles and thereby remained more calm and collected than might otherwise have been possible. An attempt was made to assassinate him due to his heretical ideas. As a Jew he was cursed and excommunicated. He was considered to be appallingly wicked for not towing the party line. But all this aggravation, if we take Spinoza's own preference for the larger perspective, is small stuff, of little consequence. Spinoza evidently thought so. He lived quietly, polishing lenses, with few and simple wants, showing little concern for power, fame or money. His major work, the *Ethics*, was published after his death.

It is no doubt true to say that, if we had the vision of the Gods, be they Greek or Spinozan Pantheistic, we would be less heated, frozen and fearful within our limited human frame and experience. What we may observe, however, is that we are *not* Gods and that therefore we *do* suffer as a result of human frailties, human preoccupations and limited human vision. The question arises, therefore, what is to be done? What is the best way of coping? Shall we try a larger Spinozan apprehension of existence? Shall we try Stoical self-discipline? Or what? What are the options? What choices are available?

According to Spinoza there was no choice at all. He argued that a larger insight calmed passions by placing them in perspective. But he did not believe that you could 'choose' to accept or reject this, or that you could choose or decide anything at all. Free will, according to Spinoza was just another illusion consequent upon our narrow understanding of existence.[7] If your imagination was sufficiently godlike the past was not 'gone' and the future was already 'here'. They were all one just as the front and back of the elephant are all one. You might imagine that you were travelling 'towards' the future, but this was simply because the stage of 'here and now' that you could imaginatively embrace was so small.

Therefore the whole discussion about 'shall I go this way, that way and what will be the consequence?' was a function of my limited grasp of the whole picture. If I extended my imagination I would see that the whole map, the whole story, every map, every story, was by its nature whole and complete. So questions about which road, which direction, which consequence only made sense for as long as we failed to apprehend the big picture. We could not 'decide' and were not 'forced', pulled or pushed except within the confines of our narrower agendas and perceptions. All these fantasies of labour, loss, gain, defeat, victory, freedom, imprisonment arose from a limited apprehension of existence.

The pantheistic vision may well have healing properties for those who can hold it. With a felt sense of being 'as one' with other people and other things, their 'otherness' becomes less evident to us. We cease to feel 'at war' with our surroundings. Time no longer 'runs' and we do not therefore have to run after it. We do not have to get 'on top of', or fear that we will be 'buried by', our problems.

Our interaction with existence becomes more like a dance. Harmony is perceived more than having to be achieved. Ethical, co-operative, loving behaviour become integral to our vision of the underlying unity of existence; they no longer have to be seen as impossibly high ideals or commandments. You do right because right actions are part of the means to a full whole life. You 'feed yourself' on right action, just as you do on right thinking and right feeling. These all become part of the food of life. A person who asks 'why must I eat?' is indeed deluded and ignorant. Where is their insight and appetite? Likewise, a person who asks 'why must I do right?' is sadly unaware of the unifying forces of existence.

Within a secular, atomised, individualistic perspective on existence, we are driven by insecurity and our lives are an unending struggle to make more of ourselves and assemble more around us that is 'us and ours'. Threats are perceived to be everywhere. Fear of loss grows the more we gain. Time, circumstance and other people are enemies or potential rivals. We keep trying to master them, beat them, catch up with them, get on top of them. Time, eventually will 'run out' on us. It will 'take' from us all that we have and hold. We are, ultimately, alone within our impermanent alliances, networks, triumphs and tragedies.

With a spiritual, pantheistic apprehension of existence we are 'at home' everywhere. We have arrived at every move we make, we are centred within every time and outside of all time. We are balanced in every movement. We are mirrored in each other. We move from *within* our wholeness and completeness rather than *in order to* become whole and complete. We dance within, rather than triumphing over, the larger symphony of existence. There is no winning or losing since all these secular nightmares are based on the illusion of a separate, struggling self. We are neither pushed, pulled nor can we push or pull anything or anyone else, since all this, too, only makes sense within the illusion of a separate self. We do not have to struggle to reach another; we merely open our eyes to the way we are already in contact. We cannot run away from one another. Where on earth could we go that could remove the reality of our interconnection and mutual obligation?

Such ethics can perhaps be made to work more easily if you live quietly, grind lenses, and avoid the hurly burly or everyday hassle and compromise where all too human individuals evidently fail to take a godlike perception of existence. The problem is that, as well as valuing an embrace of universal oneness, most of us put most of our energy and attention in to remembering our postcode, standing on our own limited piece of turf, cultivating it, and defending it if necessary, although it is just a small speck on the infinite and integrated surfaces of space and time. Presumably our emotions of elation, despair and all the rest that accompany the triumphs and tragedies of our ant-like antics have some place in the scheme of things? Somehow, these have to be incorporated within this vision of unity.

So maybe we would not be so wise if we were *always* trying to see existence from an eternal perspective? Our own headache bothers us more than the death of a stranger. The suffering of our own children concerns us more than the vast tragedies of whole continents. From Mount Olympus this shows a lack of perspective. But it is *our* perspective and if *we* won't take it who will? We are not contemplating the whole universe from an astral plane as an interconnected unity. We are down in the mud, covered in it and with limited vision in every direction. Perhaps we are there because that is where we belong; because that is who we are and where we are. We might well be foolish if we never tried to achieve a larger view. We might be equally absurd if we thought that we could vacate the leaf we were floating on, and be like Zeus or, more pantheistically, be everywhere, and take every time, at once. Perhaps that really would leave us nowhere at all? Perhaps we really need to take, and use, the time we have, however little it is?

The weakness of Spinoza's, Descartes', Leibniz's and other rationalist approaches is most evident within one of Spinoza's 'propositions':

> He, who has a true idea, simultaneously knows that he has a true idea, and cannot doubt of the truth of the thing perceived. (Prop. XLIII)

If only this were true! In fact, we can get very excited about 'the truth' of a wide variety of our ideas. Some turn out to be true, many prove to be false, most may prove to be less original and significant than we may have originally imagined. We may imagine that we know, 'quite definitely', all kinds of things that turn out to be fond fictions, ill-advised illusions, practically worthless propositions. Our thoughts about the truth of our thoughts are inevitably of interest to us; but they do not make the thoughts themselves any more or any less true.

It is not true to imagine that we can uncover truth just by constructing edifices of propositions, notes, consequences and corollaries from the comfort of our own armchairs. A certain amount of observation and testing are also helpful and nothing ever seems to get finally 'proved'. As Spinoza himself observed, human minds are very narrow and limited. It therefore seems unwise to imagine that, from such a narrow base, we can offer final 'proofs' about the ultimate nature of the universe.

Spinoza had no reputation during and at the end of his life, except as a wicked heretic. He was rediscovered around a century after his death by the German Romantics[8] who much admired his simple living, his reverence for all of existence, and his ability both to feel, and find intellectual justification for, a sense of the oneness of life. To the romantics, Spinoza pointed the way to a felt sense of the spiritual that was not encumbered with traditional theological dogma. His rationalism has, I think, no future. His lived apprehension of indivisible existence, and the lifestyle that he evolved from it, deserves to remain of considerable interest to counsellors, carers and clients.

People generally *do not*, possibly *cannot*, and probably *should not*, spend their whole lives in Olympian detachment from their own lives. But occasional glimpses of possibility that take us beyond our current triumphs and tragedies can undoubtedly be healing, inspiring and informative. I will take time and space for just one example: How shall we look at the 'self'? The most commonplace view is that we are trapped within time, we travel on a 'timeline' and that, with the passing of time, we decay. Certainly our bodies age but, with the passing of time, I find that the people I know *emerge*. The larger our glimpse of the time dimension the more rounded a picture we get of a person. Our understanding of ourselves and others may not become more flattering with the passing of time, but it can surely become deeper.

The retinas of our eyes receive two-dimensional images of the world. Our brains infer a third dimension and this is what we learn to 'see'. Perhaps if we observed a little more carefully – over time – we could learn to comprehend in four dimensions? The body will still decay in time but the personality, we will learn, is dimensioned, as well as constrained, by time. Perhaps it is in this sense that, as mystics have so often claimed, the personality, or 'soul', lives beyond time?

❓ Questions

1. How many of your own clients might benefit from a philosophy that helps them to see themselves as *of* the world rather than in triumphant control *over*, or oppressed *beneath*, their circumstances?

2. Spinoza, the arch rationalist, was idolised a century later by arch Romantics such as Goethe and Coleridge. What irony and insight does this offer us?

3. If God is in all things, the enchantment is certainly brought back into daily existence, especially if you feel it rather than merely believe it. Is enchantment the remedy to disenchantment? Is it of relevance to your clients?

4. How far is a larger, less self-centred, perspective achievable? When can it be of assistance to clients? When is it just an avoidance tactic? Can you think of specific examples?

EXERCISES

1. Compare Spinoza's pantheistic spirituality with more contemporary versions, for example, that of Jung. Compare also with Leibniz and Berkeley.

2. *Samadhi*, in Hinduism and Buddhism, is the highest point of spiritual and mental concentration. It can be arrived at by several routes. Consider how far Spinoza's teaching itself provides one such road. (This might take a few years!)

3. Consider what you are trying to achieve with which of your clients. To *find* themselves? *Improve* themselves? *Transform* themselves? *Transcend* themselves? How far might Spinoza be of help with the last?

Conclusion

Mystics in every century and culture have claimed to glimpse the universe as one interconnected totality. This vision, and way of being, has been offered as a source of healing, inspiration and understanding. Spinoza considered the unity of existence via mathematical analysis and deduction. Oriental philosophies suggest that, to get to the top of this peak of spiritual development, a great deal of self-discipline and insight are required. Disciples may work within mind, beyond mind, via the body, through love or from good works (right actions). Within each of these options, along each of these paths, a host of different strategies have been offered. Spinoza's intellectual route appears to have provided him with a sense of peace and communion within existence. Is the destination the same regardless of the route? Or is the mystic's vision no more than an hallucination?

Notes

1. Prop. I Thought is an attribute of God, or God is a thinking thing.
2. Prop. XXXI We can only have a very inadequate knowledge of the duration of particular things external to ourselves.
   Prop. XXXV Falsity consists in the privation of knowledge, which inadequate, fragmentary, or confused ideas involve.
3. Prop. XLV Every idea of every body, or of every particular thing actually existing, necessarily involves the eternal and infinite essence of God.
4. Prop. X Corollary. Hence it follows, that the essence of man is constituted by certain modifications of the attributes of God.
5. Prop. XI Corollary ...the human mind is part of the infinite intellect of God; thus when we say, that the human mind perceives this or that, we make the assertion,

that God has this or that idea, not in so far as he is infinite, but in so far as he is displayed through the nature of the human mind, or in so far as he constitutes the essence of the human mind; and when we say that God has this or that idea, not only in so far as he constitutes the essence of the human mind, but also in so far as he, simultaneously with the human mind, has the further idea of another thing, we assert that the human mind perceives a thing in part or inadequately.

6. Axiom Ia All bodies are either in motion or at rest. Axiom IIa Every body is moved sometimes more slowly, sometimes more quickly.

7. Prop. XLVIII In the mind there is no absolute or free will; but the mind is determined to wish this or that by a cause, which has also been determined by another cause, and this last by another cause, and so on to infinity.

8. For example, Goethe, Herder.

Websites

http://members.aol.com/Heraklit1/spinoza.htm
http://www.erols.com/jyselman/index.htm
http://frank.mtsu.edu/~rbombard/RB/spinoza.new.html
http://spinoza.tau.ac.il/hci/dep/philos/links.htm

Bibliography:

D. Garrett (ed.) *Cambridge Companion to Spinoza*, Cambridge University Press, 1996
L. Lermond, *Form of Man: Human Essence in Spinoza's 'Ethics'*, Brill, 1988
G. Lloyd, *Routledge Philosophy Guidebook to Spinoza and the Ethics*, Routledge, 1996
R. Scruton, *Spinoza*, Oxford University Press, 1986
B. de Spinoza, *Ethics*, Princeton University Press, 1994

Chapter 15

John Locke (1632–1704)

Key Points

- Individuals and institutions are all prejudiced by self-interest
- Institutional checks and balances can reduce damage done by self-interest
- No individual has privileged insight
- Truth therefore lies between competing perceptions
- Matter in motion is the primary reality, individuals provide their own colour.

Application

- Therapist/carer claims to privileged insight are invalid
- Carer and client self-interest will sometimes conflict
- No organisation can realistically represent the interests of both carers and clients; they require their own body to check and balance the collective interest of the other
- Locke argues that life's magic and enchantment is provided by the observer; 'in reality' there is just matter in motion
- Locke is the last serious philosopher to claim that 'self' is readily and directly observable.

Leibniz sought to assemble, via deductive reasoning, a large inverted pyramid of knowledge from the relative pinpoint of a few basic axioms. John Locke was much more circumspect about the possibility of building intellectual structures purely by the power of reason. As an empiricist, rather than a mathematician, he thought it wiser to be more pragmatic, work by trial and error and rely more on direct perception. From a wide base in a large number of observations he moves cautiously, narrowing up to a few, and tentative, generalisations.

Locke's agenda for 'personal development' involved clarifying how and why, for our own well-being, we needed to come together within a society under one government. Government, he was certain, was essential. The question was, what kind of government? On what basis? With what justification?

Hobbes' answer, as we have seen, was that our lives would be nasty, brutish and short without the overriding control of a king. Therefore we would be wise to submit freely to this power, and the king would need to be strong enough to crush those who stubbornly failed to see what was in their own long-term interests.

Locke saw the need for central authority, since without it our lives would indeed be most 'inconvenient', unpleasant and insecure, if not quite as starkly brutish as Hobbes believed. As a Parliamentarian, however, Locke argued that this authority needed to be democratic rather than absolute or regal:

> The end of civil society being to avoid and remedy those inconveniences of the state of nature which necessarily follow from every man's being a judge in his own case, by setting up a known authority, to which every one of that society may appeal upon any injury received, or controversy that may arise, and which everyone of the society ought to obey. (*An Essay Concerning the True Original Extent and End of Civil Government*, Para. 90, 1690)

Locke was convinced that absolute power should never be in the hands of one man, be it king, czar, 'or *Grand Signior, or how you please*', since the relationship between the authority figure and other people would still be one of a 'state of nature'. There would be no power overriding the relationship between king and citizen. Was this acceptable and safe? Certainly not:

> For he that thinks absolute power purifies men's bloods, and corrects the baseness of human nature, need but read the history of this, or any other age, to be convinced of the contrary. (ibid. Para. 92)

Notice Locke's appeal, not to abstract reason, but to pragmatic observation. We must say 'no' to kings because, *observe*, they do not work well enough. Let us try to improve on them.

Locke had a healthy scepticism about the dangers of giving too much power to any individual or group. Hence it was he who proposed the system of checks and balances between executive and legislature that were subsequently incorporated into the US Constitution.

Government of some kind, however, was essential. Without it we were all forced to be sovereign judges of how to deal with the people around us. This created problems because:

> Self-love will make men partial to themselves and their friends: and on the other side, ill nature, passion and revenge will carry them too far in punishing others; and hence nothing but confusion and disorder will follow; and that therefore God hath certainly appointed government to restrain the partiality and violence of men. (ibid. Para. 13)

Locke, without quite the pessimism of Hobbes, takes it for granted that people are partial towards themselves and their own clan and that, therefore, checks and balances of power need to be put into place to ensure that corruption and selfishness do not creep, or sweep, into human affairs. Locke assumes, as observable matter of fact, that every individual and institutional perception is prejudiced, but that, if we are wise in the way we organise government and society, we can mitigate the worst influences of our unavoidable bias.

This view of human nature is a salutary one for counselling. Too often, within the various strands of the counselling movement, it is assumed that, if individual clients are sufficiently 'enabled', encouraged and 'empowered' by the advanced and active empathy of the counsellor, then they will quite automatically 'find themselves', grow, develop, and become more autonomous, competent, confident, and able to pass on the same spirit of mutual respect, regard and empowerment to others.

Alternatively, it is assumed that, even if not every client can do this, a suitably trained counsellor can 'know themselves' and know and assist their clients with a degree of insight not available to other, untrained, mortals. Locke, by way of contrast, considered that it is perfectly obvious that there is a *base* nature within all of us, and it is there to be observed if we look within, around, and at the history of any and every society. Therefore we would be fools to think that we can rely solely on our own judgement or that of anyone else however 'expert' they are.

Individuals, it must be assumed, will rationalise, will seek power but often pretend otherwise, will look after their own interests first, will be disproportionate in their view of their own achievements and in the hurts they imagine others have inflicted on them. Therefore the 'truth', whatever that may be, about anything, will never be found via the observations and opinions of any one individual or interest group, but somewhere *between* the conflictual views of various players, performers and observers. Given everyone's bias, a great deal of humility will be needed in determining who is more nearly right about anything.

The consequence of Locke's (in my view, entirely wise) scepticism about human objectivity is interesting if applied to the counselling movement. For example, it will involve accepting that clients may be seeking rationalisations more than truth, and power more than goodness. Also, that, in this regard, counsellors are no different from their clients. So, if a British Association for Counsel*ling* comprises counsellors and other professionals, a Lockean observer might suggest that it be renamed the British Association for Counsel*lors*. Why? Because counsellors, being human, are bound to seek the interests of counsellors before that of their clients and it would be naïve to imagine that client and counsellor interests never conflict. Therefore, operating as a check and a balance, a British Association for Clients (in Counselling) would need to be created to act as a watchdog, and kerb the inevitable excesses, arrogance, defensiveness and self-regard that a group of counsellors are bound to develop when acting to preserve and promote their own interests.

It is precisely because people cannot be trusted to make judgements and find remedies for themselves that a society, government, and framework of law are so essential. If people were as good and trustworthy as some counsellors seem to believe, then we really would be able to live in a state of anarchy, with each individual and group being trusted to make its own local judgements about what is right, what is important and what needs to be done next. The civilisation of individuals is very often more apparent than real. It is essentially propped up by the civilisation of the government and the society of which they are a part. Take that away and just see how civilised people can afford to be. The Balkans are in chaos, the UK and US are not. Is this because of the character of the people or the nature of the government, the society, the geography, the history? There, but for fortune, go you and I.

Personal growth, within the counselling movement, involves focusing on *inner* lives and *individual* circumstances and opportunities. The evidence of history suggests that, on the contrary, personal and collective growth have more to do with the soil, that is, the society within which we find ourselves, with its history, its culture, its government, its economy, its geographical advantages and/or constraints.

Only when social interconnectedness and support become as reliable and omnipresent as they are today does it become possible for people to create our contemporary illusions about how much we can achieve on our own. The body that really counts in promoting our well-being is not the individual body but the body politic:

> For, when any number of men have, by the consent of every individual, made a community, they have thereby made that community one body, with a power to act as one body, which is only by the will and determination of the majority. (ibid. Para. 96)

Locke is naïve in imagining that *every one* of its individuals could conceivably assent to any community or that there ever was a moment in history when such a democratic society was ever formally brought into being. Societies are not in fact formed by the egalitarian activity of autonomous sovereign individuals. But, neither unanimity nor such a 'moment' in history are required to justify democratic government, so these blindspots of Locke do not ultimately weaken his argument. As a matter of history, the king, with his claim to rule by Divine right, was overthrown by barons and powerful merchants, not by the 'common people'. It just suited the barons to claim the voice of the peasantry when arguing their cause. The commoners soon discovered the truth when they themselves tried to improve their own democratic representation. In England they were crushed with just as much force and ruthlessness as would have been employed by an absolute monarch. Given that Locke himself was representative of the more comfortably situated, it is consistent with his own thesis that he himself shows the very partiality, prejudice and corresponding ignorance that he sees as inherent within any pressure group.[1]

Locke provided some of the most important philosophical foundations to the liberal political tradition that grew from the eighteenth century on. He was likewise one of the key founders of the empirical approach to theories of knowledge. One such achievement would have been formidable enough. His views about the best way to acquire knowledge are to be found in his *Essay Concerning Human Understanding* (1690):

> This, therefore, being my purpose – to inquire into the original, certainty, and extent of human knowledge, together with the grounds and degrees of belief, opinion, and assent. (ibid. Introduction)

Locke's empirical approach is very different from the more rationalist style of Descartes, yet their ideas about *self*-knowledge, of particular interest to counsellors, are rather similar:

Our knowledge of our own existence is intuitive. As for our own existence, we perceive it so plainly and so certainly, that it neither needs nor is capable of any proof. For nothing can be more evident to us than our own existence. I think, I reason, I feel pleasure and pain: can any of these be more evident to me than my own existence? If I doubt of all other things, that very doubt makes me perceive my own existence, and will not suffer me to doubt of that. For if I know I feel pain, it is evident I have as certain perception of my own existence, as of the existence of the pain I feel: or if I know I doubt, I have as certain perception of the existence of the thing doubting, as of that thought which I call doubt. Experience then convinces us, that we have an intuitive knowledge of our own existence, and an internal infallible perception that we are. In every act of sensation, reasoning, or thinking, we are conscious to ourselves of our own being; and, in this matter, come not short of the highest degree of certainty. (ibid. Chapter IX)

For Locke, my own existence is a fact to be observed. It is self-evident and requires no proof. For Descartes it was 'proved' by the fact that 'I think'. Starting with themselves, each then moves on to infer God's existence:

To show, therefore, that we are capable of knowing, that is, being certain that there is a God, and how we may come by this certainty, I think we need go no further than ourselves, and that undoubted knowledge we have of our own existence.

For man knows that he himself exists. I think it is beyond question, that man has a clear idea of his own being; he knows certainly he exists, and that he is something. He that can doubt whether he be anything or no, I speak not to; no more than I would argue with pure nothing, or endeavour to convince nonentity that it were something. If any one pretends to be so sceptical as to deny his own existence (for really to doubt of it is manifestly impossible), let him for me enjoy his beloved happiness of being nothing, until hunger or some other pain convince him of the contrary. This, then, I think I may take for a truth, which every one's certain knowledge assures him of, beyond the liberty of doubting, viz. that he is something that actually exists.

He knows also that nothing cannot produce a being; therefore something must have existed from eternity. In the next place, man knows, by an intuitive certainty, that bare nothing can no more produce any real being, than it can be equal to two right angles. If a man knows not that nonentity, or the absence of all being, cannot be equal to two right angles, it is impossible he should know any demonstration in Euclid. If, therefore, we know there is some real being, and that nonentity cannot produce any real being, it is an evident demonstration, that from eternity there has been something; since what was not from eternity had a beginning; and what had a beginning must be produced by something else.

And that eternal Being must be most powerful. (ibid. Book IV, Chapter X)

The arguments that derive God's existence from my own have fewer adherents now than they did in the eighteenth century. Yet Locke's view that 'myself' is self-evident and requires no further evidence or argument is probably, still, the 'common-sense' view today. In fact, if we observe still more carefully than Locke, we see that young children do *not* have a clear and unambiguous sense of who they are. Personal identity is constructed over a period of many years. It becomes less fluid only insofar as we become sluggish, set and prejudiced in our ways of seeing ourselves and our surroundings. Notions of personal identity are nothing like as straightforward as Locke and Descartes believed. From David Hume onwards, concepts of self have come under a sceptical scrutiny that so-called common sense does not easily or successfully dismiss. Subsequent chapters will explore the problem of personal identity, and its relevance, more deeply.

Locke also delivered something close to our contemporary common-sense view of perception. He distinguished between 'primary' and 'secondary' qualities. The first are real and 'out there' in the object:

> Primary qualities of bodies. Qualities thus considered in bodies are, First, such as are utterly inseparable from the body, in what state soever it be; and such as in all the alterations and changes it suffers, all the force can be used upon it, it constantly keeps; and such as sense constantly finds in every particle of matter which has bulk enough to be perceived; and the mind finds inseparable from every particle of matter, though less than to make itself singly be perceived by our senses: For example, take a grain of wheat, divide it into two parts; each part has still solidity, extension, figure, and mobility: divide it again, and it retains still the same qualities; and so divide it on, till the parts become insensible; they must retain still each of them all those qualities. (ibid. Book II, Chapter VIII)

Bodies were solid, extended in three dimensions of space, had a shape. All these primary qualities were independent of the observer. Secondary qualities, by the same token, were 'in' the observer more that in the object itself:

> Such qualities which in truth are nothing in the objects themselves but power to produce various sensations in us by their primary qualities, that

is, by the bulk, figure, texture, and motion of their insensible parts, as colours, sounds, tastes, &c. These I call secondary qualities. (ibid.)

Locke's views about primary and secondary qualities gained wide acceptance. It became the role of science to examine primary qualities: solidity, extension, figure, motion/rest and number. Essentially, the natural world of science was the study of matter in motion. This, it came to be believed, was all that 'really' existed in the external world. This simple, clear, foundation was a helpful framework from which the studies of sound, heat, light and electricity could, and did, prosper. The outside world was one of matter in motion. Locke provided the empirical philosophy that justified this world view, Newton developed the mathematics. The results are still subjects of study within advanced level school physics, chemistry and mathematics syllabuses. Such mechanistic materialism could, however, leave people somewhat disenchanted since, quite literally, it was a philosophy that removed all the enchantment, the spirits, the auras, the magic, the mystique, the mystery of existence, leaving us in a colourless clockwork universe (we provided the colour as a 'secondary' quality).

George Berkeley, Gottfried Leibniz and many subsequent philosophers challenged this view of matter and motion. Some of their alternative models seem counterintuitive, far removed from common sense. Yet history, via growing evidence and theorising in contemporary physics, seems to be supporting some of the more 'strange' variations on everyday views of self and world.

For Locke, the inanimate world consisted of matter in motion, and living bodies, too, were themselves machines comprising this same movement of inanimate material. From such a basis biology progressed. Biology was founded in chemistry which itself was based in physics. Where did ideas fit into this picture?:

All ideas come from sensation or reflection. The mind thinks in proportion to the matter it gets from experience to think about... The next thing to be considered is, how bodies produce ideas in us; and that is manifestly by impulse, the only way which we can conceive bodies to operate in.

By motions, external, and in our organism. If then external objects be not united to our minds when they produce ideas therein; and yet we perceive these original qualities in such of them as singly fall under our senses, it is evident that some motion must be thence continued by our nerves, or animal spirits, by some parts of our bodies, to the brains or the seat of sensation, there to produce in our minds the particular ideas we have of them... we may conceive that the ideas of secondary qualities are also produced, viz. by the operation of insensible particles on our senses. (ibid. Book II, Chapter VIII)

So, some motion or other got to work on our ears, eyes, taste buds and other sense receptors. This, as we now know, stimulates patterns of electro-chemical activity from nerve endings into our brains and, hey presto, ideas 'appear' in our minds. Just *how* this inanimate physical motion manifests as psychological mental reflection seems as much a mystery now as it was three hundred years ago.

Certainly Locke was not slow to confess his own modesty and uncertainty:

> I am apt to imagine, that, were the imperfections of language, as the instrument of knowledge, more thoroughly weighed, a great many of the controversies that make such a noise in the world, would of themselves cease; and the way to knowledge, and perhaps peace too, lie a great deal opener than it does.
>
> This should teach us moderation in imposing our own sense of old authors. Sure I am that the signification of words in all languages, depending very much on the thoughts, notions, and ideas of him that uses them, must unavoidably be of great uncertainty to men of the same language and country. (ibid. Book IV, Chapter 9)

? Questions

1. 'I think it is beyond question, that man has a clear idea of his own being'. Is it? Do we?

2. Do you think that the interests of counsellors/carers and clients should be represented by separate organisations?

3. Is beauty, colour, magic, enchantment merely in the eye of the beholder? Or is the universe magical whatever we think and perceive?

4. If we cannot abolish the effects of self-interest what can we do to protect the interests of the client?

EXERCISES

1. Try to think of a time when your own self-interest conflicted with the interests of a client. Consider what action, if any, you took to protect the client.

2. Think of a time when your own perception and interpretation clashed with those of the client. What did you do about this?

3. Write down examples you have observed of self-interest and self promotion at work among counselling and care sector organisations that may not be in the best interests of clients.

Conclusion

Locke was sceptical about the inherent objectivity and trustworthiness of human beings. He was not, however, cynical or pessimistic about human co-operation. Through knowledge built on observation we could improve our existence. Democracy required that individual and collective self-interest be organised within a system of checks and balances. This would ensure that no interest group had a disproportionate influence over others. Objective reality was essentially the world described by physics. The observer added the colour and enchantment. We knew who we were by introspection, a kind of inner observation. Memory advised that the same person was 'looking within', years previously. This view has been systematically challenged by subsequent philosophers.

Note

1. As for my own current blindspots, prejudice and partiality – they are, to me at least, invisible.

Websites

http://www.geocities.com/Athens/Forum/5507/locke.html

Bibliography

J. Locke, *A Letter Concerning Toleration*, Prometheus Books, 1990
J. Locke, *Two Treatises of Government*, Everyman, 1993
J. Locke, *An Essay Concerning Human Understanding*, Penguin, 1998

Chapter 16

Gottfried Wilhelm von Leibniz
(1646–1716)

Key Points

- Atoms cannot be the basic units of existence since they are divisible

- The basic stuff are 'monads'. They occupy no space, since space can be divided. If they were divisible, monads would not be basic

- Each monad is unique, independent, eternal and dances within the pre-established harmony provided by God

- The 'objects' that we observe are patterns of dancing monads that arise and pass away. Only the dance and the monads are eternal

- Observation provides knowledge of appearances only. Reason, alone, connects us to the underlying realities of existence.

Application

- Leibniz's vision is more enchanting than mechanical and material philosophies that have so permeated contemporary 'common sense'
- His monads and metaphysics are closer to our contemporary physics and mathematics than is at first apparent
- His style is dry but the content, when comprehensible, sparkles
- If counselling is concerned with underlying harmonies, then here is an epic and heroic effort to locate such harmony.

Descartes 'reasoned' that there were three basic kinds of stuff: God, mind and matter. Spinoza concluded that there was only one, God, and that everything else was, as it were, a wave, flame, event, or wrinkle that rose and fell briefly from this underlying substrate. Leibniz's rationalism, in contrast, produced an *infinite number* of basic substances, indivisible, fundamental constituents of the world, which he called 'monads'.

For Leibniz, the by-products, the passing events of existence were all those things that were in any way complex and which could be subdivided into something simpler. This included anything that occupied space, since every object in space could be broken into bits. It followed from this that the simplest, most basic 'stuff' of existence did not occupy space at all, because if it did you could, at least in principle, cut it in half, and in half again ad infinitum. Atoms, therefore, were too large to be acceptable as fundamental constituents of the universe. They were extended in space and could be cut (at least in imagination). It was the same with any smaller debris produced after atoms were repeatedly smashed. Fundamental constituents, said Leibniz, could not just be very small, they had to have no size at all.

Therefore the basic stuff of the universe, the monads, occupied no space whatsoever. Therefore they could not be physical. Therefore they must be mental.[1] Therefore Leibniz's universe consisted of an infinity of unextended, non-physical, point-like spiritual/mental/soulful units called monads. In Leibniz's own words:[2]

1. The Monad, of which we shall here speak, is nothing but a simple substance, which enters into compounds. By 'simple' is meant 'without parts'.
2. And there must be simple substances, since there are compounds; for a compound is nothing but a collection or aggregatum of simple things.
3. Now where there are no parts, there can be neither extension nor form (figure) nor divisibility. These Monads are the real atoms of nature and, in a word, the elements of things. (*Monadology*)

Sometimes, when a new word is coined, it enters everyday language and is used regularly. Sometimes it is stillborn. 'Monad', as we all know, since most of us know we have never heard of it, does not fly these days as a concept. It lies dead in the water. It looks strange, fantastic, ridiculous. What does it mean?:

7. The Monads have no windows, through which anything could come in or go out.
8. Yet the Monads must have some qualities, otherwise they would not even be existing things.
9. Indeed, each Monad must be different from every other. For in nature there are never two beings which are perfectly alike and in which it is not possible to find an internal difference, or at least a difference founded upon an intrinsic quality.

10. I assume also as admitted that every created being, and consequently the created Monad, is subject to change, and further that this change is continuous in each.

11. It follows from what has just been said, that the natural changes of the Monads come from an internal principle, since an external cause can have no influence upon their inner being. (ibid.)

Leibniz therefore took the view that monads could not be influenced by external causes, yet somehow the result of this universe of independent monads was harmonious. Each monad provided an independent 'voice', as it were, yet the result was not a noise but a symphony. How so? For Leibniz it was because they were all independently singing from the same hymn sheets, provided by God:

78. The soul follows its own laws, and the body likewise follows its own laws; and they agree with each other in virtue of the pre-established harmony between all substances, since they are all representations of one and the same universe.

85. Whence it is easy to conclude that the totality (assemblage) of all spirits must compose the City of God, that is to say, the most perfect State that is possible, under the most perfect of Monarchs.

86. This City of God, this truly universal monarchy, is a moral world in the natural world, and is the most exalted and most divine among the works of God; and it is in it that the glory of God really consists, for He would have no glory were not His greatness and His goodness known and admired by spirits. It is also in relation to this divine City that God specially has goodness, while His wisdom and His power are manifested everywhere. (ibid.)

So, despite appearances, the universe consists most ultimately and fundamentally in an infinity of independent monads, operating as spirits rather than physical things, in harmony by each functioning according to the Divine order. To modern ears it is truly fantastic. Or is Leibniz more modern than may at first be apparent? The language of 'souls' sounds rather archaic, medieval. Yet Leibniz also described 'infinitesimals' within the language of mathematics, and invented the differential and integral calculus,[3] still in continuous use today. Most modern minds have not yet caught up with this since most people abandon mathematics with just a smattering of arithmetic and algebra.

If we scrap the word 'monad' and instead propose that the concept of *energy* as more fundamental than inert physical mass, the discussion sounds rather more contemporary. If we go one stage further and suggest that *mass energy* is in fact the fundamental concept, and that the two components cannot be considered as logically distinct, we have then moved away from a Newtonian clockwork universe of inert masses acted upon by external forces and have caught up fast with an Einsteinian world view. In Hinduism, the intrinsic dynamism of the universe has been referred to as the dance of Shiva. Leibniz, as a rationalist philosopher and exceptionally brilliant mathematician and polymath, derived his picture via abstract analysis. Mystics have, sometimes literally, danced to the beat and felt it in every cell in ecstatic visions of communion.

Contemporary common sense, which is very different from contemporary physics, assumes a material world of inanimate objects pushed and pulled around by a variety of non-material forces (energies). Leibniz described a non-material world of active, energetic, purposeful, 'perceptive' (that is, sensitive), infinitely small objects/subjects each, as it were, operating its own agenda/script which was part of God's pre-established harmony.

So what is the relevance of any of this to contemporary readers more interested in ordinary human happiness and misery than esoteric metaphysics? Well, who are you, that feels your joys and woes? A Cartesian 'mind' somehow controlling/occupying/trapped within a body? A brief Spinozan wrinkle on the underlying bedcover/substrate of the universe that is God? A soul, among an infinity of independent spirits, sensing the world within God's pre-established harmony? If so, then there is none of the disenchantment of a dead and inert world. Every inanimate object sparkles with spirit. The universe is dancing and you are part of the dance. This is what is implied within Leibniz's *Monadology*, but you will not feel the beat within his dull prose.

For those who fear chaos and meaninglessness, Leibniz's rationalist, essentialist philosophy is a powerful antidote. Each monad operates according to the pre-established harmony of the universe as a whole which is why this infinity of independent and unique monads creates a coherent result of great beauty. Another outcome is that each monad is, as it were, a mirror of the whole universe. Its beat is the throb of the cosmos. Each monad, while unique, is also a reflection of every other. Therefore there is nothing in the universe that is cut off, empty, useless, fallow, separated, dead. There is no chaos or confusion if we look beneath mere surfaces.

I suggest it matters if we do, or do not, believe and feel ourselves to be in a barren impersonal clockwork universe of dead matter that moves only if acted upon by an external force. This has been the world view taught and assumed most often in contemporary society. It was not the outlook of any of Europe's rationalist philosophers. It is not the perspective of any contemporary physicist (of which more later).[4]

Leibniz was eloquent in distinguishing between truths derivable via processes of reasoning and facts that needed to be assembled via empirical observation. He suggested that this is the 'best of all possible worlds'; which is not, perhaps, the best of all possible observations and was much derided by Voltaire in his satire *Candide*. He explored the possibility of 'possible worlds' other than our own, another topic of considerable interest within contemporary physics.[5]

For Leibniz, God could be known to exist by reason alone. Observation was not necessary. The concept of God was one of a perfect being. Perfection had to include existence since existence was obviously more perfect than non-existence. Therefore God existed. It is an unconvincing argument if only because, as Bertrand Russell observed, there is no reason to believe that existence is nearer to perfection than non-existence. Nor does it seem to me to make sense to talk about 'perfection' in this highly abstract way.

Leibniz found a useful way of mathematically defining, expressing and exploring infinitesimals. His notion that fundamental substance cannot occupy space seems strange, but his argument shows insight and consistency. Sure enough, within contemporary quantum physics and the very small regions it explores, we find that continuous motion does not exist as we understand it, neither does space or time. And at the macro level? The latest version proposes not just three dimensions of space and one of time; but ten or eleven dimensions, six of which are 'enfolded' and a basic 'stuff' consisting of 'string'. Compared to this, Leibniz's monads look positively ordinary.

Monads look (a little) more sensible within the context of a clearer understanding of calculus, and the 'music of the spheres', be they very large or very small, may best be appreciated via mathematics. Ordinary everyday prose struggles to cope when the most 'real' and most 'fundamental' appears to be so unreal, fantastic, contradictory and incoherent to us.

But health and well-being surely require that we try, as far as we can, to understand the world we live in. It is presumably unhealthy if scientific and philosophical understanding appears alien, absurd and irrelevant to the rest of the world. Historically, an understanding of self has developed in conjunction with a growing grasp of the world within which selves operate. If we want to know how to look 'inside' we also need to know how to look around, since the two may not be so very different. Wide gaps between specialist insight and the (so-called) 'common-sense' and 'everyday' understandings of the world are unwelcome. In recent decades they seem to have been getting larger. This book is one small effort to make a bridge. I hope it will not be seen as too simple and impertinent by professional philosophers, or too complex and irrelevant by lay readers.

? Questions

1. What is real? What is merely apparent? How do we distinguish a fact from a story, from an opinion, from a prejudice? Do these questions matter?

2. Does it really matter what the client believes to be the underlying reality and shape of their existence?

3. How far do we need to understand the world if we are to understand ourselves?

4. Does it matter if 'the basics' are material substances or non-material spirits singing in harmony?

5. In what ways are 'basics' like this of intrinsic importance to people in their everyday lives?

EXERCISES

1. Think of clients who have wished to take stock of their lives. How far have they wanted to go in this stocktaking? Has God, or some other fundamental pattern or principle been important to them? Would notions of 'pre-established harmony', 'dance', 'spirit' be relevant and useful to them?

2. Here is an exercise in 'advanced empathy'. Empathise with Leibniz's vision of existence and your experience of the interconnectedness and integrated wholeness of being is transformed! Leibniz's monads may seem dry and irrelevant from the outside, but if you can climb into them they have a life worthy of serious attention. Leibniz's thought is a cathedral for the mind, but you have to be willing to let go of existing presuppositions in order to appreciate it.

Conclusion

Leibniz's exceptional mathematical reasoning led him to a fantastic metaphysics far removed from common sense. Today, mathematicians and physicists, through similar intellectual effort and imagination, produce still more fantastic descriptions of 'underlying reality'. They then test the results by observation and confirm predictions of unimaginable accuracy. Can ordinary people keep up with all this? Should they try? Is science becoming too difficult for ordinary people or are its enchanting insights well worth trying to fathom?

Notes

1. This 'followed' because Leibniz accepted Descartes' notion of matter and mind as the two basic kinds of substance.
2. Leibniz numbered all the sentences in his *Monadology*, so there are no problems with editions or page numbers.
3. Isaac Newton independently invented it a little earlier, but Leibniz's notation is considered to be superior.
4. Science is still seen as dead and mechanical as opposed to the arts which are thought to be warm, human and personal. In fact, many artists presuppose a meaningless wasteland, or engage with morally trivial subjective introspection. Many scientists, on the contrary, address the bigger questions of existence within a holistic framework that promotes awe and wonder. Moreover, there is much poetry in mathematics, if you can understand it.
5. If Leibniz's philosophy seems esoteric compared with today's 'staid' science, try David Deutsch's *The Fabric of Reality*, Penguin, 1997. This Oxford physicist argues for a 'many worlds' interpretation of quantum theory. Never mind Leibniz's 'possible' worlds. A minority of quantum physicists propose that all the 'possibles' are 'actuals', running parallel with our own universe. 'They are *parallel* in the sense that within each universe particles interact with each other just as they do in the tangible universe, but each universe affects the others only weakly, through interference phenomena' (p. 47). Perhaps, it is argued, we can get a quantum computer to carry out computations in more than one universe at a time? It would certainly speed up the calculations!

Websites

http://www.biography.com/cgibin/biography/biographyrequest.pl?page=/biography/data/L/L.8424.txt.html
http://www.maths.tcd.ie/pub/HistMath/People/Leibniz/RouseBall/RB_Leibnitz.html

Bibliography

N. Jolley (ed.) *Cambridge Companion to Leibniz*, Cambridge University Press, 1995
G.W. Leibniz, *Philosophical Essays*, Hackett Publishing Company, US, 1989
G.W. Leibniz, *Monadology*, University of Pittsburgh Press, 1991
G.W. Leibniz, *Discourse on Metaphysics*, Prometheus Books, US, 1993
G.W. Leibniz, *New Essays on Human Understanding*, Cambridge University Press, 1996
G.W. Leibniz, *Philosophical Texts*, Oxford University Press, 1998

Chapter 17

George Berkeley (1685–1753)

─────────────── **Key Points** ───────────────

■ Objects do not exist independently of observers

■ God's continuous understanding and observation is therefore the bedrock of all existence

■ Nothing, therefore, can exist, or be described or imagined, except through, and with reference to, God

■ God, is therefore the central component of all truly meaningful explanation

■ To find yourself, or any other person or thing, you must first find God. God is above, below, before, behind, within all.

Application

● For Berkeley, God is not to be excluded from any explanation

● Is underlying reality colourless matter in motion? Is this a depressing and disenchanting prospect? Berkeley thought so and he was sure this secular vision was incorrect

● How can we know others and be connected with others? How do we know that their experience relates in any way to ours? Secular sceptics did not know the answer. Berkeley believed only God could link us all together

● Berkeley challenged our common-sense notions of absolute space and time. His challenge, if not his answer, is supported by contemporary physics.

What is real? What is certain? And how far can we infer other certainties and realities from whatever starting base we may manage to establish? Locke and Descartes, as we have seen, started with 'myself', moved on to God and, in different ways, built up a world of minds and matter presided over by God.

Currently we still tend to take it for granted that this is a material world although we still have difficulty explaining how 'consciousness', whatever that may be, fits into and relates to this material reality. Bishop George Berkeley was greatly concerned that, so-called, conventional wisdom was increasingly presupposing a mechanical universe that operated like some vast clockwork mechanism. God, it was generally assumed, had created the mechanism but now, it seemed, it was capable of operating all by itself. No doubt God could interfere with his creation, slow it, stop it, shift a few wheels here and there. But Divine interference with the cosmic mechanism would spoil our ability to make scientific advances in our understanding of this vast machine. In any case, we had to assume that God's first effort was splendid enough. It should and would therefore have been his last effort. So God, the creator, having completed his work, now appeared to be redundant, permanently unemployed.

This was not good enough for Bishop Berkeley. The world envisioned by Descartes and Locke was faceless, flat, colourless, meaningless. God, for Berkeley, was surely in continuous activity. It was absurd to imagine that God was now pensioned off, redundant and that, having done His work, he could now just disappear and have the machine tick away without Him. And why all this attention to machinery? Where was soul/mind/spirit in all of this? If not actually redundant it seemed to get driven to the edge of the story; its nature, its role, its status seemed dubious, limited, uncertain. Berkeley was having none of it. In his view God was the centre, minds were the stuff of everyday existence and bodies? Matter?:

> It is indeed an opinion strangely prevailing amongst men, that houses, mountains, rivers, and in a word all sensible objects, have an existence, natural or real, distinct from their being perceived by the understanding. But, with how great an assurance and acquiescence soever this principle may be entertained in the world, yet whoever shall find in his heart to call it in question may, if I mistake not, perceive it to involve a manifest contradiction. For, what are the fore-mentioned objects but the things we perceive by sense? And what do we perceive besides our own ideas or sensations? and is it not plainly repugnant that any one of these, or any combination of them, should exist unperceived? (*Treatise Concerning the Principles of Human Knowledge*, para. 4)

You might have thought you lived in a material world, and that material objects were most real and most tangible. However, for Berkeley, the underlying reality was not the world but your *idea* about this world. Matter, material, the physical; these were all far less real than the fact that they were ideas through which we sought to provide ourselves with coherence and meaning. Locke believed, and contemporary common sense concurs, that objects continued to exist regardless of whether or not human beings were perceiving them. Berkeley thought otherwise:

> So long as they are not actually perceived by me, or do not exist in my mind or that of any other created spirit, they must either have no existence at all, or else subsist in the mind of some Eternal Spirit – it being perfectly unintelligible, and involving all the absurdity of abstraction, to attribute to any single part of them an existence independent of a spirit. To be convinced of which, the reader need only reflect, and try to separate in his own thoughts the being of a sensible thing from its being perceived. (ibid. Para. 6)

For Berkeley, his ideas were not fantastic and strange; they were obvious and inevitable. It was our current conventional wisdom that was absurd, and we believed in it because we did not look carefully enough beneath the surface of existence. So, for example, we take it for granted that the tree we can see out in the street exists when we are looking at it, exists when the neighbours are looking at it and, most crucially, goes on existing all night even when nobody is looking at it. 'Nonsense', thought Berkeley. What is real is that we have ideas of trees; when we stop having the ideas there is nothing else and there needs to be nothing else:

> 7. From what has been said it follows there is not any other Substance than Spirit, or that which perceives.
> 8. But, say you, although the ideas themselves do not exist without the mind, yet there may be things like them, whereof they are copies or resemblances, which things exist without the mind in an unthinking substance. I answer, an idea can be like nothing but an idea; a colour or figure can be like nothing but another colour or figure. If we look but never so little into our thoughts, we shall find it impossible for us to conceive a likeness except only between our ideas. (ibid.)

So, we imagined that our idea of a tree was 'like' a tree. How could we say such a thing? We could not compare our tree idea/perception with a tree since we only ever had the perception, the experience. In that case, how did we know if our experiences had any similarity with the experiences of others? For Berkeley it came down to God, the eternal Spirit. God was having ideas of trees and every other idea we had ever had plus more besides, even as we slept. God created every other spirit. God it was that ensured that there was coherence in all the ideas. God was continuously at work. God was the centre, the periphery and everywhere in between. God was the ground of our spirit, the ground of our ideas, the ground of there being any possibility of coherence in the life of minds. Without God there was nothing, and instantaneously. So much for the idea that the universe, and the so-called machines in it, could tick away for one instant without God. As for external bodies:

> 20. In short, if there were external bodies, it is impossible we should ever come to know it; and if there were not, we might have the very same reasons to think there were that we have now. (ibid.)

At this stage Berkeley feels the need to apologise. His views are so obviously true that he really has been taking too long in trying to explain them. It can all be summarised quickly and easily:

> 22. I am afraid I have given cause to think I am needlessly prolix in handling this subject. For, to what purpose is it to dilate on that which may be demonstrated with the utmost evidence in a line or two, to any one that is capable of the least reflexion? It is but looking into your own thoughts, and so trying whether you can conceive it possible for a sound, or figure, or motion, or colour to exist without the mind or unperceived. This easy trial may perhaps make you see that what you contend for is a downright contradiction.
>
> 23. But, say you, surely there is nothing easier than for me to imagine trees, for instance, in a park, or books existing in a closet, and nobody by to perceive them. I answer, you may so, there is no difficulty in it; but what is all this, I beseech you, more than framing in your mind certain ideas which you call books and trees, and the same time omitting to frame the idea of any one that may perceive them? But do not you yourself perceive or think of them all the while? This therefore is nothing to the purpose; it only shews you have the power of imagining or forming ideas in your mind: but it does not shew that you can conceive it possible the objects of your thought may exist without the mind. To make out this, it is necessary that you conceive them existing unconceived or unthought of, which is a manifest repugnancy. (ibid.)

So what is real? For Berkeley, God is the most overwhelmingly real and continuously necessary eternal spirit. To find yourself and any real serenity, therefore, you must find God. Mind/spirit is real. 'Matter' is most unreal. It is just another idea that minds have. And they have it wrong. People just do not think hard enough:

> Philosophy being nothing else but the study of wisdom and truth, it may with reason be expected that those who have spent most time and pains in it should enjoy a greater calm and serenity of mind, a greater clearness and evidence of knowledge, and be less disturbed with doubts and difficulties than other men. Yet so it is, we see the illiterate bulk of mankind that walk the high-road of plain common sense, and are governed by the dictates of nature, for the most part easy and undisturbed. To them nothing that is familiar appears unaccountable or difficult to comprehend. They complain not of any want of evidence in their senses, and are out of all danger of becoming Sceptics. But no sooner do we depart from sense and instinct to follow the light of a superior principle, to reason, meditate, and reflect on the nature of things, but a thousand scruples spring up in our minds concerning those things which before we seemed fully to comprehend. (ibid. Para. 1)

To find serenity then, you can be one of the unthinking multitude, or you can think hard, suffer the insecurities arising from a scepticism capable of analysing the ground beneath you out of existence. (What ground? It is just another idea of yours.) The deepest serenity, coupled with real insight, comes to you when, through serious study, you discover that your real ground of being, the real base on which you stand supported, is in that eternal spirit, in God. Praise Him!

Berkeley genuinely believed his idea. It is not, of course, an idea shared by most others. If it had been, I am sure the churches would be much fuller than they are today.

Berkeley's idea of there being only ideas was challenged by subsequent philosophers as we shall see. Yet, beware! Some of the primary quality absolutes that Locke presumed, Berkeley challenged, and contemporary wisdom takes for granted, have themselves been overturned by twentieth century science. For example, we still tend to believe that there is an absolute space through which we are all travelling and an absolute time that defines our rate of travel. 'Here', 'there', 'now' and 'then'. These, we presume, are primary qualities which exist independently of the observer and which are the same from wherever and howsoever you perceive them. Three dimensions of space and one of time provided the absolute framework within which matter in motion was measured.

Berkeley, however, suggested that there was *no* absolute space or time: We had ideas of bodies; and space was just another idea about the relationships between our ideas of bodies. Time, likewise, was an idea we had to construct the succession, or train, of our ideas. Absolute space and time were unperceivable and meaningless; all we had was the process of our drawing ideas of relationship between ideas. Berkeley's idealism may not have stood the test of time (however analysed); but Berkeley's relativism, has proven itself against twentieth-century science more than Locke, Newton and contemporary common sense.

Where such relativism leaves individuals and their ideas of personal identity is a question still to be considered. We shall begin to do so in the next chapter.

❓ Questions

1. What do you do with a client who believes that no explanation makes sense that does not refer to God?

2. Do we need to change our own understanding of space and time?

3. Are we trapped in space and time?

4. What could it mean to transcend them?

5. Can we find ourselves without an external principle or being?

6. How many clients suffer because there is no magic in their vision of existence?

EXERCISES

1. Consider societies and cultures where God is still central to any inner or outer exploration. What would counselling and care mean within such a culture?

2. Consider how far counselling assumes that individuals, with or without counsellors, can 'go it alone' in developing insight. What might be the strengths and weaknesses of such an assumption?

Conclusion

Eighteenth-century sceptical philosophy questioned the basis of what we knew about ourselves and the world around us. Berkeley sought to solve the problem by asserting God's central place within all existence, understanding and explanation. Without God, individual minds could know and do nothing at all. The secular humanist project of progress driven by the power of reason was an unacceptable displacement of Divine power and purpose. God did not fill the gaps in our otherwise secular knowledge. He was not above, beyond or outside; and could not be pushed to one side. He was the ground, basis and nature of all our knowledge. Without God it did not even make sense to talk of meaning, purpose, identity, existence. Therefore a counsellor who was not a Christian was, for Berkeley, a complete absurdity and a contradiction in terms.

Berkeley showed, more powerfully than any other theologian, how God might be apprehended not just as a Divine addition to an otherwise secular world, but as the very ground of all being and experience. It is useful to attempt to empathise with such fundamentally nonsecular understanding. The new millennium requires that we learn how to negotiate between a secular west and, for example, Islam. If secular humanism can only offer shopping as a vision of the future, we may also expect that the fundamentalist Christian right, already powerful, will become more attractive to those who find secularism empty and arid as a basis for life.

Websites

http://www.cpm.ll.ehime-u.ac.jp/AkamacHomePage/Akamac_E-text_Links/
    Berkeley.html
http://www.ilt.columbia.edu/academic/digitexts/berkeley/bio_berkeley.html

Bibliography

G. Berkeley, *Three Dialogues Between Hylas and Philonous*, Hackett Publishing Company, US, 1988

G. Berkeley, *Philosophical Works*, Everyman, 1993

G. Berkeley, *Treatise Concerning the Principles of Human Knowledge*, Oxford University Press, 1998

Chapter 18

David Hume (1711–1776)

Key Points

■ I never can catch 'myself' at any time without a perception, and never can observe anything but the perception

■ We never observe causes, merely the constant conjunction of one event followed by another

■ We are but a bundle or collection of different perceptions, which succeed each other with an inconceivable rapidity, and are in a perpetual flux and movement

■ Morals and criticism are not so properly objects of the understanding as of taste and sentiment

■ We assent to our faculties and employ our reason only because we cannot help it.

Application

- Clients may share Hume's uncertainty about who they are
- If morality is not 'for the glory of God' then its secular basis needs clarifying
- Causal explanations are barren without deeper underlying principles. 'A caused B'; the question remains 'why B?'
- To know we must look, but how reliable are we as observers?
- Hume undermines previous certainties. Subsequent philosophers have sought to meet his challenge or, in our own time, have taken his scepticism further still.

For John Locke, it was beyond question that *man has a clear idea of his own being; he knows certainly he exists, and that he is something.*

Subsequent philosophers have challenged this most fundamental of assumptions and, in our own time, the reality, identity and 'something-ness' of self is less self-evident, not only to philosophers but also to many laypeople. Perhaps that helps to explain why people are willing to spend considerable sums of money to be 'facilitated' or told by others who they are and in what they, and their options, consist. David Hume was one of the earliest, and most potent, critics of the supposedly self-evident self:

> There are some philosophers who imagine we are every moment intimately conscious of what we call our SELF; that we feel its existence and its continuance in existence; and are certain, beyond the evidence of a demonstration, both of its perfect identity and simplicity. The strongest sensation, the most violent passion, say they, instead of distracting us from this view, only fix it the more intensely, and make us consider their influence on self either by their pain or pleasure. To attempt a farther proof of this were to weaken its evidence; since no proof can be deriv'd from any fact, of which we are so intimately conscious; nor is there any thing of which we can be certain, if we doubt of this (*Treatise of Human Nature*, 1739, Book 1, Part 4, sec. VI)

Hume, the arch sceptic, took an empirical approach. He looked 'within' and found that he never came across 'himself' at all. Instead he witnessed what we would now describe as a 'stream of consciousness':

> For my part, when I enter most intimately into what I call 'myself', I always stumble on some particular perception or other, of heat or cold, light or shade, love or hatred, pain or pleasure. I never can catch 'myself' at any time without a perception, and never can observe any thing but the perception. (ibid.)

Practitioners of various forms of meditation make a similar observation. Witness the flow of experiences, changing, changing, rushing on and on like a never-ending river. Where are 'you' in all this? Where is the 'self' you thought you knew? And what about when you are asleep? Where are you then?:

> When my perceptions are remov'd for any time, as by sound sleep; so long am I insensible of 'myself', and may truly be said not to exist. (ibid.)

And in death? If you no longer had experiences, because you no longer had a body with receptors to trigger experiences, what then? Hume could make little sense of disembodied 'souls' or of non-physical 'essences' of self:

And were all my perceptions remov'd by death, and cou'd I neither think, nor feel, nor see, – nor love, nor hate after the dissolution of my body, I shou'd be entirely annihilated, nor do I conceive what is farther requisite to make me a perfect non-entity. (ibid.)

Yet Hume allowed there were some, like Locke, who claimed that their own selfhood was the most obvious and overwhelming fact of life. What could Hume say to such people?:

If any one, upon serious and unprejudic'd reflection thinks he has a different notion of 'himself', I must confess I can reason no longer with him. All I can allow him is, that he may be in the right as well as I, and that we are essentially different in this particular. He may, perhaps, perceive something simple and continu'd, which he calls himself; tho' I am certain there is no such principle in me. (ibid.)

For all his apparent modesty, Hume was convinced that those who experienced 'themselves' were suffering an illusion:

But setting aside some metaphysicians of this kind, I may venture to affirm of the rest of mankind, that they are nothing but a bundle or collection of different perceptions, which succeed each other with an inconceivable rapidity, and are in a perpetual flux and movement. Our eyes cannot turn in their sockets without varying our perceptions. Our thought is still more variable than our sight; and all our other senses and faculties contribute to this change; – nor is there any single power of the soul, which remains unalterably the same, perhaps for one moment. The mind is a kind of theatre, where several perceptions successively make their appearance; pass, re-pass, glide away, and mingle in an infinite variety of postures and situations. There is properly no 'simplicity' in it at one time, nor identity in different; whatever natural propension we may have to imagine that simplicity and identity... The identity, which we ascribe to the mind of man, is only a fictitious one, and of a like kind with that which we ascribe to vegetables and animal bodies. It cannot, therefore, have a different origin, but must proceed from a like operation of the imagination upon like objects. (ibid.)

'Self' for Hume, then, was not to be observed at all. Existence consisted of a stream of ideas and impressions and an idea was formed of their being *of* a single 'something'/self. Impressions were stronger and more vivid than ideas. Impressions were the raw material from which ideas were constructed. We had an impression of a face, we built up an idea of a mother to which it belonged. This idea takes many years to be constructed. We looked in a mirror and saw another face. We constructed an idea of a 'self' to which it belonged, and this complex idea, also, was built up, developed and changed, over many years.

Patterns were constructed of impressions and ideas in order to make them coherent. The patterns arose from the connections that were drawn between ideas, and an idea was formed that these connections were necessary and real:

> What is our idea of necessity, when we say that two objects are necessarily connected together. Upon this head I repeat what I have often had occasion to observe, that as we have no idea, that is not deriv'd from an impression, we must find some impression, that gives rise to this idea of necessity, if we assert we have really such an idea. In order to this I consider, in what objects necessity is commonly suppos'd to lie; and finding that it is always ascrib'd to causes and effects, I turn my eye to two objects suppos'd to be plac'd in that relation; and examine them in all the situations, of which they are susceptible. I immediately perceive, that they are contiguous in time and place, and that the object we call cause precedes the other we call effect. In no one instance can I go any farther, nor is it possible for me to discover any third relation betwixt these objects. I therefore enlarge my view to comprehend several instances; where I find like objects always existing in like relations of contiguity and succession. At first sight this seems to serve but little to my purpose. The reflection on several instances only repeats the same objects; and therefore can never give rise to a new idea. But upon farther enquiry I find, that the repetition is not in every particular the same, but produces a new impression, and by that means the idea, which I at present examine. For after a frequent repetition, I find, that upon the appearance of one of the objects, the mind is determin'd by custom to consider its usual attendant, and to consider it in a stronger light upon account of its relation to the first object. 'Tis this impression, then, or determination, which affords me the idea of necessity. (ibid. Book 1, Part 3, sec. XIV)

From impressions, ideas were formed of 'selves' and of causal relations and of the supposedly necessary connections between units of experience. All that could be directly observed was that impressions came one after another. A ball hit the ground, bounced up again, and we formed an idea that it was 'caused' to do so by the ground. This was an idea of ours but causation was not something we could actually observe. All that we observed was, as Hume put it, the 'constant conjunction' of one impression – ball travelling down – followed by another – ball moving up again.

'Common sense', supposedly, tells us that balls move downwards because of 'forces' of gravity and then bounce upwards because of the immovable ground they meet. Hume notes that we do not observe 'forces' at all. This is just an idea we have constructed or, in fact, borrowed from Isaac Newton who did all the serious thinking about it for us. The most current ideas about these balls is that large objects curve space around them and that it why balls 'fall'. But Newton will suffice as an approximation for small relative velocities.

Hume's scepticism about selves, worlds, deities and ethical principles was remorseless. Nothing seemed to remain standing after Hume had moved in to examine the basis of our knowledge. We did what we did, but the 'justifications' for what we did were nothing like as strong as we imagined. Even the 'we' that imagined was nothing like as solid as it thought. The path that Hume follows disintegrates the path, the Hume, God, the reader and the world within which the path lies. Socrates observed that he knew more than others because he knew that he knew nothing. Hume asks who is this self that thinks it is a knower of nothing? And as for ethics:

> Morals and criticism are not so properly objects of the understanding as of taste and sentiment. (*An Enquiry Concerning Human Understanding*, sec. XII, Part III)

If scepticism is taken to such lengths what is to become of us? Social chaos? Personal disintegration? In fact Hume acted as though he did actually exist, complete with ethical principles. In his daily life he did not abandon his ideas despite his discovery that their roots were shallower than we may imagine. His approach was meant to help us cultivate humility and a deeper insight into the relatively shallow basis of our insight. It was not designed to lead us to despair:

> By all that has been said the reader will easily perceive that the philosophy contained in this book is very skeptical and tends to give us a notion of the imperfections and narrow limits of human understanding. Almost all reasoning is there reduced to experience, and the belief which attends experience is explained to be nothing but a peculiar sentiment or lively conception produced by habit. *And yet:* we assent to our faculties and employ our reason only because we cannot help it. (ibid. Appendix II)

Therefore, because Hume cannot help it, he is quite prepared to consider how a society could best be organised to accommodate the interests of those 'selves' whose actual existence he has elsewhere questioned. He observes that:

> The necessity of justice to the support of society is the sole foundation of
> that virtue. (*Enquiry Concerning the Principles of Morals*, 1777, sec. III,
> Part II)

Justice is required to keep a society functioning, and society is essential to preserve peace and order. Without these, human affairs are impossible. Without society, there would be a war of all against all. Societies cannot exist without laws, magistrates and means of enforcing their decisions, because people are not wise and unselfish enough to be relied upon to act always according to what is necessary for the maintenance of society. Individual freedom must therefore be constrained because it is not always innocent and beneficial. In the longer term such constraints are in everyone's interests. Without them there would be no society because the bonds holding strangers together are relatively weak compared with our own self-regard and concern for the people close to us. Without law, society would disintegrate into feuding families and individuals:

> Sympathy, we shall allow, is much fainter than our concern for ourselves,
> and sympathy with persons remote from us much fainter than that with
> persons near and contiguous. (ibid. sec. V. Part II)

Hume believed that, although people can see the value of living in an orderly society, they will still tend to cheat in favour of their own selfish interests. Education, he thought, would help in fostering more civilised behaviour:

> In order to judge aright of a composition of genius, there are so many views
> to be taken in, so many circumstances to be compared, and such a know-
> ledge of human nature requisite, that no man, who is not possessed of the
> soundest judgement, will ever make a tolerable critic in such performances.
> And this is a new reason for cultivating a relish in the liberal arts. Our
> judgement will strengthen by this exercise: We shall form juster notions of
> life: Many things, which please or afflict others, will appear to us too frivo-
> lous to engage our attention. (*Of the Delicacy of Taste and Passion*, 1741)

A sound, serious, disciplined and comprehensive liberal education is, for Hume, not an effete cultural accessory; it is a means by which

people develop a deeper, more subtle and sophisticated understanding
of themselves and the society of which they are a part:

> Nothing is so improving to the temper as the study of the beauties, either
> of poetry, eloquence, music, or painting. They give a certain elegance of
> sentiment to which the rest of mankind are strangers. The emotions which
> they excite are soft and tender. They draw off the mind from the hurry of
> business and interest; cherish reflection; dispose to tranquillity; and
> produce an agreeable melancholy, which, of all dispositions of the mind, is
> the best suited to love and friendship. (ibid.)

Having elsewhere poured scepticism over the basis of the 'self' we
think we know, Hume can nonetheless show sophisticated insight into
human nature and its strong, weak, admirable and ugly dimensions:

> Nothing is in general so disagreeable to the mind as the languid, listless
> state of indolence, into which it falls upon the removal of all passion and
> occupation. To get rid of this painful situation, it seeks every amusement
> and pursuit; business, gaming, shews, executions; whatever will rouze the
> passions, and take its attention from itself. No matter what the passion is:
> Let it be disagreeable, afflicting, melancholy, disordered; it is still better
> than that insipid languor, which arises from perfect tranquillity and
> repose... the movement of pleasure, pushed a little too far, becomes pain;
> and that the movement of pain, a little moderated, becomes pleasure.
> Hence it proceeds, that there is such a thing as a sorrow, soft and agreeable:
> It is a pain weakened and diminished. The heart likes naturally to be
> moved and affected. Melancholy objects suit it, and even disastrous
> and sorrowful, provided they are softened by some circumstance. (*Of
> Tragedy*, 1757)

Hume's scepticism endlessly undermines our sense of certainty about
what we think is obvious and self-evident. But he seeks humility rather
than despair. He does not wish us to abandon all our ideas, merely to
hold them less closely and desperately to us. In this way, Hume argues,
we will be more ready and able to adopt new ideas when our present
'certainties' prove to be inadequate. When we look back on the ideas of
our ancestors, it is easy for us to be somewhat amazed that they entertained notions that, to us, are self-evidently inadequate. Only by
probing more carefully at their lives and circumstances do we see how
their thoughts made sense from where they were standing and given
what they knew and did not know.

It is similarly difficult for us to see that our great great grandchildren will find many of our own cherished beliefs antique, absurd, idiotic, and they will have similar difficulty understanding how we could have been 'deceived' by such 'self-evident' absurdity. Their constructions even of who they are as individuals are unlikely to be the same as ours. Indeed they may prove to be different in quite fundamental ways. All we can know, more or less for certain, is that ideas are likely to change and change again, often fundamentally, as they have done in the past. If anything, the rate of change is accelerating. What we can be sure of, is that we have no means of guessing what will change, or how, or why, or what will replace it, or what will be its consequences.

Hume's scepticism/open-mindedness was not welcomed by his contemporaries, and the power of his thinking remained obscure until it was essentially rediscovered by a German philosopher of equal or perhaps greater stature, Immanuel Kant. Hume's contemporaries could easily grow frustrated with what appeared to be an endless demolition of all the foundations of our being and doing. In our own time a similar irritation with the 'silly' speculations of philosophers is not uncommon. Yet Hume, because of his flexibility, would have almost certainly adapted to, learned about, and moved on towards, the thoughts and insights of our own time more quickly than most of his contemporaries simply because he was not so wedded and welded into eighteenth-century certainties.

Humean scepticism sought to explore, rather than undermine, the foundations of our lives. He did not counsel despair, indeed his writings show a quiet but strong faith that life is worth living and that there is much that can be savoured. Hume did advise against the extremes of emotion; he preferred a cultivated 'middle way' but recognised that some are born more excitable than others:

> People of this character have, no doubt, more lively enjoyments, as well as more pungent sorrows, than men of cool and sedate tempers: But, I believe, when every thing is balanced, there is no one, who would not rather be of the *latter* character, were he entirely master of his own disposition. Good or ill fortune is very little at our disposal: And when a person, that has this sensibility of temper, meets with any misfortune, his sorrow or resentment takes entire possession of him, and deprives him of all relish in the common occurrences of life; the right enjoyment of which forms the chief part of our happiness. Great pleasures are much less frequent than great pains; so that a sensible temper must meet with fewer trials in the former way than in the latter. (*Of the Delicacy of Taste and Passion*, 1741)

Hume's style is consistent with his message. 'Great pleasures are much less frequent than great pains.' Hume makes the point without drama, with no wailing and gnashing of teeth or calls to Stoic heroism. This is how it is. There is no need to make a show either of weakness or toughness. Refinement of temperament prefers discernment and discretion to vulgar display of any sort.

Ideas change, but often this only occurs when the people who believed in the contemporary certainties have died and thereby left room for something new. Habits, as Hume observed, do not change easily, yet they may be the real basis of many of our conceptions. They are held onto strongly; too strongly, perhaps. If we let go of our tight habitual grip on what we hold to be 'obvious', we may discover, not chaos and meaninglessness, but wonder, awe, reverence, humour, flexibility, power. If so, then the questions Hume raises are not abstract, academic and irrelevant to the layperson. They are part of the process of our being able to learn, to change, to grow. Hume makes for awkward reading. But his views deserve attention.

? Questions

1. Do some of your clients have problems establishing their identity? Is the priority to 'find', define, reassure or to question 'myself'?

2. Do clients need primarily to accept, or challenge, explanations and understandings developed during counselling?

3. Do clients discover new truths or new stories?

4. If God is dead, are morals really no more than sentiments and acquired tastes?

EXERCISES

1. Consider how far you encourage clients to question assumptions. Do you, should you, go as far as Hume in sceptical questioning?

2. Hume undermines arguments in favour of God's existence. Consider what bearings your clients tend to find in establishing meaning.

3. Consider the role of refinement, understatement, cultivation and a 'sensible temper' as a means of dealing with the 'great pleasures' and the (much more frequent?) 'great pains' of life.

Conclusion

Hume takes the process of sceptical questioning further even than Socrates. Hume is nonetheless urbane, confident, positive and perfectly willing to live within the habits, customs and social mores that are part of the culture to which he belongs. He shows that much of the framework of our lives may be difficult to justify by reason yet he is not, thereby, an irrationalist. On the contrary, Hume believed that reason could show us the limits of our certainties and thereby encourage within us a suitable humility, tolerance and reverence. Would a grasp of Hume throw some readers into despair about the problems of finding meaning? Can we do better than base our actions and explanations on habit and custom? As we shall see, many subsequent thinkers have tried to answer Hume's challenge and improve on his sceptical conclusions.

Websites

http://www.geocities.com/Athens/4753/menu.html
http://www.ilt.columbia.edu/academic/digitexts/hume/bio_hume.html
http://www.ilt.columbia.edu/academic/digitexts/hume/enquiry/enqhum.txt

Bibliography

D. Hume, *Enquiry Concerning the Principles of Morals*, Open Court Publishing Company, US, 1977
D. Hume, *Essays Moral, Political and Literary*, Liberty Fund, 1985
D. Hume, *Of Miracles*, Open Court Publishing Company, US, 1985
D. Hume, *An Enquiry Concerning Human Understanding*, Open Court Publishing Company, US, 1988
D. Hume, *Treatise of Human Nature*, Prometheus Books, US, 1992

Chapter 19

Jean Jacques Rousseau (1712–1778)

——————————— **Key Points** ———————————

■ *Cities are the abyss of the human species*

■ *Observe nature and follow the path it maps out for you*

■ *Temperance and work are the two true doctors of man*

■ *I hate books. They only teach one to talk about what one does not know*

■ *With a slow and carefully arranged gradation, man and child are made intrepid in everything.*

—— *Application* ————————————————————

● Rousseau probed and praised person-centred and cognitive therapy more lucidly than many current practitioners
● He is the source of contemporary romance with nature and pessimism about human society
● He saw education and personal development as utterly inseparable
● He praised 'authentic, natural, humanity' in preference to the pretensions and delusions of 'civilised' society
● He sought to 'facilitate' natural human curiosity and individual goodness.

> Everything is good as it leaves the hands of the Author of things; everything degenerates in the hands of man.

This is Rousseau's opening sentence in *Émile: ou, de l'éducation* (1762). It is a pessimistic start to an eighteenth-century version of Dr Spock's guide to child rearing. Émile is an imaginary youngster and the book explores what Rousseau would do as Émile's mentor and tutor. Can a teacher who equates 'man-made' with 'degenerate' be a healthy influence? In fact, Rousseau is not morbid about life, provided it is lived fully and authentically:

> The man who has lived the most is not he who has counted the most years but he who has the most felt life. (*Émile*, p. 42)

However, to feel life you must get away from other people as much as possible and return to 'nature', its beauty, mystery and 'simplicity'. This vision is in stark contrast to that of Plato, for example. For the ancient Greeks, barbarism was any life lacking the democracy and culture that could only be found within a Greek city-state. For Rousseau, in contrast, cities were to be avoided:

> Cities are the abyss of the human species... Men are not made to be crowded into anthills but to be dispersed over the earth which they should cultivate. The more they come together, the more they are corrupted. (ibid. p. 59)

Where, then, should you take your child? And how should you educate him or her?:

> Nursed in the country amidst all the pastoral rusticity, your children will get sonorous voices, they will not contract the obscure stuttering of city children.

> Instead of letting him stagnate in the stale air of a room, let him be taken daily to the middle of a field. There let him run and frisk about; let him fall a hundred times a day. So much the better. That way he will learn how to get up sooner. (ibid. p. 73, 78)

For centuries, the educated and cultivated, everywhere, had routinely and instinctively sought to get as far away as possible from the peasantry. Rousseau advocated a return to rustic living if we were to find our true, whole, natural, authentic and honest selves. He thereby began the romantic movement which has ebbed and flowed ever since through art, music, politics, literature, fashion, religion, psychology and, albeit least of all, philosophy:

> Observe nature and follow the path it maps out for you. It exercises children constantly; it hardens their temperament by tests of all sorts; it teaches them early what effort and pain are. (ibid. p. 47)

For the Greeks, within classical values and the classical vision, the core was to become as 'cultivated' as possible. In this way, you *made* yourself civilised, disciplined and worthy of respect. For Rousseau and subsequent romantics, to this day, the aim is to be as 'natural' as possible. Thereby, you would *find* yourself, simple, tempered by nature, and authentic. Yet what is meant by 'natural'? Are birds' nests natural? Or are they an alien intrusion of avian technology on the natural development of the tree? Is human technology 'unnatural'? Or are human beings just nature's way of producing a Mercedes?

Today, on all our 'environmentally friendly' products, we are promised 'natural' ingredients produced in natural, pastoral surroundings. They are kind and caring to our hands, digestion, hearts and minds. For Rousseau, too, the natural approach is the best approach; nature's way is the human path to healing, health, happiness and wholesome wholeness:

> Naturally man knows how to suffer with constancy and die in peace. It is doctors with their prescriptions, philosophers with their precepts, priests with their exhortations, who debase his heart and make him unlearn how to die. (ibid. p. 55)

We are cut off from ourselves with too many people around us, too many books, too many authorities who supposedly know better than we do. We need to turn away from politicians, priests, physicians, psychologists and philosophers, and move back to the peasantry in order to relearn how to live. So, fresh air and exercise, in this at least, Rousseau agrees with the Greeks:

> I will not stop to prove at length the utility of manual labour and bodily exercise for reinforcing constitution and health. That is disputed by no one. (ibid. p. 56)

But, if you wanted to stay healthy, you needed to keep away from doctors who knew nothing about health at all.[1]

> The only useful part of medicine is hygiene. And hygiene is itself less a science than a virtue. Temperance and work are the two true doctors of man. Work sharpens his appetite, and temperance prevents him from abusing it. (ibid. p. 55)

Work meant manual work, not the idle and empty speculations of philosophers like Rousseau. To know was to act, not to read books:

I hate books. They only teach one to talk about what one does not know.

Always books! What a mania. Because Europe is full of books, Europeans regard them as indispensable, without thinking that in three-quarters of the earth they have never been seen. (ibid. p. 184, p. 303)

You demonstrated what you knew and believed in through what you did. Actions counted above all, and were certainly more important than thoughts or speeches:

I do not like explanations in speeches. Young people pay little attention to them and hardly retain them. Things, things! I shall never repeat enough that we attribute too much power to words. With our babbling education we produce only babblers. (ibid. p. 180)

Rousseau's plea for freedom and authenticity begins with the birth of a child. Mothers should care for, and breastfeed, their own. From this, real bonds of love and support would be built up:

But let mothers deign to nurse their children, morals will reform themselves, nature's sentiments will be awakened in every heart, the state will be re-peopled. This first point, this point alone, will bring everything back together. (ibid. p. 46)

Children should not be swaddled, they should be allowed to explore; their natural curiosity and eagerness to learn should be fostered. Education should also include what we would now call 'confidence building' and 'personal development'. The existing system too often was inhumane and careless of individual development and individual concerns:

(It) teaches him everything, except to know himself, except to take advantage of himself, except to know how to live and to make himself happy. (ibid. p. 48)

Education was not just a formal activity:

We are born weak, we need strength; we are born totally unprovided, we need aid; we are born stupid, we need judgement. Everything we do not have at our birth and which we need when we are grown up is given us by education. This education comes to us from nature or from men or from things. (ibid. p. 38)

Families were crucial in the education of children, and that included fathers:

> Men, be humane. This is your first duty. What wisdom is there for you save humanity? Love childhood; promote its games, its pleasures, its amiable instincts. (ibid. p. 79)

Rousseau wrote this over two hundred years ago and yet it is still often urged and repeated as though new and important. After two centuries, it is no longer new, but, given its importance, it no doubt deserves repeating down the generations. *Émile* is perhaps the very first text on the value of discovery learning, person-centred learning, learning by experience. Rousseau is not, however, 'permissive' in the sense of believing that the child always knows best. He believed that teachers should set the agenda, but covertly and with careful planning so that the child discovered the bounds and possibilities of its own nature and the surrounding world.

The child did not always know best and often there was no point even in trying to reason with it. Adults simply had to set the boundaries and not even negotiate about them:

> If children understood reason, they would not need to be raised. (ibid. p. 89)

The wise adult, though, would confront the child with the *boundary*, not with a personal confrontation, antagonism, and battle of wills:

> Do not forbid him to do that from which he should abstain; prevent him from doing it without explanations, without reasonings. It is thus that you will make him patient, steady, resigned, calm, even when he has not got what he wanted, for it is in the nature of man to endure patiently the necessity of things but not the ill will of others. The phrase 'There is no more' is a response against which no child has ever rebelled unless he believed that it was a lie. (ibid. p. 91)

Similarly, on the matter of punishment, it was unwise for adults to punish children. They would be far more likely to learn from their mistakes if they were punished by natural consequences rather than punishing adults:

I have said enough to make it understood that punishment as punishment must never be inflicted on children, but it should always happen to them as a natural consequence of their bad action. (ibid. p. 101)

Perhaps if the adult is 'naturally' angry there is more justification?[2]
Rousseau also shows keen awareness of the value of 'cognitive-behavioural' programmes:

I want him habituated to seeing new objects, ugly, disgusting, peculiar animals, but little by little, from afar, until he is accustomed to them, and, by dint of seeing them handled by others, he finally handles them himself... With a slow and carefully arranged gradation, man and child are made intrepid in everything. (ibid. pp. 63–4)

This is a more succinct summary than can be found in many contemporary textbooks, and every bit as sophisticated. Rousseau's is, to my knowledge, the earliest version of cognitive-behavioural therapy, although no doubt the technique was in regular use long before the invention of the printing press and, quite probably, before writing of any kind existed.

Rousseau stressed the importance of 'person-centred' learning. The teacher needed to empathise with the child in order to understand what was important for it and how topics were experienced from the child's perspective. Otherwise, the child would lack both the motivation and the ability to learn:

Let the child do nothing on anybody's word. Nothing is good for him unless he feels it to be so. In always pushing him ahead of his understanding, you believe you are using foresight, and you lack it. (ibid. p. 178)

This required that the teacher, too, was real, genuine and humane, since their actions would always speak louder than their words in any case. If the child were suitably nurtured and 'natured', its own natural curiosity would ensure that it learned:

In the first place, you should be well aware that it is rarely up to you to suggest to him what he ought to learn. It is up to him to desire it, to seek it, to find it. It is up to you to put it within his reach, skilfully to give birth to this desire and to furnish him with the means of satisfying it. (ibid. p. 179)

Rousseau even included reading within this non-directive approach. If you forced books on the child, it would resist. It you demonstrated how books were of relevance and value to it, the child would thirst to read:

> I am almost certain that Émile will know how to read and write perfectly at the age of ten, precisely because it makes very little difference to me that he knows how before fifteen. (ibid. p. 117)

When Émile sought to read, he would begin by deciphering notes and letters whose contents were of real interest to him. But what would be the best kind of full-length book to begin with?

> Is it Aristotle? Is it Pliny? Is it Boffon? No. It is *Robinson Crusoe*. (ibid. p. 184)

Never mind cultivation and history. The child would best identify with this individual, Robinson Crusoe, fashioning a life, on his own, out of a natural wilderness. But herein lies one of the great weaknesses of Rousseau. He keeps on imagining that the best strategy is to get away from all these other people crowded around you. Even Rousseau admits that this is not possible in practice for most people, and so it is a utopian fantasy that does not provide practical support for those of us who actually do need, and may wish and choose, to get along with the people around us.

Rousseau is fiercely radical in his criticism of the artificiality and inauthenticity of the cultivated, rich and powerful.

> One sees from the first that in their mouths 'If you please' signifies 'I please' and that 'I beg you' signifies 'I order you'. (ibid. p. 86)

For Rousseau, social 'manners' and rules of etiquette are mostly lies, posture and imposture designed to display power, self-aggrandisement and social status. They were not really humane, genuine and ethical at all. Society cluttered the person with empty rituals and pointless accessories and status symbols that got in the way of honest self-awareness and authentic communication:

> One no longer knows how to be simple in anything, not even with children: rattles of silver and gold, and coral, cut crystal glasses, teething rings of every price and kind. What useless and pernicious affectations! Nothing of all that. (ibid. p. 69)

Society weakened individual confidence, genuineness and autonomy. It made us interdependent in every facet of our lives and this, for Rousseau, was not to be welcomed given that his role model was Robinson Crusoe:

> Society has made man weaker not only in taking from him the right he had over his own strength but, above all, in making his strength insufficient for him. (ibid. p. 84)

This was written over two hundred years ago, and since then our mutual interdependence has grown far more, along with our inertia, lack of exercise and proneness to panic at the smallest imagined 'danger' and adversity. Rousseau knew nothing of TV couch potatoes. He would have been utterly horrified.

He would not have shared the view that children, or adults, should 'express', 'unload', release and 'let go of' every emotion, be it sadness, fear, anger, frustration or anything else. On the contrary, the child who knew that nature was a university of hard knocks would not weep over every small battering and block to progress. In this respect, Rousseau shared the Stoic view that emotion must be put into perspective. Our expectations about what the world could deliver needed, above all, to be realistic. If they were, we would not whine and whinge just because what we got was not as good as what we might have preferred:

> He whose strength surpasses his needs, be he an insect or a worm, is a strong being. He whose needs surpass his strength, be he an elephant or a lion, be he a conqueror or a hero, be he a god, is a weak being... Let us measure the radius of our sphere and stay in the centre like the insect in the middle of his web; we shall always be sufficient unto ourselves; and we shall not have to complain of our weakness, for we shall never feel it. (ibid. p .81)

Rousseau shared, indeed he inspired, many of our contemporary views about progressive education. But he was not a hedonist. He did not believe in a right to happiness. On the contrary, he was shrewdly aware that a search for, and expectation of, happiness was almost certain to diminish it. Rousseau is full of succinct and useful one-liners. The following, for example, still deserves to be pasted on many a notice board:

> It is by dint of agitating ourselves to increase our happiness that we convert it into unhappiness. (ibid.)

Imagination was a great source of unhappiness, more so, even, than the tough world around us. We could imagine possible setbacks and disasters in far greater abundance than the real ones. We could suffer from an imagined rock in the face only a little less than a real one; and we could picture it hitting us over and over again. We could dwell on disappointments and frustrations and injustices endlessly and make ourselves ever more miserable:

> The real world has its limits; the imaginary one is infinite. Unable to enlarge the one, let us restrict the other, for it is from the difference between the two alone that are born all the pains which make us truly unhappy. (ibid.)

This was another reason why Rousseau was suspicious of the value of sophisticated, cultivated, urban living. It stimulated our imaginations and expectations to fever pitch. It turned desires into 'needs'. The process has continued into our own consumer culture. It would have horrified Rousseau:

> The closer to his natural condition man has stayed, the smaller is the difference between his faculties and his desires, and consequently the less removed he is from being happy. (ibid.)

Hence, Rousseau was very much opposed to spoiling the child and being overprotective:

> Do you know the surest means of making your child miserable? It is to accustom him to getting everything; since his desires grow constantly due to the ease of satisfying them. (ibid. p. 87)

Given that Rousseau did not think he could keep Émile perpetually absent from city life, he considered what lessons his imaginary pupil could learn when they came into town. They would become part of 'society'. They would be invited to meals. These would be elaborate, ostentatious, formal, mannered. What should Rousseau say to Émile about all this?:

> While the meal continues, while the courses follow one another, while the boisterous conversation reigns on the table, I lean towards his ear and say, 'Through how many hands would you estimate that all you see on this table has passed before getting here?' What a crowd of ideas I awaken in his brain with these few words! (ibid. p. 190)

No wonder Marx appreciated Rousseau's radicalism. Rousseau approved the Christian teaching that the rich man could achieve the Kingdom of Heaven as readily as a camel could travel through the eye of a needle:

> The comparison of a simple, rustic dinner, prepared by exercise, seasoned by hunger, freedom, and joy, with his magnificent formal feast will suffice to make him feel that all the apparatus of the feast did not give him any real profit, and that since his stomach left the peasant's table as satisfied as it left the financier's, there was nothing more in the one than in the other that he could truly call his own. (ibid. p. 191)

Rousseau's radicalism in relation to the church got him into particular trouble. He promoted a non-theistic spirituality that was not destined to make him popular with the clergy:

> I serve God in the simplicity of my heart. I seek to know only what is important for my conduct. As for the dogmas which have an influence neither on actions nor on morality, and about which so many men torment themselves, I do not trouble myself about them at all. (ibid. p. 308)

Rousseau believed that education needed to assist the person in finding himself, and that the individual self could find his own way to God. This authentic self lay far deeper than mere social roles, power, prestige and status. These might fade and pass away, and what then?:

> Happy is the man who knows how to leave the station which leaves him and to remain a man in spite of fate! (ibid. p. 194)

To find ourselves we needed to work, not merely contemplate. In this sense Rousseau is in the tradition of, for example, William Morris and the Arts and Crafts movement that appeared a century later:

> The letter kills, and the spirit enlivens. The goal is less to learn a trade in order to know a trade than to conquer the prejudices that despise trade. You will never be reduced to working to live. Well, too bad – too bad for you! (ibid. p. 196)

We would be most unwise to attach ourselves to, and identify ourselves with, our social roles since, in Rousseau's view, the times they were a-changing, and radically:

You trust in the present order of society without thinking that this order is subject to inevitable revolutions, and it is impossible for you to foresee or prevent one which may affect your children. The noble become commoners, the rich become poor, the monarch becomes subject. Are the blows of fate so rare that you can count on being exempted from them? We are approaching a state of crisis and the age of revolutions. (ibid. p. 194)

This, let us remember, was a mere twenty five years before the cataclysm of the French Revolution. Rousseau was prone to rhetoric, but in this respect, his prediction was quite literally correct for many hundreds of thousands of people.

Rousseau's radicalism did not, however, extend to his view about the relations between men and women:

One ought to be active and strong, the other passive and weak. One must necessarily will and be able; it suffices that the other put up little resistance. Once this principle is established, it follows that woman is made specially to please man. (ibid. p. 358)

Also, Rousseau takes a traditional Eurocentric view of history and white supremacy:

It appears, moreover, that the organisation of the brain is less perfect in the two extremes. Neither the Negroes nor the Laplanders have the sense of the Europeans. If, then, I want my pupil to be able to be an inhabitant of the earth, I will get him in a temperate zone – in France, for example – rather than elsewhere. (ibid. p. 52)

His pupil needs to be French, living in France, and healthy:

I would not take on a sickly and ill-constituted child, were he to live until eighty. I want no pupil always useless to himself and others, involved uniquely with preserving himself, whose body does damage to the education of his soul. (ibid. p. 53)

His views about how societies can be held together are seriously inadequate. He speaks of the 'general will':

Thus, the will of the prince, expressed in his acts as ruler, is, or should be, nothing but the general will, or, in other words, the Law. Such power as he has is but the power of the community concentrated on his person. (*Social Contract*, p. 321)

Rousseau does not explain how to distinguish the general will from the majority will, so the key questions about how to preserve minority rights and control the crown remain unanswered by him. Given that his heart is with Robinson Crusoe, it is not surprising that he does not tackle political questions with the persistence, concern and rigour of political philosophers like Locke or Mill. Neither does Rousseau have much hope for democracy:

> Were there such a thing as a nation of Gods, it would be a democracy. So perfect a form of government is not suited to mere men. (ibid p. 333)

People are too stupid and immature to govern as equal citizens but most kings are stupid and exploitative too. Hence the inequality that arises once people come together and societies are formed:

> The first man who, having enclosed a piece of ground, bethought himself of saying 'This is mine', and found people simple enough to believe him, was the real founder of civil society. From how many crimes, wars and murders, from how many horrors and misfortunes might not any one have saved mankind, by pulling up the stakes, or filling up the ditch, and crying to his fellows, 'Beware of listening to this imposter; you are undone if you once forget that the fruits of the earth belong to us all, and the earth itself to nobody'.(Rousseau, 1755/1992)

No wonder, then, that Rousseau keeps thinking about Robinson Crusoe. No wonder that every romantic since Rousseau has a vision of getting away from it all, dreaming alone, or with just a few friends, tending one's own back yard. This sentiment of withdrawal and escape from society still runs very strong. But it does not help us learn to live together, work and play together, contribute as active citizens and tackle real social problems:

> In a word, it is the best and most natural arrangement that can be made that the wise should govern the masses, provided that they govern them always for their good, and not selfishly. (*Social Contract*, p. 335)

But who are the wise? How are they to be identified? Rousseau has no answers.

Rousseau identifies problems, warns that it is probably too late to solve them, and that we should not ideally be starting from here. He then walks away to his desert island, lake, mountain or cabin to dream, paint, sing, meditate and play music. But you can be sure that he will be back from time to time to tell you that your own efforts to live as a citizen are still not working. Countless other comfortably situated romantics have followed Rousseau in condemning the status quo, living well off it, but proposing remedies that could not conceivably apply to the majority who cannot afford, or find work within, an idyllic rural arcadia.

Man is born free; and everywhere he is in chains.

This is the stirring opening sentence of Rousseau's *Social Contract*. Yet Rousseau really had no idea how such chains could be broken. Marx tried, impressed by the need to be practical. Rousseau would have judged his efforts to be a failure, and no wonder. Utopianism can be of little value when practised either in one's head or in one's actions. Pessimism can be an easy option when hope finds it hard to triumph over experience. So where does this leave us?:

> Although in general Émile does not esteem men, he will not show contempt for them, because he pities them and is touched by them. Unable to give them the taste of things that are really good, he leaves them with the things that are good according to popular opinion, with which they are contented. (*Émile*, p. 336)

This is morally unsatisfactory and smug; but how many romantic escapists and elite aesthetes, although less honest than Rousseau, in fact adopt this condescension?

Nonetheless, Rousseau's impatience with our obsession with words and books may strike a chord among many readers. For so many of us, cyber-reality's screens, words, faxes, emails, lists, talk, take up more time than physical contact or physical action of any sort. Our air is conditioned, we rarely see the sky above us or feel the earth beneath our feet. The stars are eclipsed by street lighting, even eye contact becomes rare. To Rousseau, our 'Microsoft'© present existence, and virtual® future, would have exceeded anything in his worst nightmare of alienated 'life'.

❓ Questions

1. Shall we best 'find ourselves' more easily in pastoral seclusion with a few friends? What do you think?

2. Does Rousseau help us find our real selves as individuals? Does he encourage irresponsible withdrawal from social duty and social concern? Which, do you think, is most true?

3. In what ways do you find Rousseau's account to be better/worse than contemporary person-centred and cognitive-behavioural writers?

4. Does contemporary counselling pay sufficient attention to the development of the client as 'citizen'?

EXERCISES

1. Read *Émile*. For all its faults it should be required reading in all counsellor training since it underlies both person-centred and cognitive-behavioural programmes.

2. Explore 'classical' and 'romantic' tendencies within your own experience of counselling and care.

3. Consider whatever visions you have of client development. Is the developed client alone? With a few friends? An active, urban, citizen?

4. Compare Rousseau with Carl Rogers and consider their similarities and differences. Are they both Romantics? In what ways?

Conclusion

Prior to Rousseau, human development was a shared activity, best achieved in society, in cities, more than among the peasantry. You would find yourself, not on a hillside, but within your civilisation, culture, society and its advances. Personal development, for Rousseau, was achieved *despite* the unhealthy constraints, dishonesty and double dealing of social life. To find yourself you needed to get *away* from others rather than co-operate and interact with strangers. Society was an obstacle to finding yourself, not the framework within which your identity was formed. Was Rousseau's romanticism a step backwards from the classical Greek view? Can worthwhile human beings only be grown from cultures, cities and civilisations? Do selfishness and superstition run riot in the absence of society? Is the 'state of nature' to be avoided, admired or is it, itself, just a romantic fiction?

Notes

1. Rousseau may not have been far wrong given the abysmal ignorance of eighteenth-century medicine. Medicine works better now: '80% of health care expenditure goes on therapies of unknown cost effectiveness, 10% goes on care that damages us and

10% on care that improves our health.' Alan Maynard, Professor of Health Economics, *Times Higher Education Supplement*, 30 January 1998.

2. 'If you strike a child, take care that you strike it in anger, even at the risk of maiming it for life. A blow in cold blood neither can nor should be forgiven'. George Bernard Shaw, *Man and Superman*, 'Maxims for Revolutionists'. Viking, 1988.

Websites

http://members.aol.com/Heraklit1/rousseau.htm
http://www.wabash.edu/Rousseau/
http://www.wabash.edu/Rousseau/WorksonWeb.html
gopher://gopher.vt.edu:10010/02/137/1

Bibliography

J.J. Rousseau, *Social Contact*, Oxford University Press, 1966
J.J. Rousseau, *Émile, or On Education*, Penguin Classics, 1991
J.J. Rousseau, *Discourse on the Origin of Inequality*, Hackett Publishing Company, US, 1992

Chapter 20

Immanuel Kant (1724–1804)

Key Points

- There is no such thing as direct observation. Presuppositions cannot, even in principle, be 'put to one side'

- Observations are always, by their very nature, constructions of events

- Constructions of human perception are determined by individual mental sets and also by categories of thinking that we all share and cannot avoid

- The underlying conditions, without which no experience can be read at all, include space, time, causality, freedom and order

- Act only on that maxim through which you can at the same time will that it should become a universal law.

Application

- What can I know? Kant's answer to the question challenges the possibility of 'empathy' as it is variously described within contemporary counselling theory

- Too much counselling theory presupposes a naïve (Lockean) empiricism demolished by Hume and Kant over 250 years ago. It does so with almost no acknowledgement of any of these philosophers

- Counsellors are taught to put their agendas 'to one side'. Kant shows that we must consider what we bring to any situation that cannot, in principle, be set aside

- Given that we live and develop in societies, personal development cannot divorce itself from consideration of what 'ought' to be.

If we take in our hand any volume; of divinity or school metaphysics, for instance; let us ask, Does it contain any abstract reasoning concerning quantity or number? No. Does it contain any experimental reasoning, concerning matter of fact and existence? No. Commit it then to the flames:

for it can contain nothing but sophistry and illusion. (Hume, *An Enquiry Concerning Human Understanding*, sec. XII, part III)

Kant was deeply impressed with David Hume's sceptical bonfire, engulfing, as it did, so much woolly thinking and careless attention to evidence. Kant believed that, via Hume, he had been awakened from his 'dogmatic slumbers'. However, he was concerned about the size of Hume's bonfire, and did not wish to burn everything that was neither a truth of reasoning nor of direct observation.

What else was there, though? Did anything else deserve to be preserved and, if so, how? Truths derived purely by reasoning from self-evident, or accepted, propositions are know as *a priori* or *analytic* truths. Those dependent on observation are known as *synthetic*. The first involve a process of logical/mathematical analysis of concepts, the second requires a synthesis built, preferably, from a large number of observations.

Kant argued that there was a third category of truth, which he called *synthetic a priori* propositions. They were synthetic in that through them direct empirical knowledge was built up; they were analytic in that they were unavoidable givens, or frames, within which our experience was constructed. They were not observable *objects* of experience. They were not read *out* of our experience, neither were they read *into* our experience. They were, rather, the underlying conditions without which no experience could be read at all.

Leibniz believed that reason was the prime tool for understanding the universe. Thus, by a process of purely abstract thought, he posited 'monads' as basics of the universe.[1] Hume did not think that truths could be derived purely via reason from the comfort of our armchairs. We needed to build up knowledge from direct observation. We should use our five senses, but caution was essential since these senses were themselves so vulnerable to our limited understanding and unlimited prejudices. Habit, more so than reason, Hume believed, was the basis of our actions.

Kant agreed with Hume that Leibniz was seriously in error. But Kant was not happy to talk merely of 'habit'. He asked why we have particular (so-called) habits of perception, action and understanding? Why do we experience anything at all? Experience shapes us, but how do we shape experiences? What laws of logical and psychological necessity determine our encounters with the world? How do we construct or construe experience? Within what categories? According to what conditions? What is essential if I am to experience anything at all?

Leibniz believed that the world must conform with the laws of thought and could thereby be understood by abstract thinking. Hume countered that our thoughts, on the contrary, needed to fit in with the way the world actually was, insofar as we could know it at all via our senses. Kant observed that whatever we knew about the world needed to conform to the perceptual tools available to us. With these we would construct, categorise and make sense of existence. Anything that lay outside our grasp would be unknown to us, so all that we knew had to fit our conceptual categories in some way. What 'handles' did information need if we were to be able to get a hold of it? Against what templates did raw experience need to match? What 'shape' did the data of existence need to fit with our frames of observation? What 'colours' could they have to be visible to us at all?

Kant proposed a variety of examples of the sort of thing he meant: We 'see' that there are three dimensions of space and one of time. This, we may imagine, is the way the world is. Or is it? Kant suggested that it was the way we constructed the world rather than the way the world actually was:

2. Space then is a necessary representation a priori, which serves for the foundation of all external intuitions. We never can imagine or make a representation to ourselves of the non-existence of space, although we may easily enough think that no objects are found in it. It must, therefore, be considered as the condition of the possibility of phenomena, and by no means as a determination dependent on them, and is a representation a priori, which necessarily supplies the basis for external phenomena. (*Critique of Pure Reason*, sec. 1)

1. Time is not an empirical conception. For neither coexistence nor succession would be perceived by us, if the representation of time did not exist as a foundation a priori. Without this presupposition we could not represent to ourselves that things exist together at one and the same time, or at different times, that is, contemporaneously, or in succession.

2. Time is a necessary representation, lying at the foundation of all our intuitions. With regard to phenomena in general, we cannot think away time from them, and represent them to ourselves as out of and unconnected with time, but we can quite well represent to ourselves time void of phenomena. Time is therefore given a priori. In it alone is all reality of phenomena possible. (ibid. sec. 2)

These dimensions were categories without which we could not think or experience the world at all. They were more to do with the way our brains were constructed than the real nature of the universe. Kant's observation may seem fantastic, except when you learn that serious physicists now suggest that the universe does indeed seem to consist of eleven dimensions, many of which are 'enfolded', and that this provides a more accurate and complete account of our environment. Immediately we wonder how can we possibly think about eleven dimensions. What does this mean? How can we imagine it or talk about it? In fact, without the language of mathematics it seems impossible and, if so, it strengthens Kant's view that three dimensions of space and one of time are indeed the necessary building blocks of human thinking and perception regardless of whether or not they comprise the scaffolding of the world itself.

'Orderliness' was another *synthetic a priori* truth for Kant. To think and observe at all required that we saw patterns, structure, shape, continuity. Insofar as the world remained a booming, buzzing confusion it was impossible for us to see it, taste it, touch it, talk or think about it at all. Likewise, there had to be an observer, itself a continuous phenomenon, an object of observation rather than random events, there had to be world to be observed, otherwise there could be no distinction between fantasy and observation. All this was necessary if we were to talk, reflect, communicate, compare notes. We had to believe that there was something 'out there' which it made sense to compare notes about.

We say that the psychotic individual has lost contact with reality. They cannot distinguish hallucination from real perceptions. This presupposes that there is a reality that can be contacted, discussed, analysed, synthesised, shared. How are we to think and talk coherently about it? There has to be a 'substance' to it, Kant argued. Substances have to occupy four dimensions and thereby have permanence and duration. If they do not, there is no 'they' for us to perceive, think and discuss. These substances must act and interact according to orderly causal principles or else, again, they cannot be grasped at all.

Hume had observed that there was no cause 'out there' in the world, but merely the 'habit' of human beings to assume that A 'caused' B when A and B were frequently observed together in sequence. Kant thought that our inserting causation into our observations was not just a habit, but a condition of experience. Why? Because we can develop a variety of habits, but we cannot form an alternative concept, or habit, to causation. We cannot habitually explain the conjunction of A and B in any other way at all except to refer to the notion of causation:

It resulted, (however), from my inquiries, that the objects with which we have to do in experience are by no means things in themselves, but merely phenomena; and that although in the case of things in themselves it is impossible to see how, if A is supposed, it should be contradictory that B, which is quite different from A, should not also be supposed (that is, to see the necessity of the connection between A as cause and B as effect); yet it can very well be conceived that, as phenomena, they may be necessarily connected in one experience in a certain way (for example, with regard to time-relations); so that they could not be separated without contradicting that connection, by means of which this experience is possible in which they are objects and in which alone they are cognisable by us. And so it was found to be in fact; so that I was able not only to prove the objective reality of the concept of cause in regard to objects of experience, but also to deduce it as an *a priori* concept by reason of the necessity of the connection it implied. (*The Critique of Practical Reason*, p. 31)

So causation was a condition of experience, not just a psychological preference or habit. Similarly free will was a requisite category for there to be observing agents discussing an external world and acting morally or immorally. Therefore, instead of asking, for example, 'How do we know that people have choice?' Kant turns the question around and, as it were, asks: Do you really think that you could discuss a world consisting of people observing, analysing and communicating if there were *not* choices being made? There are selves, worlds, others, choices, dimensions, ethics, responsibilities because all these constitute the very ground of thought and experience. If they were not in place you would not even be able to ask about them at all and attempt to deny, or be sceptical about, their validity.

The framework of this book is not large enough to allow us to examine the arguments for and against Kant's frameworks, or categories, of possible experience. Some have argued that he cannot keep all his candidate *synthetic a priori* truths. Others, that his concept needs to be refined or replaced. Kant's answers to the questions he raises remain controversial. The questions themselves seem ever more relevant and important.

Kant's style of writing is terribly dry and difficult, and it is impossible to recommend his works to lay readers unless they are so highly motivated that they are willing to labour and suffer more than can be imagined in advance. Yet Kant's agenda is in fact relevant and important. As he himself observes:

The whole interest of reason, speculative as well as practical, is centred in the three following questions:
1. What can I know?
2. What ought I to do?
3. What may I hope?
(*Critique of Pure Reason*, sec. II)

What was true? What could we know? Kant agreed with Hume that empty speculations needed to be committed to the flames, but what should be preserved? Truths of reasoning. Truths of observation. In addition, though, there were the truths that determined our very ability to reason and observe and which determined the very existence of selves that had a capacity to reason and observe. This was descriptive, as opposed to speculative, metaphysics. It was not empty speculation that moved uselessly beyond what we saw and inferred. It was, rather, a sober and thorough examination of the framework of observation and inference, the ground on which observations were made, the tools via which thought and perception became coherent possibilities.

On the question 'what ought I to do?', Kant examined the status of ethical judgements. What did it mean to say that someone 'ought'? Emphatically, Kant did not accept that 'ought' was merely a statement of subjective preference. It never meant the same as 'I want, I like, I prefer' and so on. 'Ought' was not merely an individual opinion, emotion or intention. It did not simply describe the state of an individual. Neither was 'ought' true by definition or logic in the way that it is true that a triangle has three sides. Nor was it a truth that could be simply observed. For Kant, it was rather a truth derivable as soon as you accepted that society was a desirable or necessary component for human existence. For society to exist at all there had to be coherent rules governing the actions and interactions of individuals. 'You ought' was essential, in order to challenge 'I want'. Why? Because, if every 'I want' had its way, human interactions descended into chaos and warfare. Society, then, simply ceased to exist.

A key feature of 'ought' as opposed to 'want' was that it was universalisable. It could be expressed as a coherent rule applicable to all. For example, act only on that maxim through which you can at the same time will that it should become a universal law.

Kant was the stereotypical academic. He rose, apparently, at five a.m., every day, studied for two hours, lectured for two more, and spent the rest of the morning at his desk. He dined at a restaurant and spent the afternoon in conversation with friends. He then walked for about an hour, exactly the same walk, studied some more, went to bed between nine and ten p.m. every day. People, it was said, set their watches according to his habits.[2] In eighty years he never traveled more than forty miles from Königsburg. These, let us hope, are not necessary *a priori* conditions for successful philosophy. The work of a truly successful philosopher ought to be both important (as Kant's work certainly was) and accessible (as Kant's writing certainly was not). It could be argued that the more you understand what you are talking about the more you are able to speak in a language that others can readily understand. If so, Kant was not at all clear what he was saying since his language is atrocious and academic in the worst possible sense of being virtually incomprehensible and incoherent, if not always then often, too often. No wonder that prose described as 'complete Kant' became a term of abuse; signifying that it was incomprehensible and probably meaningless.

To be sure, Kant was breaking such new ground in his questions that there was no readily available way of talking about the subject. But, at the very least, an effort to construct shorter sentences would have helped, although perhaps more responsibility for this should be laid at the door of the translator? German as a language allows for larger sentence constructions since the grammar and endings show which bits of the Lego bricks are joined to which. English works differently; imagery, allusion, metaphor are more important. Perhaps to really appreciate Kant requires that it be read in the original. If so, then here is a *synthetic a priori* condition of understanding that I myself cannot meet.

Kant sought to unite empiricist and rationalist philosophies by subsuming them into something altogether larger that embraced both. We could not know the world purely by reason nor purely by observation. Our observations were constructed by basic synthetic *a priori* categories. Our reasoning needed to be informed by observation. Kant agreed with Hume that there were limits to our ability to understand the phenomena of the world but he did not think that this meant that the world was chaotic. On the contrary, there was a noumenal world that underlay all the phenomena we experienced. Hence past history, prejudice and preference influenced experience but always within fundamental parameters that were the conditions of any experience. There was an underlying, noumenal, order. Hence there was a pattern to the disorderly and prejudiced ways in which we tried to make sense of phenomena.

Kant's interest in 'deconstructing' the process of, and conditions for, perception catapults him into a postmodern mind-set two centuries before postmodernist scepticism and pluralism. He differs from the more chaotic, anarchic and subjectivist versions of postmodernism in that he believed in an essential, underlying coherence and pattern to all reality; a noumenal stability beneath phenomenal confusion. Kant was no existentialist.[3] He was an essentialist as are most contemporary physicists. The theoretical physics of our own time, far from being dull, mechanical and naïvely empirical, explores fundamental relativism and uncertainty within a framework of mathematical theory which is coherent, elegant and objective. For physicists, unlike Sartre, essence precedes existence in their belief in an underlying, meaningful pattern and coherence to existence which we can unravel. Mass energy is neither arbitrary nor governable by our own preferences. We do not simpy make meaning, we uncover meaningful patterns that exist quite independently of our own preferences. Nonetheless, our own perspective, process and presupposition influence what and how we see.

This intelligent exploration of the interconnection between the objective and the subjective was, above all, begun by Kant. In this respect we owe him a great debt. Far from moving beyond a Kantian synthesis, many contemporary naïve empiricists (at one extreme) and chaotic postmodern subjectivists (at the other) have not yet reached Kant.

? Questions

1. What ideas do your clients need in order to be able to understand you? What do you need in order to be able to understand them?

2. How do you introduce 'ought' into client discussions? Is it irrelevant? On what basis does it have a role?

3. How far are you confident that you can empathise with clients? What do you mean by this term?

4. Are your clients searching for 'underlying truth'? Of an eleven dimensional enfolded relativistic and quantum universe? Are you/they seeking 'objective' truths? A manageable story?

EXERCISES

1. Consider how far your own counsellor/care training has examined the psychology of perception.

2. Consider the 'mental sets' that govern the way you construct counselling and professional care. This is extremely difficult precisely because our most strongly held assumptions and presuppositions are the most invisible to us. This is why it is valuable to examine 'alien' and 'exotic' ways of construing the world: esoteric ideas may be interesting both in themselves and because they allow us to see, and therefore re-assess, our own most basic assumptions more clearly.

3. Consider how far the key Kantian questions (listed in the Conclusion) and Kant's answers to them, are of relevance to clients.

Conclusion

Kant asked What can I know?, What ought I to do?, What may I hope? These are, of course, questions of concern to us all. Kant considered truths we could arrive at by reason and by observation. He then broke new ground by considering what needed to be the case if reason and observation were to be possible at all. What has to be taken as read if we are to read out of observation or read into it? This is a difficult, abstract question that has become a central part of so-called 'postmodern' enquiry into truth, perception and opinion. It is a vital question to counsellors who may imagine that they can empathise with the 'truth' as experienced by clients and with the subjects and objects of concern to clients. Too often, counselling theory assumes a kind of naïve empiricism of the form, 'I listen, I observe, I put my own agendas to one side and thereby facilitate client exploration.' This is tidy and attractive to both counsellor and client, but is it actually true? According to Kant, and subsequent philosophy, it is, emphatically, no more than a cosy, simplistic, illusion.

Notes

1. Leibniz's mathematical conception of an infinitesimal has survived far more successfully than his natural scientist's notion of a monad.
2. Apparently the only exception to this rigid pattern occurred when Kant, having become utterly engrossed in Rousseau's *Émile*, stayed at home for several days!
3. Compare him with Kierkegaard, Nietzsche, Heidegger and Sartre.

Websites

http://comp.uark.edu/~rlee/semiau96/kantlink.html
gopher://gopher.vt.edu:10010/02/107/6
gopher://gopher.vt.edu:10010/02/107/7

gopher://gopher.vt.edu:10010/02/107/2
http://www.friesian.com/kant.htm

Bibliography

D. Hume, *An Enquiry Concerning Human Understanding*, Open Court, 1988
I. Kant, *Critique of Judgement*, Oxford University Press, 1978
I. Kant, *Critique of Pure Reason*, Prometheus Books, US, 1991
I. Kant, *Critique of Practical Reason*, Prometheus Books, US, 1996
I. Kant, *Groundwork of the Metaphysics of Morals*, (Cambridge University Press, 1998

Chapter 21

Jeremy Bentham (1748–1832)

Key Points

- The greatest happiness of the greatest number is the foundation of morals and legislation

- We can calculate individual pleasures and pain and then determine our best individual actions

- We can total the individual pleasures and pains that will be consequent upon political decisions and thereby calculate the best social policies

- Ethical decision making thereby becomes a problem of accountancy. We must add up the net pleasure of each available option and select the one that delivers the most happiness.

Application

- Utilitarian principles are the basis of many definitions of counselling
- Counselling thereby shares in the weaknesses of utilitarianism
- The limits of utilitarianism ought to lead counsellors to explore in more depth their own aims and objectives
- Utilitarianism highlights the problem of reconciling individual well being with the needs of society more generally
- Utilitarian limitations raise the question of how far any deliberate search for 'well-being' is likely to be self-defeating.

Speculative philosophy, which to the superficial appears a thing so remote from the business of life and the outward interests of men, is in reality the thing on earth which most influences them, and in the long run overbears every other influence save those which it must itself obey. (Mill, 1838)

I am sure Mill is right, and hence this present sketch of philosophical ideas that underpin the practice of providing human support and attention. Today's 'common sense' is very often the offspring of an esoteric philosophy first developed centuries earlier. Likewise, the common sense of our descendants may, even now, be developing out of common sight. It is unlikely to be the same as our own.

The more influential the philosophy, the more invisible it becomes. It fills the space of our awareness and concern. It comprises the mental furniture, floor, walls and windows of contemporary thought. When a philosophy is everywhere in your thinking, it is hard for you to locate it. It determines what you think about and how you think. It drives out alternative ways of thinking. It provides no way of looking in on what was thought. It is difficult to detect the overwhelming influence of particular philosophers when they have, as it were, provided you with the very eyes by which you see everything else.

We may not know, or be able to think about, Benthamite Utilitarianism, or Cartesian Dualism. We might not have heard either of Bentham or Descartes. Yet, this may be because we think entirely within Benthamite and Cartesian categories. It is difficult to look in on such ideas precisely because they comprise the way in which we look out on the world. To repeat, when the stature of a philosophy grows so that, like air, it fills all the space available, it becomes invisible.

Take the following, for example:

> The overall aim of counselling is to provide the opportunity for the client to work towards living in a more satisfying and resourceful way.

This was agreed in a resolution proposed at the 1996 AGM of the British Association for Counselling. Utilitarianism has never been discussed within counselling conferences, yet this definition, in its circularity, is greatly influenced by a Utilitarian view of existence. It consequently suffers from precisely the problems encountered by the Utilitarians. Jeremy Bentham was the first such and although subsequent efforts were made to patch the problems arising from Bentham's approach, I do not believe that the difficulties have ever really been resolved.

Utilitarianism starts well and would appear to be quite uncontroversial. Its central principle is that we should act, individually and collectively, so as to deliver the greatest happiness for the greatest number. In this respect the philosophy is *liberal* – individuals decide for themselves in what happiness consists – and *democratic* – the happiness of everyone is a part of the calculation and not just that of kings, aristocrats or other elites. Utilitarianism also requires that we avoid selfishness and self-centredness – our own happiness is neither more nor less important than that of others.

Bentham argued that a search for the greatest happiness of the greatest number provided the most useful principle for conducting our affairs. It would create the greatest overall 'utility' in the society. He believed that we could thereby 'calculate' the best individual and social policy via what he saw as a kind of felicific/hedonistic calculus. What was right? What was wrong? In ethics, Bentham argued, you would find out by working out the likely consequences of an action. How many people would be affected by the action? How much overall pain would it produce? How much pleasure, in total, would result? When the calculations were completed, an overall measure of the 'utility' of the action would thereby be produced. If it scored higher than the alternatives it would be justifiable, or positively desirable, depending on the score. If it scored low, the action would be deemed unwise. With a very large negative score (pain greatly exceeding pleasure), the action could be defined as positively evil.

In this way, subjective judgements could be ruled out. We could take out our calculators, tot up the positives (pleasures) and the negatives (pains) and then we would know how to choose between a range of (suitably scored) options. Or would we?

The trouble is that 'happiness' is an easy concept when you look at it from a distance, but not as you move closer. What do we actually mean by happiness? Is it the same as pleasure? If our view of happiness is limited and hedonistic, then Utilitarianism provides a shallow, narrow vision of individuals as consumers of pleasures with no other meaning and purpose to their lives. Even 'pleasure' is not an easy term on closer inspection. Are some kinds of pleasure more desirable than others? Who decides and how? Is it better to be a Socrates, however dissatisfied, than a pig, however content? Socrates and the pig may have a different view of this. If the pigs outnumber Socrates, and they all have one vote, does that mean that the whole culture must inevitably move downmarket? Shall we all 'dumb down' to the lowest common denominator? What about the happiness of minorities? Public hangings and floggings might make people very 'happy' and the comfort of the crowd might 'weigh' far more heavily than the misery of the condemned prisoner. Will the consumer be king even if most consumers are fools who do not know what they want or what is good for them?

We encourage people to go to school and rise above base instincts and immediate gratification. Does this produce the 'greatest happiness for the greatest number'? Even if it did not, would we demolish the education system? If drugs could keep people endlessly blissful and with no side effects should we take them?

The maximisation of happiness gets us nowhere since the term is so vague. Similarly, the British Association for Counselling text concerning clients living more satisfyingly and resourcefully prompts more questions than answers. Why should we be 'satisfied' more often, even if we know what the term means? What are the most significant forms of 'satisfaction'? Is satisfaction really at the heart of the mystery of living? Surely there is more to life than this? Indeed, surely there is so *much* more that the utilitarian principle is fundamentally *un*satisfactory? I am not satisfied or happy with Utilitarianism. It is not even maximising my happiness. If moral philosophy can get no further than this then it is not going far enough and must be judged a failure.

'I can't get no satisfaction, although I've tried and I've tried and I've tried and I've tried.' So sang Mick Jagger and the Rolling Stones, and through this they became something of an icon of the last quarter of the twentieth century. Perhaps the problem is that the Utilitarian philosophy, that has so much underpinned individual and social practice in the twentieth century, is ultimately sterile, arid, meaningless and unfulfilling. How much dissatisfaction arises from the madness of believing that we should always, or often, be satisfied? How much misery arises from the folly of hoping that we necessarily can, and should, be happy? In previous centuries most people were not cursed with the expectation that they ought to be, or could be, more 'satisfied', 'resourceful', 'fulfilled' than they were. Consequently, with one of the paradoxes that make life such a misery and such fun, they were probably more satisfied more often than we are. Currently we are deeply immersed in a consumerist, hedonistic, individualistic view of existence that talks endlessly of 'personal growth' and fulfilment. We fail to notice that the target of 'happiness' moves away from us as fast as we approach it. We are so deeply immersed in this utilitarian, hedonistic and liberal secular ideology that it is a part of the air we breath. We have no vision of any other possibility. We cannot think of any other way of envisioning ourselves and constructing our futures. Liberal utilitarianism is everywhere inside us and around us; so much so that we cannot detect its pressure, push and pull on us. What are the alternatives? They are assembling, at least some of them, I hope, in these chapters.

> The greatest happiness of the greatest number is the foundation of morals and legislation. (Bentham, 1789/1988)

So said Bentham. When he said it, it was probably not true. It is far more often true in practice now than it was then, which shows how influential utilitarian thinking has been in the last century. But should this be the foundation of morals and legislation? I think not.

John Stewart Mill tried to patch up some of the limitations of Utilitarianism, but he highlighted one of its fateful weaknesses in pointing out yet another of life's paradoxes:

> Ask yourself whether you are happy, and you cease to be so.

Insofar as this is so, and often it is, then the Utilitarian principle disintegrates. The very act of calculating utility, said Mill, diminishes utility. This is, surely, a devastating indictment of Utilitarianism. Our pleasure diminishes when we organise our lives so as merely to seek pleasure. Even for hedonists, then, active hedonism is not the best means of finding pleasure. Pleasure, happiness, utility, however these may be defined, tend to be by-products that come and go, usually beyond our control, in the process of our getting serious and committed and involved with other matters altogether. And do we not know this from our own experience? Life seems pointless when we say that its only point is to be happy. Look around at all those who have buried themselves in hedonistic consumerism yet who feel hollow, pointless and worthless inside. It is not that pleasures are intrinsically wrong, but that there can be no really worthwhile pleasure merely in seeking them.

Mill said of Bentham:

> He could, with close and accurate logic, hunt half-truths to their consequences and practical applications, on a scale both of greatness and of minuteness not previously exemplified; and this is the character which posterity will probably assign to Bentham. (Mill, 1838)

Bentham got hold of the idea, obvious enough, that we tend to prefer pleasure to pain and that, as good democrats, we ought to maximise pleasure and minimise pain. As a rough and ready guide it is uncontroversial enough. But as a basis for providing identity, meaning, purpose and direction in the lives of individuals and societies it is barren and empty. Even if such calculations could ever be made, why should people co-operate? The option that gives me the greatest happiness might not be the one that gives the greatest happiness for the greatest number. Why, then, should I choose any collective option that makes me less happy than my own preferred personal preference? In order to solve this problem, 'rule utilitarianism' was proposed as a better alternative to 'act utilitarianism'. In other words, following Kant, we should seek to adopt the collective rules, not the individual acts, which promoted the greatest happiness of the greatest number. However, the question could still be put, *why* should we do this? Bentham, a far less profound thinker than, for example, Kant, did not see much need to explore the problem. His forte was in developing legislation and social policy. Ultimately, he was less interested in exploring the rationale for any such a policy.

Utilitarianism, while a weak force philosophically, was powerful politically when, during the nineteenth century it was used as a 'canon' that could batter down various easy targets of injustice, patrician authoritarianism and corruption. The greatest happiness of the greatest number implied that everyone ought to vote, that everyone's views were important, that societies could and should be planned; that legislation, good government and efficient management all needed attention, scrutiny and regular maintenance.

As a social reformer, then, Bentham was a powerful figure whose energies and achievement could not, and need not, be encompassed in these pages. As a philosopher providing insights into how we are to make a shape to our identity and a direction in our lives he was far less successful. This matters because he was, and still is, most influential.

? Questions

1. What do you think are the underlying aims of counselling? Pleasure? Greatest happiness? Self-actualisation? Truth? Peace of mind? Love? Achievement? Insight? Wisdom? Courage? Commitment? Faith? Resignation? Detachment?

2. Does it matter that the counselling movement has such difficulty in finding adequate ways of describing its aims and outcomes?

3. Do you think that counselling does/should adopt Utilitarian principles in defining its aims? Can you think of more desirable alternatives?

4. Do you think that we are most likely to be 'happy' if we actively seek, or expect, 'happiness'?

EXERCISES

1. Examine the counselling theorists who have been most influential within your training and consider which underlying philosophies have been most influential on them.

2. Consider how far your own vision within care for a client is that they pursue their 'happiness'.

Conclusion

Bentham's belief in the greatest happiness for the greatest number is easy to understand and digest. It sounds like common sense. It only falls apart when it is examined more closely. The idea of a common definition of happiness then becomes untenable, as Aristotle realised many centuries earlier. The greatest happiness principle can be easy to understand because we can each project into it our own notions of what happiness consists in. We can also make it true by definition; we seek to maximise happiness because happiness is defined as that which we seek to maximise. This gets us nowhere nearer to saying what happiness is. The question remains, should it be actively sought? Will we be happy if we actively seek happiness? Are there not, in any case, other, more clear and more important, goals, principles and ways of finding meaning and self-respect?

Websites

http://www.ucl.ac.uk/Bentham-Project/index.htm
http://tqd.advanced.org/3376/Benth.htm
http://www.utm.edu/research/iep/b/bentham.htm
http://www.phil.canterbury.ac.nz/Phil236/lectures/hedons/calculus.htm

Bibliography

J. Bentham, *Fragment on Government*, Cambridge University Press, 1988
J. Bentham in *The Principles of Morals and Legislation*, Prometheus 1988
J. Bentham, *Introduction to the Principles of Morals and Legislation*, Oxford University Press, 1996
P. Bhikhu (ed.) *Moral and Political Philosophy of Jeremy Bentham*, Frank Cass, 1974
John Stuart Mill, 'Bentham', *London and Westminster Review*, August 1838 (revised in *Dissertations and Discussion Volume 1*, 1859)

Chapter 22

Georg Wilhelm Friedrich Hegel
(1770–1831)

Key Points

- Absolute spirit envelopes, governs, guides, and constitutes, all reality, and unifies all opposites

- In partaking of this spirit, we are as one with each other and with the whole of existence

- A single system of explanation shows the interconnectedness of every component of existence and a 'dialectical' process of 'thesis', 'antithesis', 'synthesis' governs the development of thought and the movement of history. The last 'synthesis' becomes the next 'thesis'

- Syntheses thereby become more all-embracing and we thus move closer to an apprehension of the unity of all existence

- The mind, using reason, can explore the oneness of existence, but ultimately the absolute is to be apprehended in spirit through revelation

- We may find ourselves in freedom via an ever-larger apprehension of our place within the absolute spirit.

Application

- Visions of integration with the whole of existence are (seductively?) attractive to clients tired of isolation and meaninglessness
- Hegel may now be unfamiliar, but Hegelian philosophies of union and communion remain attractive and recur perennially
- Hegelian optimism remains attractive. We would love to reclaim a belief in an inevitable enlargement of vision to ever-greater insights of oneness and interconnection
- Integrated systems of belief offer something for everyone, since each believer can interpret their meaning to suit their own preference. Perhaps that is both their strength and their weakness?

● Nineteenth-century physics was atomistic and mechanistic. Twentieth-century physics (field theories, quantum theory, relativity theory) is more sympathetic to disciplined approaches to integrationist and unifying models of existence.

It is interesting to introduce Hegel to my computer. Every time I paste in text from any of Hegel's (translated) works, my machine promptly underlines everything and the grammar checker comes up with the following messages over and over again: 'Long sentence (no suggestions)', or 'Verb confusion (no suggestions)'. Certainly the sentences are long. Whether or not German grammar can effectively hold them together, I do not know. Certainly English grammar appears to be strained beyond its limits.

But we must start somewhere; what about with 'me'? Who is this 'self' that I think I know? Hume had observed that whenever he looked 'inside' he never found 'himself', but merely ideas and impressions. Hegel agreed:

> Certainly, it must be conceded that we have not the least conception of the 'I', or of anything whatever, not even of the Notion itself, so long as we do not really think, but stop short at the simple, fixed general idea and the name. It is an odd thought – if it can be called a thought at all – that I must already make use of the 'I' in order to judge of the 'I'; the 'I' that makes use of self-consciousness as a means in order to judge, this is indeed an x of which, as well as of the relationship of such 'making use', we cannot have the slightest conception. (*Hegel's Logic*, 1975)

In other words, in the very act of judging the nature of an 'I', there is presumably an 'I' that is doing some judging? Hegel implies that this 'I' is like x in algebra, a variable. Yet what do we know of this variable I? What circumstances give it what kind of identity according to what principles? For Hegel there was no need for Hume's scepticism:

> Surely it is ridiculous to call this nature of self-consciousness, namely, that the 'I' thinks itself, that the 'I' cannot be thought without its being the 'I' that thinks, an inconvenience and, as though there was a fallacy in it, a circle. (ibid.)

Hume merely observed that he did not observe an 'I', although he presumably answered when others called out 'David' or 'Hume'? He remained baffled about how this 'self' could be described. Hegel, on the other hand, considered that an 'I' that could reflect on 'I's must be part of something rather bigger. It all looked fragmented and arbitrary when seen from a partial perspective, but when placed within a broader picture, within the totality of existence, more coherence and meaning could emerge. Pieces of jigsaw, on their own, make no sense. To understand what they are and how they fit in you have to see the whole totality of which they are a part. Only then do they have any real identity and sense. The eye needs a physical body within which to be embedded, to function and to be contextualised. The 'I', thought Hegel, needed a context of soul within which to attain coherence and direction:

> It is this relationship through which, in immediate self-consciousness, the absolute, eternal nature of self-consciousness and the Notion itself manifests itself, and manifests itself for this reason, that self-consciousness is just the existent pure Notion, and therefore empirically perceptible, the absolute relation-to-self that, as a separating judgement, makes itself its own object and is solely this process whereby it makes itself a circle. (ibid.)

I, when describing a meaningful context to the 'I', offer the rather prosaic metaphor of a jigsaw puzzle. Hegel, much more grandly, spoke of The Absolute, the Ideal, the Spirit, the Idea, the Oneness, the World-Soul, always with capital letters. These capitals included God, although not of the personal, patrician and bearded variety. Such generalisations were not arid abstractions for Hegel; on the contrary they were what infused life, meaning, energy and coherence into individual phenomena that, without this wholeness, were isolated, incoherent, arbitrary, meaningless. Hegel posited an enveloping Absolute Spirit that governs and guides all reality. With our human reason we did not so much observe or deduce this Absolute, we were, rather, a part of it, and an expression of it. There was a World-Soul and we were a component of it. It was evident throughout all of history. It was continually in a process of change and development that Hegel called the 'dialectic'.

With our partial vision we lived with not so much half-truths as tiny fragments of truth. Thesis created an anti-thesis from which, if we were wise, we could derive a synthesis that embodied both partialities and moved beyond to something less fragmented. This then became a new thesis from which another antithesis would emerge, and so on. All the time we would piece together more fragments and move a little closer to a larger Absolute that we could glimpse, sense, but never finally know:

> Finite things are finite because they do not possess the complete reality of their Notion within themselves, but require other things to complete it – or, conversely, because they are presupposed as objects, hence possess the Notion as an external determination. The highest to which they attain on the side of this finitude is external purposiveness. (ibid.)

The whole jigsaw is the expression of the overall idea, or plan, or picture. Mere pieces of jigsaw are just physical fragments that contribute to the picture but do not themselves embody it. They are thus further from the underlying reality than the conception itself. 'What is the Big Idea?' asked Hegel (as it were). Without the Idea we had just meaningless fragments and no picture. We were, therefore, cut off from reality:

> We must recognise that everything actual is only in so far as it possesses the Idea and expresses it... the reality that does not correspond to the Notion is mere Appearance, the subjective, contingent, capricious element that is not the truth.
>
> Wholes like the state and the church cease to exist when the unity of their Notion and their reality is dissolved; man, the living being, is dead when soul and body are parted in him; dead nature, the mechanical and chemical world – taking, that is, the dead world to mean the inorganic world, otherwise it would have no positive meaning at all – dead nature, then, if it is separated into its Notion and its reality, is nothing but the subjective abstraction of a thought form and a formless matter.
>
> Spirit that was not Idea, was not the unity of the Notion with its own self, or the Notion that did not have the Notion itself for its reality would be dead, spiritless spirit, a material object. (ibid.)

This is all very well as a loose generalisation. But where does it get us when it comes to the day-to-day specifics of piecing the pieces of our lives together? For example, to take this metaphor one step further, what if we have pieces muddled up from more than one jigsaw? Why do we assume that there is just one puzzle? One big picture? What if pieces are missing? What if it is all a meaningless jumble? Why do we think that putting capitals in front of everything strengthens the power of our argument? Does Hegel have an argument at all or just a spiral of sentences that lift clean from the solid ground and float away all by themselves to who knows where?

During the nineteenth century these vast idealist abstractions became the common sense, at least of the intelligentsia. Hegel ruled, OK? And, in the UK, English variants like Francis Bradley and Bernard Bosanquet were equally in the ascendant. Yet by the beginning of the twentieth century, faced with broadsides from Bertrand Russell and others, Hegelian idealism popped like a bubble, and almost disappeared from the twentieth-century philosophical curriculum, at least within Anglo-Saxon teaching. Russell and his contemporaries took the view that the entire Hegelian edifice grew up from logical errors, misuse of language and a lack of attention to detail and clarity. It was seen as creating confusion more than insight, vague fantasy rather than understanding. It seemed to be an expression of a yearning for coherence and unity rather than a sober analysis.

Even in Hegel's lifetime there were a few sharp critics. Above all, there was Arthur Schopenhauer, who certainly did not mince his words. Schopenhauer admitted that obscure language did not mean that the ideas were necessarily without value. But there were dangers:

> The public had been forced to see that what is obscure is not always without meaning; what is senseless and without meaning at once took refuge in obscure exposition in language. (Schopenhauer, *The World as Will and Representation*, Appendix)

So where did Hegel fit into this scheme? Were his ideas better than his ability to express them? Schopenhauer left the reader in no doubt about his own views:

> The greatest effrontery in serving up sheer nonsense, in scrabbling together senseless and maddening webs of words, such as had previously been heard only in madhouses, finally appeared in Hegel. It became the instrument of the most ponderous and general mystification that has ever existed, with a result that will seem incredible to posterity, and be a lasting monument to German stupidity. (ibid.)

Many would now agree with Schopenhauer. I have offered a few pieces of the more readable Hegel. But, in his own day, students flocked to his lectures and ignored Schopenhauer's, which were on offer in Berlin at the same time. It is currently hard to see common sense, or any sense, in much of Hegel much of the time. But who knows what new fashions/insights are in store for us in a new millennium?

What new ideas are under wraps and, more likely, what old ones will come round in a circle to us dressed up as new? Already 'leading edge' transpersonal psychotherapists like Ken Wilbur[1] are introducing new syntheses of self and context that, they freely acknowledge, draw very heavily indeed from Hegel.

What new ideas will help to shape what new 'realities'? (And vice versa.) Perhaps the following will help you answer these questions. Perhaps it will not. My machine promptly underlined the whole lot and has clearly been programmed by an Anglo-Saxon out of sympathy with Hegel. Alternatively I am being unfair? Perhaps I have not grasped the text adequately? Perhaps the translator did not understand the philosophy:

> That the Idea has not completely leavened its reality, has imperfectly subdued it to the Notion, this is a possibility arising from the fact that the Idea itself has a restricted content, that although it is essentially the unity of Notion and reality, it is no less essentially their difference; for only the object is their immediate, that is, merely implicit unity. But if an object, for example the state, did not correspond at all to its Idea, that is, if in fact it was not the Idea of the state at all, if its reality, which is the self-conscious individuals, did not correspond at all to the Notion, its soul and its body would have parted; the former would escape into the solitary regions of thought, the latter would have broken up into the single individualities.
> (*Hegel's Logic*, 1975)

Is this useful, or even coherent? Does the fact that a thinker had a lot of followers who thought he was talking great sense mean that he actually was talking great sense? In his autobiography,[2] the Nobel physicist, Richard Feynman, provides a salutary story about the wisdom that may not always be found among august bodies of thinkers. A Nobel physicist was holding forth on his ideas. The world's leaders in the field listened respectfully and took notes. A bright and impertinent young Feynman dared to say that he could not understand what the great man was talking about. In discussion later with Feynman, the great man thanked him for his question; agreed that what he had been saying had been incoherent. No one could make sense of it because it did not make sense. But the whole room thought they were making sense of it, or kept quiet about any uncertainty they felt. The great man confided in Feynman that it was a terrible thing to be a great man; you could utter any nonsense and almost no one would dare challenge you or ask you what you were talking about!

Hegel's argument marches on with never a pause for breath. There are continual whiffs of meaning. Guesses and glimpses between the lines can feel fruitful at times. But I remain in the school that argues for clarity as a sign of insight. The more you understand what you are saying, the more, I believe, you can say it such that the non-specialist can grasp and enjoy it. There is not much enjoyment in reading Hegel.

But I suppose if you want to travel all the way to The Absolute without even getting out of your armchair you must expect a lot of struggle on the way:

> In philosophy at present we hear little of the soul: the favourite term is now mind (spirit). The two are distinct, soul being as it were the middle term between body and spirit, or the bond between the two. The mind, as soul, is immersed in corporeity, and the soul is the animating principle of the body. (*Hegel's Logic*, 1975)

After Hegel there was a great deal of talk about souls and spirits. Then the talk died away. It may now be on its way back again. But if our minds have as much difficulty in grasping these concepts as our eyes have in seeing them we ought, I think, to proceed with great care.

The Science of Logic, at 840 pages of dense text, is Hegel's definitive work. A shorter version is supposed to be more readable. In his *Phenomenology of Spirit*, Hegel argues that any opposition between Thought and Being can finally be overcome through Thought's recognition of itself in the reality it has attempted to comprehend. But what is meant by Being in this context? The thesis of Being, which is a term frequently used within mainland European traditions, is met by the Anglo-Saxon antithesis that 'Being' is a misuse of language that creates nothing but confusion. Are we nearer to a synthesis above and beyond these two views?

Hegel observed that:

> In regard to practical Ideas, Kant recognises that 'nothing can be more harmful and unworthy of a philosopher than the vulgar appeal to an experience that allegedly conflicts with the Idea'. This very experience would not even exist if, for example, political institutions had been established at the proper time in conformity with Ideas, and if crude conceptions, crude just because they had been drawn from experience, had not taken the place of Ideas and so nullified every good intention. (*Hegel's Logic*, 1975)

This is indeed the antithesis of Anglo-Saxon empiricism. Do ideas build from experience, or are experiences shaped by the ideas that determine what, how and where we look? No doubt the answer in each case is 'yes'. The empiricists give pride of place to experience, direct observation and measurement. The (philosophical) idealists see this as naïve and vulgar. Ideas and experience are, both, necessary to examine any question. Neither has meaning independently of the other. In this sense the Idealists have the edge. But when ideas and experiences conflict what should give way? The scientific tradition would make controlled observations the acid test. Compare this with Hegel:

> The Idea being the unity of Notion and reality, being has attained the significance of truth; therefore what now is is only what is Idea. That actual things are not congruous with the Idea is the side of their finitude and untruth, and in accordance with this side they are objects, determined in accordance with their various spheres and in the relationships of objectivity, either mechanically, chemically or by an external end. (ibid.)

Hegel does not wish to be arid. He believes that his Absolute, which is indeed God, is the root of life, the whole of life, the shape of life, the integration and meaning of life. Abstract ideas, he readily agrees, can desiccate this life. Our dead ideas and our living being can seem far apart:

> Life, Spirit, God – the pure Notion itself, are beyond the grasp of abstraction, because it deprives its products of singularity, of the principle of individuality and personality, and so arrives at nothing but universalities devoid of life and spirit, colour and content. (ibid.)

Hegel thought that Kant, with his conception of synthetic *a priori* knowledge, had failed to save humanity from Hume's scepticism about what could be known about self, world and values. Hegel therefore sought to break out of empirical scepticism by seeking wholeness and integration that could be glimpsed, which was rationally coherent and aesthetically appealing, and which could be approached more systematically via the 'dialectic' of thesis, antithesis and synthesis.

Hegel was unhappy with naïve empiricist fascination with fragments. This intoxication, he was convinced, could not take us towards the underlying essentials of Truth. Reality was a whole entity if it was anything. It could not, therefore, be found within fragments of analysis or observation. If we sought Truth by chopping it up we killed it. Hegel disliked Anglo-Saxon fidgeting with intellectual debris, endless analysis of bits of pieces. He thought this approach to philosophy ignored the underlying essentials. It was sterile, meaningless, lifeless, lacking in wholeness. In these respects Hegel may sometimes have been right. I however, am not convinced that a Teutonic 'Wort-Fest' solves the problem and integrates Ideas with Life, Spirit, Big Pictures, Cosmic String, Spaghetti or Spiritual Sauce.

Yet much of the impetus that drove Hegel may be due for a revival. His intellectual instincts, if not his writing style, may deserve serious reappraisal. For years physicists sought to reach 'ultimate' reality and basic understanding by breaking atoms into ever smaller bits. What were the fundamental particles from which everything else was built? What were the basic building blocks of life? Such atom smashing continues, but it is becoming more clear that what is perhaps most real and fundamental are not so much the basic particles as the basic principles which describe how all this activity interconnects. Fields and waves are at least as important as particles. The absolute (mathematical) essentials of their operation are more fundamental than the existential (empirical) observable fragments. To get to truth we must see the dance as a whole rather than the dead shape of a lost shoelace. And this truth appears to be more fantastic than fairytale with physicists talking, not always helpfully, of minds and god as though Hegel were writing only yesterday. I am pleased to report that the life, magic and enchantment of the universe appears to have been rediscovered by science. Physicists are seeking a 'theory of everything' which, they hope, will link within one conception, their existing theories of mass energy, wave particles. Unlike Hegel's Absolute, theoretical physics will remain experimentally testable, valuable in its predictions and, one expects, aesthetically elegant. The mathematics, I fear, will be even more daunting than Hegel's prose.

? Questions

1. Do you find philosophies of 'wholeness', 'oneness', 'transpersonal unification in spirit' reassuring and important? Or empty? Vague? Distracting? Speculative? Or what?

2. Hegelianism is 'big system' philosophy. Can this approach make progress or does it decay too easily into empty speculation?

3. Do you find it helpful or harmful to advise clients of our essential 'oneness in spirit'?

4. Do you think it makes sense to talk of 'feeling' or 'apprehending' the 'oneness' of life?

5. Atomists believe that to understand and 'get real' requires that we dissect a subject into parts. Absolutists and idealists assert that reality and understanding is only achieved when we grasp whole and entire totalities. What do you think? Or is this a false dichotomy?

EXERCISES

1. Hegelian 'oneness' went out of fashion. But theories of unification and interconnection are receiving more attention now that physics has moved away from

mechanism and atomism. See if you can make time to keep up with some of the big changes that have taken place in contemporary physics. Consider the relevance of these changes in establishing philosophies for living.

2. Compare Ken Wilbur, Roberto Assagioli and other transpersonal therapists, with Hegel. Wilbur is certainly more readable.

3. Given the current distaste for the limitations of materialism, consider how far a philosophy emphasising mind and spirit is likely to be popular and helpful.

Conclusion

Hegel was extremely important, indeed dominant, in philosophy for at least a century after his death. Neo-Hegelians of the political left, right and centre interpreted him to suit their own perspectives. Hegel became less important in Anglo-Saxon countries in the twentieth century, although Francis Bradley (1846–1924) and Bernard Bosanquet (1848–1923) were greatly influenced by him and were themselves significant voices in Britain at the end of the nineteenth century. They, too, spoke of mind as more central and fundamental than matter. As physics becomes more fantastic than fantasy, perhaps integrationist philosophies are due for renewal? If so will they adopt, not just the holistic vision of physics, but its disciplines and dogged determination to test theory rather than merely speculate?

Notes

1. See, for example, Ken Wilbur's *Up from Eden: A Transpersonal View of Evolution*, Shambhala, 1983

2. Richard Feynman, *Surely You're Joking Mr Feynmann?*, W.W. Norton, 1997

Websites

http://www.alphalink.com.au/~pashton/thinkers/hegel.htm
http://werple.net.au/~andy/index.htm
http://www.hegel.org/
http://www.radix.net/~joshua/hegel.htm
http://members.aol.com/pantheism0/hegel.htm
http://www.miami.edu/phi/hegel.htm
http://www.ultranet.com/~rsarkiss/HEGEL.HTM

Bibliography

G.W. Hegel, *Philosophy of Mind*, Oxford University Press, 1971

G.W. Hegel, *Hegel's Logic; Being Part One of the Encyclopedia of the Philosophical Sciences*, Oxford University Press, 1975

G.W. Hegel, *Introduction to the 'Philosophy of History'*, Hackett Publishing Company, US, 1988

G.W. Hegel, *Phenomenology of Spirit*, Pennsylvania State University Press, 1994

G.W. Hegel, *On Art, Religion and the History of Philosophy: Introductory Lectures*, Hackett Publishing Company, US, 1997

A. Schopenhauer, *The World as Will and Idea*, Everyman, 1995

A.W. White, *Absolute Knowledge: Hegel and the Problem of Metaphysics,* Ohio University Press, 1983

Chapter 23

Arthur Schopenhauer (1788–1860)

Key Points

- ▓ 'Self' is a noumenal subject, not a phenomenal object

- ▓ Since it is not an object, it cannot be observed

- ▓ 'Self' is, rather, the context, stage, framework within which the phenomenal and ephemeral objects of existence may be experienced

- ▓ Selves, being subjects, operate outside the spatio-temporal causal world of objects

- ▓ There is no separate self; we are, ultimately, an expression of the one subject, the single noumenon, the divine self.

Application

- Schopenhauer taught that self-centredness is a prison to be avoided by renunciation of appetite and appreciation of art, philosophy and empathy
- If you commune with the collective spirit you will be released from the unending cycle of always wanting and willing more
- But you must remember that the underlying energy of existence is blind, purposeless, amoral and essentially uncontrollable
- 'Optimism is a bitter mockery of the unspeakable suffering of humanity.'

Idealism within ethics is, of course, about ideals. However, idealism within philosophy more generally might be less confusingly described as _idea_-ism. It is the idea that ideas are more fundamental, more real and more important than any particular sensory observation.

For Plato, for example, the concept of 'cathood' was more significant than observations of, or interactions with, individual cats. For Leibniz, the notion of a monad, derived via the power of reasoning, provided a more fundamental grasp of the universe than opening your eyes and observing the flotsam and jetsam of day-to-day experience.[1]

For Kant, the *noumena* of existence, things as they were in themselves, were far more significant than mere *phenomena*, things as they appeared, for all that the latter were perceivable and the former were invisible except via the inferences of mental process.

For Hegel, the World-Soul was much more central than daily experiences of this or that, or trivial self-preoccupation.

Philosophers, being preoccupied with ideas, will have a tendency to consider that this bread and butter of their existence is even more important that bread and butter. Of course, your body and mind have to be sufficiently sustained by phenomenal bread to have energy to contemplate noumenal ideas like the more deeply real forms of 'breadness' ('breadability'?). As a matter of history, however, most people have tended to be more interested in their own, phenomenal cats, fields, crops, horses, spouses and other ephemera rather than the underlying concepts. The phenomena generally seem more 'real' to us than the abstract concept, presumably because day-to-day events occupy most people more regularly than underlying ideas. This would have neither surprised nor impressed Schopenhauer (1973) who observed: 'Intellect is invisible to the man who has none' (*Aphorismen zur Lebensweisheit*).

Schopenhauer, like Kant, considered that beneath the world of phenomena was a noumenal world, comprising the substrate of all existence. However, there were no noumena for Schopenhauer, rather there was a single noumen*on*. There were no things in themselves, rather a single thing in itself. Schopenhauer accepted Kant's argument that space and time were constructions of the mind rather than underlying realities. He further observed that phenomenal objects differed because they occupied different locations in space and time. Therefore, he thought, there could not be more than one noumenon because it existed outside of space and time. I fail to see why we can only have one non-spatial and non-temporal entity. We are quite capable of entertaining the idea of more than one non-dimensional substance. Besides which, being non-spatial, they would not occupy the same place!

Aesthetically, however, there are attractions in the notion of just one big idea/underlying reality/noumenon, call it what you will, from which everything else is just a manifestation. Indeed, contemporary physicists are battling to achieve something not dissimilar in their efforts to produce a 'theory of everything'. One current view is that the universe exploded out of an original, primordial stuff the size of an orange or smaller. Others argue that this original stuff was not any size at all, nor in any place and time since space-time (in however many dimensions) actually came into being *with* the big bang. Truly, contemporary physics is every bit as fantastic as the most extraordinary theories ever imagined by philosophers. Our 'real' world, when examined beyond mere appearance, makes the wildest dream look positively tame and predictable.

Schopenhauer believed that the noumenal world was indeed magical, and he enjoyed magic every bit as much as philosophy. Of course magic and physics tend not to be seen as having anything to do with each other. The physics most of us learned at school seems prosaic, gritty and mechanical with its atoms, electrons, molecules all spinning around like mini solar systems with clockwork precision. This mechanistic vision, however, has little to do with present-day physics with its occult-like quantum world of strangeness, charm, baryon numbers, lepton numbers, quarks and, most recently, 'string' which, to a quark, is small in the way that an atom is small in a galaxy.

So where do 'I' fit into this scheme of things? In what direction am I going when even space and time are not what I thought they were? For Schopenhauer, self was a subject, not an object, and he saw a fundamental distinction between the two.

Hume had noted that, whenever and wherever he observed, he never found 'himself'. Schopenhauer agreed that he never would since self was not an object of perception or introspection at all. Self was more like the noumenal 'stage' upon which the phenomenal objects of existence performed. Self was not an object in the world, rather it provided the boundary beyond which the world could not be known. Also, it was the vehicle within which the objects of experience were organised. The subject observed objects and thereby could know them. Subjects were themselves unobservable. As observers we were unknowable. An ology of the psyche was, therefore, impossible via the five senses.

We could not 'look inside' via introspection since:

> As soon as we turn into ourselves to make the attempt, and seek for once to know ourselves fully by means of introspective reflection, we are lost in a bottomless void; we find ourselves like the crystal ball out of which a voice speaks whose cause is not to be found in it, and wanting to understand ourselves, we grasp, with a shudder, only an insubstantial spectre. (*The World as Will and Idea*, 1995, p. 180)

As subjects we ourselves operated outside the space, time and causal world of objects. We were noumenal, therefore, but for Schopenhauer there was only one noumenon. Therefore, the notion of an individual, separate, unique, self was essentially an illusion. It was an idea rather than a reality and a misleading one at that. We were, ultimately, an expression of the one subject, the divine self, the transcendent supreme reality or being.

This is not dissimilar from versions of teaching to be found within Hinduism, and Schopenhauer acknowledged a debt, not just to Kant and Plato but also to ancient Hindu teaching found in the Upanishads:

> For the person who performs works of charity, the veil of Maya has become transparent, and the illusion of the 'principium individuationis' has left him. He recognises himself, his will, in every being, and consequently also in the sufferer. (ibid. p. 235)

Many mystics have both taught and claimed to experience a communion of self with a divine source. Within Hinduism this is the union of Âtman with Brahman, the transcendent supreme reality. Within Christian mysticism, also, the claim is that, if only we open our eyes, we will see the face of Christ in every face. The saintly person does not do good in order to be good. They do so since this is the obvious thing to do. Imagine that we are all one family. Imagine that you are not just imagining this as an abstraction but that you feel this interconnection with others to the core of your being. If this were so, then 'passing by on the other side' would be far harder for us than actually assisting another human being in need.

Versions that we have of Christ's teaching are often far more radical than the reality of the Christian Church. Give up all you have to the poor. Abandon your self-preoccupation. Only then will you discover the real meaning of wealth. You will thereby find, on earth, the kingdom of heaven. Within mystical apprehensions, heaven is here on earth when the prison wall of ego and self-preoccupation is broken down and the light of life pours into our endarkened souls. We then find that we were always one, at one, and that, in seeking our separate 'unique' self, we had been looking in to a dark and sterile cave of illusions.

The claim, generally, within Christian, Buddhist and Hindu teaching, is an optimistic one. If you can only learn to escape from the prison of self via an appropriate practice or yoga – union with God – then you will be released from the rack of striving, dissatisfaction and suffering that is the condition of individual existence. Return to communion with the underlying, noumenal, collective spirit and there will be release, bliss, freedom from the unending cycle of always wanting and wanting more.

Schopenhauer, too, thought that a transcendental escape from the 'prison ship' of an imagined self was the way to salvation. He suggested that there were three routes. The first was knowledge of the true underlying noumenal reality, which could be acquired by a study of philosophy. The second was a mature appreciation of works of art, especially music, which provided a larger perspective on, and expression of, striving, joy and suffering. The third route to the communion of spirit was that of showing real empathy for others since, in that way, one could free oneself from the sufferings that arose from self-preoccupation and achieve a larger outlook on human misery.

However, Schopenhauer was not optimistic about the likely success of those seeking salvation via these routes. He himself was able to demonstrate the scale of the problem within his own life since he was, by all accounts, selfish, self-centred, hedonistic and flirtatious, certainly not the serene hermit, monk or mystic.

For Schopenhauer the underlying energy of the universe was not bright, loving and liberating as it was for so many others who shared a similar holistic vision. It was blind, purposeless, amoral and essentially uncontrollable:

> All willing arises from need, therefore from deficiency, and therefore from suffering. The fulfilment of a wish ends it; yet for one wish that is concealed there remain at least ten which are denied. Further, the desire lasts long, the demands are infinite; the satisfaction is short and scantily measured out. But even the final satisfaction is itself only apparent; every satisfied wish at once makes room for a new one; both are delusions; the one is known to be so, the other not yet. No attained object of desire can give lasting satisfaction, but merely a fleeting gratification; it is like alms thrown to the beggar, keeping him alive today so that his misery may be prolonged till the morrow. (ibid. p. 119)

As observing subjects we were not able to survey the universe dispassionately and peacefully. We were driven by the force, will, or energy of existence that welled up in us quite outside our control. What we saw was what the will pushed us to see. What we did was what we were driven to do. The idea that we had a faculty of reason that could weigh, assess and decide objectively, systematically and logically was, for Schopenhauer, a cosy fantasy that was not borne out by the evidence all around us:

> For all endeavour springs from deprivation – from discontent with one's
> condition – and is thus suffering as long as it is not satisfied; but no satis-
> faction is lasting, rather it is always merely the starting-point of a new
> striving. (ibid. p. 195)

Schopenhauer was the arch pessimist, so much so that it is hard to see
how he could justify living at all. He did not need to, of course, since he
observed that we were driven to live. But if he really believed that living
was such unadulterated misery it might follow that suicide was the only
defiant and heroic act available to us. In fact he dined well, enjoyed
food, sex and an ability to live indefinitely and comfortably on his
father's inheritance. He observed that all these good things end just as
bubbles burst:

> We continue our life, however, with great commitment and much care, for
> as long as possible, just as we blow into a soap-bubble for as long as we can,
> making it as big as possible, although we know perfectly well that it will
> burst. (ibid. p. 197)

But it does not follow that there can be no really good and worthwhile experience just because no experience is of infinite duration.
Schopenhauer would have agreed, but within a decidedly jaundiced
vision of the options:

> The ceaseless efforts to banish suffering accomplish no more than to make
> it change its form. This is essentially need, want, concern for the preserva-
> tion of life. If we succeed (which is very difficult) in banishing pain in this
> form, it immediately reappears in a thousand others, varying according to
> age and circumstances, such as the erotic drive, passionate love, jealousy,
> envy, hatred, anxiety, ambition, avarice, sickness, and so on. If at last it can
> find access in no other form, it comes in the sad, grey garment of surfeit
> and boredom against which we try this remedy and that. If, finally, we
> succeed in driving this away, we shall hardly do so without letting pain in
> again in one of its earlier forms, and so we start the dance again from the
> beginning; for all human life is tossed backwards and forwards between
> pain and boredom. (ibid. p. 201)

Those who suffered might dream of winning in the lottery of life.
With wealth and fame, surely, we could live happily ever after? Not so,
argued Schopenhauer:

> Just as want is the constant scourge of the common people, so boredom is
> the scourge of the fashionable world. In middle-class life ennui is repre-
> sented by Sunday, just as is want by the six weekdays. (ibid. p. 199)

The 'good life' might be observable on TV but it was not a part of
real life. We kept on hoping for better and we put on a brave front if we
could. But what was the reality beneath the varnished appearance?:

> Certainly human life, like all inferior merchandise, is embellished from the
> outside with a false lustre: suffering always hides itself away; on the other
> hand, everyone displays whatever pomp or splendour he can afford, and
> the less content he is in himself, the more he desires to appear fortunate in
> the opinion of others: to such lengths does folly go, and to gain the good
> opinion of others is a priority in everyone's endeavour, although the utter
> futility of this is expressed in the fact that in almost all languages vanity,
> vanitas, originally means 'emptiness' and 'nothingness.' (ibid p. 205)

And so we scan the newspapers, dreaming of the good life lived by
the famous and powerful, searching for the scandal, suffering beneath
surface appearances, and feeling relieved that at least we were not so
badly off as those poor victims of the latest reported tragedy:

> The sight or the description of somebody else's suffering accord us satisfac-
> tion and pleasure in precisely the way Lucretius beautifully and frankly
> expresses it at the beginning of the Second Book (of 'De Rerum Natura').
> (ibid. p. 202)

When others suffer loss, their pain reminds us of the value of what
we have and the fact that we could be worse off. If the unfortunate is
rich and famous it 'brings them down a peg or two'. Misfortune in
others, then, can produce a 'feel-good' response in the reader that we
will be most unwilling to confess.

Suffering and misery, therefore, were not obstacles to living one's life,
as many currently hope and believe, they were the very warp and weft
of existence:

> To me optimism – when it is not merely the thoughtless talk of those who
> give room only to words under their low brows – appears not merely as an
> absurd, but also as a really wicked way of thinking, and as a bitter mockery
> of the unspeakable suffering of humanity. Let no one think that Chris-
> tianity is conducive to optimism; on the contrary, in the Gospels 'world'
> and 'evil' are used almost synonymously. (ibid. p. 206)

Of course, Christian teaching had a vision of heaven as well as of hell, but Schopenhauer noticed that heaven looked dull, boring, vapid and unreal and hell was only too similar to life on earth:

> For where else did Dante get the material for his hell, if not from our real world? And a very proper hell he made of it, too. When, on the other hand, he came to describe heaven and its delights, he was faced with an insuperable difficulty, in that our world offers no material at all for such a scene. (ibid. p. 205)

Similarly, art easily portrayed stories of struggle, passion, loss, frustration, and doubt. But what happened when hopes were realised and the couple lived 'happily ever after'? The story ended. Why?:

> Every epic or dramatic poem can represent only a struggle, a striving and fight for happiness, but can never present lasting and consummate happiness itself. It conducts its hero through a thousand difficulties and dangers to his destination; as soon as this is reached, poetry swiftly lets the curtain fall; for now there would be nothing left for it to do but to show that the glittering goal in which the hero imagined he would find happiness had only teased him, too, and that after obtaining it, he was no better off than before. Because true, lasting happiness is not possible, it cannot be the subject of art. (ibid. p. 203)

Freud, who aimed to lift hysterical misery into common unhappiness, acknowledged the influence of Schopenhauer, whose sights were set equally low. He does not convince me that we should abandon all hope altogether but his observation about our limited ability to observe dispassionately is well made and deserves serious attention. Schopenhauer was one of the few philosophers to notice how powerfully sex drives and constructs our lives and heavily shapes so much of what we see, say and do. As philosophers, people might seek truth, or imagine so. As human beings, people sought power, position, partners, allies, advantage, acclaim, success, security and excitement. We were not talking heads. We were embodied sexual animals, and our minds and their contents were victims more than observers of the consequences:

> Teeth, throat, and intestines are objectified hunger; the genitals are objectified sexual desire; the grasping hands, the swift feet, correspond to the strivings of the will which they represent as a grade later and more indirect. (ibid. p. 41)

Ideas were rationalisations after the event more often than first movers in a process of free choice. When truth clashed with personal advantage, truth was displaced, circumvented or crushed outright. Truth was therefore a regular casualty, since expressions of power and interest were almost always at odds with a disinterested perspective. We did not make a decision in our minds and then act. We acted and then found reasons for it. In the action we discovered the nature of what we might fondly imagine was our 'decision'. In any case, most of our actions and 'decisions' operated quite independently of any would-be mental process.

We were subjects, not objects. But we were subject to the will, or energy, of the universe. We were embodied in physical objects, bodies, whose activities we only imagined we could control. Through art we could escape. Through dissolving into the no-'thingness' of the transcendental will, we could also become free from the constraint and illusion of individualism. Ego was a prison, yet ego – its urges, advantages and preferences – almost entirely determined everything we saw and did. Most of what we called objective knowledge was simply that construction of events and their meaning that best suited our own interests. In all these respects, Schopenhauer's vision of hell on earth was similar to St Augustine's Earthly City. The key to our suffering, for both philosophers, was our self-centred and secular preoccupations. Schopenhauer, though, held out little hope of escape to a heavenly city. For him, there was no personal compassionate deity to whom we could open our hearts and thereby find salvation.

Schopenhauer's world was one of suffering and disappointment. His ethics were based on compassion, but he did not live as he wrote. His belief that irrational forces roared like a hurricane through all life and all human beings influenced, among others, Friedrich Nietzsche, Sigmund Freud, Richard Wagner, Thomas Mann and Thomas Hardy. He saw will rather than mind as the organising principle of existence, but it would be better to talk of energy since the will he describes is neither conscious, controllable or in any way personal. Schopenhauer believed that intellect was slave rather than master of the force of existence. If we were to achieve any mastery or insight at all we needed to acknowledge this fact of life. We needed to prostrate ourselves before it rather than imagine that we could posture and perceive independently of it. We did not so much see the hurricane force of being, it blew right through us, tearing us apart, spinning us, hurling and whirling us. There was no justice in the outcome.

Schopenhauer himself, whose writing was far more lucid than that of Kant or Hegel, vividly portrayed this vision of the dynamism of existence. Moreover, his transcendental will, or force, found a living embodiment in the work of the composers, novelists and painters for whom he was a very major influence.

Schopenhauer argued that a restless energy is more fundamental than any supposedly inert objects we think we know. This view is closer to contemporary physics than the clockwork universe of Newton that is still taught in schools. It is described within Hindu teaching as the dance of Shiva and mystics have claimed to feel it, and be filled by it, rather than just conceptualise it. The grim dead atoms of nineteenth-century physics were like tiny nuggets of the coal that dominated the nineteenth-century economy. They have transmuted within contemporary understanding. Nowadays atoms are a focus in and around which there is endless quantum activity whose nature defies our wildest imagination.

Contemporary 'common sense' will have it that we can choose good over evil, by ourselves, on our own, or with the help of fellow human confidantes, confessors, counsellors. This also tends to be the teaching of the contemporary Christian church. It is therefore useful to remember that the more commonly held view historically has been that we cannot achieve any kind of respite, release or salvation on our own or in any secular context. Indeed, it was blasphemous to think otherwise and to imagine that we ever could, or should, 'go it alone'. Schopenhauer argued that 'the force' governed us entirely. Christians have believed that God reigns supreme and that without His active and continuous assistance we are dashed, done for, doomed.

Far from being inherently or potentially good, humanity has more usually been seen as fundamentally wicked. Even today Christians routinely recite that they have erred and strayed like lost sheep, that there is no health in them, that they are miserable offenders, that they hope for improvement only via confession and a humble begging to be absolved from sin. We have needed baptism to cleanse us from the taint of original sin. We have needed to pray for forgiveness.

The 'I'm OK – you're OK' message of contemporary counselling would have been seen as far from OK throughout most of recorded history. The British monk Pelagius adopted a 'person-centred' approach to fulfilment in the fifth century AD. He questioned St Augustine's teaching that divine grace was essential for salvation. It followed that baptism was not essential. Perhaps people could find their own way and discover what was good and right for themselves? Pelagius was condemned by Augustine and excommunicated by Pope Innocent I in 417 AD.

Schopenhauer's pessimism, then, looks eccentric from our own perspective, but from a larger historical vantage point it is almost 'normal'. The contemporary philosophy that we can and should be happy, and that we are essentially good is almost an historical aberration. Does it allow us to behave better than otherwise we would? Does it promote happier lives? Or does it make us blind to our own wickedness and selfishness, and miserable in the absurd hope that a significant share of happiness is readily available to us? Perhaps we should be more honest about our dishonesty, and more ready to be miserable? We might then, paradoxically, manage a little more honesty and find a little more peace:

> Willing and striving is his whole being, which may be closely compared to an unquenchable thirst. But the basis of all willing is need, deficiency – in short, pain. Consequently, the nature of animals and of Man is subject to pain from its origins and in its essence. If, on the other hand, it lacks objects of desire, because their gratification is immediate and too easy, a terrible emptiness and ennui come over it, that is, its nature and existence itself becomes an unbearable burden to it. Thus its life swings like a pendulum backwards and forwards between pain and ennui, which are the elements of which it is made. This is piquantly expressed in the observation that after man had consigned all pain and torment to hell, there was nothing left for heaven but ennui. (ibid. p. 198)

> The striving after existence is what keeps all living things busy and active. But when existence is assured to them, they do not know what to do with it; thus the second thing that sets them in motion is the effort to be rid of the burden of existence, to make it cease to be felt, 'to kill time', i.e. to escape from tedium. (ibid. p. 199)

Is this pessimism, realism or comedy? Insofar as it is true, need we collapse into despair? Can we, within these awesome and awful circumstances, nonetheless seek, and sometimes find, real faith, commitment, compensation and comfort? Schopenhauer praised the life of the monk, while living the life of an aesthete and *bon viveur*. He kept pistols near his bed but did seem to enjoy good times, however fleeting. The secret, perhaps, is paradoxical: If you believe that you can and should live happily ever after and be fulfilled and 'actualised' then you are likely to feel endlessly disappointed as your life falls so far short of your ideals. If, however, you accept Schopenhauer's analysis, then any good moments will be enjoyed. You will still suffer, but at least you will not suffer (still further) via the belief that you 'should' be happy.

❓ Questions

1. How far do your own clients offer rationalisations rather than dispassionate insight? And what about you?

2. Can we really put self-interest, sex and power ploys to one side during counselling? If not, how can we use these energies rather than be used by them?

3. Is Schopenhauer a useful antidote to naïve optimism within contemporary counselling?

4. Do you find notions of transcendental will or force useful or irrelevant in your own practice as a counsellor/care worker?

5. Is 'self' a prison-like illusion from which we need to escape? Are you optimistic or pessimistic about the likely chances of success?

EXERCISES

1. Compare Schopenhauer's philosophy with the Vedanta, one of the Hindu systems.

2. Consider the role of evil in contemporary counselling and care. Is it a concept of relevance and value?

3. Examine Christian texts concerning human wickedness, limitation and sorrow. Do any of these have any relevance within contemporary care? For example, the Old Testament chapter on Job is worth attention. Who is most convincing? God? Job? Job's friends?

4. Discuss how far particular clients are made miserable in the belief that they should be happy. Could their mood lift if their expectations were more realistic?

Conclusion

Schopenhauer stressed the importance of sexuality and power as determinants of human behaviour and thereby influenced, respectively, Freud and Adler. Schopenhauer's pessimism was unremitting but possibly more cheering than utopian optimism. In any case, he did not always practice the gloom that he preached. Schopenhauer introduced Hindu conceptions of an underlying spirit that links all of reality and offered a variety of methods of escaping from the rack of self-preoccupation that are similar to various forms of yoga. Schopenhauer is beautifully lucid and offers a cutting insight on the human condition that care workers should not ignore.

Note

1. It is easy to mock monads, since they have not lasted very well. Binary numbers and differential calculus, also products of Leibniz's mind, have survived and prospered and may indeed be more fundamental and significant than many observable ephemera.

Websites

http://www.miami.edu/phi/schopnh.htm
http://www.ksc.kwansei.ac.jp/~95024w/Schopenhauer/

Bibliography

A. Schopenhauer, *Essays and Aphorisms*, Penguin, 1973
A. Schopenhauer, *Philosophical Writings*, Continuum, US, 1993
A. Schopenhauer, *On the Basis of Morality*, Berghahn Books, 1995
A. Schopenhauer, *The World as Will and Idea*, Everyman, 1995
A. Schopenhauer, *The Wisdom of Life and Counsels and Maxims*, trans. T. Bailey Saunders, Great Books in Philosophy, 1995

Chapter 24

John Stuart Mill (1806–1873)

--- **Key Points** ---

- Paths of personal development quite often collide, the consequences need careful attention
- Liberty, devoid of social responsibility, creates anarchy
- Individual rights are vital or else we suffer tyranny
- Individual freedom is unachievable without responsibility, strength, maturity, self-discipline and insight
- Personal development therefore requires a broad liberal humanist education.

--- *Application* ---

- Mill did not believe that every thought and emotion could be prized, celebrated and explored without restraint
- The general average of mankind are not only moderate in intellect, but also moderate in inclinations
- Mill celebrated individual freedom and expression but considered that these could not merely be explored; they needed to be cultivated
- While showing real concern for the dangers of authoritarianism, Mill would have considered libertarian tendencies in counselling as juvenile and anarchic.

I explored the influence of Utilitarian thinking on the counselling movement in Chapter 21. 'Satisfaction' and 'resourcefulness' were shown to be somewhat vague as fundamental aims within counselling. But there is a deeper problem. What if my efforts to achieve satisfaction, resourcefulness (and resources) conflict with you and yours? What if the counsellor's concern for the client disregards the rights, needs and interests of strangers or close contacts of the client? How can the legitimate claims of others be respected when the counsellor only ever hears the client's view?

Counselling would be so much less problematic if, in focusing on our own satisfaction, we never interfered with the rights and needs of others. The trouble, of course, is that living in societies is rarely so easy. We may tread on the toes of others more through carelessness or ignorance than malicious intent, but the damage may be real either way. Economists have often imagined that, if everyone thought and worked just for him or herself then, 'by an invisible hand,' we would thereby create the best of all possible worlds. Your self-preoccupation, while seeming to be selfish at times and damaging to others, would nonetheless be in the interests of society generally. Those of us who have not had our minds warped by such preposterous economic 'truths' know better.[1]

Mill was interested in 'personal development' as we now call it, but also, and crucially, he wished to reconcile this with the concerns of others and the advancement of society as a whole. Unlike so many contemporary individualists, Mill saw that paths of personal development quite often collide with each other. They may also conflict with the needs of the culture overall, without which personal prospects may be poor indeed. How then, could a balance be struck? It was not easy, since it was in our nature both to co-operate and to exploit:

> To prevent the weaker members of the community from being preyed upon by innumerable vultures, it was needful that there should be an animal of prey stronger than the rest, commissioned to keep them down. But as the king of the vultures would be no less bent upon preying upon the flock than any of the minor harpies, it was indispensable to be in a perpetual attitude of defence against his beak and claws. The aim, therefore, of patriots, was to set limits to the power which the ruler should be suffered to exercise over the community; and this limitation was what they meant by liberty. (*On Liberty*, p. 65)

Too much individual liberty, devoid of social responsibility, created anarchy. Too little concern for individual rights led to tyranny. A continuous balancing process was needed to avoid either extreme. How, though, did we know if an appropriate compromise was being found?:

> There has been a time when the element of spontaneity and individuality was in excess, and the social principle had a hard struggle with it. The difficulty then was, to induce men of strong bodies or minds to pay obedience to any rules which required them to control their impulses... But society

has now fairly got the better of individuality; and the danger which threatens human nature is not the excess, but the deficiency, of personal impulses and preferences. (ibid. p. 118)

Britain in 1859 was, in Mill's opinion, too conformist and insufficiently protective of personal development and individual rights. The balance was weighted too much in favour of the needs and evolution of collective society and not sufficiently respectful of individuals. Whether he would say the same if he could observe our approach to a new century is not clear. But there are clues.

Mill sought to protect individual autonomy and personal agendas against the intrusion of overly authoritarian leadership, but he did not believe, unlike so many within contemporary counselling, that every individual thought and emotion could be prized, respected, celebrated and allowed to go where it will. When he speaks of individuals and their rights to follow their own path, it soon becomes clear that, in practice, he is thinking of a minority of exceptional individuals and not the majority.

Mill believed that everyone *in principle* should be allowed to think and feel for him or herself, although this freedom would need to be constrained when the result was anti-social and destructive. The real problem, though, was that, in Mill's view, most people were neither willing nor able to think and act for themselves. They would be incapable of making use of such liberal individual freedom and terrified of the opportunity were it ever to be made available:

> The general average of mankind are not only moderate in intellect, but also moderate in inclinations: they have no tastes or wishes strong enough to incline them to do anything unusual, and they consequently do not understand those who have, and class all such with the wild and intemperate whom they are accustomed to look down upon. (ibid. p. 126)

In pre-democratic days, patrician observations about the 'ignorant herd', its shallow pleasures and foolish preoccupations, were commonplace and unremarkable. Individual freedom required individual responsibility, strength, maturity, self-discipline and insight. Since most people failed adequately to achieve any of these, how could they be recognised as mature adults? How could they vote? How could they act for themselves if they were incapable of thinking for themselves? How far was democracy possible and desirable if, despite their full-grown size, most people did not achieve full adult maturity?

Mill is recognised as a progressive force within nineteenth-century politics, believing that, via education, people from all classes could come much closer to realising their full potential and thereby earn the right to play a greater role in the political life of their country. He also argued against intrusion by government and believed that individuals tended to be better judges of what was in their own best interests than kings, politicians or professionals of any complexion.

He was suspicious of those who thought they knew what was best for others and who therefore expected to be obeyed because they were the chosen few, the vanguard, the elect, the enlightened. For example, of the Calvinists:

> According to that, the one great offence of man is Self-will. All the good of which humanity is capable, is comprised in Obedience. You have no choice; thus you must do, and no otherwise; whatever is not a duty is a sin. Human nature being radically corrupt, there is no redemption for any one until human nature is killed within him. To one holding this theory of life, crushing out any of the human faculties, capacities, and susceptibilities, is no evil: man needs no capacity, but that of surrendering himself to the will of God: and if he uses any of his faculties for any other purpose but to do that supposed will more effectually, he is better without them. That is the theory of Calvinism; and it is held, in a mitigated form, by many who do not consider themselves Calvinists. (ibid. p. 119)

In his criticism of such authoritarianism, and his support of individual autonomy and development, Mill uses the metaphor of a tree that has become so popular within contemporary movements for personal growth:

> Many persons, no doubt, sincerely think that human beings thus cramped and dwarfed, are as their Maker designed them to be; just as many have thought that trees are a much finer thing when clipped into pollards, or cut out into figures of animals, than as nature made them. (ibid. p. 120)

Calvinism is not the force that it was in 1859, but the spirit lives in the many variants of authoritarianism that have risen, prospered and fallen within the twentieth century. Tyrants may be emperors, kings or any leader who claims to speak for 'the people' or 'the masses' without doing any such thing. Tyranny may also rest in the hands of whatever category of professional may feel it knows better than you do what is best for you and who understands more than you what you think, feel, want and need:

It is not difficult to show, by abundant instances, that to extend the bounds of what may be called moral police, until it encroaches on the most unquestionably legitimate liberty of the individual, is one of the most universal of all human propensities. (ibid. p. 141)

Mill would no doubt have been appalled at the carnage that has been wreaked on the twentieth-century world by those who have known that it is their calling to save everyone else from their inadequacy. Yet Mill was also an elitist who, while welcoming the triumph of the liberal democracies over fascism and communism, would have been less than impressed with the result. His views about 'people power' in 1859 show quite clearly what he would have thought of its further development in the last few generations. Certainly he talks the language of individual sovereignty that is a part of so much current therapeutic ideology. For example:

What more or better can be said of any condition of human affairs, than that it brings human beings themselves nearer to the best thing they can be? (ibid. p. 121)

But individuality for Mill is not a status that we can all automatically or effortlessly occupy. Some are, if you like, more individual than others:

Genius can only breathe freely in an atmosphere of freedom. Persons of genius are, ex vi termini, more individual than any other people – less capable, consequently, of fitting themselves, without hurtful compression, into any of the small number of moulds which society provides in order to save its members the trouble of forming their own character. (ibid. p. 122)

For Mill, it is of no use saying to counsellors and other carers that they will support the individuality of every client. Only the heroic, exceptional individual may have the strength and insight to 'discover themselves' with the aid of a counsellor. But what of the majority of sheepish humanity who do not wish to create themselves, make something of themselves, know who they are, or find out through the hard work of thinking for themselves? These will accept, or greedily steal, off the shelf, whatever conception of their individuality the counsellor, or other authority figure, has constructed.

We can all choose the route of personal development, but the path is not easy. It is in many ways far more attractive to let others tell us who we are, what we are, where we fit in and where we have to go:

He who lets the world, or his own portion of it, choose his plan of life for him, has no need of any other faculty than the ape-like one of imitation. He who chooses his plan for himself, employs all his faculties. He must use observation to see, reasoning and judgement to foresee, activity to gather materials for decision, discrimination to decide, and when he has decided, firmness and self-control to hold to his deliberate decision. (ibid. p. 117)

Mill was convinced that only a small minority chose such a tough route. Yet democracy was about giving more power to the people. Were the people ready for it? What would happen to a society that was governed by the will of the majority? This mass did not know what it willed and did not want to find out. It was not rising to the difficult challenge of self-discipline and individual questioning and exploration. Mill was not optimistic:

In sober truth, whatever homage may be professed, or even paid, to real or supposed mental superiority, the general tendency of things throughout the world is to render mediocrity the ascendant power among mankind. (ibid. p. 123)

Was Mill right about the dominance of mediocrity in 1859? Is he more or less right for a new millennium? What, for example, would he have thought of the tabloid newspaper in the UK, those organs of 'information' through which most people read about the political life of their society?

In politics it is almost a triviality to say that public opinion now rules the world. The only power deserving the name is that of masses, and of governments while they make themselves the organ of the tendencies and instincts of masses. This is as true in the moral and social relations of private life as in public transactions. Those whose opinions go by the name of public opinion, are not always the same sort of public: in America, they are the whole white population; in England, chiefly the middle class. But they are always a mass, that is to say, collective mediocrity. And what is still greater novelty, the mass do not now take their opinions from dignitaries in Church or State, from ostensible leaders, or from books. Their thinking is done for them by men much like themselves, addressing them or speaking in their name, on the spur of the moment, through the newspapers. (ibid. p. 123)

If the newspapers of 1859 were alarming to Mill, I shudder to imagine what he would have thought of our present predicament. Cynics say that no journalist ever lost money by underestimating the intelligence of the mass of British readers. Is this unfair? Or is it painful reality? Mill tries to be sanguine:

> I am not complaining of all this. I do not assert that anything better is compatible, as a general rule, with the present low state of the human mind. But that does not hinder the government of mediocrity from being mediocre government. (ibid. p. 124)

If an electorate does not wish to think for itself, then it will prefer to have its thinking done for it by others. It will want 'thought' compressed into thirty-second sound bites. It will want to be amused, entertained, flattered, aroused. It will not want its politicians to be philosophers or statesmen. It will want its leadership to be specialists in public relations who can create 'events' that gorge an unending appetite for distraction, sentimentality, voyeurism, excitement, scapegoats and all those other agendas of cheap romance, thrillers, 'disaster' movies and soap operas. When public opinion becomes important and the public prefer soap opera, then 'the news' and political debate generally will themselves become just another kind of soap opera, indistinguishable from, and just as fictional as, the fiction and advertising with which they compete for public attention.

In an age of 'people power', the people may prefer to be placated and amused more than challenged, educated and responsible. This will not mean that they necessarily have much power. Those with real power will get on with their business in private and will create whatever illusions and 'certainties' are necessary to keep the sheep shepherded in their respective fields. So is there any way out of the sheep pen?:

> No government by a democracy or a numerous aristocracy, either in its political acts or in the opinions, qualities, and tone of mind which it fosters, ever did or could rise above mediocrity, except in so far as the sovereign Many have let themselves be guided (which in their best times they always have done) by the counsels and influence of a more highly gifted and instructed One or Few. The initiation of all wise or noble things, comes and must come from individuals; generally at first from some one individual. The honour and glory of the average man is that he is capable of following that initiative; that he can respond internally to wise and noble things, and be led to them with his eyes open. (ibid. p. 124)

Tyrants of every kind would say the same thing of course. So how do we find a path that takes us between, and prevents us from being shipwrecked upon, the two rocks of mediocrity and tyranny?:

I am not countenancing the sort of 'hero-worship' which applauds the strong man of genius for forcibly seizing on the government of the world and making it do his bidding in spite of itself. All he can claim is freedom to point out the way. The power of compelling others into it is not only inconsistent with the freedom and development of all the rest, but corrupting to the strong man himself. It does seem, however, that when the opinions of masses of merely average men are everywhere become or becoming the dominant power, the counterpoise and corrective to that tendency would be, the more and more pronounced individuality of those who stand on the higher eminencies of thought. It is in these circumstances most especially, that exceptional individuals, instead of being deterred, should be encouraged in acting differently from the mass. (ibid. p. 124)

This may sound fine in theory but in practice, of course, it is a much tougher proposition. People may claim to be eminent who are not. Boorish behaviour may be excused, especially by the boorish, as 'creative', 'exceptional' and 'individual'. Gurus rise and fall. They are followed, but hindsight is not always kind either to the leader or their followers. If we must follow because we cannot or will not judge and act wisely for ourselves, how do we find the wisdom needed to know who to follow? Mill cannot be blamed for failing to find an easy answer to this question. There is none.

Mill was nothing like so contemptuous of ordinary citizens as to suggest that they did not think for themselves at all. But he was concerned that when they did think it was very rarely about society or politics. Rather, it was their own daily work that occupied them:

There is now scarcely any outlet for energy in this country except business. The energy expended in that may still be regarded as considerable. What little is left from that employment, is expended on some hobby; which may be a useful, even a philanthropic hobby, but is always some one thing, and generally a thing of small dimensions. The greatness of England is now all collective: individually small, we only appear capable of anything great by our habit of combining; and with this our moral and religious philanthropists are perfectly contented. But it was men of another stamp than this that made England what it has been; and men of another stamp will be needed to prevent its decline. (ibid. p. 127)

So where does this leave the counsellor? If they non-directively 'prize' and 'enable' clients to follow their own agendas, might this not merely be encouraging mediocrity? Is the counsellor in any kind of educational role, in which case should they not be concerned to 'raise standards'? If so, who will define the standards? How? And how are they to be taught?

Personal development has been thought to require, not merely an individual confessional to a counsellor/confidante, but a broad liberal humanist education more generally. Certainly this was Mill's view, although he was quite sure that not everyone would be able to benefit equally from such an education. His observations about 'moral police' ring as true today as ever. He explores the problem of avoiding the extremes of anarchy and authoritarianism that, by its nature, remains perpetually difficult to resolve. His view that business preoccupations occupy too much of the lives of too many people seems as relevant and welcome now as ever it was in the nineteenth century.

Mill took the view that:

> The sole end for which mankind are warranted, individually or collectively in interfering with the liberty of action of any of their number, is self-protection. That the only purpose for which power can be rightfully exercised over any member of a civilised community, against his will, is to prevent harm to others. (ibid. p. 72)

But the difficulty remains that of deciding what constitutes 'harm to others'. Since we are all interconnected, the business and behaviour of each of us influences the interests and well-being of everyone else in one way or another even if that is no one's intention. At what stage should inconvenient self-preoccupation be construed as anti-social harm of others? Clearly people draw the line in different places and there is no easy formula that will determine who is right.

One attempted remedy is to take the utilitarian principle of 'greatest happiness of the greatest number' and to try to use this as a means of drawing a boundary between the personal/private and the social/public. Bentham, as we have seen, explored this option and Mill sought to tackle some of the criticisms Bentham had encountered. However, in so doing, Mill added so many caveats that the Utilitarian approach to personal and social decision making seems, to me at least, undermined more than supported.

For example, critics have suggested that 'happiness', however defined, is not the only goal in life. Mill agreed. Indeed, within *Utilitarianism*, he went so far as to say that it would be better to be a Socrates unhappy than to live happily as a pig. If so, then the greatest happiness principle falls to pieces. Instead, it would seem that we should be seeking to build a world of sensitive and educated philosophers, however depressive they may be.

? Questions

1. Can you think of occasions where the actions and intentions of your client may have clashed with the interests of others? What did/could/should/ you do/have done about it?

2. Can you think of clients whose expressiveness might have been improved with more self-discipline? What did/could/should you do/have done to help?

3. How often would client personal development be enhanced with further education? What examples come to mind? What did the client need to know? How did you help? How could you have helped?

4. How far, if at all, is it the counsellor's role to 'raise standards' in clients? In terms of social conscience? Social responsibility? Self-discipline? Maturity? Do counsellors have the necessary authority, knowledge and skill? Or teachers? Or clergy? Or who?

EXERCISES

1. Consider if, and how, the counselling curriculum could be changed to include wider political agendas?

2. If education is therapeutic and therapy is educational, discuss what client education might consist in. Should there be different 'levels' according to the capacity of each client?

3. Discuss how far counsellors can/should include the interests of outsiders when these clash with the concerns of clients.

Conclusion

Mill considered the personal development of individuals from broad social and political perspectives. He asked how we are to live with each other creatively and constructively so as to preserve liberty and avoid both tyranny and anarchy. Mill was one of the greatest exponents and defenders of liberal humanist principles in politics, in education and in personal development, all of which, he believed, were intimately inter-connected. Mill believed in equality of opportunity but did not think that this would produce equality. People were obviously unequal in so many respects. Each individual was unique, but so are sheep. Far from seeking to shape a life of their own, Mill thought most preferred to follow along the path of the individual in front of them.

Note

1. There is evidence that students who study classical economics do indeed become more selfish than others! See Matt Ridley, *The Origins of Virtue*, Penguin, 1997.

Websites

http://paul.spu.edu/~hawk/millh.html
http://phenom.physics.wisc.edu/~shalizi/Mill/On_Liberty/
gopher://gopher.vt.edu:10010/02/122/3
gopher://gopher.vt.edu:10010/02/122/2
http://www.socsci.mcmaster.ca/~econ/ugcm/3ll3/mill/prin/book1/bk1ch01
http://wiretap.spies.com/ftp.items/Library/Classic/women.jsm

Bibliography

J.S. Mill, *On Liberty,* Dent, 1964 (with *Subjection of Women* and chapters *On Socialism*)
J.S. Mill, *On Socialism*, Prometheus, US, 1987
J.S. Mill, *Consideration on Representative Government*, Prometheus, US, 1991
J.S. Mill, *Utilitarianism*, Oxford University Press, 1998

Chapter 25

Sören Aabye Kierkegaard
(1813–1855)

───────────────── **Key Points** ─────────────────

- Self is not simply to be found; it must be created
- Self is always seeking to *become* more than, currently, it *is*
- Self is forever becoming, yet unbecoming to itself. This is painful
- Human spirit lies in our ability to despair; but, if we succumb to despair, we are ruined
- Self, and its despair, is often avoided by immersion in the trivial.

── *Application* ──────────────────────────────

- Existentialists see self as a subject and project to be created. This abolishes the possibility of outside, third-party objectivity or neutral descriptions of humans as objects
- No one has the last word on the nature of the created self; that includes counsellors, therapists and other care workers
- Existentialists oppose any conception of self as an object to be discovered, described or manipulated
- Self is a balance between our infinite potential and our finite actuality
- For Kierkegaard, we come to know ourselves within God. Does any deity have a role in contemporary care?

Who was Sören Kierkegaard? A Danish philosopher and theologian, founder of existentialism, son of a Lutheran merchant who had converted to Christianity. Sören Kierkegaard was a prolific writer who attached playful pseudonyms to many of his works and who 'became' the fictional authors he had created.

His *noms de plume* were not serious disguises. There was evidently an underlying Kierkegaard who wished to seen to be the author of these various characters. What was his view of the underlying self of whom he was a unique example?:

> The human being is spirit. But what is spirit? Spirit is the self. But what is the self? The self is a relation which relates to itself or that in the relation which is its relating to itself. The self is not the relation but the relation's relating to itself. A human being is a synthesis of the infinite and the finite, of the temporal and the eternal, of freedom and necessity. In short a synthesis. A synthesis is a relation between two terms. Looked at in this way a human being is not yet a self. (*The Sickness unto Death*, p. 43)

Here, in one charming (and somewhat tortuous), paragraph, we have self as awareness, self-awareness, relationship, becoming as well as being, bounded as well as unbounded, bonded as well as free. We certainly do not have the comfortable platform of Descartes' 'I think, therefore I exist'. For Descartes, 'self' was an indubitable starting place; God must evidently have created such a self; and from this orderly beginning the rest of the world could be put together piece by piece.

For Kierkegaard, the problem was more about how we were to put ourselves together. What we were was always much less than what we wished to become. We were beings wishing to become more than we were, and fearful that we would not so become. We were not becoming, at least to ourselves. This was a recipe for frustration, anxiety and despair.

Descartes believed that we found ourselves through finding that we thought. Kierkegaard saw that via thought we found that we were not what we wanted to be. We wanted to make something of ourselves, to become someone. As Schopenhauer observed, our plans ran ahead of our achievements. The result could be chronic misery, anxiety and despair:

> The possibility of this sickness is man's advantage over the beast, and it is an advantage which characterises him quite otherwise than the upright posture, for it bespeaks the infinite erectness or loftiness of his being spirit. (ibid. p. 44)

Chronic anxiety and despair at our present state showed that we sought to improve upon what, where, and who, we were. This was what made us human. Anxiety arose from a desperate concern that circumstances might not improve and could even get worse. Despair was an indicator of our capacity to soar beyond our current state of being. Yet if we actually fell permanently into despair we might not get anywhere, we might just stay stuck:

> Consequently it is an infinite merit to be able to despair. And yet not only is it the greatest misfortune and misery actually to be in despair; no, it is ruin. (ibid. p. 45)

'Self', for Kierkegaard was made rather than merely discovered, and, for as long as we were alive, our potentiality was always greater than our actuality. Our being was to be always in the process of becoming; and we felt anxiety and despair when this living process became blocked or stultified:

> If, on the other hand, the self does not become itself, then it is in despair, whether it knows it or not. (ibid. p. 60)

We might well *not* know that we are anxious or in despair. We might become so despairing that we block even our experience of despair:

> He who says without pretence that he despairs is, after all, a little nearer, a dialectical step nearer being cured than all those who are not regarded and who do not regard themselves as being in despair... People who, on the other hand, say they are in despair are as a rule either those who have so much more profound a nature that they are bound to become conscious of themselves as spirit, or those who have been helped by painful experience and difficult decisions to become conscious of themselves as spirit – either one or the other, for very rare indeed is there one who in truth is not in despair... So much is spoken about wasting one's life. But the only life wasted is the life of one who so lived it, deceived by life's pleasures or its sorrows, that he never became decisively, eternally, conscious of himself as spirit, as self, or, what is the same, he never became aware – and gained in the deepest sense the impression – that there is a God there and that 'he', himself, his self, exists before this God, which infinite gain is never come by except through despair. (ibid. p. 56–7)

Like Mill, Kierkegaard believed that it was better to be a Socrates dissatisfied than a pig satisfied. To be truly human was to strive to be more than we were, to find ourselves before God, to suffer despair at our current inadequacy and incompleteness. Yet we would not do this if we merely succumbed to despair. We had to discover our inherent and noble tendency to despair; yet we needed then to rise above it by using it as a goad to act, to explore, to become, to face ourselves and our predicament.

Chronic anxiety could become a useless and self-destructive habit. To sink into despair, knowing that one had done so, could temporarily free us from anxiety but provided no solution. An even more common failure to become oneself was to avoid one's underlying despair via distraction, superficiality, day-to-day triviality:

> While one kind of despair steers blindly in the infinite and loses itself, another kind of despair allows itself to be, so to speak, cheated of its self by 'the others'. By seeing the multitude of people around it, that is, being busied with all sorts of worldly affairs, by being wise to the ways of the world, such a person forgets himself, in a divine sense forgets his own name, dares not believe in himself, finds being himself too risky, finds it much easier and safer to be like the others, to become a copy, a number, along with the crowd. (ibid. p. 64)

Kierkegaard believed that this process of avoiding oneself by immersion in the trivial, the other, the day to day, was extremely common. Indeed, it was almost entirely universal and 'normal'; it was generally thought to be the 'proper' way of adapting to oneself and one's life:

> Now this form of despair goes practically unnoticed in the world. Precisely by losing himself in this way, such a person gains all that is required for a flawless performance in everyday life, yes, for making a great success out of life. Here there is no dragging of the feet, no difficulty with his self and its infinitizing, he is ground as smooth as a pebble, as exchangeable as a coin of the realm. Far from anyone thinking him to be in despair, he is just what a human being ought to be. Naturally the world has generally no understanding of what is truly horrifying. The despair that not only does not cause any inconvenience in life, but makes life convenient and comfortable, is naturally enough in no way regarded as despair. (ibid. p. 64)

> Yes, what we call worldliness simply consists of such people who, if one may so express it, pawn themselves to the world. They use their abilities, amass wealth, carry out worldly enterprises, make prudent calculations, and so on, and perhaps are mentioned in history, but they are not themselves. In a spiritual sense they have no self, no self for whose sake they could venture everything, no self for God – however selfish they are otherwise. (ibid. p. 65)

In daily activity we could lose a grasp of who we were, and fill our underlying emptiness with busyness, distraction, calculation and manoeuvring. We lost all sense of self-as-potentiality by losing ourselves in day-to-day actuality.

Did this mean that we needed to avoid everyday responsibilities if we were to be able to 'find ourselves'? Certainly not. A balance needed to be struck between infinite potential and finite actuality. Self was a balancing act between potentiality and actuality, between the infinitude of the one and the unavoidable finitude of the other. Self with no potentiality was no self at all. But a self that merely hovered at the edge of its potential futures without making any of them an actual, albeit limited, present, suffered another kind of evasion and despair:

> Now if possibility outstrips necessity, the self runs away from itself in possibility so that it has no necessity to return to. This then is possibility's despair. Here the self becomes an abstract possibility; it exhausts itself floundering about in possibility, yet it never moves from where it is nor gets anywhere, for necessity is just that 'where'. Becoming oneself is a movement one makes just where one is. Becoming is a movement from some place, but becoming oneself is a movement at that place.
>
> Thus possibility seems greater and greater to the self; more and more becomes possible because nothing becomes actual. In the end it seems as though everything were possible, but that is the very moment that the self is swallowed up in the abyss. Even a small possibility needs some time to become actual. But eventually the time that should be spent on actuality gets shorter and shorter, everything becomes more and more momentary.
>
> Surely what the self now lacks is actuality; that at least is what would normally be said, and indeed we imply this when we talk of a person's having become unreal. But on closer examination what the self really lacks is necessity. (ibid. p. 66)

The businessman may fail to 'find himself' because he has immersed himself too much in daily business. He loses himself in the actuality of mundane demands and becomes the victim of his own, overfull, diary. The bohemian may imagine that he is finding himself by sneering at the businessman and contemplating his future potentiality above and beyond 'ordinary' preoccupation. He imagines that he is looking down on the marketplace from a more ethereal view, his diary is blank, indeed he does not use one. But without any actuality, action, commitment to choices, limitations, positions, efforts, successes, failures, who or what is he? He has never become anything, and without action and decision of some sort he never will.

Madness and despair, then, could accompany those who felt blocked by necessity, limitation, frustration and contingent actuality. Madness and despair, too, equally would await those who imagined they could inhabit a world consisting only of opportunity, options, potentiality, possibility and unlimited choice:

> The petty bourgeois is spiritless, while the determinist and the fatalist are in a state of spiritual despair. But spiritlessness, too, is despair. The petty bourgeois lacks any spiritual characteristic and is absorbed in the probable, in which the possible finds its tiny place. Thus he lacks possibility in the way needed to become aware of God. Devoid of imagination, as the petty bourgeois always is, he lives within a certain orbit of trivial experience as to how things come about, what is possible, what usually happens, no matter whether he is a tapster or a prime minister. This is the way in which the petty bourgeois has lost himself and God. For to be aware of his self and of God, a man's imagination must whirl him up higher than the dank air of the probable, it must tear him out of that and, by making possible what exceeds the measure of sufficiency of all experience, teach him to hope and fear, or fear and hope. But imagination is what the petty bourgeois mentality does not have, will not have, shrinks from with horror. (ibid. p. 71)

For Kierkegaard, then, we needed to be committed to the givens of our everyday existence while also seeing beyond the everyday. Mostly, he thought, people were simply lost in everyday trivia. A deeper awareness required a degree of solitude, yet for most this was feared and avoided:

> In general, the urge for solitude is a sign that there is after all spirit in a person and the measure of what spirit there is. So little do chattering nonentities and socializers feel the need for solitude that, like love-birds, if left alone for an instant they promptly die. As the little child must be lulled to sleep, so these need the soothing hushaby of social life to be able to eat, drink, sleep, pray, fall in love, and so on. (ibid. p. 95)

The majority therefore avoided the spiritual path altogether. Even among those who thought they were taking it, only a small minority ever succeeded. For most, 'spirituality' was merely a way of evading day-to-day duties, roles, choices and limitations. People might imagine they were transcending ordinary life; in most cases, though, they were merely escaping, dodging and running away from life.

They might, however, entertain all kinds of illusions about what they imagined to be their insight into themselves and the world. Hence, for every spiritual 'guru' who had something worthwhile to offer, there were scores of bogus variants delivering only fantasies. Illusion, it seemed, was far more common than real insight. Youth might have little foresight and many illusions about the future, but what of age? Even our claims to hindsight might be much weaker than we imagined:

> What affects the adult is not so much the illusion of hope as, no doubt among other things, the grotesque illusion of looking down from some supposedly higher vantage point, free from illusion, upon the illusions of the young.
>
> This 'we have been', which we so often hear from older people, is just as great an illusion as the younger person's illusions of the future; they lie or invent, both of them. (ibid. p. 89)

Even our claims to progress might often be illusions. For example the youth emerges into adult status, develops plans that exceed actualities, finds frustration and limitation and may fall into anxiety and despair. Older adults may imagine that they tackled this problem and come to terms with life. Or have they? Have they found a mature balance between the finite and infinite? Or have they merely settled for the trivial and insignificant?:

> And perhaps over the years one leaves behind that little bit of passion, feeling, fantasy, that little bit of inwardness one had, and comes as a matter of course (for such things come as a matter of course) to see life from the commonplace point of view. This 'improved' condition, which has indeed come over the years, he now looks upon in despair as something good; he convinces himself easily (and in a certain satirical sense nothing can be more certain) that it could never now occur to him to despair – no, he has secured himself, he is in despair, spiritlessly in despair. (ibid. p. 90)

For Kierkegaard the lowest potentiality of human existence was to settle for a life without spirit in a despair that did not face up to itself. Progress, then, consisted in facing up to the depths of one's anxiety or despair. This was the unavoidable consequence of seeing the gaping chasm that existed between what was and what might be. Further progress meant living through both anxiety and despair, but not allowing oneself to become mired within it. Ultimately one might find oneself not as an end product, but as a movement balanced between potentiality and actuality.

For Kierkegaard, this connection to oneself meant connection with God. But, when he meditates on these matters, God is not so ever present in dialogue in the way that is found in, for example, St Augustine:

The despair is intensified in proportion to the consciousness of the self. But the self is intensified in proportion to the standard by which the self measures itself, and infinitely so when God is the standard. The more conception of God, the more self; the more self, the more conception of God. Only when a self, as this particular individual, is conscious of being before God, only then is it the infinite self; and that self then sins before God. (ibid. p. 112)

Kierkegaard attacked the Church that, in his view, was too often un-Godly in its experience and its practice:

It has to be said, and as bluntly as possible, that so-called Christendom (in which all, in their millions, are Christians as a matter of course, so that there are as many, yes, just as many Christians as there are people) is not only a miserable edition of Christianity, full of misprints that distort the meaning and of thoughtless omissions and emendations, but an abuse of it in having taken Christianity's name in vain. In a little country, scarcely three poets are known to each generation... and yet a true priest is an even greater rarity than a true poet. (ibid. p. 134)

He also had little time for those who sought to 'defend' God via intellectual argument:

Just picture a lover. You agree, don't you, that he'd be capable of speaking of his beloved day in and day out, as long as the day lasted, and the night as well? But do you suppose it could occur to him, do you think it would be possible for him, don't you think he would find it disgusting to speak in such a way as to offer three reasons for concluding that there was after all something to being in love – more or less as when the pastor gives three reasons for concluding that it pays to pray, as though the price of prayer had fallen so low that three reasons were needed to help give it some crumb of esteem? (ibid. p. 135)

Yet Christianity had often managed to run on and on via the power of the argument and the power, or blind momentum, of the institution. Kierkegaard took both of these away. This was fine for those who could find God via their own faith and experience. Yet, as Kierkegaard had himself argued, only the tiniest minority had ever found spiritual expression on their own and without the support of rational argument or a living institution. It is scarcely surprising, then, that most of those who followed Kierkegaard in other ways did not find God. Instead they sought to find coherence without such a deity. Thus it is that, nowadays, the existential agenda tends to be associated with the human task of coping *without* rather than *within* God. Existentialism is now far more part of the humanist agenda, although there are still those within Christian teaching who would also seek to embrace an existential practice.

Having said that, perhaps it is time to ask just what on earth is meant by existentialism. There is no easy answer, but it is best to begin by looking, from an historical perspective, at just what it was that Kierkegaard was trying to oppose. Here, a one-word answer is possible – Hegel!

Hegel was forty three years older than Kierkegaard. His was the voice of authority. Hegelianism was the conventional wisdom within philosophy during, and beyond, Kierkegaard's lifetime. Hegelianism was about building systems of thought and placing human experience within this broad intellectual context. Hegel sought an 'absolute'. Via the dialectical process of thesis creating antithesis, we moved to a higher intellectual synthesis. This then itself became a thesis creating a new antithesis, and so on. In this way we moved closer to the underlying essences of existence.

Individual experience was of little account when compared to this collective, but elitist, intellectual system building. Existence was determined by underlying essences that could be apprehended intellectually by Hegelian heavyweights. This view of knowledge is in the tradition of Plato and continues today among those who, for example, would say that understanding of ten-dimensional spaces requires maths and mind power rather than meditation and individual self-awareness. For Kierkegaard this was not the way.

Each of us required individual self-awareness before God, but not before Hegel. Each of us was unique. None of us was confinable or coherent within human intellectual system building, however comprehensive or complex. Each of us needed to find, face, explore, trust and come to terms with our experience. Each of us needed to balance between knowing and not knowing, finite and infinite. Any attempt to put a system of understanding around the whole of life and the whole of self was a form of blasphemy, hubris, madness. As Sartre later put it, existence precedes essence.[1]

For Kierkegaard, we could travel through anxiety and despair rather than stay stuck within them, since we found ourselves within God. For many of the existentialists who followed Kierkegaard, there was no finding God but plenty of despair and 'angst'. The question then remained, and remains, are we to use our anxiety well or merely be used up by it? Can we face anxiety without God?

In *Fear and Trembling*,[2] Kierkegaard marvels at the way Abraham could stay within a God who could demand:

> Take now my son, thine only son Isaac, whom thou lovest, and get thee into the land of Moriah; and offer him there for a burnt offering upon one of the mountains which I will tell thee of. (Genesis 22.1)

Kierkegaard wrestles to make sense of this divine demand for the entire length of the book. What kind of God requires such an inhuman sacrifice? What kind of human is prepared to act in such a bestial, slavish, amoral way? Is such a God petty? Arrogant? Overweening? Arbitrary? Does Abraham 'know' that God will not in the end demand this sacrifice? If so, is not God Himself behaving like some childish godfather requiring cheap demonstrations of servitude from overly demeaning disciples? The questions go on and on. But they, at least, are compelling. The answers are less than convincing. Questions like this were repeated over and again by subsequent explorers of biblical texts. The result was that more and more came to the view that they did not experience God, neither did they believe in the arguments for the existence of God. Worst of all, growing numbers of people came to believe that they did not think much of this Christian God. As Alan Watts put it,[3] this God of the scriptures was not the sort of being you would much wish to invite to dinner! He was far too demanding, unforgiving, arbitrary, invasive and severe.

Kierkegaard's anxiety seems to have outlived his God. It can itself become a kind of modish indulgence and he himself appeared to be aware of this danger. But Kierkegaard was surely right to remind us that anxiety and despair are not 'obstacles' to life but part of the very warp and weft of lived existence. This is particularly of relevance to every therapist and counsellor. Their client may complain of anxiety. Does this mean that there is something 'wrong' with them? Do progress and effectiveness in counselling require that clients should end their sessions feeling less anxious? Might they, should they, sometimes feel more uneasy? How much will they know, or not know?

How will a balance be found between finite actuality and infinite possibility? Who will decide? Will I 'find myself' just a little more if I think and feel according to the hints provided by my counsellor? Should I follow Kierkegaard or Hegel, or whom?

The existentialist values experience before essence. But is this a meaningful distinction? If existentialism is an 'ism' that opposes 'isms' generally, does that mean that it is self-contradictory? If so, does it matter?

Can I belong to a school of thought that seeks to do away with schools of thought? If I do then perhaps the only consistent response is for me to deny that I am a member?

I seek to 'find myself' rather than become too immersed in daily demands and daily clichés. Yet doesn't 'finding myself' itself, and easily, become a cliché? Everyone routinely seems to be trying to 'find themselves' using methods and jargon that suggests triteness, superficiality and empty modishness. What is the solution? Or, since there are no final solutions, what is your best next move?

Whatever you may choose there will be no final escape from uncertainty, insecurity and looming despair:

'How can we cure ourselves of life, when life and its everyday mysteries is all that we have got?' (van Deurzen, *Everyday Mysteries*, p. 3)

? Questions

1. Which of your clients suffer not from what they think they *are* but from what they think they are *not*?

2. How far are counsellors in danger of imprisoning clients within new accounts of who they are?

3. Who will fund counselling as an open-ended encounter between two searching and co-creating subjects/ souls? Do you think they should?

4. Infinite potential transforms to finite actuality via our choices. What kind of link, if any, can you thereby make between existentialism and behaviourism?

5. How far does existentialism itself find a suitable balance between self as infinite potential subject and self as finite and actual object?

EXERCISES

1. Consider how far existential perspectives inform your own counsellor/care training? Should they? How? With what consequence?

2. As a detached student, compare Kierkegaard with other existentialists summarised in this book, that is, Nietzsche, Heidegger and Sartre.

3. As a committed existentialist, *resist* comparing Kierkegaard with Nietzsche, Heidegger or Sartre. They are subjects that you as subject will create and explore for yourself. They are not objects to be compared. Or are they?

4. Of the old, and the young, and their perceptions of past and future, Kierkegaard observed that, they lie or invent, both of them. Consider your experiences of this, and your ability to determine truth.

5. Discuss the notion that confronting one's own anxiety and despair can often be a sign of progress.

Conclusion

Kierkegaard is seen as the founder of existentialism. True to its imperative, he explored, as subject/mystery, the mystery of human subjectivity. Therefore he did not declare a new object of study or objective academic discipline. Kierkegaard's prime target was Hegel, the arch essentialist system builder; but he would have opposed all subsequent efforts to turn people into objects of impersonal description and manipulation. Kierkegaard's existentialism was grounded in God, but subsequent explorers had trouble finding a Christian deity although some claimed to find a transcendent spirit, as, of course, had Hegel. Kierkegaard's anxiety could become a modish indulgence but he was more aware of this danger than many subsequent existentialists. For existentialists we are not objects, nor detached observers, therefore they resist efforts to describe the essential nature of humanity. They stress freedom more than frameworks, subjective choice rather than impersonal objectives. But perhaps the subject–object split itself needs to be transcended? The differences between existentialists like Kierkegaard, Nietzsche, Heidegger and Sartre are profound. It is hard to find a common 'essence' that they all share. Does this thereby undermine and/or reinforce the validity of existentialism?

Notes

1. 'The appearance does not hide the essence, it reveals it; it *is* the essence'. *Being and Nothingness*, Routledge, 1996, p. xxii.
2. Penguin, 1985.
3. *God*, Celestial Arts, 1975.

Websites

http://www.users.interport.net/~dstorm/danpage2.htm
http://www.webcom.com/sk/
http://www.webcom.com/kierke/

Bibliography

Emmy van Deurzen, *Everyday Mysteries*, Routledge, 1997

S. Kierkegaard, *Fear and Trembling*, Penguin, 1985

S. Kierkegaard, *The Sickness unto Death*, Penguin, 1989

S. Kierkegaard, *Concluding Unscientific Postscript*, Princeton University Press, 1992

S. Kierkegaard, *Either/or*, Princeton University Press, 1992

Chapter 26

Karl Marx (1818–1883)

Key Points

- The ruling ideas of each age have ever been the ideas of its ruling class

- The bourgeoisie has resolved personal worth into exchange value

- All old-established national industries have been destroyed or are daily being destroyed

- The work of the proletarians has lost all individual character. We have become an appendage of the machine

- We shall have an association, in which the free development of each is the condition for the free development of all.

Application

- Marx is adept in showing how individual suffering, uncertainty and identity is shaped by wider material circumstances
- For Marx, much internal 'angst' is best understood by examining interpersonal and international processes of change
- Marxists explore how individual esteem and meaning is greatly determined by social class and global relationships
- Marxists argue that we can oppress others without intending to, or knowing that we oppress. This is a salutary warning to those who tend to 'psychologise' and individualise every problem.

The revolutionary collapse of Communism after 1989 was even more rapid and complete than its rise. What need, then, is there to talk of Karl Marx? In any case, Marx wrote of class, power, politics, economics. What is there in Marx, therefore, of interest to anyone seeking to provide individual care and attention? Is Marxism an essentially twentieth-century phenomenon that has no place within the thinking of a new millennium?

Marx will seem irrelevant to those counsellors and other care workers who imagine that individual identity, well-being and personal development run on an entirely separate track from political, social, cultural and economic processes of change. But wherever else Marx may have been wrong, he was surely right in stressing and exploring ways in which our own individuality and personality is shaped, and deformed, by the broader social, political and material contexts within which we live:

> What else does the history of ideas prove, than that intellectual production changes its character in proportion as material production is changed? The ruling ideas of each age have ever been the ideas of its ruling class. (*Communist Manifesto*, p. 72)

For Marx, our thought and attention, whether we realised it or not, was focused according to the priorities of whoever were the victors in the last power struggle. Truth, for Marx, was not some pure commodity available to liberal intellectuals trained in dispassionate thought and closeted in ivory towers. There were only versions of truth, each born out of Hegel's dialectical process of thesis, anti-thesis leading to a new, but never final, synthesis. For Hegel this dialectical struggle was essentially abstract, logical and intellectual. Ideas battled with ideas and thereby gave birth to new ideas. The whole process was essentially a manifestation of the movement of the underlying 'spirit' within all existence. For Marx the real battle was a material one, on the ground, between antagonistic social classes. The ideas that struggled to emerge or survive were essentially by-products of this underlying conflict rooted in material and social reality.

So what, for Marx, and co-author Frederick Engels, was the state of play of ideas and social realities in 1848, when the first edition of their *Communist Manifesto* appeared?:

> The bourgeoisie, wherever it has got the upper hand, has put an end to all feudal, patriarchal, idyllic relations. It has pitilessly torn asunder the motley feudal ties that bound man to his 'natural superiors', and has left remaining no other nexus between man and man than naked self-interest, than callous 'cash payment'. It has drowned the most heavenly ecstasies of religious fervour, of chivalrous enthusiasm, of philistine sentimentalism, in the icy water of egotistical calculation. It has resolved personal worth into exchange value, and in place of the numberless indefeasible chartered freedoms, has set up that single, unconscionable freedom – Free Trade. (ibid. p. 44)

This is rousing stuff; some would say 'rabble rousing'. But there are surely many that, while never describing themselves as communist, would have a great deal of sympathy with it. Our material circumstances assuredly do construct and constrain what we do and do not do, think and do not think, feel and do not feel. There is not a 'me' that I know, who then goes out and explores its world. There is a world that shapes me far more profoundly than I can shape it. It was there before me. It will still be there after I am gone. It determines, not entirely, but to a very large degree, who and what I think I am, how I feel about myself, what goes on in my head, what I do and what I think is important:

> All old-established national industries have been destroyed or are daily being destroyed. They are dislodged by new industries, whose introduction becomes a life and death question for all civilised nations, by industries that no longer work up indigenous raw material, but raw material drawn from the remotest zones; industries whose products are consumed, not only at home, but in every quarter of the globe. (ibid. p. 46)

Marx and Engels' Manifesto first appeared in 1848. Much of it could equally well be describing 1948 or 1998. Perhaps it will sound just as relevant in 2048? How many personal problems are the consequence of these huge social changes and dislocations? Many who think their problems are essentially personal suffer from forces that are essentially social. Perhaps the most therapeutic intervention for such social casualties would be a course in Marxism? Would proletarian self-esteem rise a little if they could glimpse the vast waves of social and economic change upon which they are being carried – or beneath which they are being drowned?:

> The bourgeoisie, by the rapid improvement of all instruments of production, by the immensely facilitated means of communication, draws all, even the most barbarian, nations into civilisation. The cheap prices of its commodities are the heavy artillery with which it batters down all Chinese walls, with which it forces the barbarians' intensely obstinate hatred of foreigners to capitulate. (ibid. p. 47)

> Owing to the extensive use of machinery and to division of labour, the work of the proletarians has lost all individual character, and, consequently, all charm for the workmen. He becomes an appendage of the machine, and it is only the most simple, most monotonous, and most easily acquired knack, that is required of him. (ibid. p. 51)

In the north east of England, communities of disaffected young and old surround me, who are demotivated, depressed, disillusioned. Should they be offered individual counselling so that they can each explore their personal circumstances, feelings and self-esteem? Should greater efforts be made to replace the traditional industries that have, on such a scale and in such a short space of time, collapsed? Should people be told that very little can be done if you do not have the skills needed in the changing marketplace? It depends, of course, on whether you think markets have an autonomous existence or governments can, and should, have a hand in shaping our economic destiny. 'Depression' is a personal experience and an economic concept. The two can be, in fact, very closely interlinked. But it is certain that psychological depression is often an effect, never a cause, of the economic variety.

> The less the scale and exertion of strength implied in manual labour, in other words, the more modern industry becomes developed, the more is the labour of men succeeded by that of women. (ibid. p. 52)

Here, too, in just one sentence, is a root cause of many of the profound changes in gender relations and gender identity that preoccupy counsellors and their clients. If anything, Marx's observation about female employment is far more relevant now than when it was first published:

> The lower strata of the middle class – the small tradespeople, shopkeepers, and retired tradesmen generally, the handicraftsmen and peasants – all these sink gradually into the proletariat, partly because their diminutive capital does not suffice for the scale on which modern industry is carried on, and is swamped in the competition with the large capitalists, partly because their specialised skill is rendered worthless by new methods of production. (ibid. p. 53)

Marx observed a globalisation of economic competition, a growth of companies operating on a global scale, a growing sense of individual powerlessness ('alienation') in relation to these vast forces. I am sure that if he returned today he would assert that his forecast had been entirely vindicated. Now even nation-states can feel relatively powerless when compared with these huge market forces. Will there be a collapse of the stock exchange next year? Will Japan bring down Korea? Would Europe and America be able to survive the results? Who will be the winners and losers? Will any single government be able to control or combat these social-economic processes? Will even a union of European governments, pooling their sovereignty, be strong or smart enough to steer events?

Marx was an optimist, not to say a romantic and a utopian for all his claims to 'scientific' socialism. For Marx these vast global economic forces could be tamed, directed and humanised, not so much by existing governments, but by 'the people':

> In place of the old bourgeois society, with its classes and class antagonisms, we shall have an association, in which the free development of each is the condition for the free development of all. (ibid. p. 76)

Clearly Marx should have read his Machiavelli, and contemporary liberal philosophers like Mill, who were much more sensible of the difficulties in achieving constructive co-operation between human beings. In the real world, no association of humanity has ever existed that managed to free itself of struggle, antagonism, manoeuvre, egocentricity and factional in-fighting. How did Marx think that his own 'association' would avoid these problems?:

> The Communists disdain to conceal their views and aims. They openly declare that their ends can be attained only by the forcible overthrow of all existing social conditions. Let the ruling classes tremble at a Communist revolution. The proletarians have nothing to lose but their chains. They have a world to win. Working men of all countries, unite! (ibid. p. 96)

Thus ends the *Communist Manifesto*. The working men (and women?) are to unite. Class struggle will thereby be abolished. The state will act in the interests of the majority and remove all the irrationalities of a global market based on capital and private greed:

> The proletariat will use its political supremacy to wrest, by degrees, all capital from the bourgeoisie, to centralise all instruments of production in the hands of the State, that is, of the proletariat organised as the ruling class; and to increase the total of productive forces as rapidly as possible. (ibid. p. 74)

Hooray, hurrah, alleluia, hosanna - but how? Marx is long on his analysis of political and economic deficiencies and some of it remains of interest. Like so many revolutionaries, however, he falls badly short when it comes to providing a coherent remedy.

Marx did, in fact, not feel the need to provide a detailed plan since he felt quite sure that revolutionary change towards a communist society was an inevitable next step in the process of change based on dialectical materialism. The 'bourgeois' had once been a force for progress in relation to medieval power relations, and arose as a new synthesis from previous clashes of thesis and anti-thesis. Their time would expire, by historical necessity. Capitalism contained within it its own contradictions that would bring about its demise. In particular it was always going to create crises of overproduction because workers were never paid enough to purchase all they produced. Wars removed some of the surplus but this state of affairs could not go on:

> The conditions of bourgeois society are too narrow to comprise the wealth created by them. And how does the bourgeoisie get over these crises? On the one hand by enforced destruction of a mass of productive forces; on the other, by the conquest of new markets, and by the more thorough exploitation of the old ones. That is to say, by paving the way for more extensive and more destructive crises, and by diminishing the means whereby crises are prevented.
>
> The weapons with which the bourgeoisie felled feudalism to the ground are now turned against the bourgeoisie itself.
>
> But not only has the bourgeoisie forged the weapons that bring death to itself; it has also called into existence the men who are to wield those weapons – the modern working class – the proletarians. (ibid. p. 50)

Hindsight gives some of these words a bitter taste. This florid language demonises 'the bourgeoisie' (a term stronger in its power to abuse than to enlighten) and romanticises the 'working class'. This way lies intolerance, utopianism, fascism and totalitarianism. Hindsight indicates that governments do not necessarily manage economies very well; that 'people's' governments may not pay much attention to the people; that no one has produced an organisation within which the free development of each can necessarily work harmoniously for the free development of all.

For so many philosophers, ideas are sovereign and have to be used to determine, or 'prove' the nature and very existence of material reality. For Marx, material realities shaped the nature of our ideas rather than vice versa, and he was highly critical of those philosophers who merely wished to observe and ruminate upon the nature of the world:

> Philosophers have only *interpreted* the world in various ways, but the real task is to *alter* it. (quoted in *The German Ideology*, 1998)

There is now substantial evidence that we do very often assess ourselves according to the quantity and quality of the material goods with which we surround ourselves.[1] Marx believed that this fetish of equating status with material possessions was driven by capitalism. In the Socialist International that would 'inevitably' replace it, people would recognise themselves beyond mere commodities and would attach value according to use and labour more than to exchange value (price).

We were obsessed with commodities; we saw the market as a part of nature rather than the product of history and society. With the triumph of the working class, confidently predicted by Marx as a dialectical inevitability, commodity fetishism would disappear. We would be less cut off from ourselves, less alienated, less exploitative, more co-operative, more rational in terms of what we produced and why. Yes, and pigs would fly through the sky on little wings manufactured in the workers' communes.

Marx seems to me to be far better in analysing contemporary problems than in offering believable solutions. His argument that we may be exploiting each other, not because of the contents of our consciousness, but because of the nature of our social and political organisation is surely well made. It is of particular value to counsellors with a penchant for individualising problems and exploring them purely in terms of the intentions and conscious thoughts and feelings of personal clients.

Marx examined the social, political and economic determinants of human suffering. In his view, it was naïve to believe that individuals had very much control over their own destiny. Only if they came together in the mass could they influence the course of history. We suffered, we were confused and we were less than honest with ourselves and with others. We felt helpless, uncertain, depressed and unsure of our identity. People could exploit each other and act amorally regardless of their individual make up and intentions. It just was not adequate to examine individual psycho-dynamics if we wished to understand how and why we helped and, more often, hurt each other. We needed to understand the social and political dynamic.

Individual actions were obviously important, but what people do is shaped by what they understand to be social and political 'reality'. Liberal economists, from Adam Smith on, thought that markets were benevolent and that the best social outcome came from people pursuing their own private interests. Marx believed that the existing social order was perniciously exploitative of the proletariat and that, in addition, 'bourgeois' society destroyed the souls of 'the bourgeoisie'. For the capitalist, to exploit means 'to utilise'. For the Marxist, capitalist exploitation meant oppression. Which of the two connotations is more appropriate? The answer is debatable. Less contentious is Marx's observation that our identity and our actions are shaped by social forces many of which we do not understand or perceive at all.

We interpret what we see of the social world around us, but much of it we do not see at all. We are not conscious of many social forces since we do not have the concepts to isolate and analyse them. Consequently, the large 'social waves' on which we are carried are largely invisible to us. They might make us seasick, but we tend to see this queasiness as a personal problem and do not notice how far we share it with others. Marx analysed the invisibility of social process with far more sophistication than his liberal contemporaries; and for this I think he still deserves appreciation.

Freud, as everyone knows, focused on the unconscious. Marx was more preoccupied with what would now be called 'false consciousness'. The capitalist economy cut us off from the product and real value of our labour and thereby could give us a false sense of who we were and what we amounted to. It prevented us from finding true pride in our work, mystified the real bonds and interconnections between us, and led to a fixation on things as expressions of value. To transpose this into a Christian perspective, capitalism deliberated on the price of everything and the value of nothing.

Hence the *Communist Manifesto* sought the abolition of private property, so that people no longer walled themselves in with material goods:

> Private property has made us so stupid and one-sided that an object is only ours when we have it – when it exists for us as capital, or when it is directly possessed, eaten, drunk, worn, inhabited, etc. – in short, when it is used by us. (*Economic and Philosophic Manuscripts*, p. 139)

People would co-operate; there would be an ethical economy – from each according to his ability, to each according to his need. The government, which, after the revolution, would magically and mystically remain democratic, uncorrupted and efficient, would supervise what was to be produced and how best to produce it. Communist party members would be at the 'vanguard' of this change, but they would not, of course, take advantage of this position of power. Since we would all be getting what we needed we would not need to privately own anything. Property could be shared:

You are horrified at our intending to do away with private property. But in your existing society, private property is already done away with for nine-tenths of the population; its existence for the few is solely due to its non-existence in the hands of those nine-tenths. (*Communist Manifesto*, p. 66)

This principle, apparently, could be applied to wives as well:

Abolition of the family! Even the most radical flare up at this infamous proposal of the Communists.

On what foundation is the present family, the bourgeois family, based? On capital, on private gain. In its completely developed form this family exists only among the bourgeoisie. But this state of things finds its complement in the practical absence of the family among the proletariat, and in public prostitution. (ibid. p. 68)

Families treated people as commodities, shut them off from wider society, enslaved women and focused on the bourgeois fetish of accumulation rather than on wider co-operation, caring and sharing. These immature obsessions would die all by themselves as Communism provided a wider collective means by which people could give and receive support:

Our bourgeois, not content with having the wives and daughters of their proletarians at their disposal, not to speak of common prostitutes, take the greatest pleasure in seducing each other's wives.

Bourgeois marriage is in reality a system of wives in common and thus, at the most, what the Communists might possibly be reproached with, is that they desire to introduce, in substitution for a hypocritically concealed, an openly legalised community of women. (ibid. p. 71)

This is more sloganeering and abuse than intelligent observation, argument and evidence. But insofar as you can believe that a wider community of people can work and play co-operatively and compassionately with each other, it may be said to 'follow' that there is less need of such a private monogamous haven of marriage. In theory, do we need to 'possess' our partner? If we enjoy each other, do we not want each other to enjoy those others beyond our own front door? And why do we have our own front door? Do we need a front door at all? Why not knock the walls down between our neighbours and ourselves? Why not share a kitchen? Shall we use just one bed? Or rotate? On a rota basis? In which case, how big do kitchen and bed each need to be?

Such experimentation pre-dated Marx and will no doubt be tried again. Certainly we have no cause to feel complacent about the current state of the institution of marriage. The material basis of many social mores, that Marx was so skilled at uncovering, appears to have become more evident in the years since his death. For example, women are far more independent financially than ever before. Hence they seek to withdraw from an unsatisfactory marriage more often than in the past. Does this mean that they are less happy with marriage now than were their grandparents? Or were women equally unhappy with their status one hundred years ago? If so, they were almost entirely unable to do anything about it since they were so completely dependent, financially, on their husbands. Material dependence kept the woman with her man and allowed the man to be exploitative. Material independence may free the woman but what future does this leave for the family? For Marx, if the family was exploitative then let it end. Is individual isolation, with more people living alone, a preferred alternative? Marx was an optimist. We would come together and form groups on an equal basis. Community life would improve; indeed international relations more generally would become more peaceful and constructive:

> In proportion as the exploitation of one individual by another is put an end to, the exploitation of one nation by another will also be put an end to. (ibid. p. 72)

Communism hoped to put an end to the exploitation of one individual by another and thereby of one nation by another. It has not achieved either. Stalin butchered tens of millions of people in the name of the people's party, two superpowers glowered at each other and provided arms for smaller nations to fight their proxy wars. Is this because the people were not good enough for Communism? Is it because they suffered the wrong leaders in the wrong circumstances? Is it that 'real' communism was never actually tried? In my view it is none of these. Communism was an essentially utopian adventure that was naïve about the hard realities of individual personalities, social structures and political economies. It was totalitarian in its notion of 'false consciousness', party 'vanguards' and 'inevitable forces of progress'. It was lethal in its demonising of all opponents of 'the people'. It was crude in its talk of 'the masses', and thereby showed a lack of concern and respect for individual variety. It was simplistic in analysing so much of human life in terms of class struggle and it was absurdly naïve in imagining that all the shadows and follies in the human psyche would be removed when the working class came to power.

Russia, under Communism, showed what was wrong with Communism. But there is no cause for complacency about the alternatives. Russia under capitalism is showing, even more rapidly and revoltingly, what is wrong with capitalism when it is not tempered by shared values, humanity, an effective and vaguely democratic government. Perhaps western regimes are currently the least worst available. But let us not be so foolish or complacent as to assume that they are the best achievable. They may work 'well enough' for as long as circumstances are not too unkind. But for how much longer will comfortable circumstances continue? And is the current 'well enough' really good enough?

? Questions

1. How many of your client issues seem to be primarily social, political, economic rather than psychological?

2. If you assist clients to cope psychologically with political and economic injustice, how far are you thereby colluding with injustice?

3. How far do you agree that Marx scores high in his analysis of socio-economic problems but low in his proposed remedies?

4. Do you find the notion of 'false consciousness' of value as a counsellor?

5. Should counsellors in deprived communities focus primarily on job search skills or on the reasons why jobs have disappeared from these communities?

EXERCISES

1. Consider how far socio-economic components of human distress are, and should be, included within your counsellor/care training.

2. Discuss how far personal identity and personal meanings are socially constructed. How far should you 'look out' in order to understand the ways in which your clients 'look in'?

Conclusion

Marx sought to explain the forces of history and his ideas were widely and variously, feared and revered for most of the twentieth century. Marxism itself became, almost overnight, an historical period piece.

Marx's analysis of socio-economic problems still deserves attention even though his proposed remedies, insofar as he had any, were hopelessly naïve and utopian. People shape and are shaped by wider political realities. Counsellors might achieve greater understanding of the human psyche if they spent more time examining the nature of the socio-economic soil from which we all emerge and via which we are nurtured, defined and constrained.

Note

1. In a consumer society it is not so much the Cartesian 'I think, therefore I exist' that predominates, but rather, 'IKEA, therefore I exist.'

Websites

http://paul.spu.edu/~hawk/marx.html
http://csf.colorado.edu/psn/marx
http://www.alphalink.com.au/~pashton/thinkers/marx.htm
http://www.marx.org/
http://english-www.hss.cmu.edu/marx/

Bibliography

K. Marx, *Capital* (student edition), Lawrence and Wishart, 1992

K. Marx, *Poverty of Philosophy*, Prometheus, US, 1995

K. Marx and F. Engels, *Economic and Philosophic Manuscripts*, Lawrence & Wishart, 1973

K. Marx and F. Engels, *Communist Manifesto*, Progress Publishers, 1977

K. Marx in *The German Ideology: Including Thesis on Feuerbach*, ed. F. Engels, Prometheus Books, 1998

Chapter 27

Friedrich Wilhelm Nietzsche
(1844–1900)

───────────────── **Key Points** ─────────────────

■ Christianity was from the beginning... life's nausea and disgust with life

■ An attack on the roots of passion means an attack on the roots of life: the practice of the church is hostile to life

■ What can be loved in man is that he is an overture and a going under

■ Surpass the sand-grain considerateness, ...the pitiable comfortableness, the happiness of the greatest number!

■ He who seeth the abyss, but with eagle's eyes, he who with eagle's talons graspeth the abyss: he hath courage.

Application

- Nietzsche challenged cheap fantasies that life can be, or should be, just, fair and rewarding
- Authentic humanity involved finding the courage to face hard realities and abandoning cosy nursery stories of comfort and consolation
- Nietzsche assumed that most do not have the courage, character or strength to undertake an authentic journey of self-expression
- There is no self to discover. Self is to be transcended, to be left behind
- Counsellors and clients like to believe they are on a heroic psychic journey. How often are they just tending a psychic garden?

God hath died: now do we desire – the Superman to live. (*Thus Spoke Zarathustra*, Chapter 73, Para. 2)

Christianity was from the beginning, essentially and fundamentally, life's nausea and disgust with life, merely concealed behind, masked by, dressed up as, faith in 'another' or 'better' life. (*The Birth of Tragedy*, p. 23)

Nietzsche claimed repeatedly that God had died. The 'superman', 'overman', (Übermensch) would therefore inherit the earth free of the shackles of a cowardly, corrupt, decadent, dishonest, life-and-soul sapping church.

He liked to shock, and often succeeded. The result is a crazed, manic, metaphor-driven style that weakens his case via ludicrous overstatement. Yet he deserves careful attention. Like contemporary counsellors, he examined questions of identity and authenticity. His inflammatory words serve both as a lesson and a warning:

The church fights passion with excision in every sense: its practice, its 'cure,' is castration. It never asks: 'How can one spiritualize, beautify, deify a craving?' It has at all times laid the stress of discipline on extirpation (of sensuality, of pride, of the lust to rule, of avarice, of vengefulness). But an attack on the roots of passion means an attack on the roots of life: the practice of the church is *hostile to life*. (*Twilight of the Idols*, Para. 7)

Perhaps this is not true of all forms of Christian teaching. Yet what of the belief that we will only really live to the full *after we have died?* Is this not an avoidance of our responsibilities and opportunities in this life on earth? Nietzsche saw it as an act of bad faith, a loss of confidence and courage within earthly existence. He is, I believe, quite right. Too much puerile fantasy is allowed to shelter under country spires and too many outside are too polite to say what they really think about it. Too much of what passes for Christian teaching is not just rationally incoherent and absurd, it is morally repugnant, feeble, cowardly and dishonest. What kind of hope do we really have in this life on earth if we imagine that it is just a preparation for the supposedly more real and eternal life to come? Should we 'do good' in order to arrive in a heavenly eternity? Or simply because it is right? Why does heaven seem so boring? Why does the devil have all the best tunes? Should we really model ourselves on lost sheep and lambs?

Children want everything to be fair and believe in Father Christmas. Adults prefer whatever notion they may have of fairness but surely we are fools if we expect life to deliver? Parents can pick us up, wipe us down, arbitrate when we squabble and clean up the mess. Supposedly grown adults hope their deity will do the same and get down on their knees to pray. Counsellors may easily succumb to secular versions of these fantasies of cosmic justice and fairness and clients may beg them to provide. Nietzsche was disgusted at such behaviour and said so, loudly and repeatedly.

'Oh, God I have sinned. Please forgive me.' 'Oh God, we are innocent, please free us of our suffering.' 'I am trying hard but life is so unfair. Will there be pie in the sky when I die?' 'We are as lost sheep.' Are we? Is this an attractive vision of humanity? Nietzsche did not think so.

For Nietzsche the history of the church was one of bowing, scraping, cringing, whinging, apologising, pleading for special favours. It was demeaning, disgraceful, despairing, dishonest and despicable behaviour. It was time we all grew up. God, Nietzsche claimed, is dead. God, for Nietzsche, was just a bad idea all along. He argued that we should have faith and hope in ourselves, our potential, our actual existence. We should stand on our own feet and behave like independent adults. Life could be very tough. But, in a more contemporary idiom, when the going gets tough, the tough get going:

> He who seeth the abyss, but with eagle's eyes, he who with eagle's talons graspeth the abyss: he hath courage. (*Thus Spoke Zarathustra*, Fourth Part, Chapter 73, The Higher Man, Para. 4)

There was no personal celestial accountant keeping track of whoever was, and was not, getting their 'fair' share. Nietzsche was glad of it. Not everyone received what they hoped were their just deserts. Why should they? Feeble individuals, struck down by misfortune, might cry 'why me?' The Übermensch would observe 'Why *not* me?'.

What kind of faith and courage required life to be just and fair? Real courage meant you got up and got on in full knowledge that tomorrow might well be harsh, arbitrary, chaotic and random. If we were to shape up we had to make our own shape and sense of self and circumstance. We would make, and tell, our own story. It would not always, or often, end 'happily ever after':

> Hungry, fierce, lonesome, God-forsaken: so doth the lion-will wish itself. Free from the happiness of slaves, redeemed from deities and adorations, fearless and fear-inspiring, grand and lonesome: so is the will of the conscientious. In the wilderness have ever dwelt the conscientious, the free spirits, as lords of the wilderness; but in the cities dwell the well-foddered, famous wise ones – the draught-beasts. (ibid. Second Part, Chapter 30, The Famous Wise Ones)

'O Zarathustra,' said they, 'gazest thou out perhaps for thy happiness?' 'Of what account is my happiness!' answered he, 'I have long ceased to strive any more for happiness, I strive for my work.' (ibid. Fourth Part, Chapter 61, The Honey Sacrifice)

Contemporary adherents of personal growth often think of oak trees. Nietzsche's images were far more carnivorous. We were to be wolves, lions and eagles, not cows, sheep or lambs, lost or found. If a lamb were ever to lie down beside you, why, eat it!

In any case, most of our contemporary depression and despair was an indulgence resulting from our all too easy lives. We had forgotten what real pain and suffering really were. Psychology was a pastime for the underemployed. We were cut off from the real gales of existence as we tended our own back garden and ruminated in our own parlours. We were enfeebled, physically, mentally, spiritually, morally:

> The emergence of pessimistic philosophies is by no means a sign of great and terrible misery. No, these question marks about the value of all life are put up in ages in which the refinement and alleviation of existence make even the inevitable mosquito bites of the soul and the body seem much too bloody and malignant and one is so poor in real experiences of pain that one would like to consider painful general ideas as suffering of the first order.
>
> There is a recipe against pessimistic philosophers and the excessive sensitivity that seems to me the real 'misery of the present age' – but this recipe may sound too cruel and might itself be counted among the signs that lead people to judge that 'existence is something evil.' Well, the recipe against this 'misery' is: misery. (*The Gay Science*)

Nietzsche has a point. How much counselling, and other forms of care and attention, are given over to people who have more time and money than real suffering or tragedy? How many want to pretend to explore their supposedly deep wickedness in order to avoid the deeper truth that they are deep down shallow, dull, mediocre and cowardly?

If we were to discover anything worth finding, we should stop being clones of each other, and make our own way for ourselves. We should not be sheep, lost or found, following others and their tired conventions. All this arose from a fear of life. We should express ourselves and explore for ourselves. What might we find?:

> I teach you the overman. Man is something that shall be overcome. What have you done to overcome him?

> All beings so far have created something beyond themselves; and do you want to be the ebb of this great flood and even go back to the beasts rather than overcome man? What is the ape to man? A laughingstock or a painful embarrassment. And man shall be just that for the overman: a laughingstock or a painful embarrassment... Man is a rope, tied between beast and overman – a rope over an abyss...What is great in man is that he is a bridge and not an end: what can be loved in man is that he is an overture and a going under. (*Thus Spoke Zarathustra*, Prologue, Paras. 3–4)

Our task, then, was not to 'find' ourselves, but to go beyond ourselves or, as every *Star Trek* fan knows, '*to boldly go where no man has been before*'.

And, if we were to get to this 'beyond', we would probably need to tread over all those lambs, ox and asses of humanity who did not want even to face themselves and their timid mediocrity, never mind move beyond themselves. Nietzsche, unlike so many within the contemporary human potential movement, knew that self-realisation and self-transcendence required that we learn about, and utilise, *power*, in all its myriad forms. It could often be a rough game:

> Anything which is a living and not a dying body... will have to be an incarnate will to power, it will strive to grow, spread, seize, become predominant – not from any morality or immorality but because it is living and because life simply is will to power... 'Exploitation'... belongs to the essence of what lives, as a basic organic function; it is a consequence of the will to power, which is after all the will to life. (*Beyond Good and Evil*, aphorism 259)

This Darwinian mentality, nature red in tooth and claw, clashes immediately with liberal ethical principles. Ever since Darwin, efforts have been made to reconcile evolution with ethics. Nietzsche wanted none of it. No reconciliation was required. Nietzsche, echoing Thrasymachus in Plato's *Republic*, saw justice as nothing but the interests of the stronger and history as the story of the victorious:

> Morality, as it has so far been understood, has in the end been formulated once more by Schopenhauer, as 'negation of the will to life' – is the very instinct of decadence, which makes an imperative of itself. It says: Perish! It is a condemnation pronounced by the condemned. (*Twilight of the Idols*, Morality as Anti-Nature, Para. 5)

> There is nothing we envy less than the moralistic cow and the fat happiness of the good conscience. One has renounced the great life when one renounces war. (ibid. Morality as Anti-Nature, Para. 3)

In places like this, Nietzsche is so eager to shock and shake his readers that he shakes any potential subtlety out of his own argument. Anyway, he cries, he does not want to argue and persuade and be part of that whole ghastly, complicated, self-controlling, liberal rationality. He wants to follow his instincts and be 'real'. This is what we must all do. As a result, his observations turn into a rant, a shout, and a childish indulgent scream. More sinister, they become a wilful Faustian flirtation with evil.

Nietzsche knows he is playing a dangerous game, and he revels in it. Away with Mill and those other 'blockhead' philosophers who try to weigh and balance and assess and find formulae and 'on the one hand' and 'on the other hand'. Nietzsche is a romantic, yet he is often a victim more than a master of his bedazzling prose. When he can no longer dazzle, he tries to bludgeon. He resorts to base insult, shocking for the sake of shock. He becomes an adolescent more than a sage. Eventually he became insane.[1]

> To call the taming of an animal its 'improvement' sounds almost like a joke to our ears. Whoever knows what goes on in menageries doubts that the beasts are 'improved' there. They are weakened, they are made less harmful, and through the depressive effect of fear, through pain, through wounds, and through hunger they become sickly beasts. It is no different with the tamed man whom the priest has 'improved.' In the early Middle Ages, when the church was indeed, above all, a menagerie, the most beautiful specimens of the 'blond beast' were hunted down everywhere; and the noble Teutons, for example, were 'improved.'
>
> But how did such an 'improved' Teuton who had been seduced into a monastery look afterward? Like a caricature of man – like a miscarriage: he had become a 'sinner,' he was stuck in a cage, imprisoned among all sorts of terrible concepts. And there he lay, sick, miserable, malevolent against himself: full of hatred against the springs of life, full of suspicion against all that was still strong and happy. In short, a 'Christian'. (*Twilight of the Idols*, The 'Improvers' of Mankind, Para. 2)

At this stage, Nietzsche's ranting is no longer amusing. It is one thing to say that ethics can block the individual. It is quite another to suggest that every ethical individual is a blockhead, and that ethics are whatever the victorious want them to be. This wilfully ignores the complexities and dilemmas painstakingly explored by serious writers, for example, those mentioned in previous pages. Nietzsche was not, in fact, a German nationalist, his 'overmen' were to be found treading on the backs of others all over the world. He was contemptuous of nationalist melodrama, seeing it as a cheap solution to each individual's need to create meaning. But *Thus Spoke Zarathustra* was part of the basic kit in the knapsacks of German infantrymen in World War One, and his description of the 'free Teuton' rings harsh in the ears of those who know anything of that other great feast of self-expression, the Second World War:

> You say it is the good cause that hallows even war? I tell you: it is the good war that hallows every cause. (*Thus Spoke Zarathustra*, Part 1, Of War and Warriors)

Is it? Are we to support liberal humanist principles merely because the liberals won the war? Is that all there is to it? What role is there for philosophy if it is soldiers who settle every argument?:

> How I understand the philosopher – as a terrible explosive, endangering everything… my concept of the philosopher is worlds removed from any concept that would include even a Kant, not to speak of academic 'ruminants' and other professors of philosophy. (*Ecce Homo*, sec. 3.2.3)

Well, Nietzsche certainly was a terrible explosive. He was generally overlooked in his own lifetime, but he truly did become alive and potent after his own death. Soldiers and statesmen no doubt choose the philosopher, if they ever do, who best fits their own prejudices and preferences. Nazi Germany certainly admired Nietzsche and, given his more rabid foaming, it is easy to see why. From a philosophical perspective the Second World War might be caricatured as (the beliefs of) Mill allied with Marx versus Nietzsche. Then Mill and Marx fell out, as was inevitable. Now Marx has fallen.

Does that mean that Mill was right? Or more right than the others? Or that he and liberal humanism are safe? Or will they all become, when old and replaced by the new, 'a laughing-stock or a painful embarrassment?':

> The most careful ask today: 'How is man to be maintained?' Zarathustra however asketh, as the first and only one: 'How is man to be surpassed?' (*Thus Spoke Zarathustra*, Fourth Part, Chapter 73, The Higher Man, Para. 3)

Here is the human potential movement at its most energetic. Do not merely find and nurture yourself on some feeble care and maintenance basis. You must break out of yourself, go beyond yourself. Not, like Schopenhauer and the Buddhists, via renunciation, but via a turbo-charged, all out, uncompromising, self-assertion. Go for it. Do it.

Think about how you will be in a year's time. Start from there right here right now. You must move beyond anything you think you know you are. Do it.

The result, of course, can be social chaos, personal catastrophe and psychic disintegration. Boundaries do not merely hem us in. They provide a shape and framework from which we can make an identity. We are social beings. We find, and even transcend, ourselves within and not despite our community. We express ourselves within the grain and disciplines of our circumstances. We do not express, find or transcend very much if we just shout and smell our way 'instinctually'. Also, we are not eagles. Generally, we move and express ourselves in packs. Mill tried to engage with the resultant complications. Nietzsche did not:

> But he who is hated by the people, as the wolf by the dogs – is the free spirit, the enemy of fetters, the non-adorer, the dweller in the woods. (ibid. Second Part, Chapter 30, The Famous Wise Ones)

We cannot all be lone wolves, although there is, let us hope, a place for them. Nietzsche, like Rousseau, loved woods and wilderness and because they, too, are part of the story of humanity, Nietzsche and other romantics are not to be dismissed. Of course, it is easy to laugh. He praised wolves but sat writing and writing. He loved strong brave men on horses riding ruthlessly over their victims. But he was no soldier himself:

> The true man wants two things: danger and play. For that reason he wants woman, as the most dangerous plaything. (ibid. Part 1, 'Of Old and Young Women')

> Man shall be trained for war and woman for the recreation of the warrior. All else is folly. (ibid.)

Most women would have been too strong for Nietzsche to 'play' with. He roared on the page but, by his own reckoning, writers were not so lion-like as soldiers, tyrants, men of action, John Wayne, Captain Kirk. In a feminist, post-feminist, postmodern age these pathetic conceptions of 'strength' and 'assertion' impress only those unreconstructed dinosaur men who are not new men. Machines do the heavy lifting. Men with muscles may become toy boys of female executives. They do not have the status they once had. Power still has sex appeal, of course, but powerful men do not so much lift heavy weights as make heavy-weight decisions affecting whole corporations or nations.

Yes, and here Nietzsche was probably more right than we would care to believe. Power can, still, make its own rules, or can, at least, make special exception for itself. But power, too, now, works mainly in packs, in networks. The power mover does not sit alone, but is on the phone, connecting, persuading, aligning and manoeuvring. Machiavelli will have more to offer this operator than Nietzsche.

Nietzsche might think that this is a triumph of the baboons over the lone wolf. He would prefer the wolf. But the baboons get to write the history books and by his own rules they are therefore to be respected right up to the moment they are overthrown:

> Democratic institutions are quarantine arrangements to combat that ancient pestilence, lust for tyranny: as such they are very useful and very boring. (*The Wanderer and his Shadows*, sec. 289)

Perhaps that is why Nietzsche is so rabid. He despises efforts to 'civilise' and democratise but suspects that his own heroes are going to lose. He worshipped Napoleon, who lost to a congressional alliance. What would he have made of Hitler? There is a more reflective insightful Nietzsche waiting to be seen and heard within all the shouting. This is a Nietzsche that does not, for example, condemn all religion as imprisonment; but only those dead institutions that come to replace the living, spirited, revolutionary first principle:

> As soon as a religion comes to dominate it has as its opponents all those who would have been its first disciples. (*Human, All Too Human*, sec. 118)

But overstatement so easily drowns out potential Nietzschean concerns about originality, integrity and courage:

> For believe me, the secret of realizing the greatest fruitfulness and the greatest enjoyment of existence is: to live dangerously! Build your cities on the slopes of Vesuvius! Send your ships out into uncharted seas! Live in conflict with your equals and with yourselves! Be robbers and ravagers as long as you cannot be rulers and owners, you men of knowledge! The time will soon be past when you could be content to live concealed in the woods like timid deer! (*The Gay Science*, aphorism 283)

Remarks like these are silly, but dangerously so. They soon become offensive:

> The invalid is a parasite on society. In a certain state it is indecent to go on living. To vegetate on in cowardly dependence on physicians and medicaments after the meaning of life, the right to life, has been lost ought to entail the profound contempt of society. (*Twilight of the Idols*, 'Expeditions of an Untimely Man, aphorism 36)

Given that Nietzsche was himself an invalid for so many years, during which time he wrote much of his best work, these observations are richly ironic. Fortunately, Nietzsche does not always want to approve of the victors:

> Even today many educated people think that the victory of Christianity over Greek philosophy is a proof of the superior truth of the former – although in this case it was only the coarser and more violent that conquered the more spiritual and delicate. So far as superior truth is concerned, it is enough to observe that the awakening sciences have allied themselves point by point with the philosophy of Epicurus, but point by point rejected Christianity. (*Human, All Too Human*, sec. 68)

In statements like this he shows a concern for notions of truth and principle that mean more than the view of the victorious. Elsewhere, he is more contemptuous, and more contemporary:

> What then is truth? A mobile army of metaphors, metonyms, and anthropomorphisms – in short, a sum of human relations, which have been enhanced, transposed, and embellished poetically and rhetorically, and which after long use seem firm, canonical, and obligatory to a people: truths are illusions about which one has forgotten that is what they are; metaphors which are worn out and without sensuous power; coins which have lost their pictures and now matter only as metal, no longer as coins. (*On Truth and Lies in an Extra-moral Sense*, pp. 46–7)

Observations like this make it possible to categorise Nietzsche as an early postmodernist, with all the anarchic and irresponsible tendencies that can go with it. If not contemptuous of all notions of truth such postmodern perspective can be overly tolerant of anyone's 'truth'. Opinions disappear since everyone, supposedly carries their own truth as determined from their own 'experience'. Quite a bit of this sort of philosophy has rubbed off on components of the contemporary human potential movement. Truth becomes 'my truth', 'my thing'. 'I do my thing, you do your thing' and who is left to clean up afterwards? Absurdities like this lead (some) counsellors to the judgement that they should not judge at all!

Nietzsche plays with the idea that truth is play and personal perspective, but he then hankers for the truth of the Übermensch and other beautiful losers. Certainly he was out of line with (ahead of?) the conventional truths and wisdom of his, and our own, time. For example:

> Surpass, ye higher men, the petty virtues, the petty policy, the sand-grain considerateness, the ant-hill trumpery, the pitiable comfortableness, the 'happiness of the greatest number! (*Thus Spoke Zarathustra*, Fourth Part, Chapter 73, The Higher Man, Para. 3)

> The doctrine of equality!... There exists no more poisonous poison: for it seems to be preached by justice itself, while it is the end of justice. (*Twilight of the Idols*, Expeditions of an Untimely Man, aphorism 48)

> In the stream – Mighty waters draw much stone and rubble along with them; mighty spirits many stupid and bewildered heads. (*Human, All Too Human*, sec. 541)

Perhaps Nietzsche sensed himself as another beautiful loser:

> I know my fate. One day there will be associated with my name the recollection of something frightful – of a crisis like no other before on earth, of the profoundest collision of conscience, of a decision evoked against everything that until then had been believed in, demanded, sanctified. I am not a man I am dynamite. (*Ecce Homo*)

Nietzsche imagined that he would become 'something frightful' rather than the discoverer of truth and goodness redefined. He was right. Tigers have less space on a crowded earth, and the Nazi's Tiger tanks, for all their magnificent power and superiority, were steadily ground to pieces by weight of numbers, packs of mass-produced T34s from the east and Shermans to the west. In the air, it was the same. The Jagdverband 44 'top gun' air aces in their Me262 jets were overwhelmed by the productivity and (mercifully) greater weight of democrats working in teams. It was (self-defined) elite versus mass attrition. The 'elite' lost. Wagner wrote the music, Nietzsche supplied the poetry and philosophy.[2] The one-thousand-year Reich went down.

It *was* frightful, and liberals can, I believe, say so with good and coherent reasons and not just because liberalism won. In any case, no victory remains eternally secure. What new philosophy, carried within the rucksacks of what new army, will march into the sun to claim its space and time?

❓ Questions

1. How often can you, and should you, challenge clients to the degree that Nietzsche challenges his own readers?

2. Which clients are seeking to tear down masks? To go beyond them? To repaint them?

3. Which clients are seeking authenticity, however painful? A plausible narrative? A consoling rationalisation?

4. Are there various truths from various perspectives? Various perspectives on one truth? Various prejudices, stories and metaphors posing as truth?

EXERCISES

1. Counsellors challenge and support clients, one more than the other depending on counsellor, client and circumstance. Nietzsche is all challenge. He thought that anything else was cowardly and unsupportable if we were to be heroically and authentically human. But what if a client does not seem ready, willing or able to confront painful truth as you see it? Consider what you would do, or should do. Do you, should you, collude with client fiction, pettiness or mediocrity? Discuss whatever examples come to mind.

2. Consider clients who might prosper if they left 'themselves' behind and created a new story rather than merely rehearsing an old one.

Conclusion

Nietzsche confronted cosy liberal and Christian illusions about the nature of truth, identity, power and co-operation. His was a challenge against easy, comfortable answers. Nietzsche's own remedies were often romantic, irresponsible, indulgent and immature. But he was right to highlight shallow theology, tepid morality and lazy versions of liberalism when they fudged more often than faced issues. Nietzsche tore huge holes in 'greatest happiness' conceptions of existence. He showed that these begged key questions rather than answering them. They provided a thin, milky, indolent and complacent vision of psyche, circumstance, principle and purpose. Nietzsche roars that we need to find the courage to celebrate the red blood running in our veins. I think he is right. However, the real challenge, surely, is to do so without over-heating and spilling too much blood in the process. Nietzsche, Mill and Marx, all in different ways, fall short of an adequate answer.

Notes

1. Was Nietzsche's long mental illness primarily a physiological or a psychological phenomenon? I do not know. He died, apparently, of paralysis caused by dormant tertiary syphilis. Certainly he suffered acute physical pain for many years.
2. For Nietzsche, the Übermensch was a transnational, 'transhuman', hero; he had no interest in nationalist agendas. But there is no doubt that his strident teaching was co-opted by German Nationalism in both world wars.

Websites

http://www.usc.edu/dept/annenberg/thomas/nietzsche.html
http://www.pitt.edu/~wbcurry/nietzsche.html
http://ourworld.compuserve.com/homepages/_ahimsa_/w-f_n~.htm
http://userzweb.lightspeed.net/~tameri/nietz.html
http://members.aol.com/KatharenaE/private/Philo/Nietz/nietz.html

Bibliography

F. Nietzsche, *The Gay Science*, trans. W. Kauffmann, Vintage, 1974
F. Nietzsche, *Beyond Good and Evil*, Penguin, 1990
F. Nietzsche, *Ecce Homo*, trans. W. Kauffmann, Penguin, 1992
F. Nietzsche, *Human, All Too Human*, Penguin, 1994
F. Nietzsche, *Thus Spoke Zarathustra*, Prometheus, US, 1994
F. Nietzsche, *The Birth of Tragedy*, Dover, 1995
F. Nietzsche, *On the Genealogy of Morals*, Oxford University Press, 1997
F. Nietzsche, *On Truth and Lies in an Extra-moral Sense*, in *Complete Works of Nietzsche*, trans. R.T. Gray, Stanford University Press, 1998
F. Nietzsche, *Twilight of the Idols*, Oxford University Press, 1998
F. Nietzsche, *The Wanderer and his Shadows*, in *Complete Works of Nietzsche*, trans. R.T. Gray, Stanford University Press, 1998

Chapter 28

Sigmund Freud (1856–1939)

Key Points

- ■ (Psychoanalysis) can become indispensable to all the sciences which are concerned with the evolution of human civilisation

- ■ The religions of mankind must be classed among the mass delusions

- ■ No one has a right to join in a discussion of psychoanalysis who has not had particular experiences which can only be obtained by being analysed oneself

- ■ I am actually not a man of science at all... I am nothing but a conquistador by temperament, an adventurer

- ■ As we see, what decides the purpose of life is simply the programme of the pleasure principle.

Application

- • 'To us he is no more a person now but a whole climate of opinion'. (W.H. Auden, *Another Time* (1940) 'In Memory of Sigmund Freud')
- • A great deal of therapy has, to a greater or lesser degree, used the models, metaphors and methods of Freud
- • This chapter argues that Freud had been far too influential and deserves to continue to decline in significance in the twenty-first century
- • Freud's views about the influence of society and civilisation on the development of personality were pessimistic and damaging
- • Freud had few constructive proposals to make about how citizens and cities, together, could be improved.

Freud is not generally recognised by philosophers as a philosopher, but Auden is, I believe, right in stressing how influential Freud has been in determining how we think about ourselves and our circumstances. Freud's agenda was monstrous in the scale of its ambition:

For we do not consider it at all desirable for psycho-analysis to be swal-
lowed up by medicine and to find its lasting-place in a text-book of psychi-
atry under the heading 'Methods of Treatment'. (*The Essentials of
Psycho-Analysis*, p. 63)

Freud did not want psychoanalysis to be just one of a variety of psychi-
atric treatments. On the contrary, the aim was that Freudian teaching
would underlie and construct culture, arts, social science, the humanities and child rearing. It would replace religion and the priest as the
source of support and inspiration and become a secular religion in its
own right:

> As a 'depth-psychology', a theory of the mental unconscious, it can become
> indispensable to all the sciences which are concerned with the evolution of
> human civilisation and its major institutions such as art, religion and the
> social order. It has already, in my opinion, afforded these sciences consider-
> able help in solving their problems... Psycho-analysis has yet another
> sphere of application... Its application, I mean, to the bringing up of chil-
> dren. (ibid. p. 64)

Parents, teachers and every kind of professional could turn to psychoanalysis for advice and support. In the past they may have relied upon
the priest, but Freud saw religion of any kind as a form of neurosis:

> The religions of mankind must be classed among the mass-delusions of
> this kind. (*Complete Psychological Works of Sigmund Freud*, Vol. 21)

> The whole thing is so patently infantile, so foreign to reality, that to anyone
> with a friendly attitude to humanity it is painful to think that the great
> majority of mortals will never be able to rise above this view of life. (ibid.)

> At this price, by forcibly fixing them in a state of psychic infantilism and by
> drawing them into mass-delusion, religion succeeds in sparing many
> people an individual neurosis. (ibid.)

We needed to grow up and consult someone who really did understand our problems and opportunities, the psychoanalyst. Pastoral work
would still be important, but it ought not to be in the hands of the
clergy, weighed down as they were with medieval mumbo-jumbo:

> A professional lay analyst will have no difficulty in winning as much respect
> as is due to a secular pastoral worker. Indeed, the words, 'secular pastoral
> worker', might well serve as a general formula for describing the function

which the analyst, whether he is a doctor or a layman, has to perform in his relation to the public. (*The Essentials of Psycho-Analysis*, p. 70)

The church had often been criticised for its authoritarianism. The Pope was all powerful and, supposedly, infallible. The hierarchy was non-negotiable. God revealed Himself to those in authority and His Truth was disseminated via the institution that was the Church. Presumably with Freud, who claimed to be a scientist, there would be free discussion, exploration, experiment and concern for evidence? In fact Freud believed that only those who had themselves been 'analysed' could possibly discuss analysis:

> You can believe me when I tell you that we do not enjoy giving an impression of being members of a secret society and of practising a mystical science. Yet we have been obliged to recognise and express as our conviction that no one has a right to join in a discussion of psycho-analysis who has not had particular experiences which can only be obtained by being analysed oneself. (ibid. p. 495)

Could individuals analyse themselves and thereby become eligible to discuss psychoanalysis with Sigmund Freud? According to Freud, only one individual had managed to carry out self-analysis. His name was Sigmund Freud. Everyone else needed to be analysed by someone who could trace their analyst's analysis on a path back to Freud. Freud had apprehended truth and passed it down the line of approved analysts. No other route to insight was legitimate:

> Dear Wilhelm,
> My self-analysis is in fact the most essential thing I have at present and promises to become of the greatest value to me if it reaches its end. (Masson, 1985)

Freud's analysis did reach its end and so he was thereby able to save everyone else from their own delusions if only they would seek suitable guidance. Was this really science? Freud admitted to Fliess in 1900:

> I am actually not a man of science at all... I am nothing but a conquistador by temperament, an adventurer. (ibid.)

That certainly does have a ring of truth to it. Moreover, Freud's conquests were considerable. Socrates believed he was wiser than the norm because he knew that he knew nothing. Freud, on the other hand, had seen psychic truth and could pass it on through a hierarchy of approved Freudian analysts. Is this progress? Personally, I prefer the Socratic insight. It seems to me to be altogether deeper, more humble and more worthwhile.

If you submitted to Freudian teaching, what could you learn, and how?:

> At first the analysing physician could do no more than discover the uncon-scious material that was concealed from the patient, put it together, and, at the right moment, communicate it to him. Psychoanalysis was then first and foremost the art of interpreting. Since this did not solve the thera peutic problem, a further aim came quickly into view: to oblige the patient to confirm the analyst's construction from his own memory. In that endeavour the chief emphasis lay upon the patient's resistances: the art consisted now in uncovering these as quickly as possible, in pointing them out to the patient and in inducing him by human influence – this was where suggestion operating as 'transference' played its part – to abandon his resistances. (*The Essentials of Psycho-Analysis*, p. 227)

The analyst interpreted, brought the patient's memories back to consciousness, and uncovered the resistances that patients utilised in order to avoid facing the truth. If only the patient dropped their resis-tance, what might they learn?:

> Pressing out the contents of the blackheads is clearly to him a substitute for masturbation. The cavity which then appears owing to his fault is the female genital, that is, the fulfilment of the threat of castration (or the fantasy representing that threat) provoked by his masturbation. (ibid. p. 170)

A patient might, of course, dare to argue that he pressed blackheads for other reasons; that the cavity had very little relation or resemblance to the female genital; and that masturbation was generally unconnected with picking blackheads. Such a patient would be deemed 'resistant' and their interpretations were illegitimate. It was the therapist's role to interpret and the patient's task was to overcome resistance to thera-peutic interpretation. You could not pick and choose interpretations. It was all or nothing. And you could not yourself become a therapist if you had not accepted the interpretations of your own therapist.

In the process, you would therefore have no choice but to accept a great deal of new, secular, Freudian terminology. And, given that Freud wished to colonise the entire culture with his ideas, we would all have to think whatever Freud thought. For example:

> Sooner or later the child, who is so proud of his possession of a penis, has a view of the genital region of a little girl, and cannot help being convinced of the absence of a penis in a creature who is so like himself. With this, the loss of his own penis becomes imaginable, and the threat of castration takes its deferred effect. (ibid. p. 397)

> The wish to get the longed-for penis eventually in spite of everything may contribute to the motives that drive a mature woman to analysis… One cannot very well doubt the importance of envy for the penis. (ibid. p. 424)

> The discovery that she is castrated is a turning-point in a girl's growth. (ibid. p. 424)

Do women believe that they have been castrated? Is this a turning point in their development? Are boys really so proud and girls so envious? Do boys really fear castration, either literal or symbolic? Where is the evidence? Where is the methodology for assembling evidence? Freud claimed to be a scientist but he seems nearer to being honest in his confession to Fliess that he was a 'conquistador by temperament, an adventurer', (not to say confidence trickster).

Jung became increasingly impatient with the guruism and with Freud's low opinion of religion. It was all very well for analysts to treat their patients like ignorant children. But Jung believed that the relationship should be different with trainee analysts. He wrote:

> Your technique of treating your pupils like patients is a blunder. In that way you produce either slavish sons or impudent puppies (Adler-Stekel and the whole insolent gang now throwing their weight about in Vienna). I am objective enough to see through your little trick. You go about sniffing out all the symptomatic actions in your vicinity, thus reducing everyone to the level of sons and daughters who blushingly admit the existence of their faults. Meanwhile you remain on top as the father, sitting pretty. (McGuire, 1974)

No wonder that Jung broke with Freud, as did most other heavyweight rivals who decided that they could, and should, carve reputations of their own. The Church of Freud thereby broke up, as churches do, into sects of many kinds.

292 Philosophy for Counselling and Psychotherapy

Freud, like Locke and Descartes before him, believed that 'self', at least on the surface, was something we each felt confident we knew and could know:

> Normally, there is nothing of which we are more certain than the feeling of our self, of our own ego. This ego appears to us as something autonomous and unitary, marked off distinctly from else. (*Complete Psychological Works of Sigmund Freud*, Vol. 21)

Freud thereby echoes, although does not acknowledge, Locke. But he shows little awareness of subsequent critics of this naïve introspectionism, from Hume onwards. Freud's 'self' was more troubled, turbulent and divided, though, than the self of Locke or Descartes:

> We are warned by a proverb against serving two masters at the same time. The poor ego has things even worse: it serves three severe masters and does what it can to bring their claims and demands into harmony with one another. These claims are always divergent and often seem incompatible. No wonder that the ego often fails in its task. Its three tyrannical masters are the external world, the super-ego and the id. (*The Essentials of Psycho-Analysis*, p. 502)

Because these three sub-personalities are so familiar, I will be very brief with them:

> We approach the id with analogies: we call it a chaos, a cauldron full of seething excitations. (ibid. p. 498)

> The super-ego is the representative for us of every moral restriction, the advocate of a striving towards perfection – it is, in short, as much as we have been able to grasp psychologically of what is described as the higher side of human life. (ibid. p. 493)

Ego tried to compromise between the demands of the pleasure-seeking animal ego and the perfectionistic super-ego while at the same time coping with the demands of other people and circumstances. But what were these sub-personalities? Were they real, albeit mental or metaphysical entities, or just ways of thinking about self? Were they just analogies, metaphors?:

> In psychology we can only describe things by the help of analogies. There is nothing peculiar in this; it is the case elsewhere as well. But we have

constantly to keep changing these analogies, for none of them lasts us long enough. (ibid. p. 17)

In fact, Freud did not pay much attention to analogies and models of self that had preceded his own thinking. Since philosophers and others prior to Freud had not benefited from psychoanalysis and were, unlike Freud, incapable of analysing themselves, none of them had the status of Freud. Indeed, it was Freud who would take it upon himself to analyse what and why they 'really' thought and felt as they did. Leonardo da Vinci, for example, may have been a highly original thinker, but Sigmund Freud knew Leonardo better than the Italian knew himself, and thus felt quite free to tell the world what he had 'discovered' in his 'researches'.

The Greeks, as we have seen, had been concerned to show how human beings were different from animals and how civilisation was preferable to barbarism. Hume, likewise, extolled the virtues of cultivation, discretion, reflection, refinement. Freud, contrariwise attended to how we were *similar* both to animals and to machines. This was an attractive package to those tired of Victorian hypocrisy and sceptical of an establishment that could bring us to the barbarities of the First World War. Our basic drives operated according to the 'pleasure' principle. We sought to maximise pleasure and avoid pain. But what was pleasure? Were the pleasures of philosophers the same as the pleasures of the pig? If pleasure was simply defined as those many and various things that we sought then yes we sought pleasure. But the term, because it could mean anything, then meant nothing at all. Freud, like the Utilitarians, failed to see the problem but did distinguish between 'lower' and 'higher' courses of action:

> It is impossible to escape the impression that people commonly use false standards of measurement – that they seek power, success and wealth for themselves and admire them in others, and that they underestimate what is of true value in life. (*Complete Psychological Works of Sigmund Freud*, Vol. 21)

Freud did not show how the 'true', 'better' and 'higher' could be distinguished from inferior versions and he tended to the mechanistic and atomistic view that what was most 'real' were the instincts, the basic drives, the animal within.

> As we see, what decides the purpose of life is simply the programme of the pleasure principle. (ibid.)

This was a bleak picture. It shared none of the Greek optimism concerning the power of city-states to civilise and enhance the options, identity and sophistication of its inhabitants:

> Generally speaking, our civilisation is built up on the suppression of instincts. (ibid.)

Instinctual man needed to be suppressed if city life was to be achievable at all. However, Freud suspected that civilisation frustrated, twisted and stunted people at least as much as it did them much good:

> Civilised man has exchanged a portion of his possibilities of happiness for a portion of security. (ibid.)

Plato and Aristotle would have been appalled at the idea that cities only provided security. They created possibilities of personal identity, development, discipline, detachment and fulfilment that simply did not exist within 'natural' or barbaric settings. For the Greeks, cities were the cradle of civilisation. For Freud, as with Rousseau, cities were more like a cage:

> If civilisation imposes such great sacrifices not only on man's sexuality but on his aggressivity, we can understand better why it is hard for him to be happy in that civilisation. In fact, primitive man was better off in knowing no restrictions of instinct. (ibid.)

Freud, like Rousseau, thereby played with the idea that primitive people were happier and more authentic than city dwellers. Freud failed to see, as Hobbes had proposed, that without society our lives would be nasty brutish and short. He did accept that, within cities and a civilised society, some could produce and others could appreciate great art, culture and creation of many kinds. But all this creativity was 'essentially' and 'really' just a displacement, or 'sublimation', of sexual energies that could not find a relief in their 'natural' outlet:

> To extend this process of displacement indefinitely is, however, certainly not possible, any more than is the case with the transformation of heat into mechanical energy in our machines. A certain amount of direct sexual satisfaction seems to be indispensable for most organisations. (ibid.)

In this chapter of his writing Freud put inverted commas around 'civilised'. He did not share Rousseau's romanticism about primitive wholesomeness, and was as pessimistic as Schopenhauer (though less of a *bon viveur*). His description of civilised humanity was not a Greek celebration of personal and collective progress and development. On the contrary, Freud saw mainly crippled, stunted, frustrated, miserable and confused individuals struggling to reconcile their 'drives' with their conscience and their circumstances. Above all, they suffered because they did not know what to do with their sexuality:

> This brings us to the question whether sexual intercourse in legal marriage can offer full compensation for the restrictions imposed before marriage. There is such an abundance of material supporting a reply in the negative that we must give only the briefest summary of it. (ibid.)

> In the vast majority of cases the struggle against sexuality eats up the energy available in a character and this at the very time when a young man is in need of all his forces in order to win his share and place in society. (ibid.)

> The result is that when the girl's parental authorities suddenly allow her to fall in love, she is unequal to this psychical achievement and enters marriage uncertain of her own feelings. In consequence of this artificial retardation in her function of love, she has nothing but disappointments to offer the man who has saved up all his desire for her. (ibid.)

This neurosis around our sexuality was destructive because it set the pattern for so much else in our lives. Other components became correspondingly twisted:

> The sexual behaviour of a human being often *lays down the pattern* for all his other modes of reacting to life. (ibid.)

> His behaviour will be conciliatory and resigned rather than vigorous in other spheres of life as well. (ibid.)

Sexual mores damaged everybody, but, in Freud's view, they were absolutely lethal for women:

> I think that the undoubted intellectual inferiority of so many women can rather be traced back to the inhibition of thought necessitated by sexual suppression. (ibid.)

No wonder we were all so miserable. But Freud could not see any easy solution or escape from the unavoidable struggle between super-ego and id. In any case, it was a part of our nature that happiness of any kind was very difficult to feel for more than a fleeting moment:

> We are so made that we can derive intense enjoyment only from a contrast and very little from a state of things. Thus our possibilities of happiness are already restricted by our constitution. Unhappiness is much less difficult to experience. (ibid.)

If we could reduce our hysterical misery to common unhappiness that would be progress of a kind. In any case, why on earth should we expect to be happy?:

> One feels inclined to say that the intention that man should be 'happy' is not included in the plan of 'Creation'. (ibid.)

Perhaps we could find happiness and fulfilment within religion? Perhaps, thought Freud, but only by living in illusion. God was a father substitute for people who would not, or could not, grow up. Mystical experience was an 'oceanic feeling' for those seeking to return to the nirvana of the womb. The oriental route to 'happiness' could only be achieved by entirely cauterising all our expectations and drives. This, for Freud, was a delusional remoulding of reality:

> The extreme form of this is brought about by killing off the instincts, as is prescribed by the worldly wisdom of the East and practised by Yoga. (ibid.)

Western religions tried another tack, pleasure was not renounced altogether, but was postponed to the life hereafter:

> Following consistently along these lines, *religions* have been able to effect absolute renunciation of pleasure in this life by means of the promise of compensation in a future existence; but they have not by this means achieved a conquest of the pleasure principle. (ibid.)

Freud, unlike Rousseau, did not believe that we could, or should, escape the cities and become 'real' again within some pastoral Eden. Civilisation was necessary, but:

> The price we pay for our advance in civilisation is a loss of happiness through the heightening of the sense of guilt. (ibid.)

If anything, though, the sum total of happiness ought to be decreased still further since, in Freud's view, too many people did not feel guilty *enough:*

> The stars are indeed magnificent, but as regards conscience God has done an uneven and careless piece of work, for a large majority of men have brought along with them only a modest amount of it or scarcely enough to be worth mentioning. (*The Essentials of Psycho-Analysis*, p. 488)

It was an altogether miserable, gloomy and jaundiced view, but it was not one that could be discussed with Freud on equal terms since he was analysed, and thereby self-aware, and we, most of us, were not. According to Freud, our quintessentially human characteristics, our highest goals, ideals and achievements, were displacements of the more 'real' sexual energies that society could not afford to let us indulge. So what were we to do? What was the point of it all?:

> The question of the purpose of human life has been raised countless times; it has never received a satisfactory answer and perhaps does not admit of one. (*Complete Psychological Works of Sigmund Freud*, Vol. 21)

Could we not bond together in caring, sharing concern and compassion for each other? Could we not learn to co-operate and cultivate our society and ourselves?:

> It is always possible to bind together a considerable number of people in love, so long as there are other people left over to receive the manifestations of their aggressiveness. (ibid.)

Was our technical progress a reason for hope and/or consolation? What about all the improvements we had made in our control over Nature, our labour-saving gadgetry, our toys, our status symbols and our cultural and artistic exploration?:

> Men have gained control over the forces of nature to such an extent that with their help they would have no difficulty in exterminating one another to the last man. They know this and hence comes a large part of their current unrest, their unhappiness and their mood of anxiety. (ibid.)

Freud's stoicism and pessimism was no doubt influenced by the First World War, the clear onset of the second, and painful illness in old age. He promised that, via analysis, we could come to know ourselves better and learn ways of coping with our contradictory inclinations and less than wonderful circumstances:

> Its intention is indeed to strengthen the ego, to make it more independent of the super-ego, to widen its field of perception and enlarge its organisation, so that it can appropriate fresh portions of the id. Where id was, there shall ego be. It is a work of culture – not unlike the draining of the Zuider Zee. (*The Essentials of Psycho-Analysis*, p. 504)

But Freud had no basis for imagining that psychoanalysts had a privileged insight into themselves, others or reality at large. His views of the self were interesting, as metaphor, but nothing like as new as he claimed. He paid insufficient heed to the equally worthy views of so many others. Many of his ideas, as with all of us, were stillborn dead. Worst of all, Freud's effort to give psychoanalysis complete hegemony on western society's arts, culture and education was an act of megalomania almost unheard of in our cultural history.

? Questions

1. Is the concept of 'the unconscious' a useful form of metaphysics? Or are we merely *not* conscious of much within and around us?

2. How far does Freud influence your own thinking and practice?

3. What, in your view, remains of Freud's teaching that is worth keeping?

4. Which of Freud's ideas were really new? Which were old dressed in what, at the turn of the Nineteenth century, were modern metaphors?

5. When clients disagree with the Freudian analyst they are being 'resistant'. If so, how can valid objections to analysis ever be considered?

EXERCISES

1. Write down your ideas concerning why Freud was so influential among twentieth-century intelligentsia.

2. Compare Freud's super-ego, ego and id with Christian teaching of angels, humans and demons. Note the similarities and differences.

3. Compare Freud's analyses of internal conflict with those of Plato and Aristotle. What are their strengths and weaknesses?

4. Consider how far Freud's criticisms of religion are valid.

5. Consider the problem of therapist interpretation. Why should, should not, clients accept therapist interpretations?

Conclusion

Freud created a narrative about human development that combined mythical themes with contemporary (pseudo) scientific metaphors. It was an appealing brew since it filled the gap left by a decaying Christianity. It offered both excitement and (the illusion of) dispassionate and heroic self-enquiry. Freud's view that societies were essentially oppressive and constraining, albeit necessary, has been destructive. It has distracted too many intelligent people away from the ever-pressing problem of nurturing, defending and developing a civilised society. Societies protect and define individuals, but require the active and mature participation of committed citizens. Freud has thereby contributed to the twentieth-century preoccupation with 'self'. This navel gazing has been sterile for individuals and damaging to society. Freud's views about personal identity were philosophically naïve and took little account of the development of the subject since John Locke. His claims to be a 'scientist' and to have based his theories on biological principles have not stood the test of time.

Websites

http://www.geocities.com/Athens/4753/menu.html
http://plaza.interport.net/nypsan/
http://plaza.interport.net/nypsan/freudarc.html
http://www.csulb.edu/~mfiebert/freud.htm

Bibliography

S. Freud, *Totem and Taboo*, Ark, 1983
S. Freud, *Beyond the Pleasure Principle*, W.W. Norton, 1990
S. Freud, *Interpretation of Dreams*, Penguin, 1991
S. Freud, *Introductory Lectures on Psychoanalysis*, Penguin, 1991
S. Freud, in A. Freud, *The Essentials of Psycho-Analysis*, Penguin 1991
S. Freud, *Two Short Accounts of Psychoanalysis*, Penguin, 1991
S. Freud in *Complete Psychological Works of Sigmund Freud*, ed. J. Strachey Norton, 1999
W. McGuire (ed.) *The Freud/Jung Letters: The Correspondence between Sigmund Freud and Carl Jung*, Princeton University Press, 1974
J.M. Masson (ed.) *The Complete Letters of Sigmund Freud to Wilhelm Fliess, 1887–1904*, Harvard University Press, 1985

Chapter 29

Carl Gustav Jung (1875–1961)

_____ **Key Points** _____

- ■ Jung criticised Freud for reducing human motivation to sexual drives and the 'pleasure principle'

- ■ The spiritual dimension of existence was not, as Freud believed, an infantile avoidance of adulthood, but a feature of growing maturity and insight

- ■ Philosophy underpinned therapy; we needed to look far and wide, and include oriental teaching, for ideas and inspiration

- ■ We were still beginners in our understanding of therapy. Therefore we needed humility concerning the extent of our ignorance

- ■ Human qualities mattered more than professional qualifications.

_____ *Application* _____

- • Jung explored the relation between the growth of therapy and the decline of the church
- • He encouraged an exploratory attitude rather than a rigid allegiance to systems
- • His preoccupation with the successful and the sophisticated is less helpful for those seeking more basic skills and insights
- • Jung was an elitist who believed that most wanted to do as others did rather than find out who they were.

My life has been permeated and held together by one idea and one goal: namely, to penetrate into the secret of the personality. (Storr, p. 253)

Jung, as first president of the International Psychoanalytic Association, was closely involved with Freud. Eventually each went his own way, and Jung's criticism (see Chapter 28) helps to show why. Freud, as we have seen, thought he could explain our 'higher' aspirations in terms of displaced sexual energy. Jung disapproved of Freud's focus on sex and on Alfred Adler's preoccupation with power:

> Both schools, to my way of thinking, deserve reproach for over-emphasising the pathological aspect of life and for interpreting man too exclusively in the light of his defects. A convincing example of this in Freud's case is his inability to understand religious experience, as is clearly shown in his book: 'The Future of an Illusion'. (*Modern Man in Search of a Soul*, p. 134)

Jung claimed to owe a great debt to Freud and denied that they were opponents. However, his criticism of Freud was sharp:

> Freud began by taking sexuality as the only psychic driving power, and only after my break with him did he grant an equal status to other psychic activities as well. (ibid. p. 138)

Sometimes Jung was positively damning of Freud:

> It was a great mistake on Freud's part to turn his back on philosophy. Not once does he criticise his premises or even the assumptions that underlie his personal outlook. (ibid. p. 135)

Jung was more hesitant, humble and tentative about the state of psychological knowledge:

> The very number of present-day 'psychologies' amounts to a confession of perplexity. (ibid. p. 33)

But Jung was convinced that any kind of reductive approach that analysed personality purely in terms of drives and material circumstances was doomed to miss the essence of humanity. Even the Freudian 'super-ego', with its perfection principle and its embodiment of human ideals was, to Jung's taste, overly mechanistic and devoid of life:

> As for Freud's idea of the 'super-ego', it is a furtive attempt to smuggle in his time-honoured image of Jehovah in the dress of psychological theory. When one does things like that, it is better to say so openly. For my part, I prefer to call things by the names under which they have always been known. (ibid. p. 141)

In Jung's view, Freud too often sought to explain human personality in terms of human pathology. We were not all neurotic all the time.

Admittedly, we could suffer if we did not feel normal, functioning, average and effective members of society. But Jung was actually more interested in successful patients; people who had already 'made it' in society by all the usual criteria of social success, yet who still did not know what to make of it:

> To be 'normal' is a splendid ideal for the unsuccessful, for all those who have not yet found an adaptation. But for people who have far more ability than the average, for whom it was never hard to gain success and to accomplish their share of the world's work – for them restriction to the normal signifies the bed of Procrustes, unbearable boredom, infernal sterility and hopelessness. (ibid. p. 55)

> About a third of my cases are suffering from no clinically definable neurosis, but from the senselessness and emptiness of their lives. (ibid. p. 70)

Jung's patients tended to be rich, intelligent, confident, successful and powerful. So what was the matter with them? They did not suffer material or psychological deprivation; rather, many seemed to be going through a spiritual crisis:

> Among all my patients in the second half of life – that is to say, over thirty-five – there has not been one whose problem in the last resort was not that of finding a religious outlook on life. (ibid. p. 264)

Jung's patients did not need to explore ways in which they could make their mark, establish a position or an identity. They had done all that. Now they were bored by position, weighed down by their own weight, impatient with, and imprisoned within, their image. What was the point of it all? What did it matter? Why go on, and how?:

> I said just now that we have no schools for forty-year-olds. That is not quite true. Our religions were always such schools in the past, but how many people regard them as such today? How many of us older persons have really been brought up in such a school and prepared for the second half of life, for old age, death and eternity? (ibid. p. 125)

Established religion no longer carried the authority it once did. People did not so readily turn to the priest for explanation, comfort or absolution. Nietzsche, as we have seen, had pronounced on the non-existence of any deity:

When Nietzsche said 'God is dead', he uttered a truth which is valid for the greater part of Europe. People were influenced by it not because he said so, but because it stated a widespread psychological fact. The consequences were not long delayed: after the fog of -isms, the catastrophe. (Storr, p. 247)

Jung was alarmed by the result. Could we really manage on our own?:

The individual who is not anchored in God can offer no resistance on his own resources to the physical and moral blandishments of the world. (*The Undiscovered Self*, p. 24)

Clearly our culture was in crisis. Even the clergy seemed to have lost faith in their own institution and were beginning to turn to Freud and other analysts for insight and understanding:

The fact that many clergymen seek support or practical help from Freud's theory of sexuality or Adler's theory of power is astonishing, inasmuch as both these theories are hostile to spiritual values, being, as I have said, psychology without the psyche. They are rational methods of treatment which actually hinder the realisation of meaningful experience. (*Modern Man in Search of a Soul*, p. 263)

Christian teaching seemed to have lost its way. Jung did not believe that a secular-based psychotherapy could fill its place. So where could we turn if we were to find meaning, direction and inspiration? Jung looked both to the orient and at the mystical roots within early western teaching. Our contemporary culture could learn a great deal from these:

Western man is held in thrall by the 'ten thousand things'; he sees only particulars, he is ego-bound and thing-bound, and unaware of the deep root of all being. Eastern man, on the other hand, experiences the world of particulars and even his own ego, like a dream; he is rooted essentially in the 'Ground', which attracts him so powerfully that his relations with the world are relativized to a degree that is often incomprehensible to us. (Storr, p. 257)

Contemporary western philosophy was mechanistic and materialistic. It was disenchanting, demoralising and it disconnected us from any renewing sense of ourselves and our environment. Since it had no place for soul, it was itself soul destroying. Philosophy mattered to Jung. It was not mere academic abstraction. It could be life making or life breaking, arid or empowering. It fed or starved the psyche. It celebrated or ignored our humanity. It defined or dissolved the self. It was the floor and foundation upon which other activity stood, or through which it, and we, would fall.

Oriental philosophy might not pay enough attention to the material, but in the west we were too much in the thrall of day-to-day stuff and we lost sight of underlying spirit or principle:

> The Western attitude, with its emphasis on the object, tends to fix the ideal – Christ – in its outward aspect and thus to rob it of its mysterious relation to the inner man. It is this prejudice, for instance, which impels the Protestant interpreters of the Bible to interpret the Kingdom of God as 'among you' instead of 'within you'. (ibid. p. 258)

'The Kingdom of God is *within* you'. What did this mean? That we should make a God of 'self'? This was Sartre's view but Jung disagreed. We needed to hold a sense of awe, wonder and reverence both about God and about self, each was larger and more mysterious than we knew. People might think they knew who they were, and everyone felt free to contribute an opinion on the nature of psyche, personality and other psychological questions:

> But anyone who really knows the human psyche will agree with me when I say that it is one of the darkest and most mysterious regions of our experience. (ibid. p. 253)

Who are you? At one level the question is simple, self evident, immediate, obvious and familiar. But as you push at it more deeply it can become ever more mysterious:

> Most people confuse self-knowledge with knowledge of their conscious ego-personalities. Anyone who has any ego-consciousness at all takes it for granted that he knows himself. But the ego knows only its own contents, not the unconscious and its contents. (*The Undiscovered Self*, p. 351)

We were unconscious (although I prefer '*not* conscious') of most of what went on within and around us. Jung studied Kant, Schopenhauer, Nietzsche, the early gnostics, Hinduism and alchemy in order to break beneath surface appearances of self. Contemporary psychology was nothing like so new as it claimed and should borrow from, and acknowledge its debts to, earlier thinkers. For example:

It is a fact that the beginnings of psychoanalysis were fundamentally nothing else than the scientific rediscovery of an ancient truth; even the name catharsis (or cleansing), which was given to the earliest method of treatment, comes from the Greek initiation rites. (*Modern Man in Search of a Soul*, p. 40)

Within gnostic teaching (Greco-Roman, *c.* second century AD), God was within self and self was within God. The spiritual dimensions of existence were more fundamental than the material and existed outside our categories of space and time. This teaching drew from oriental and Platonic philosophies. Jung adapted it and drew in Kant's notion of synthetic *a priori* categories. There was a 'collective unconscious' that we all shared. There were 'archetypes', pre-existing structures and categories of thought and feeling, which connected and formed us and pointed to the underlying unity of all existence. There was more to heaven and earth than could be divined in all our philosophies. Our arid mechanical and material conception of existence sapped and undermined our spirit. It was narrow, shallow and false. It had been a productive model within nineteenth-century physics but had been entirely jettisoned within the thinking of twentieth-century physicists:

Even physics volatilizes our material world. (ibid. p. 245)

Jung was fascinated by this and kept abreast of contemporary developments within natural science via his collaboration with the physicist Wolfgang Pauli. We could imagine that material reality was substantial and solid in relation to metaphysics. But look at the reality. Physicists had sought to discover the 'basic grit' of material objects by breaking them down into smaller and smaller units. They had imagined that atoms were the basic building bricks, solid spheres moving in vast empty spaces. But they too could be broken further, they were waves as much as particles, their movement was discontinuous, they disappeared and reappeared, they interacted with each other mysteriously and instantaneously over immense distances, their position and velocity were not both precisely knowable even in principle. The observer influenced the nature of their reality. It was anything but prosaic; it was literally fantastic:

We delude ourselves with the thought that we know much more about matter than about a metaphysical mind, and so we overestimate physical causation and believe that it alone affords us a true explanation of life. But matter is just as inscrutable as mind. (ibid. p. 205)

So we needed to retain a sense of humility, awe and wonder about both the physical and the mental or spiritual. Did we know much about either and were they so different at more fundamental levels of understanding?:

> The distinction between mind and body is an artificial dichotomy, a discrimination which is unquestionably based far more on the peculiarity of intellectual understanding than on the nature of things. (ibid. p. 85)

Certainly we had a long way to go in understanding mind and we would be most unwise to think that we had moved ahead of previous thinking on the subject. Since westerners were so focused on the material, and disinclined to look within, we would do well to consider oriental efforts to understand the psyche:

> Psychoanalysis itself and the lines of thought to which it gives rise – surely a distinctly Western development – are only a beginner's attempt compared to what is an immemorial art in the East. (ibid. p. 249)

In 'finding oneself', therefore, one needed to draw as widely as possible from sources within both western and oriental philosophy, both ancient and modern. In so doing, was the 'self' ever to be realised as a final destination? Of course not:

> Personality, as the complete realisation of our whole being, is an unattainable ideal. But unattainability is no argument against the ideal, for ideals are only signposts, never the goal. (Storr, p. 196)

In fact Jung did not believe that self-realisation was a serious agenda for most people:

> To develop ones own personality is indeed an unpopular undertaking, a deviation that is highly uncongenial to the herd. (ibid. p. 198)

Most of us wanted to fit in, to do as others did, to live like sheep, to jump as, and when, others jumped. Thinking and feeling for oneself was far too painful, dangerous and inconvenient. Jung was an elitist much influenced by Nietzsche:

> The great liberating deeds of world history have sprung from leading personalities and never from the inert mass, which is at all times secondary and can only be prodded into activity by the demagogue. (ibid. p. 191)

To be truly human, to find one's own vocation and personality was a rare event. Most of us were lost in habit, convention, fashion and convenience. We adopted whatever mask, or 'persona', was offered to us. We wanted someone to tell us who we were rather than find out for ourselves. We took a 'personality' off the peg along with the clothing and other accoutrements with which it was dressed:

> Personality is the supreme realisation of the innate idiosyncrasy of a living being. It is an act of high courage flung in the face of life, the absolute affirmation of all that constitutes the individual, the most successful adaptation to the universal conditions of existence coupled with the greatest possible freedom for self-determination. (ibid. p. 195)

To find ourselves we needed to look around. But, above all, we had to look and listen within and not be carried away by the noise and patter of everyday chatter and action.

> The inner voice is the voice of a fuller life, of a wider, more comprehensive consciousness. (ibid. p. 208)

Was the voice within authentic or illusory? It could be hard to know but this was no excuse to ignore it. We were part of a larger mystery of existence. We did not need to listen to the herd. If we stayed quiet we might hear that voice within and thereby discover our vocation. Nowadays, 'vocational education' tends to describe humdrum day to day training for daily paid employment. For Jung, however, our vocation was to find our highest self, our individual personality, our role and function as determined by deeper, noumenal, spiritual forces:

> Anyone with a vocation hears the voice of the inner man: he is called... It is what is commonly called *vocation*: an irrational factor that destines a man to emancipate himself from the herd and from its well-worn paths. (ibid. p. 199)

Finding oneself might best be achieved, however, in the company of a fellow traveller, guide, soul mate or therapist. Jung did not advise a reductive, mechanistic Freudian psychoanalyst. Neither was Adlerian preoccupation with power of much use:

> Adler himself does not call his teaching 'psychoanalysis', but 'individual psychology'; while I prefer to call my own approach 'analytical psychology', (*Modern Man in Search of a Soul*, p. 32)

Jungian analytic psychology, as you might expect, was recommended as the most suitable system for the person on a spiritual quest, but Jung was quick to acknowledge that much of what he, and other contemporary therapists, were doing had been done by others, for centuries, within other cultures and traditions. The style, the accoutrements, the language might be different; but much of the underlying substance was the same. For example, healing had a great deal to do with confessing one's own limitations and preoccupations to another. Established religions had been dealing in this activity for centuries:

> It is only with the help of confession that I am able to throw myself into the arms of humanity freed at last from the burden of moral exile. (ibid. p. 41)

Jung was highly critical of any attempts to mechanise such healing activity. It could not be neatly boiled down into checklists, quality standards and learning outcomes:

> The meeting of two personalities is like the contact of two chemical substances: if there is any reaction, both are transformed. (ibid. p. 57)

Because both individuals were transformed it was absurd to imagine that the therapist, psychologist, or whoever, could be detached, disinterested, neutral and objective:

> It is futile for the doctor to shield himself from the influence of the patient and to surround himself with a smoke-screen of fatherly and professional authority. (ibid. p. 57)

This raised questions about how you could train people in such healing activity. Which professional training route would reliably deliver what results?:

> The medical diploma is no longer the crucial thing, but human quality instead. (ibid. p. 61)

This debate continues to this day, of course, and I am not convinced that we have made much progress with it in the last fifty years. Perhaps we have not done so in the last five hundred years?

Jung himself introduced 'new' concepts such as 'anima' and 'animus' (the male and female components within all personalities), and 'introvert' and 'extravert', which have become so much a part of the language that they hardly need explaining. But Jung was exploratory rather than dogmatic about these ways of thinking about people. He searched far and wide for ideas and inspiration concerning what was helpful, healing, and transforming.

Given our poor sense of history, it is easy to imagine that our ideas are new when they are not. For example, the ecumenical movement within contemporary Christianity would do well to explore Manichaeism. Mani, born in the third century AD in Babylonia, spread his message over most of the Roman world. He believed he was one of a long line of prophets that included Adam, the Buddha, Zoroaster and Jesus. What they had in common was, for Mani, far more important than the differences. This was considered heretical within Christianity. But millions have died in order to maintain the 'purity' of Christian teaching.

Jung's exploration of alchemy is more difficult to appreciate. Matter may be more fantastic than we think but this does not give us a licence to engage in fabulous metaphysical speculation about mind unless we discipline the activity in some way. Alchemists, apparently, were not merely trying to turn base metals into gold; they were also trying to find the 'gold' within the base components of the human soul. In other words to find the way of bringing out the best in each of us. This is worthy enough but I, myself, do not find any enlightenment on the subject of personal development within the various formulae, mantras and mandala paintings of Jung. But perhaps I am being too rigid?:

> My aim is to bring about a psychic state in which my patient begins to experiment with his own nature – a state of fluidity, change and growth, in which there is no longer anything eternally fixed and hopelessly petrified. (ibid. p. 76)

This makes sense, and I am more impressed with Jung's playful, exploratory approach to dreams and other material, as compared with Freud's doctrinaire and arbitrary interpretations.

I also admire Jung's awareness of the way in which introspection could itself become indulgent and fanciful. Catharsis was right when the time and place were right, but there were other goals and we needed to maintain a sense of perspective:

> Self-restraint is healthful and beneficial; it is even a virtue. This is why we find self-discipline to have been one of man's earliest moral attainments. (ibid. p. 38)

Jung was primarily concerned with spiritual questions yet he operated outside all the established religions and within an essentially secular quasi-medical profession. The young might have difficulty engaging with, and establishing themselves within, their lives; but Jung was most interested in the spiritual concerns of more elderly patients:

> Just as the youthful neurotic is afraid of life, so the older one shrinks back from death. (ibid. p. 67)

What could Jung offer such people?:

> From the standpoint of psychotherapy it would therefore be desirable to think of death as only a transition – one part of a life-process whose extent and duration escape our knowledge. (Storr, p. 129)

People more readily sacrificed their lives when they believed that there was pie in the sky when they died. But could we, and should we, try to convince ourselves in the belief in a cosmic Father Christmas?

Jung drew back from such dogmatic fantasy. He explored the questions, and the efforts of previous seekers, but did not pretend to be able to peddle definitive answers. In any case, if we were brave and strong we did not need to have certainties and securities about these, or other matters. But Jung had no illusions. Those who found and expressed even the smallest part of their own individuality were but a tiny fraction of the population as a whole. Jung drew back (but not very far back) from the contempt felt by Nietzsche for 'the herd'. His elitism does not seem to have put him at odds with Nazi fantasies of 'Aryan superiority'. But he certainly did not share Nietzsche's rejection of the past as backward and inferior to the developing 'overman'. On the contrary, the self we ever managed to know was just the tip of an iceberg. What we did not know, was vast, drawn from the past, and shared within the communion of humanity and life more generally:

> If it were permissible to personify the unconscious, we might call it a collective human being combining the characteristics of both sexes, transcending youth and age, birth and death, and, from having at his command a human experience of one or two million years, almost immortal. (*Modern Man in Search of a Soul*, p. 215)

With study and effort we could make some of this heritage of humanity more conscious and available to us. But, how far could we manage to turn wise words into brave actions?:

And where are the great and wise men who do not merely talk about the meaning of life and of the world, but really possess it? (ibid. p. 261)

❓ Questions

1. What proportion of your own clients are suffering primarily a spiritual crisis? How do you know? How do you respond?

2. How far do you think philosophy is important for counselling, therapy and other care work? Which philosophies most influence your own practice?

3. Jung's clients were generally very prosperous. Do we have to be materially comfortable before we can attend to spiritual matters? Or is poverty and simplicity the preferred route to the kingdom of heaven?

4. 'Wonderful. Counsellor. Almighty God, the everlasting father. The Prince of Peace' (from Handel's *Messiah*). Can, and should, counselling practice be separated from spiritual practice?

EXERCISES

1. Review your own theory and practice. What, if any, changes and additions do you envisage over the next three years?

2. Consider the proliferation of therapeutic theories and practices. Is an ecumenical movement possible/desirable?

3. Discuss your own relations with clients. Who have most influenced and changed you? How? Why? What 'chemical reactions' with clients have been most significant?

4. Assess the efforts of counsellors to be detached and impartial. In what ways is this desirable and appropriate? Illusory and unhelpful?

Conclusion

Jung explored the relation between psychotherapy and religion. Therapy could not ignore philosophy since the latter provided the foundations, the concepts, the values and the boundaries of therapeutic activity. Philosophies, east and west, deserved attention and Jung combined an interest in medieval alchemy, early Christian occultism and twentieth-century physics. He was not much interested in unsophisticated, unsuccessful people suffering from basic social dysfunction.

But meaning, purpose and inspiration matter to all of us, therefore it seems to me incorrect and unjust to exclude 'the masses' from spiritual agendas and concerns. Jung's 'analytic psychology' was a platform for exploration more than a rigid or introverted school of practice. We still have much to learn, from other cultures and generations, about what is healing and helpful. Therefore Jung's reluctance to impose another 'school' of therapy on contemporary practice seems impressive and appropriate.

Websites

http://onlinepsyche.com/jungweb/
http://www.cgjung.com/cgjung/
http://www.uga.edu/~counseling/jung/

Bibliography

C.G. Jung, *Answer to Job*, Ark, 1984
C.G. Jung, *Psychology and the East*, Ark, 1986
C.G. Jung, *Psychology and Western Religion*, Ark, 1988
C.G. Jung, *Man and His Symbols*, Penguin, 1990
C.G. Jung, *Development of Personality*, Routledge, 1992
C.G. Jung, *Two Essays on Analytical Psychology*, Routledge, 1992
C.G. Jung, *Freud and Psychoanalysis*, Routledge, 1993
C.G. Jung, *Modern Man in Search of a Soul*, Ark, 1995
C.G. Jung, *The Undiscovered Self*, Routledge, 1996
A. Storr, (ed.) *Jung, Selected Writings*, Fontana, 1986

Chapter 30

Ludwig Wittgenstein (1889–1951)

_____ **Key Points** _____

- 🔳 Wittgenstein does not sit easily within any 'school' of philosophy, although he greatly influenced both logical and linguistic analysis

- 🔳 His interests moved from logic to language, as lived and used, and finally to psychology

- 🔳 Wittgenstein's Socratic, question-based enquiry knew no boundaries. It included questions concerning how we know others, the nature of consciousness, personal identity and the status of ethics.

___ *Application* _____

- Reading Wittgenstein's questions about the nature of psychology provides a kind of shock therapy
- Wittgenstein's questioning is provocative, unsettling, enigmatic, challenging, thought provoking
- Wittgenstein is less of a system builder than an antidote to anyone becoming too complacent within whatever system of ideas they currently occupy.

> Roughly, it must be the case that in general I can give a more coherent report about my actions than someone else. (Wittgenstein, *Last Writings on the Philosophy of Psychology*, Vol. 2, p. 34)

Surely we know ourselves better than others know us? We like to think so. Yet we also, sometimes, and in some respects, claim to know others better than they know themselves. People (other people) can be so lacking in self-awareness. Does Ray Monk know Ludwig Wittgenstein better than that philosopher knew himself? After reading Monk's award-winning biography[1] I am inclined to think he does. It provides a far more coherent report on this philosopher's mind, personality, life and work than Wittgenstein's own notes, books or recorded conversations.

Wittgenstein's personality, life and legacy have intoxicating qualities. I can imagine a (big budget) film being produced from Monk's biography that could make a (still bigger) cult of Wittgenstein and a modish fashion out of philosophy. Unfortunately, it would reinforce all the stereotypes of philosophers as unworldly, highly eccentric, slightly mad and utterly incomprehensible. Wittgenstein makes Einstein seem positively ordinary.

His story and background provide a vivid and dramatic backdrop to his extraordinary personality. He was a son of one of the wealthiest industrialists in Europe, living in palatial luxury in turn of the century Vienna at the height of its cultural vitality. Members of the family, of Jewish background, were cosmopolitan benefactors of the arts and prominent, somewhat *avant garde*, citizens of a declining Austro-Hungarian Empire. Wittgenstein scribbled in his notebooks while fighting (and earning medals) in the Austrian army. He gave away all his vast fortune. His homosexuality was expressed elliptically in writing more than directly in action. He often contemplated suicide (several brothers did actually kill themselves), he was a perfectionist and suffered long bouts of depression.

Wittgenstein became a professor of philosophy at Cambridge without any formal training in the subject. He did not read anything written by most of the philosophers mentioned in this book, yet is highly influential and regarded as one of the foremost twentieth-century thinkers. What does that say about philosophy, Cambridge and, not least, about Wittgenstein?

Wittgenstein entitled all his lectures 'philosophy'. He did not like large audiences, he made no preparations, wrote no lecture plan, there were long pauses, many claimed that he was usually incomprehensible, he dominated discussions, he had no social graces and cared nothing for them. He wrestled with questions rather than delivering any package of answers. He often did not even explain why he was asking the questions and they frequently followed one another in no observably coherent pattern. He showed the *process* of (a particular approach to) philosophy more than describing or delivering the product of it.

Wittgenstein had only one book published in his lifetime, the *Tractatus Logico-Philosophicus* (1922). His other major work, *Philosophical Investigations*, appeared posthumously in 1953. Subsequently, an enormous literature has been sold of private musings by Wittgenstein and lecture notes of students. They are fragmented, enigmatic, mysterious, stimulating and thought provoking. Wittgenstein generally encouraged his philosophy students to abandon the subject and take up manual work.

So why include a chapter on Wittgenstein in these pages? Because he was clever yet incomprehensible? If so, what kind of cleverness is this and how are we to assess it? Clearly it is time to consider what it is of relevance to readers that Wittgenstein was actually trying to say.

The *Tractatus* began with a very small circulation and after its publication he abandoned philosophy and became a highly eccentric, demanding, exciting and essentially unsuccessful primary school teacher in various remote Austrian villages. During this time he also became something of a legend among Anglo-Saxon philosophers and of 'The Apostles', a fashionable elite of the English intelligentsia. J.M. Keynes playfully referred to him as 'God' (which he was not) and as a 'maniac' (which he perhaps was). Wittgenstein, along with the 'Vienna Circle' of philosophers, became of central importance in the development of Anglo-Saxon as opposed to 'Continental' philosophy. This distinction is thus problematic from the start: the Vienna circle was based, as might be guessed, in Vienna and Wittgenstein, as already mentioned, was himself Austrian.

So what is this supposed 'Anglo-Saxon' philosophy? In the early part of the twentieth century, English philosophers became tired and impatient with Hegelian and neo-Hegelian mysticism and dialectics. Bradley and Bosanquet, much influenced by Hegel, were no longer rising stars. Bertrand Russell's *Principia Mathematica* (1903) sought to show that the whole of mathematics could be derived from a small number of basic logical principles and that language, too, could be analysed down to, and built up from, basic 'logical atoms' of thought and 'atomic facts' in reality.

Large-scale syntheses of thesis and antithesis, creeping ever closer to integration with a metaphysical absolute, went out of style. Russell was impatient with the muddled, vague, over-general thinking. It was time to analyse details, piece together logical atoms and their interconnections, abandon warm fuzzy sentiment for cool clarity and rationality.

Wittgenstein, working as an aeronautical research student, was greatly impressed by Russell's book, discovered that philosophy captured him more than aeronautics, and soon impressed Russell with the power and energy of his intellect. Russell was becoming exhausted after his labours with the *Principia* and thought that Wittgenstein, and his *Tractatus*, was the means by which logical atomism could be further developed and refined.

The *Tractatus*, only seventy five pages long, is a series of statements numbered in complex decimal notation. Each place of decimal provides a qualifying remark to the previous. Hence statements 2.011 and 2.012 refine on statement 2.01; statements 2.0121 and 2.0122 elaborate on 2.012. Wittgenstein moves into several places of decimals and the whole effect seems to be very much in Russell's spirit of analysing the logical atoms of thought in order to proceed further in the direction set by Russell's *Principia*.

In fact, however, Wittgenstein was a poet and free-fire thinker as much as he was a logician. He danced within literary analogies as much as logical analysis. Logical atomist philosophers were both impressed by the power of Wittgensteinian analysis and perplexed by Wittgensteinian mysticism. Surely the two could not go together? The logician Frege did not think so and was sharply critical of the *Tractatus* from the first statement onward. Wittgenstein's response was that only a tiny handful of people ever understood his work, and Frege was not one of them. If true this is odd. How can a book that seeks to underpin and clarify the foundations and structure of logic be incomprehensible to most prominent professional logicians? Was the book poor in organisation and expression? Did the logicians lack imagination and intelligence? Wittgenstein answered 'yes' on all counts:

1   The world is all that is the case.
1.1   The world is the totality of facts, not of things.

Frege asked, why talk of both 'facts' and 'the case'? What was the difference?:

1.12   For the totality of facts determines what is the case, and also whatever is not the case.

What did this mean? Frege observed that:

From the very beginning I find myself entangled in doubt as to what you want to say, and so make no proper headway.[2]

Frege was not alone. There are few mathematical poets or poetical mathematicians who might be best placed to proceed with the *Tractatus*. Is it worth the labour? Wittgenstein's writing is a process of investigative thinking more than a summary of previous effort. He offers a laser-like intensity of analysis that is both (harmfully) mesmerising and (helpfully) challenging and thought provoking.

Wittgenstein (as embodied in the *Tractatus*) suggested that propositions were 'pictures' of reality. They could be analysed and were orderly and so, likewise, was the world that they represented. Representation and reality shared the same logical form; both were coherent and well formed but there were limits to what we could know about either. Consequently, as we came to the edge of our knowledge we likewise found ourselves beating against the boundaries of our language. Often, we could not even say of which we did not know. We might not even know what to ask.

These components of the *Tractatus* were readily open to consideration by logical atomists and logical positivists in Britain, the US and Vienna.[3] But what were they to make of Wittgenstein's more enigmatic observations? For example:

> 5.631 There is no such thing as the subject that thinks or entertains ideas. If I wrote a book called The World as I found it, I should have to include a report on my body, and should have to say which parts were subordinate to my will, and which were not, etc., this being a method of isolating the subject, or rather of showing that in an important sense there is no subject; for it alone could not be mentioned in that book.

There are echoes of Hume here who, likewise, never managed to observe 'myself':

> 5.632 The subject does not belong to the world: rather, it is a limit of the world.

This is similar to Schopenhauer. It was seen to be closer to metaphysics than any self-respecting logician ought to be. There was altogether too much open ended suggestion and mystery in Wittgenstein's sentences for them to sit easily within an atomist agenda. He spun fresh questions and new lines of enquiry faster than pinning down definitions, axioms and procedures in the fashion preferred by Russell or (much earlier) Euclid:

> 5.641 Thus there really is a sense in which philosophy can talk about the self in a non-psychological way. What brings the self into philosophy is the fact that 'the world is my world'. The philosophical self is not the human being, not the human body, or the human soul,

with which psychology deals, but rather the metaphysical subject, the limit of the world – not a part of it.

Here Wittgenstein even dares to mention metaphysics. His intellect is continually breaking out of whatever intellectual framework he is supposedly constructing and thereby posing new questions. Russell was hoping for a work that would buttress and fill the gaps in his own *Principia*, but here was Wittgenstein moving beyond a technical analysis of logical propositions and their interconnection. Off and away he went into speculation about the nature of psychology and experience and anything and everything else that came before his restless enquiring spirit.

Logic was still important to Wittgenstein:

> 6.124 The propositions of logic describe the scaffolding of the world, or rather they represent it. They have no 'subject-matter'. They presuppose that names have meaning and elementary propositions sense; and that is their connection with the world.
>
> 6.13 Logic is not a body of doctrine, but a mirror-image of the world. Logic is transcendental.

But other statements move him to broader agendas to which, later, he would return:

> 6.41 The sense of the world must lie outside the world. In the world everything is as it is, and everything happens as it does happen: in it no value exists – and if it did exist, it would have no value. If there is any value that does have value, it must lie outside the whole sphere of what happens and is the case. For all that happens and is the case is accidental. What makes it non-accidental cannot lie within the world, since if it did it would itself be accidental. It must lie outside the world.

Here Wittgenstein is suggesting that all that is the case in the universe of discourse for logical analysis is not all that is the case. 'Something', he implied, lay outside this world. What could it be? Could we talk about it? Was it important? These were just the kind of metaphysical statements from which logical positivists wished to divorce themselves.

Wittgenstein assisted logicians in improving their analytical edifice, and then proceeded to climb right out of it:

6.54   My propositions are elucidatory in this way: he who understands me
       finally recognizes them as senseless, when he has climbed out
       through them, on them, over them. (He must so to speak throw
       away the ladder, after he has climbed up on it.)

Wittgenstein ended the *Tractatus* with:

7   What we cannot speak about we must pass over in silence.

Or, in more traditional, and poetic, translation: 'Whereof we cannot
speak, thereof we must remain silent.'

True to his message, he went silent as a practicing philosopher for
many years.

When Wittgenstein returned to philosophy, it was to overturn much
of what he had said in the *Tractatus*. He decided that there was nothing
to be gained from imprisoning oneself and one's questions within a
framework of logical analysis. He had been wrong in the *Tractatus*:
Logic was *not* a mirror image of the world; the world was a much bigger
place than that. Propositions were not pictures of reality, and logical
analysis did not provide scaffolding for most of existence. The seeds of
this change of sentiment are already in place within the *Tractatus*:

4.112 Philosophy aims at the logical clarification of thoughts. Philos-
      ophy is not a body of doctrine but an activity. A philosophical
      work consists essentially of elucidations. Philosophy does not
      result in 'philosophical propositions', but rather in the clarification
      of propositions.

Within the *Philosophical Investigations* Wittgenstein's philosophical
activity went way beyond logic per se and moved on to language. It was
not enough just to consider and elucidate the logic of the language. We
also had to examine and clarify the enormously various ways in which
language was used in the stream of life and in conjunction with all the
non-verbal activity that was an integral part of understanding its
meaning and its place.[4] Philosophy did not need a new language, nor
should it provide a structure to existing languages:

124.   Philosophy may in no way interfere with the actual use of language;
       it can in the end only describe it.
       For it cannot give it any foundation either.
       It leaves everything where it is.

But the world 'where it is' was, in Wittgenstein's second phase of philosophical activity, a much more varied, complex, multifaceted place than ever. Linguistic analysis replaced logical analysis and where Wittgenstein moved so followed large cohorts of Anglo-Saxon philosophers. There was not one set of rules of language, there were many. They were not written down. They were not just contained in what people said, but also in what they did. The whole stream of interaction of living people needed to be examined. How did their gestures, tone, actions relate with what they said? What kinds of games, linguistic and otherwise were they playing and how did they operate? What was going on 'inside their heads' when they said and did this or that? How could we know? How far did it matter? Who was this 'me' that did this or that?

Wittgenstein did not provide answers to these general questions. Instead he explored them as they showed themselves to be important to him in relation to many and various particular situations. The whole point was that we should avoid generalising and look at the specificity of language use in all its multiplicity.

The result of Wittgenstein's labour was to show, rather than describe, the richness of human activity, and to show the extent to which it transcended any philosophical, or other, generalisation that had ever previously been made about it. Many of his numbered paragraphs within *Philosophical Investigations* are in fact exercises, where the reader is invited to explore the questions, consider the ways in which particular metaphors are used, how truth is determined in particular situations, what distinctions are significant and why. In footnote a to paragraph 151, for example:

> 'Understanding a word': a state. But a mental state? – Depression, excitement, pain, are called mental states. Carry out a grammatical investigation as follows: we say
> 'He was depressed the whole day'.
> 'He was in great excitement the whole day'.
> 'He has been in continuous pain since yesterday'.
> We also say 'Since yesterday I have understood this word'. 'Continuously', though? – To be sure, one can speak of an interruption of understanding. But in what cases? Compare: 'When did your pains get less?' and 'When did you stop understanding that word?'.

The questions go on and on. Wittgenstein is in many respects like a reincarnation of Socrates; restless, unsettling, destabilising, not a system builder, a great threat to any system you think you have, yet concerned to probe, to elucidate, to clarify, to assess, to compare:

Now what takes place when, say, he reads a newspaper? (156)
I want to remember a tune and it escapes me; suddenly I say 'Now I know
it' and I sing it. What was it like to suddenly know it? (184)
How do words refer to sensations? (244)
In what sense are my sensations *private*? (246)
What would it be like if human beings showed no outward signs of pain?
(257)
What gives us *so much as the idea* that living beings, things, can feel? (283)
What does it mean to understand a picture, a drawing? (526)

Rather than seeking a generalisation as an answer, Wittgenstein is
primarily concerned to examine the rules of evidence, actions and
procedures that we in fact utilise in our daily lives in order to answer
these questions. He does not assume that the way we establish answers
will be the same in different situations. Indeed he tends to the view that
our efforts to elucidate truth are likely to be different. There are not so
much large generalisations to be found. Instead there are 'family resem-
blances' between some efforts at verification and others. The world is
indeed a (magically) complex place. Wittgenstein's philosophy attempts
to honour and unravel its complexity rather than compress it within
inadequate generalisation:

Look at a stone and imagine it having sensations. (284)
Suppose everyone had a box with something in it: we call it a 'beetle'. No
one can look into anyone else's box, and everyone says he knows what a
beetle is only by looking at *his* beetle. – Here it would be quite possible for
everyone to have something different in his box. (293)
Is thinking a kind of speaking? (330)
The chair is thinking to itself: ... WHERE? In one of its parts? (361)
Is calculating in the imagination in some sense less real than calculating on
paper? (364)

Wittgenstein shows the dangers of generalisation by illustrating just
how subtle and varied are circumstance and our means of apprehension. Like Heidegger, he saw that much of what we apprehend is assim-
ilated without any conscious 'act' of apprehension at all:

Asked 'Did you recognise your desk when you entered your room this
morning? – I should no doubt say 'Certainly!' And yet it would be
misleading to say that an act of recognition took place. (602)

He became more fascinated with the poetry, as well as the logic, of language:

> Understanding a sentence is much more akin to understanding a theme in music than one may think. (527)

He grew more and more interested in what we meant by, and how we used notions of, 'inner' and 'outer' worlds and their interconnection:

> How should we counter someone who told us that with him understanding was an inner process? – How should we counter him if he said that with him knowing how to play chess was an inner process? (*Philosophical Investigations*, Part II, sec. vi)

What he does not do, however, is show that we ought to avoid all generalisations. Indeed, it is self-evident that generalisations are a part of the stream of our lives and they have a role (many multifaceted roles) in human activity. Wittgenstein focuses on the language of everyday life and, in his later work, he uses everyday and non-technical language. The result is that at times it is very clear what he is saying, but less than clear why he is saying it and where it fits in to anything else that he says. Sign posting has its place, but Wittgenstein tends to point to the road, invite you to walk with him along it, but is very reluctant to examine or draw any maps.

Wittgenstein refers to all kinds of language games within the complex stream of life, but he prefers to consider 'ordinary' languages as spoken by the layperson. Yet professional language games, including the languages of philosophy, are themselves part of the rich cultural process of human activity. Wittgenstein might have been wiser, therefore, to have attended, not just to the variety of conversation and interaction in everyday life, but to the wealth of ideas devised and explored by philosophers in previous centuries. Given that he had studied so little philosophy, it seems to be something of a rationalisation on his part to try to exclude professional philosophy altogether from the process of doing philosophy.

Ray Monk observes that Oxford University would never have employed as professor of philosophy someone who had read so little of it. Yet colleagues agreed that to refuse a professorship to Wittgenstein would have been like refusing Einstein (a patent office clerk) a chair in physics. Wittgenstein was one for whom the rules needed to be rewritten. He also illustrates why the rules, more generally, have a place.

Wittgenstein did not wish to promote or leave behind a 'school' of philosophy. He feared that mediocrity would misunderstand and trivialise what he was trying to do, or turn it into a set of wooden procedures that would serve no useful purpose. For Wittgenstein every moment in the study of (the doing of) philosophy was an existential moment. We had to be alive to the whole broad and intricate circumstance under investigation, with our whole being and without (unexamined) presupposition. Less brilliant disciples might not manage this. They might fiddle and fidget with language usage with much less clarity of point, purpose or penetration. Thus Anglo-Saxon philosophy, subsequent to Wittgenstein, slipped into a tendency to make a fetish of the examination of ordinary language usage, as though by this means alone all philosophical questions could be elucidated.

We can be sure that Wittgenstein would have been routinely disgusted with this legacy. We can also be sure that, had he lived on, he would have moved on, either to a phase three of Wittgensteinian philosophy, or to something else altogether. He grew more and more interested in psychology but saw it as, at present, a barren subject:

> The existence of the experimental method makes us think we have the means of solving problems which trouble us; though problem and method pass one another by. (ibid. Part II, sec. xiv)

Wittgenstein combined a sharp ability to examine psychological questions with an almost total inability to perceive the effects he had on others. He scored very high on analysis, elucidation and creativity, but almost nil on empathy. This might not, however, have disqualified him from practice as a psychologist, although perhaps it should have.

Wittgenstein has much to say about psychological matters that do not summarise easily, or at all. He was brilliant but, like all of us, fallible. We should resist being mesmerised by him. He was quite capable of making inaccurate statements. For example, from the *Tractatus*:

> 4.1212 What can be shown, cannot be said.

Think about this statement. Wittgenstein is wrong here. We can show and we can say what we show. Both have their place. Further:

> 4.116 Everything that can be thought at all can be thought clearly. Everything that can be put into words can be put clearly.

Quite obviously, much that is thought is neither thought nor put into words at all clearly, nor is there reason to think that one day it will. Wittgenstein was often unclear and, given that he was beating at the boundaries of what can be said and thought, this is to be expected. He himself said of his book, in the preface to *Philosophical Investigations:*

> It is not impossible that it should fall to the lot of this work, in its poverty and in the darkness of this time, to bring light into one brain or another – but, of course, it is not likely.

He also advised that:

> I should not like my writing to spare other people the trouble of thinking. But, if possible, to stimulate someone to thoughts of his own.

In this Wittgenstein was hugely successful and he cannot be blamed for the fact that few minds operated with the same tenacity and brilliance. Wittgenstein thought that his book was not good but that he could not improve on it. By conventional criteria it is a terrible book; a jumble of poorly organised, badly signposted, totally unexplained ideas. There is no coherent crown, but of the gems, many, but not all, shine in spite of all that.

? Questions

1. Do the questions posed by Wittgenstein, as quoted in this chapter, strike you as useful? Can you see their point and relevance? Which? Why?

2. Can you think of the reasons why Cambridge should, and should not, have appointed an 'unqualified' candidate as professor of philosophy?

3. Wittgenstein combined a sharp ability to observe and ask questions about psychology with a poor capacity to see himself as others saw him. Is this important? Relevant? Common?

4. Who determines a person's powers of empathy and how?

EXERCISES

1. Look again at Wittgenstein's questions and exercises quoted in this chapter. Explore them, assess them, discuss them and write down why you think he posed them and why they are worth considering.

2. If this whets your appetite, there is no substitute to reading Wittgenstein himself and considering actively, and for yourself, the questions he raises. Wittgenstein did not want to summarise philosophy, he wanted readers to do philosophy for themselves and thereby discover for themselves its power and its relevance. If you appreciate Wittgenstein you will not become a 'follower' (of Wittgenstein or of anyone else).

Conclusion

Wittgenstein's exploration of language as it is used, and of the nature and status of psychology and identity is highly relevant to anyone interested in talk as a means of healing. He was a prime influence within two schools of philosophical thinking although he did not wish to belong to any school. His ignorance of the history of philosophy allowed him to look afresh at philosophical questions but prevented him from learning from what others had to offer. Most of the work published in his name is in fact a jumble of private notes that he did not want published at all. It is chaotic, creative, confusing, stimulating. Wittgenstein so much fits the stereotype of the eccentric genius philosopher that it is impossible to provide a caricature of his story. Truth, in his case, is stranger and more fascinating than any fiction.

Notes

1. R. Monk, *Ludwig Wittgenstein: The Duty of Genius*, Vintage, 1991.
2. Quoted in Monk, 1991, p. 163.
3. Positivism: The view that theology, mysticism and metaphysics are either inchoate muddled fantasies or, if coherent, are beyond the reach of human discussion, analysis and understanding. Either way, the positivist agenda consists in seeking to abolish all such systems from the 'proper' conduct of philosophy and rational thought.
4 Heidegger explored similar territory. A serious meeting of these two minds would have been interesting.

Websites

www.sbg.ac.at/phs/alws/alws.htm
www.hd.uib.no/wab/wabhome.htm
www.utm.edu/research/iep/w/wittgens.htm
www.unc.edu/~elliott/witt.htm

Bibliography

L. Wittgenstein, *Philosophical Investigations* 3rd edn, Macmillan, 1973

L. Wittgenstein, *Remarks on the Philosophy of Psychology* Vols 1 and 2, University of Chicago Press, 1989

L. Wittgenstein, *Last Writings on the Philosophy of Psychology*, Vols 1 and 2, Blackwell, 1994

L. Wittgenstein, *Tractatus Logico-Philosophicus* (English tr. Pears and McGuinness), Routledge, 1995

L. Wittgenstein, *Culture and Value*, Blackwell, 1998

Chapter 31

Martin Heidegger (1889–1976)

───────────────────────── **Key Points** ─────────────────────────

- The person exists only in the performance of intentional acts, and is therefore essentially not an object

- 'Being-in-the-world' indicates in the very way we have coined it, that it stands for a unitary phenomenon

- There is no such thing as the 'side-by-side-ness' of an entity called 'Dasein' with another entity called 'world'

- Only he who already understands can listen

- The Self of everyday Dasein is the they-self, which we distinguish from the authentic Self – that is, from the Self which has been taken hold of in its own way.

Application

- For Heidegger, we do not start with self and venture into world. The everyday common-sense self, derived from Descartes, is a fallacious idea torn out of the self-world engagement that we are
- Time is a dimension of our identity more than a line on which we travel. We are characterised by our intentions and our past
- Spaces and objects likewise characterise us – home, workware, leisureware, car, and so on, do not just surround us, they, and our interaction and pattern of intention, make up part of who we are
- We communicate via our shared interaction and our communion of intention far more than by exchanging supposedly 'inner' experiences
- If Heidegger is right, then the most basic common-sense assumptions within counselling – about self, world, interaction and communication – must be abandoned.

Heidegger's *Being and Time* (1927) is considered to be one of the major existentialist works of the twentieth century. Sartre's *Being and Nothingness* (1943) is another. Heidegger thought that Sartre's work was unreadable rubbish, that Sartre entirely failed to understand the central thesis of *Being and Time* (in this I think he was right) and that Heidegger was not himself an existentialist at all. Consistent existentialism may indeed require that you deny that you are an existentialist. What are we to make of all this and why does it matter?

Heidegger is crucially, and radically, important on questions of personal identity, meaning, choice, authenticity and relationship, all pretty central stuff for counsellors. His ideas are difficult to express because they fundamentally challenge a great deal of the contemporary wisdom and 'common sense' that is embedded in our existing language. Heidegger, in English translations, is explained using hyphenations. These weld together seemingly disparate concepts that, for Heidegger, were inseparable. It does not make for easy reading.

Much of Heidegger *is* usefully quotable, however, provided a few explanations are attached. I shall start with personal identity:

> Essentially the person exists only in the performance of intentional acts, and is therefore essentially not an object. Any psychical Objectification of acts, and hence any way of taking them as something psychical, is tantamount to depersonalisation. A person is in any case given as a performer of intentional acts which are bound together by the unity of a meaning. (*Being and Time*, p. 73)

For Heidegger, intentions, meanings and actions were not merely performed or experienced by the person, they formed and expressed the person and were an integral part of their identity. It was not that I existed and then formed intentions. My intentions formed me more than I shaped them and were not ultimately separable from me. Neither were intentions merely mental phenomena. I did not exist, form a (mental) intention and then go and do something physical. On the contrary, the sequence was more nearly the other way round. I did something and in so doing discovered my intentions through which I came to learn about my identity. This is obvious when you consider the actions of babies. They have not formed an identity or clarified their intentions. They act, and in so doing their mother and later they themselves, build up a picture of who they are and where they are trying to go. The process takes years of endless activity.

One consequence of this was that it was absurd to think that you could bracket off your supposed 'inner life' from its material context. We were doers and what we imagined was our inner world was not separate from the physical world at all. To imagine otherwise created endless confusion about the supposed 'relationship' between self and world. Einstein introduced the concept of 'mass energy', thereby underlining that each was an aspect of the other and could not be thought of separately. Heidegger spoke of 'Being-in-the-world', and with a similar purpose:

> The compound expression 'Being-in-the-world' indicates in the very way we have coined it, that it stands for a unitary phenomenon. This primary datum must be seen as a whole. (ibid. p. 78)

Again, a comparison with contemporary physics may be useful. The identity of a particle is not so much determined by its basic 'stuffiness' as by the principles that describe its action and interaction. These mathematical equations integrate the particle in time and space such that the time-space-stuff-wave-function-in-foreground-background-in-n-dimensions become one unitary concept and mathematical function. Similarly, for Heidegger, person-place-context-purpose-intention-meaning was one concept. You just could not have one without the others and there was no meaning in any one component except within its dynamic relation with the others:

> There is no such thing as the 'side-by-side-ness' of an entity called 'Dasein' with another entity called 'world'. (ibid. p. 81)

In other words, there was no meaningful distinction that could be made between self and world. Self-world was one concept, one reality. We were not so much *in* the world as *of* the world:

> It is not the case that man 'is' and then has, by way of an extra, a relationship-of-Being towards the 'world' – a world with which he provides himself occasionally. Dasein is never 'proximally' an entity which is, so to speak, free Being-in, but which sometimes has the inclination to a 'relationship' towards the world. (ibid. p. 84)

Therefore we could not possibly go within and 'find ourselves'. Identity, meaning, purpose was discovered through committed and coherent action and connection, or not at all:

When Dasein directs itself towards something and grasps it, it does not somehow first get out of an inner sphere in which it has been proximally encapsulated, but its primary kind of Being is such that it is always 'outside' alongside entities which it encounters and which belong to a world already discovered. (ibid. p. 89)

We were 'spread out' over the world in (metaphorically) the same way as particles are now considered to exist in a superposition (pattern of all-places-potentially-as-one) wave function over space-time.

What mattered was not so much what we perceived as what we did. Indeed, what we saw, and did not see, was structured very much by what we did. Philosophers had got it all back to front:

The kind of dealing which is closest to us is as we have shown, not a bare perceptual cognition, but rather that kind of concern which manipulates things and puts them to use; and this has its own kind of 'knowledge'. (ibid. p. 95)

Babies did and in so doing began to see. What they saw was determined by what they could do and wished to do. So it was with adults:

We shall call those entities which we encounter in concern 'equipment'. Equipment is essentially 'something in order to… ' Equipment… always is in terms of its belonging to other equipment: ink stand, pen, ink, paper, blotting pad, table, lamp, furniture, windows, doors, room. These 'Things' never show themselves proximally as they are for themselves, so as to add up to a sum of realia and fill up a room. What we encounter as closest to us (though not as something taken as a theme) is the room; and we encounter it not as something 'between four walls' in a geometrical spatial sense, but as equipment for residing. (ibid. p. 97)

We never just 'saw' in a detached and disinterested fashion. We were always interested and seeking our interests. What we saw was selected, structured and integrated accordingly. Our perceptions were a coherent, unified construct formed by our intentions, our past experiences, the meanings and purposes, programmes and plans we were making for today. We noticed what was of interest and concern to us and we understood it in relation to all those other objects that were an integral part of our purpose. Pen, ink, study, room, office and city centre, all these were integrated in the sense we made of existence. Accountant, office, contract, today, deadline, that's 'me'. Trees? Ants? Bag lady? I cannot say I noticed those:

What we 'first' hear is never noises or complexes of sounds, but the creaking wagon, the motorcycle. We hear the column on the march, the north wind, the woodpecker tapping, the fire crackling. It requires a very artificial and complicated frame of mind to 'hear' a 'pure noise'. The fact that motorcycles and wagons are what we proximally hear is the phenomenal evidence that in every Dasein, as Being-in-the-world, already dwells alongside what is ready-to-hand within-the-world; it certainly does not dwell alongside 'sensations'. (ibid. p. 207)

Can we 'just' listen? It would be an unusual, artificial, contrived and difficult task. Listening is always a creative act structured by experience, knowledge, values, priorities and purposes. You hear according to what you understand. Hence so many witnesses hear, and see, so very differently according to how they construe events. We do not hear and then understand. More nearly, we understood, and hear accordingly. The relevance of all this to counselling is, I hope, obvious and overwhelming.

Both talking and hearing are based upon understanding. And understanding arises neither through talking at length nor through busily hearing something 'all around'. Only he who already understands can listen:

Speaking at length about something does not offer the slightest guarantee that thereby understanding is advanced. On the contrary, talking extensively about something, covers it up and brings what is understood to a sham clarity – the unintelligibility of the trivial. (ibid. p. 208)

For Heidegger, actions did indeed speak louder than words. We had evolved as animals that *did*. Only later, as language evolved, did we learn to talk about what we did. Language was more likely to be an effect of what we intended than a cause. Underlying reality lay in what we did. Language could hide such reality as easily as reveal it. Consequently, the idea that we would naturally 'get to the bottom of things' by talking about them was suspect. We got to the bottom of who we were and where we were heading by facing up to what we *did* more than to what we *said*. In practice, what counted, was what we did:

'Practical' behaviour is not 'atheoretical' in the sense of 'sightlessness'. The way it differs from theoretical behaviour does not lie simply in the fact that in theoretical behaviour one observes, while in practical behaviour one acts, and that action must employ theoretical cognition if it is not to remain blind; for the fact that observation is a kind of concern is just as primordial as the fact that action has its own kind of sight. (ibid. p. 99)

Observation and commentary were not more fundamental ('primordial') than action and intention. Intention itself was often derivable from what we did rather than being the primary cause. We did not so much form an intention and then act; we often discovered the form of our intentions from our actions. In any case, most of what we did, we just did, without conscious intention or commentary at all. Only exceptionally were our actions embellished with conscious mental activity and cerebral cogitation:

> Interpretation is carried out primordially not in a theoretical statement but in an action of circumspective concern – laying aside the unsuitable tool, or exchanging it, 'without wasting words'. From the fact that words are absent, it may not be concluded that interpretation is absent. (ibid. p. 200)

When we know what we are doing, and usually we do, we just get on with it, without words or discussion. We may thereby co-operate and communicate silently in our shared agreed knowledge of what needs to be done next. Only when we become uncertain does the conscious mental representation of possible options begin and the open discussion with others. For example, we drive along, expert as motorist and navigator, unconscious. The learner driver, on the other hand, says: 'Now first gear, increase revs, pedal, gearstick, forward, sideways.' The lost driver says: 'Second on left after hill, or was it?'

Conscious cogitation, mental representation, extensive discussion and argument, all this can be a sign that we have lost the control we had when we were silent, unconscious, directed, efficient, competent. Similarly, when we are working most closely, constructively, co-operatively, skilfully, with another, there may be less and less that is needed to be said and discussed. When I am typing at my word processor most energetically and effectively, when I feel most productive, I have no inner conversation with myself. I just type. The words just keep on coming:

> Communication is never anything like a conveying of experiences, such as opinions or wishes, from the interior of one subject into the interior of another. Dasein-with is already essentially manifest in a co-state-of-mind and a co-understanding. (ibid. p. 205)

We were not just here, in this one physical place. Within our world of commitment and concern, we were alongside those others with whom we co-operated. We were not just now, at this time. Our concern stretched back into the past and forward into a future. Here and now we were continually forming and formed by the whole pattern of meaning that was our story. Bodies were located in one space at one time. People were positioned in a space-time of concern, coherence and intention. The dimensions of personal identity stretched over decades and among scores of people, places and projects:

> But ontologically, Being towards one's ownmost potentiality-for-Being means that in each case Dasein is already ahead of itself in its Being. Dasein is always 'beyond itself'. (ibid. p. 236)

> Its own past – and this is always means the past of its 'generation' – is not something which *follows along after* Dasein, but something which already goes ahead of it. (ibid. p. 41)

Choices that are obvious to us are invisible and are not construed as choices at all. They are often inevitable consequences of larger choices we have already made. I have decided to see my mother who is unwell. I shall drive. Everything after that is automatic. Shall I change gear? Steer to the left or right? Stop at these lights? Avoid that pedestrian? I do not consciously consider any of these options. I do not construe them as options or as problems needing effort and analysis:

> When equipment cannot be used, this implies that the constitutive assignment of the 'in-order-to' to a 'towards-this' has been disturbed. The assignments themselves are not observed; they are rather 'there' when we concernfully submit ourselves to them. But *when an assignment has been disturbed* – when something is unusable for some purpose – then the assignment becomes explicit. (ibid. p. 105)

So, the idea that we get more control over our affairs by consciously revisiting, discussing and analysing everything we do is absurd. We could not, and do not need to, analyse every component of our activity. Most of it is not so much *un*conscious, it is *not* conscious. There is no unconscious world within which I am saying 'change gear', 'stop at the red light'. Neither is there is any point or purpose in trying to become conscious of the components of driving. If it works, do not fix it. As individual organisms we are each a vast empire of cells acting and interacting. We only become conscious of all the work being done in our shoulders, say, when they start to ache, when something is going wrong.

The principle is the same with the making of meaning. Usually we construe who, what and why without conscious reflection. Sometimes the answer it is not clear. Only then do we become aware of the question, or of the need to formulate a question. This meaning making was ultimately a shared activity:

> The world of Dasein is a *with-world* (Mitwelt). Being-in is Being-with Others. (ibid. p. 155)

Each of us was inherently interconnected with others, but this could pose problems. Too easily we lost a proper sense of boundary. We lost ourselves in others. We avoided our own responsibilities:

> This Being-with-one-another dissolves ones own Dasein completely into the kind of Being of 'the Others', in such a way, indeed, that the Others, as distinguishable and explicit, vanish more and more. In this inconspicuousness and unascertainability, the real dictatorship of the 'they' is unfolded. We take pleasure and enjoy ourselves as they take pleasure; we read, see, and judge about literature and art as they see and judge; likewise we shrink back from the 'great mass' as they shrink back; we find 'shocking' what they find shocking. The 'they', which is nothing definite, and which all are, though not as the sum, prescribes the kind of Being of everydayness. (ibid. p. 164)

Constructive co-operation and interconnection easily turned into mindless conformity and mediocrity. A tyranny of the 'norm' established itself. We did not do this and that. Why? Because 'it was not done':

> This care of averageness reveals in turn an essential tendency of Dasein which we call the 'levelling down' of all possibilities of Being. (ibid. p. 165)

> Everyone is the other, and no one is himself. The 'they', which supplies the answer to the question of the 'who' of everyday Dasein, is the 'nobody' to whom Dasein has already surrendered itself in Being-among-one-another. (ibid. p. 166)

The self, for Heidegger, was, therefore, a complex emergent phenomenon. Philosophers, historically, had made the grave error of bracketing it off from the environment of which it was a part. So how were we to 'find myself', and what did this question actually mean? Heidegger's answer was that in the process of authentic, intentional action and interaction we made meaning and defined and established our identity. However, this was an ideal rather than a reality since Heidegger did not believe that many people ever actually achieved it. Instead, most individuals preferred to behave like the sheep and lambs that Nietzsche so despised. They wanted to be told who they were, what to think, what to do, how to act, how to respond, what to feel, what to wear. They wanted options ready packaged, off the shelf, easy wrapped and colour co-ordinated. They wanted others to do the thinking and deciding for them. They wanted to do, 'as you do', in order to belong to whatever social group and lifestyle commodity packaging they had signed up to:

> The Self of everyday Dasein is the *they-self*, which we distinguish from the authentic Self – that is, from the Self which has been taken hold of in its own way. As they-self, the particular Dasein has been dispersed into the 'they', and must first find itself. (ibid. p. 167)

Thus counsellors might imagine that they could 'facilitate' clients to 'find themselves'. Heidegger's view was that Joe Average would be most keen to be led by the counsellor, or any other authority figure, to be told, implicitly or explicitly, who they were, what they were, how to talk and think about themselves, where to go, what to do.

Within different schools of therapy, each psycho-style consultant offers a range of 'psychic interiors' that the customer may purchase to renovate and redecorate their 'inner world'. There are different languages, concepts, priorities and narratives to describe the nature of the self and its story. Some counsellors offer the inner child, some the id, some the transpersonal self, some a primal scream, and so on. Sure enough, the vast majority of clients come away using just the language, concepts, priorities and narratives offered by the (quite possibly 'non-directive') counsellor. They seek their inner child, or id, or transpersonal self. Why? Because it is easier to take these ideas 'off the shelf' than to weigh and assess within the vast range of options available. Thinking for oneself, originally and creatively, is hard work. Mostly people seem to prefer to avoid it. Similarly, most education, is even now not a process of drawing out the person. By and large, we are asked to repeat what someone else did and thought.

I believe that Heidegger is of profound and radical importance in the story of our efforts to understand who we are and what it is to be 'real'. He challenges all those philosophers who start with 'me' as an indubitable given of existence and who then go out to derive, observe and construct the world:

> The question of whether there is a world at all and whether its Being can be proved, makes no sense if it is raised by Dasein as Being-in-the-world; and who else would raise it? (ibid. p. 247)

We are embedded in, interconnected with and products of, our world. Our identity is inseparable from this dynamic interconnection. Even the concept of ourselves is inseparable from the world of which we are. Deprive a person of all sensory stimulation from their environment and they quickly disintegrate as persons. The notion of soul or self as an isolated non-physical unit is incoherent. Therefore it is an absurdity to imagine that we can in any way 'start' with 'me':

> That Kant demands any proofs at all for the 'Dasein of Things outside of me' shows already that he takes the subject – the 'in me' – as the starting point for this problematic. (ibid. p. 248)

Moreover, much of what goes on does so without conscious intention or choice, and rightly so. The art of living involves knowing when conscious attention, thought, questioning, decision making, creation and review are required. On those occasions we need to stand in our own integrity with courage and independence of thought, feeling and action. We will still, of course, remain interdependent.

In practice, Heidegger believed, this authenticity and individuality was often not achieved because we were lost in others, lost in things, and because, indeed, we saw ourselves as a thing, a commodity, to be bought and sold, traded, exchanged.

To be oneself required courage because there was no easy description of self and identity. Self was not fixed and unmoving. It was not separable from its world and from others, although it should not lose itself in others. It was changing, moving, seeking, intending and endlessly forming itself, endlessly incomplete. We felt a sense of incompleteness because we were always seeking to move forward into the next part of the story, the next agenda and the next chapter. To move forward and make a new shape was indeed what it was to be alive. As in the river of Heraclitus, we shaped the bank and were shaped by it and we were both. It was a dizzying thought that most people preferred to avoid. So when would there ever be solidity, finality and completion?:

> In Dasein there is undeniably a constant 'lack of totality' which finds an end with death. (ibid. p. 286)

All would be still, and fixed, and final, for us, when we died, on our extinction, of which we could not, of course, conceive and from which we drew back. Perhaps we could at least have a good death and, just before, just in time, could we wind up all our affairs, as we wanted them to be? Could we say 'goodbye', complete all our assignments, achieve all the recognition, respect and love that we craved? Could we finally get on top of life, of ourselves, before we died? For Heidegger, death would go to plan about as often as life. We might die too soon, too late, and certainly our real death might not bear much relation to any death we might have envisioned:

> So little is it the case that Dasein comes to its ripeness only with death, that Dasein may well have passed its ripeness before the end. For the most part, Dasein ends in unfulfilment, or else by having disintegrated and been used up. (ibid. p. 288)

Death was terrifying because we were always trying to make something of ourselves/our lives. Death made us nothing, non-existent. Death seemed to undo all that we sought to put together. It seemed to mock us. Here we were, boldly going forward, or so we hoped, and to what, to non-existence? It was inconceivable:

> In this state-of-mind (anxiety), Dasein finds itself face to face with the 'nothing' of the possible impossibility of its existence. Being-towards-death is essentially anxiety. (ibid. p. 310)

It was all too difficult, too painful. It was easier to draw back, to follow the crowd, to distract oneself as best one may:

> It remains indefinite who has 'really' done the choosing. So Dasein makes no choices, gets carried along by the nobody, and thus ensnares itself in inauthenticity. (ibid. p. 312)

There *was* a way out. It was not from God. (Heidegger abandoned Catholicism). It was from listening to the call of our own conscience:

> If we analyse conscience more penetratingly, it is revealed as a *call*. Calling is a mode of discourse. The call of conscience has the character of an appeal to Dasein by calling it to its ownmost potentiality-for-Being-its-Self; and this is done by way of *summoning* it to its ownmost Being-guilty. (ibid. p. 314)

Heidegger listened and for some time decided that the way forward was via the Nazi Party. It was strong, brave, committed and critical of consumer distraction and shallow pleasure. It saw self-fulfilment via heroic integration within a greater national cause. It joined with Nietzsche in its praises of the Ubermensch. Heidegger eventually drew back from the horrific consequences. He was not to write another book with the same scale and sweep as *Being and Time*. It is unlikely that he thought much of the culture of Mickey Mouse that now so predominates contemporary thought and aspiration:

> Everydayness takes Dasein as something ready-to-hand to be concerned with – that is, something that gets managed and reckoned up. 'Life' is a 'business', whether or not it covers its costs. (ibid. p. 336)

So, here we are, marketing ourselves as desirable commodities, carrying our portfolios, buying and selling ourselves. Is there any place or any need for heroism and resoluteness when our cabbages come in plastic and our concerns can be shrink wrapped by the local counsellor?:

> When Dasein is resolute, it can become the 'conscience' of Others. Only by authentically Being-their-Selves in resoluteness can people authentically be with one another – not by ambiguous and jealous stipulations and talkative fraternizing in the 'they' and in what 'they' want to undertake. (ibid. p. 345)

Perhaps we could, despite death, transcend time:

> 'As long as' Dasein factically exists , it is never past, but it always is indeed as already having been, in the sense of 'I am-as-having-been'. Therefore Dasein, in existing, can never establish itself as a fact which is present-at-hand, arising and passing away 'in the course of time', with a bit of it past already. (ibid. p. 376)

Here is Heidegger, he is dead. Something of his spirit I try to relay to you. He reached back in time to form his identity. He reaches forward to us, beyond his death, a star. Much of what he said deserves to be taken forward. He is not widely enough known. He will, I hope, reach way beyond the time of many brighter celebrities who will, much sooner, be forgotten:

> Dasein does not fill up a track or stretch 'of life' – one which is somehow present-at-hand – with the phases of its momentary actualities. It stretches itself along in such a way that its own Being is constituted in advance as a stretching-along. The 'between' which relates to birth and death already lies in the Being of Dasein. (ibid. p. 426)

Once one has grasped the finitude of one's existence, it snatches one back from the endless multiplication of possibilities which offer themselves as closest to one – those of comfortableness, shirking, and taking things lightly – and brings Dasein into the simplicity of its fate. This is how we designate Dasein's primordial historizing, which lies in authentic resoluteness and in which Dasein hands itself down to itself, free for death, in a possibility which it has inherited and yet has chosen. (ibid. p. 435)

? Questions

1. 'Speaking at length about something does not offer the slightest guarantee that thereby understanding is advanced'. What is the place of silence and non-verbal communication within your own practice of counselling/care?

2. 'Only he who already understands can listen'. How do you know if you understand? What did you need to know in order to understand? What examples come to mind?

3. How far do you get caught up in trying to look 'within' to the client's experience?

4. How do you engage with the intentions, history, actions and accoutrements that comprise the client's identity?

5. Who are you, and how are you, to assess authenticity in the client?

EXERCISES

1. Consider the conceptions of personal identity, responsibility and authentic communication explored within your own counsellor/care practitioner training. How far does Heidegger challenge these? How far do you feel ready, willing and able to incorporate Heidegger's thinking within your own practice?

2. Much psychotherapy advises that, to gain insight, we must talk. Many oriental teachers, on the contrary, suggest that we would often do better to shut up for a few hours, attend to what we are doing, and on a regular basis. Examine the role of silence within healing programmes, east and west.

Conclusion

Heidegger's notions of personal identity, communication, experience, and responsibility are radically different from conventional 'common sense'. Much of what he says, though, is less fantastic and more plausible than the idea of a disembodied soul 'inferring' the existence of a world and divorcing talk from action. Perhaps we should admit that listening without preconception or prior understanding – is impossible. There is no 'outside', 'detached, 'objective' stance available to counsellors or anyone else. We are part of the pattern of human life rather than outside observers of it. We understand before speech, and what others say is the least important component of communication. Above all we express via what we do, as formed by what we intend. We communicate in what we have and what we hold, what we use or abuse, presuppose and preconceive. Heidegger's is a dynamic world, whose motion, emotion, time and space is what we are rather than what we are in.

Websites

http://www.wavefront.com/~contra_m/cm/reviews/cm13_rev_heidegger.html
http://www.geocities.com/Athens/Delphi/9994/heidher.html
http://www.webcom.com/~paf/ereignis.html

Bibliography

M. Heidegger, *Being and Time*, Blackwell, 1978
M. Heidegger, *Basic Problems of Phenomenology*, Indiana University Press, 1982
M. Heidegger, *Concept of Time*, Blackwell, 1992

Chapter 32

Jean-Paul Sartre (1905–1980)

---------- **Key Points** ----------

▣ The 'self' – a little God which inhabits me and which possesses my freedom as a metaphysical virtue

▣ Human reality is its own surpassing toward what it lacks

▣ 'Being-for-itself' – that restless spirit that moves on from whatever we had made of ourselves

▣ 'Being-for-others' – the 'me' that is an observed object for others making something of themselves

▣ It is absurd that we are born; it is absurd that we die.

Application

- Sartre described existential psychoanalysis as seeking 'to determine the original choice'
- The client locates, reassesses and takes responsibility for important decisions, interpretations and intentions. Each of these is regarded as more fundamental than particular thoughts or feelings
- Sartre saw preoccupation with, so-called, past influences as irresponsible – an act of 'bad faith'
- Decisions and intentions count for more than past circumstances. What matters is what we make of environments and events
- We make meaning within what we choose, engage with and intend. Meaning is not to be 'found', since there is no meaning in any absolute sense.

Kierkegaard's existentialism consisted in finding oneself within and before God. Nietzsche's self was a bridge leading to 'superman'. For Heidegger, self was inextricably interwoven with, and emergent from, its larger context. Hegel's self was part of the absolute idea. For Sartre, self was similar to Descartes' self, but without God. Self, for Sartre, was its own God:

> It is a matter of envisaging the self as a little God which inhabits me and which possesses my freedom as a metaphysical virtue. (*Being and Nothingness*, p. 42)

Nietzsche's supermen went down in flames in 1945. But Sartre's deification of the self has been most influential in the latter half of the twentieth century. The self that was described by Sartre has in many ways been the self subsequently created. The nauseous consequences were eloquently explored in his novel *Nausea*.

So how does Sartre's 'self' differ from Heidegger's or Kierkegaard's? Can we select to 'be' one or the other? Is one nearer to 'the truth' than the others? What are we to make of ourselves? How? And which, if any, of these philosophers can help us? Who are we? What are we to do? What is our reality?

> Human reality is its own surpassing toward what it lacks; it surpasses itself toward the particular being which it would be if it were what it is. (ibid. p. 89)

For Sartre, as with Kierkegaard and Schopenhauer, we were beings that always wanted to be more than we were. We wanted to boldly go, and be and do, and, wherever we were, whatever we were, we had not yet arrived. We wanted to move on, to grow, to reach out. Whatever 'something' we thought we had made of ourselves felt like nothing compared to the something and someone we wanted to be. No wonder we often felt frustrated:

> The being of human reality is suffering because it rises in being as perpetually haunted by a totality which it is without being able to be it, precisely because it could not attain the in-itself without losing itself as for-itself. Human reality therefore is by nature an unhappy consciousness with no possibility of surpassing its unhappy state. (ibid. p. 90)

Sartre, like Heidegger, hyphenated concepts. Being-in-itself, the being that, in some sense, we were, was not all that we were. We wanted to get out of ourselves, move on from ourselves make more of ourselves then more again, without end. Being-for-itself was that restless spirit that moved on from whatever we had made of ourselves. To finally make ourselves would be to die. To be alive was to be forever renewing, remaking, remodelling, removing and getting out of the current 'in-itself'. Sartre spoke of the for-itself 'nihilating' the in-itself. I myself would choose to 'nihilate' this clumsy concept.

Sartre also spoke of a 'Being-for-others'. This was the 'me' that was an observed object for others making something of themselves. 'Every man for himself' would seem to be the consequent principle, which, as we have surely learnt, does not leave much room for Society. Sartre, more than Heidegger, tended to think that, in being-for-others, I would lose myself and become an alienated object. He did not sufficiently appreciate that social beings could find themselves within community. Too much self-centred me-for-myself can become indulgent, arid and sterile for me. It can be positively destructive for the society of which I am a part:

> If we happen to appear 'in public' to act in a play or to give a lecture, we never lose sight of the fact that we are looked at, and we execute the ensemble of acts which we have come to perform in the presence of the look; better yet we attempt to constitute a being and an ensemble of objects for this look. (ibid. p. 281)

We were conscious of ourselves as being looked at. What we made of ourselves was influenced by what we imagined others were making of us. We attempted to influence what others made of us by making a certain offering, or presentation, of ourselves to others. We made something of ourselves and we made something of each other. We allowed ourselves to be made, in some degree, by what others made of us. But what was the self that resulted from all this mutual making over? Was it a real authentic self or a made up self? Who could decide?

Sartre did not think the answer could be found via introspection. Actions could speak louder than words or thoughts, and, in fact, all were interconnected and inseparable, one from another. It was not helpful to think of internal 'motives' operating independently of, or independently causing, external 'acts':

> The resolute project toward a change is not distinct from the act, the motive, the act, and the end are all constituted in a single upsurge. Each of these three structures claims the other two as its meaning. (ibid. p. 438)

This echoes Heraclitus's view of reality as flux. Heidegger gave similar attention to the centrality of 'process', and, indeed, sought to relate his thinking to that of Heraclitus. But, in trying to make sense of oneself, this eternal movement of life was frightening. We wanted to nail down the internal furniture of our lives:

> Psychologically in each one of us this amounts to trying to take the causes and motives as *things*. We try to confer permanence upon them. We attempt to hide from ourselves that their nature and their weight depend each moment on the meaning which I give to them; we take them for constants. (ibid. p. 440)

For Sartre, we were not so much made by our motives as makers of motives. We made them, we interpreted them and we re-interpreted them. We acted with motive rather than because of it. Our motives and our actions arose from the free potential that we were. We were what we made of ourselves, and for as long as we were alive we could remake, make more, make less, make something new of ourselves, then move on again:

> Man can not be sometimes slave and sometimes free; He is wholly and forever free or he is not free at all. (ibid. p. 441)

For Sartre it was an act of 'bad faith', moral cowardice, irresponsibility leading to illusion, for us to see ourselves as 'caused' and determined by our motives and circumstances. The circumstances were, to some degree, a given, but it was what we made of them that counted. The motives were all our own work:

> Past motives, past causes, present motives and causes, future ends, are all organised in an indissoluble unity by the very upsurge of a freedom which is beyond causes, motives, and ends. (ibid. p. 450)

The idea that I had to think about and deliberate on all these causes and circumstances before I could act freely and responsibly was itself a deception:

> A voluntary deliberation is always a deception. How can I evaluate causes and motives on which I myself confer their value before all deliberation and by the very choice which I make of myself? (ibid. p. 450)

> Further: if I am brought to the point of deliberating, this is simply because it is a part of my original project to realise motives by means of deliberation rather than by some other form of discovery (by passion, for example, or simply by action). (ibid. p. 451)

Sartre, surely has a point. We may act responsibly when we pause and consciously deliberate but, as Heidegger observed, we do not always, or often, need to engage in conscious cogitation. We often act, and/or feel, and we know what we are doing and choosing, without having to have an inner monologue or dialogue about it. This does not mean that we are less responsible. It often means that we are more in control. Good drivers do not consciously deliberate, but they drive deliberately and they are certainly responsible for the consequences.

So, the irresponsible and dishonest could feel weighed down and oppressed by external causes and internal motives, but the individual who felt and faced up to the reality of their freedom knew that it was we who gave weight, shape, size and influence to causes and motives. We did so depending on the decisions, the projects and the excuses that we had already set up for ourselves:

> Actually causes and motives have only the weight which my project - that is, the free production of the end and of the known act to be realised – confers upon them. (ibid. p. 451)

So we found ourselves in what we did, in our projection of ourselves towards the self we wanted to be. Hume was right, we did not look inside and find 'myself'. Neither was there a 'myself' to be found in this instant and immediate here and now:

> To assume self-consciousness never means to assume a consciousness of the instant; for the instant is only one view of the mind and even if it existed, a consciousness which would apprehend itself in the instant would no longer apprehend anything. I can assume consciousness of myself only as a particular man engaged in this or that enterprise, anticipating this or that success, fearing this or that result, and by means of the ensemble of these anticipations, outlining his whole *figure*. (ibid. p. 462)

There was not an 'essential' self to find at all. Moreover, because time was one of the dimensions that comprised the shape of self, there was no self to be observed in this, that, or any other instant. Self could not be observed in two dimensions or, more crucially, in three. Any essential self we imagined we had found was an essentially inessential self. It was a temporary construct we had made through our own existence of choice and action. I could not find myself and then determine what projects and ends to embark upon. On the contrary (as being-for-itself), I freely chose my projects and my ends and in so doing created myself and thereby (temporarily) found myself (as being-in-itself):

Adam is not defined by an essence since for human reality essence comes after existence. Adam is defined by the choice of his ends. (ibid. p. 468)

Here, then, is the essence of the existentialist project: Existence precedes essence. I exist, and in so doing I choose, I project, I take action, I thereby construct and discover myself:

Thus human reality does not exist first in order to act later; but for human reality, to be is to act, and to cease to act is to cease to be. (ibid. p. 476)

All this, I hope, is reasonably clear. I have chosen the most lucid moments within Sartre's philosophical writing, much of which, sadly and in sharp contrast to his novels, is tortuous in the extreme. However, to what extent, if at all, is Sartre's existentialism actually true? Sartre was both an existentialist and a Marxist. This is quite an achievement given the vast differences and disagreements between these two philosophies. Towards the end of his life, he abandoned both. Let us look at some of the problems. First, and most obvious, this vexed question of individual freedom and responsibility.

Sartre was well aware that his views about human freedom and responsibility were at odds with conventional wisdom and common sense:

Much more than he appears 'to make himself', man seems 'to be made' by climate and the earth, race and class, language, the history of the collectivity of which he is a part, heredity, the individual circumstances of his childhood, acquired habits, the great and small events of his life. (ibid. p. 482)

Our circumstances appeared to surround, overwhelm and loom over us like vast mountains. How could we get over them? How could we blame ourselves if we failed to get on top of them?:

The coefficient of adversity in things can not be an argument against our freedom, for it is by *us* – that is, by the preliminary positing of an end – that this coefficient of adversity arises. A particular crag, which manifests a profound resistance if I wish to displace it, will be on the contrary a valuable aid if I want to climb upon it in order to look over the countryside. (ibid. p. 482)

We did not see buildings as obstacles blocking our path. We saw them as a given from and around which we made choices and took action.

The mountain might not be moveable, but what we made of it and what we did or did not do with it was in our hands. We were free to make what we chose of our circumstances. But were we free to do what we liked with them?:

> 'To be free' does not mean 'to obtain what one has wished' but rather 'by oneself to determine oneself to wish' (in the broad sense of choosing). In other words success is not important to freedom. (ibid. p. 483)

The freedom that Sartre explores is the freedom to interpret our world and its mountains. It is not the freedom to move mountains since, self-evidently, we are generally not able to move them at all:

> Thus we shall not say that a prisoner is always free to go out of prison, which would be absurd, nor that he is always free to long for release, which would be an irrelevant truism, but that he is always free to try to escape (or get himself liberated). (ibid. p. 484)

Suddenly, Sartre's notion of freedom looks less intoxicating, and less significant. We are free, he says, even in gaol. We are free to try to escape even though our chances of success (Sartre's 'coefficient of adversity') might be extremely, and almost infinitely, small. Is this going to be of much consolation to most prisoners? In the same way, we are all 'free' to dine at the Ritz. We will need some money of course. So we are 'free' to make a project of choosing to earn, find or steal the money, make the grade, buy the suit, get the car, establish a credit rating, drive off and select the meal.

There is no doubt that, when circumstances are tough, it is useful to find out what options we have and to work with them. Prisoners of war, prisoners of conscience, may discover that they have an inner freedom of control over their own thoughts and feelings that cannot be reached by their gaolers. They even have a few active options within the daily life of their cell. We only feel trapped in gaol because we want to get out. But does that mean we must take full responsibility for being in gaol? And does it really make sense to pretend that we can choose to be there? Zen teaching explores the problem in the story of the Zen master who achieved control of a situation when, having been thrown out of the window, declared: 'I am going down!'

Here is insight, and also an awareness of the absurdity of taking this kind of argument too far. A building is not an obstacle to us even if its absence would allow us to get from A to B more quickly:

What is an obstacle for me may not be so for another. There is no obstacle in an absolute sense, but the obstacle reveals its coefficient of adversity across freely invented and freely acquired techniques. (ibid. p. 488)

This is all very well, up to a point. By changing our attitudes, projects and expectations, we can redefine the meaning and the nature of our circumstances. As Dale Carnegie suggested in his best-selling *How to Make Friends and Influence People* (1994), 'When fate hands you a lemon, why not turn it into a lemonade?' Popular self-help psychology is full of this sort of thing. Choose positive attitudes, take positive action, redefine circumstances in a positive way and you can create a positive cycle, get on your bike, get up and away, get on, do it. And so on. It is all true, and important, up to a point.

But you need water and sugar to turn your lemon into lemonade, and some people's sour circumstances are a desert that they never deserved and from which they cannot, on their own, be expected to escape.

Sartre realises that we have freedom only within our circumstances, many of which are the 'givens' of existence within which we must work:

Human-reality everywhere encounters resistance and obstacles which it has not created, but these resistances and obstacles have meaning only in and through the free choice which human-reality *is*. (ibid. p. 489)

In the second part of this sentence, Sartre is seriously in error. These givens of existence do not only have meaning through my projects, actions, choices and interpretations. The mountain was there before me; it will be there after me. It is a mountain whatever I imagine it to be. I will not be able to climb twenty nine thousand feet unaided whatever I might think and do:

Thus our freedom itself creates the obstacles from which we suffer. (ibid. p. 495)

Yes and no, but 'no' more than 'yes'. Our circumstances create the obstacles from which we suffer more than we do. Our nature is a given as much as our circumstances. We have needs as well as options. I need water. I have no choice. If there is no water, I shall want water, I shall crave water and I shall not be able to 'choose' not to care about the lack of water. I shall die from the lack of water.

Heidegger realised, as Sartre did not, that meaning is not entirely, or even primarily, constructed on an individual basis. Most meaning making is a social activity. We discover what Trafalgar or Waterloo mean and we are moving into psychosis if we imagine that we can make anything we like out of them. There will be some room for individual freedom and choice but what we make of them will also be greatly determined by whether, for example, we are French or English citizens. Sartre realised that history, like everything else, was constructed and reconstructed according to our current projects, ends, choices and circumstances. But his focus on individual choice did not sit easily with his Marxism:

> Who shall decide whether the period which I spent in prison after a theft was fruitful or deplorable? I – according to whether I give up stealing or become hardened. (ibid. p. 499)

This is true enough, and it is important. It is also true that Sartre realised that there were limitations on the extent to which we could interpret our history. Moreover Sartre goes beyond so much naïve empiricism in realising that what we are trying to do, and where we are trying to go, has a great influence on where we think we have been, what we think has happened to us, and what we believe went on before us:

> Now the meaning of the past is strictly dependent on my present project. This certainly does not mean that I can make the meaning of my previous acts vary in any way I please; quite the contrary, it means that the funda-mental project which I am decides absolutely the meaning which the past which I have to be can have for me and for others. I alone in fact can decide at each moment the bearing of the past. (ibid. p. 498)

Just as Freud gave primacy to the power of the past to influence, explain and determine our present actions, so Sartre believed that it was the future that counted. The past mattered, but it was defined, shaped and described in terms of our planned future:

> Thus the urgency of the past comes from the future. (ibid. p. 499)

The therapist needed to unravel, not so much key influences from the past, but key decisions about, and visions we had for, our future. Even beginnings and endings only had meaning in terms of the story we were telling of ourselves:

The actual project therefore decides whether a defined period of the past is in continuity with the present or whether it is a discontinuous fragment from which one is emerging and which is put at a distance. (ibid. p. 501)

Consequently as our current story about ourselves changed, both individually and collectively, so our history would be rewritten. How, for example, were we to interpret the storming of the Bastille?:

> He who would like to decide the question today forgets that the historian is himself historical; that is, that he historicizes himself by illuminating history in the light of his projects and those of his society. Thus it is necessary to say that the meaning of the social past is perpetually 'in suspense'. (ibid. p. 501)

We could, and would, rewrite our history in the process of changing our projects for the future. But, having chosen our future project, the past was certainly important:

> We choose our past in the light of a certain end, but from then on it imposes itself upon us and devours us. (ibid. p. 503

For Sartre, we were free to choose, and the therapist needed to help clients become aware of, and take responsibility for, the choices that they had already made:

> Of course my freedom to *choose*, as we have seen, must not be confused with my freedom to *obtain*. (ibid. p. 505)

Sartre believed that we stayed free, in this sense of being free to choose, regardless of our circumstances:

> Even the red hot pincers of the torturer do not exempt us from being free. (ibid. p. 506)

But what kind of freedom is this? What, in all honesty, are our options when faced with red hot pincers? Can we choose not to scream or burn or die? We might choose not to give away information to 'the enemy' but even this is not certain. Torturers claim to be able to break the will of most people. They may have good reason to know:

> I am absolutely free and absolutely responsible for my situation. But I am never free except *in situation*. (ibid. p. 509)

This kind of observation can, for example, be used as a handy excuse for governments who do not choose to improve the situation of the poor, the underprivileged, the oppressed. 'You are all absolutely free, get on your bikes. Take a positive attitude, help yourselves and be more responsible.' Your situation is a 'given'.

Sartre, as a Marxist, did not accept this excuse, and would have added that governments are absolutely free to improve the miserable circumstances within which the poor act with 'absolute freedom'. But it is something of a misuse of common parlance to talk of absolute freedom in these straightened circumstances, and more may be lost than gained by this attempt to change everyday meanings and understandings of freedom.

Faced with this 'freedom', we might feel afraid, daunted, alone, lost and arbitrary. Certainly we would feel alone since Sartre had defined freedom in Cartesian and individualistic terms. Choose Heidegger's freedom, by the same token, and you need never feel alone:

> It is absurd that we are are born; it is absurd that we die. (ibid. p. 547)

Are there any absolute foundations to our lives? The world is flat and is supported by four great elephants standing on a tortoise floating in a vast ocean of milk. But what lies under the milk? Is it in another, larger saucer? There is no end to the storms we can create and questions we can ask about teacups large and small. No explanation is final in that we can, if we so choose, ask, 'but why, and how?' of that, and that. We can then imagine a mysterious 'nothing' lying 'behind' or 'beneath' whatever fundamental 'something' we have constructed, and it can feel absurd. Beyond the limit of what we sense and make sense of there lies, not surprisingly, senselessness.

But absurdity does not have to be allowed to wallow around in the centre of our lives even it can hover on the edge. Self-evidently, those who project themselves and are happy with their projects feel more fulfilled than do those who lose, or fail to find, impetus and who sink into depression and despair. According even to his own theory, we may ask who is Sartre to say that life is absurd? It can be absurd when we make it and interpret it as absurd. It is, unavoidably, nonsense when we make no sense of it. After Sartre's fame, all kinds of 'me-too' philosophers, intellectuals and café dwellers joined in on the game of feeling angst ridden, nauseous, absurd. A whole 'theatre of the absurd' came into vogue with lost individuals sharing hopeless hopes in a desert of meaninglessness and pointlessness. It became a badge whereon one showed that one was 'sensitive' and 'avant garde'.

Then America got hold of existentialism and tended to focus more on its 'can-do' components. Life is what you make of it. Go forward, think and grow rich, and so on. This project, like any other, could also become simplistic, indulgent and naïve.

At times Sartre did seem to realise that there were limits on the control we had of our projects:

> We have, in fact, every chance of dying before we have accomplished our task, or, on the other hand, of outliving it. There is therefore a very slim chance that our death will be presented to us as that of Sophocles was, for example, in the manner of a resolved chord. (ibid. p. 536)

From many a North American perspective we could be what we wanted to be. We could make any project we wished to make of ourselves. The therapist's task was to uncover the client's project. This the client would have chosen, but they might well not be aware of, or take responsibility for, the choice they had made:

> Existential psychoanalysis seeks to determine the original choice. (ibid. p. 570)

Sartre saw this existential approach to psychoanalysis as very different to the Freudian project. He was also rather humble about his own role:

> This psychoanalysis has not yet found its Freud. (ibid. p. 575)

For Sartre, though, there was a fundamental project that we all shared, whether we realised it or not:

> The best way to conceive of the fundamental project of human reality is to say that man is the being those project is to be God. (ibid. p. 566)

Christians, and even humanists, throughout most of history would have seen this view as a form of blasphemy. After all, it was an act of evil to defy the will of God. It was the devil's work. It was hubris to imagine that we could choose without respect for, and understanding of, the warp and weft of existence. It was arrogance and folly to become self-preoccupied, insular and introverted. By any sensible interpretation of freedom we are not absolutely free. Our freedom is highly constrained by our circumstances and we do no service to each other and ourselves if we pretend otherwise.

Sartre's narrative can be useful as a means of assisting people to gain a fuller understanding of their powers, options and responsibilities. But it is also liable to lead people to overestimate the extent of their powers, options and resources. We are, in Sartre's sense, 'free' to dine at the Ritz. But never mind subjective resourcefulness, we also need objective resources and most people do not, and will not, have them. Therefore Sartre's 'freedom' is not personally or politically of much interest except for those who wish to obfuscate fundamental structural inequality and injustice.

Sartre's hero, in the novel *Nausea*, becomes more and more detached from the world around him and, unsurprisingly, moves closer to psychotic depression. It is a brilliant account of what can happen, but ought to serve more as a warning than as a viable philosophy:

> Everything is gratuitous, that park, this town, and myself. When you realise that, it turns your stomach over and everything starts floating about. (*Nausea*, p. 188)

The hero, Antoine Roquetin, is detached, disengaged, and sees absurdity, blind habit and avoidance of individual freedom and responsibility in every direction:

> What can I do? Is it my fault if, in everything he tells me, I recognise borrowings, quotations? Is it my fault if, while he speaks, I see all the humanists I have known reappear? (ibid. p. 168)

He sees the same within himself:

> They aren't dead, my habits, they go on bustling about, gently, insidiously weaving their webs, they wash me, dry me, dress me, like nursemaids. Was it they too who brought me up on this hill? (ibid. p. 224)

Roquetin is also able to look with a detachment that allows him to see with more wonder and awe than is available to those busy with their projects:

> I saw clearly that you could not pass from its function as a root, as a suction-pump, to that, to that hard, compact sea-lion skin, to that oily, horny, stubborn look. The function explained nothing; it enabled you to understand in general what a root was, but not that one at all. That root, with its colour, its shape, its frozen movement, was... beneath all explanation. (ibid. p. 186)

So there are some benefits in idling in cafés on a private income for long periods of time. Eventually, however, Roquetin hits on a project that might free him from his sense of listlessness and purposelessness:

> Couldn't I try... Naturally, it wouldn't be a question of a tune... But couldn't I in another medium?... It would have to be a book: I don't know how to do anything else. Then, through it, I might be able to recall my life without repugnance. (ibid. p. 252)

Roquetin finds a project, finds a connection with others and moves on from sterile introspection. Ironically, he only manages to think of one viable option ('I don't know how to do anything else') and this may be a common experience for many of us, regardless of Sartre's notion of 'absolute' freedom. Nonetheless, we may have reason to believe that he therefore moves away from depression and psychosis and rejoins the community of which he is a part. We may also imagine that Roquetin's existentialism thereby comes more under the sway of Heidegger than of Sartre. No wonder, then, that Sartre himself moved on from his own creation. To move on from his philosophy is, in any case, consistent with the reality that his philosophy seeks to describe.

❓ Questions

1. What do you think of the idea of self as 'a little god within'? Is it insight or folly that our culture has made a deity of self?

2. How far is it helpful to encourage clients to take responsibility for their circumstances? Do they shape, or are they primarily shaped by, their environment? What examples come to mind?

3. Do we really make our own meanings? If self is sovereign how far can meanings be shared and on what basis can they be challenged?

4. How far do you, or will you, utilise existential approaches within your own practice of counselling/care?

EXERCISES

1. Compare Nietzsche, Kierkegaard, Heidegger and Sartre. What do you consider to be the strengths and weaknesses of each?

2. Consider Sartre's view that we make our motives more than being driven by them. What is your view? Do motives impinge on, or emerge from, the self?

Conclusion

Sartre's 'self' was similar in some respects to Descartes', but without God. Self, for Sartre, became its own God and I believe that this view of self has been hugely influential within, and thereby destructive of, our culture. Sartre gives 'self' autonomy from its circumstance that entirely fails to take into account the more sophisticated interaction explored by Heidegger. It is not surprising, therefore, that Heidegger had such a low opinion of *Being and Nothingness*. But Sartre's exploration of freedom, motive, intention, meaning making and responsibility deserve attention even though he underestimates the defining influence of circumstance over person power.

The existentialist assertion that 'I make my own meanings' seems as wrong-headed as the essentialist, idealist alternative of absolute meaning independent of any observer. The next 'big name' in philosophy might, hopefully, provide a synthesis that incorporated and transcended this thesis and antithesis. Unfortunately, no philosopher, to my knowledge, has yet achieved such integration. In the meantime, it is not progress to be shipwrecked in subjectivity, or to meander in meaninglessness, or to wallow destitute within one's own deconstruction. Neither is it honourable to celebrate the triumph of Machiavellian public relations over liberal concern for truth. Modernity, as previously understood, is being left behind. The shape of the postmodern, if it is ever to be attempted or achieved, remains unclear; but the next chapter will attempt at least to explore some of the issues.

Websites

http://www.nobel.se/laureates/literature-1964-1-bio.html
http://www-phil.philengl.dundee.ac.uk/staff/jdb/existent/sartre2.htm

Bibliography

Dale Carnegie, *How to Make Friends and Influence People*, Pocket Books, 1994
J.P. Sartre, *Existentialism and Humanism*, Eyre Methuen, 1974
J.P. Sartre, *Essays in Existentialism*, Citadel, US, 1987
J.P. Sartre, *Nausea*, Penguin, 1990
J.P. Sartre, *Being and Nothingness: An Essay on Phenomenological Ontology*, Routledge, 1996

Chapter 33

What next?

────────────────────────── **Key Points** ──────────────────────────

- ■ It is too early to know which contemporary philosophers will have left a mark a century from now

- ■ The current position within philosophy appears to be one of considerable disillusion with 'grand narratives'

- ■ Marxism and psychoanalysis have suffered major losses of prestige and influence. Christianity continues its long decline and liberal humanism has come under attack from many quarters

- ■ The statement that no large statements can be made is itself a large statement.

── *Application* ──────────────────────────────────────

- ● A vision of the future that provides us with no more than shopping and the sale of personal portfolios is a barren, depressing, prospect
- ● Health, personal and collective progress are not served by sterile secularism or postmodern nihilism
- ● A vision of no vision should carry a government health warning. It provides no future either for governments or individuals
- ● The liberal humanist agenda can continue, but there is no room for complacency.

Sartre died in 1980. His major work, *Being and Nothingness* was written in 1956. This was modern writing for a modern age. We are now, supposedly, in a *post*modern period. What does that mean? What has been happening in the development of ideas since Sartre? How are we to make sense of our current circumstances? What is changing? What is to be done? Which voices within contemporary discussions will carry down the centuries and influence our great great grandchildren?

The concept of postmodernism first appeared within architecture. The modern was functional, undecorated, new and provided a clean break from past, backward-looking, forms. The postmodern, on the contrary, plays with decoration, style, performs with itself and borrows without much concern for 'authenticity'. So can we also have postmodern art? Is there a postmodern philosophy? Are we now a postmodern humanity? Or are there not essentials within the human spirit and human circumstances that transcend any particular period in, perspective on, or fashion from, history?

As everyone splashes about with their ideas it is almost impossible to see who is making the deeper waves that really will carry forward beyond one century. It takes time to see who is most profoundly shaping the way others think, feel and act. Enough decades have passed to show the nature and scale of Sartre's influence. But who has a similar stature among more recent names? I think it is too early to know. Something, at least, can be said about the pattern of discussion that comprises the (so-called) postmodern agenda.

From Hume onwards, naïve ideas about a simple core self have become increasingly implausible. Self has been analysed and contextualised; the nature of its would-be internal dynamics, boundaries and external circumstances have been hotly debated. But all serious commentators have agreed that, even among those who avoid crises of identity, there is no simple unchanging self-essence that exists independently of a changing world. The question 'Who am I?' is relatively easy to answer in terms of conventional 'identity', but it becomes much more complex and mysterious when questions continue to be asked about the basis of previous answers.

Existentialists, critical of grand theories, warned against simplistic labelling of 'myself'. Self was not, in any case, an object at all. Subsequent to Sartre, the scepticism has been taken still further with, for example, Jacques Derrida (b. 1930) proposing that we 'deconstruct' the basis of not just our concepts but also of our experiences. There was no system or self to be built but we could take apart other people's efforts to construct such selves and systems. The aim was not to cultivate a new philosophy of life, but merely to see by what assumptions and prejudices others had assembled such philosophies and identities. There was no Mount Olympus, no 'neutral' or dispassionate standpoint, no philosophical doctrine to be held, merely positions, languages, narratives to be analysed.

A similar interest in linguistic analysis preoccupied post-war Anglo-Saxon philosophy. Its style was very different from continental approaches, but the danger was the same: What happens if you do nothing but take everything apart? You ought not to be surprised if you end up with nothing but very small pieces. Nothing will be whole and intact. Moreover, on what basis will you distinguish between ephemeral trivia and eternal truth? A 'grand narrator' would have no problem, but if you have deconstructed all supposedly grand narratives how do you measure the relative significance of whatever is left? If none of these smaller sketches carries particular authority how are judgements to be made? On what authority do you judge anything? Surely the act of deconstruction itself requires authority and judgement? If so who provides the authority? On what basis is any judgement distinguished from mere prejudice or lower-brain habits and preoccupation?

A great deal of the philosophy we have examined shows that absolute truth is neither as absolute nor as true as medievalists or contemporary believers in 'common sense' would like to believe. But we descend into chaos if we move to the opposite polarity and assume that 'truth' is indistinguishable from opinion and that anybody's 'truth' is as significant as anyone else's. If 'anything goes' in our efforts to make sense then soon nothing will make sense at all.

Postmodern thinking, therefore, is an asset insofar as it explores the limitations of a narrowly defined 'rationality'. It is a dangerous liability, however, if it suggests that there is no rationality at all but only rationalisations. If there are only opinions and appearances then nothing is real, nothing is true and nothing is important. Moreover no one then has any basis to say that there are only opinions. Such a statement is not 'true'; it is merely another opinion. Postmodernism thereby castrates itself before it is in a position seriously to break into, and break down, the activities and interests of anyone else.

Modern advertising showed modern people living in modern houses and taking the advice of modern scientists in white coats. Postmodern advertising laughs at the idea of selling products but goes on selling them anyway. It jokes at all its efforts to attract attention and goes on attracting attention. It invokes not so much a modern environment as a surreal world wherein every fantasy can be made real, but nothing is really real, except that advertisers are trying, and succeeding, in making a sale.

Modern life was shared via broadcast technology. Postmodern life fragments into 'narrow-cast' networking. Its more developed technologies may keep you abreast of what is new and real. Still more likely, its technology may merely distract you, taking you further into fantasy, play, imagery, restless surfing of (in)attention.

If Jacques Derrida is the arch deconstructionist, Claude Lévi-Strauss (b. 1908) is the arch structuralist. For Lévi-Strauss, we do not inhabit a world of mere appearances, prejudices, opinions and plausibilities. On the contrary, there was a deep structure that underlay cultural systems and which transcended particular fashions or the specific cultural preoccupations of any one period in history. There was, as the Greeks would have called it, a *logos* underlying the ways in which cultures were constructed and developed. Cultures were systems of communication and there were fundamental essentials governing their structure that transcended the cultures themselves. Lévi-Strauss is more than willing to generalise about the entire human condition just as deconstructionists pour scorn on any such efforts to generalise. They do, of course, make generalisations about the limits of generalisation.

As ever there are dangers and insights within both styles of thinking: Deconstructionists may end up dissecting trivial pieces into still more trifling components; structuralists may make such broad generalisations that it no longer is clear what is being generalised.

Occasionally the worst kinds of French philosophy appear to manage both kinds of meaninglessness at the same time. Broad and sweeping statements are made about how the most specific species of utterance can be broken down still further into – nothing much at all. This kind of thing, I am sure, will not survive another century. Poorer versions of Anglo-Saxon philosophy are much more concerned about clarity of communication. A chummy, down-to-earth specificity is employed to talk very carefully about – not very much at all. The moral is that there are morals, values and priorities, and that philosophers need to believe that some topics are more significant than others are. Philosophers need to talk more about what is important and less about what is not. They need to believe that (widely) shared and serious talk is possible and desirable. Otherwise their philosophy, not surprisingly, will be insignificant.

The seventeenth and eighteenth centuries have been described as an Age of Enlightenment. At this time, it is claimed, we moved beyond superstition and theological dogma and trusted in the powers of reason and humanity. Human beings, with their big brains, could think, feel and act intelligently for themselves, learn from their mistakes, harness the powers of nature and make a more comfortable, fair and enlightened world. In earlier chapters, we have considered some of the flagship thinkers of this tradition, including Descartes, Locke and Hume, and continuing into the nineteenth century with Mill. In many respects this tradition was stimulated by the rediscovery of the Greek humanist tradition. The Greeks once again became role models and liberal education drew from the thinking of two and a half thousand years previously in preference to monastic dogmas and blind habit. Public schools and public architecture both took their inspiration from this, would-be, Golden Age of Ancient Greece.

Such liberal humanism lives on but its limitations were exposed by Schopenhauer, Kierkegaard, Marx and Nietzsche, and the onslaught has continued in our postmodern era. Where does that leave us? I will give you an illustration: I go to a presentation on the latest thinking in education at the turn of the century, and I find that 'humanities', as a subject area, is offered as logically and organisationally equivalent to 'hotel and hospitality management'. Something, surely, is going badly wrong? I come home and see an advertisement for what claims to be the largest shopping centre in Europe. The 'Metro Centre', I am reassured, is not just a shopping centre, it is a Way of Life. And I think, yes, this advertisement is telling the truth. Shopping is our way of life. Tradesmen, as Plato would see them, now run the world. In a postmodern era, hotel and hospitality management is equivalent to, and possibly the same as, the Humanities. But should this be the case? Is it legitimate to talk about what 'should' be or am I merely airing a tired old liberal and patriarchal preference?

I hope the reader can see how all these generalisations are important to anyone who wants to make sense of existence or help someone else do the same. If shopping really is a way of life then we are in deep trouble if we really want to come to terms with ourselves, get real and communicate with others. If we think there are no realities but only more or less plausible appearances then, again, this is a sign that our culture is in deep crisis. I hope that this whole book will have shown why and why it is absurd to see all these chapters as the mere airing of opinions. These philosophers took their own, and other people's, ideas seriously. They reacted seriously to each other and their thinking consequently formed patterns, shapes and directions that can, at any time, be explored and considered.

The fact that definitive conclusions do not get drawn from such analysis, and that an easy consensus does not exist, is not to say that any old prejudice and opinion will suffice. That is a cheap solution for those who, disappointed at the lack of simple answers, will not work seriously with the complexities, uncertainties and paradoxes of real life.

The liberal humanist tradition had always been a 'grand narrative' in the sense that it sought to integrate experience, individual and collective development. Liberal humanism, in its essence, revealed and explored the interconnections between the big questions that mattered. Scientists, in contrast, tended to have a reputation for being narrow specialists less than interested in human dimensions and rounded personalities. Yet in some modern and postmodern developments within the humanities there has been a withdrawal into ever more introverted, self-preoccupied and sceptical visions of life's possibilities. The world has looked more grey, less hopeful, more mechanical and there has been growing uncertainty about the self that is to perform each day. Is there a self at all? Are we merely storytellers? Are there only masks to wear and no original face to unmask? Can we tell any lies we like if, in reality, there is only fantasy? Why bother to get up in the morning? Is God dead? Are all that remain in a secular wilderness shopping and self-promotion? What values, projects, adventures are worth getting serious about?

These questions will always be important and progress with them is not assisted by a scepticism that does not merely test but actually seeks to destroy the basis of value judgements and individual identity. Yet just as confidence dissipates in the Enlightenment agendas of progress, reason, justice, co-operation and self-determination so the vision of science moves way beyond grey mechanism and takes us into a world more awesome and magical than anything in a Lewis Carroll novel. At first the worlds of contemporary science may seem just as frightening and chaotic as anything encountered by Alice in Wonderland or through the looking glass. Yet the arbitrariness of it all is only apparent, and there is an underlying and essential beauty, coherence and sheer awesome splendour to reality that exceeds the best efforts of poets to describe it. Indeed, it does not require poetry; it is already poetic in its succinctness, elegance and power.

So, just as postmodern language is used to deconstruct and disintegrate any grand vision of coherence, sense and meaning that we might wish to live by, so postmodern mathematics comes in to provide ever larger syntheses, patterns and constructions of an organised, elegant and beautiful universe. Traditionally we assume that words are central to making sense of, and bringing together, our existence. Yet mathematics, for those who have been shown how to grapple with it, provides more of a vision of integration now than much of the latest prose, which tends to be more about fragmentation and disintegration.

In sharp contrast to science's efforts to develop a 'theory of everything', Jean-François Lyotard (b. 1924) describes postmodernism as 'incredulity towards metanarratives':

> The grand narrative has lost its credibility, regardless of what mode of unification it uses, regardless of whether it is a speculative narrative or a narrative of emancipation. (Lyotard, 1984, p. 489)

This itself is a large statement that large statements cannot be made. Should we be depressed?:

> Most people have lost the nostalgia for the lost narrative. It in no way follows that they are reduced to barbarity. What saves them from it is their knowledge that legitimation can only spring from their own linguistic practice and communicational interaction. (ibid., p. 493)

Here we are back in our networks once again. The wider picture within which our 'communicational interactions' take place cannot be talked about. Or, at least, the kind of talk I have in my network will be incommensurable with the various kinds of talk in other networks. If you come from another network then there will be no metanarrative via which we can try to engage with each other. We will presumably, therefore, be mutually incomprehensible. We may make value judgements about what we observe in each other, but neither judgement will have any transcendental authority over the other.

To put it another way, according to this vision of no vision, there is no history of humanity, but merely different histories of different tribes and networks each with its own spin and rationalisations and interests to protect.

If this is really the case, then there will not and cannot be any new big idea from any new major thinker. No one will be able to make a large wave that travels through time and society as a whole. If metanarrative is impossible, there is no society as a whole and maybe no society at all. There will be no one ocean of existence which we all share. Instead, each network will occupy its own small, drying and fragmenting pond, its own private and bounded universe of shared experience more or less hermetically sealed from others. Lyotard will not be able to be a big name from a big university. If he succeeds then he fails. He becomes a name known only to those who talk and think like he does and who move within narrow university circles:

> We are all stuck in the positivism of this or that discipline or learning... the diminished tasks of research have become compartmentalised and no one can master them all. Speculative or humanistic philosophy is forced to relinquish its legitimation duties, which explains why philosophy is facing a crisis wherever it persists in arrogating such functions. (ibid. p. 492)

The authority of universities will be itself suspect and, in any case, there will not even be a university in any shared sense, merely different departments and small teams each focused on its own agenda, indifferent to, and uncomprehending of, the work of people in other corridors. Perhaps this explains why Lyotard and many contemporaries make so little effort to be comprehensible to those who do not belong to the world of postmodern French philosophy? These philosophers assume that others will not understand them and that there is no reason why they should try.

Insofar as Lyotard is right, I fear that he is describing a malaise, a disintegration, a loss of shared vision and communal values that should be a cause of collective alarm rather than self-congratulation. If Lyotard is right, then there is not only no history but, by implication, no future either. Instead there are just individual 'futures' which, if not shared, will be essentially of the aimless channel-hopping, distraction-seeking, meaningless variety.

Postmodernists, consistent with their own grand narrative of no grand narratives, will deny that there can, or should, be any wide and shared understanding of the term 'postmodernism'. They will deny that the word can ever mean the same thing to different networks of people. They will, if serious, not expect that you, from your perspective, should necessarily take them seriously.

This kind of clowning suggests a serious loss of morale among 'leading-edge' academics and intellectuals. How is this nihilism to be explained? To try at all is, of course, to engage in another 'grand narrative'. I will try not to be too grand but there is fairly clear evidence of a pattern to this postmodernist development. The current fragmentation makes sense when it is remembered that two grand narratives of the twentieth century appear to have almost collapsed as this century came to a close. On the one hand, there is Marxism. In the mid-twentieth century many western intellectuals sincerely hoped or feared that Communism was the ideology of the future. Now it sounds like a voice from the past, and many postmodernists would appear to be refugees from Marxism who became disillusioned with this ideology from 1968 onwards. On the other hand, there is psychoanalysis. This was once seen as the royal road to the unconscious, to our underlying and authentic individual reality. Now it is becoming more and more clear that Freud's work had always been pseudo-scientific, vague and untestable indoctrination.

Two main routes, then, to finding ourselves, one individual and one collective now both look untenable. In addition, the Christian tradition has continued the decline already well under way in the nineteenth century. Another important narrative, the liberal humanism whose history and development has been explored in so many earlier chapters, has likewise been heavily criticised throughout the last one hundred years. Now it is commonplace to say of liberal humanists, of whatever kind, that they are nothing like as dispassionate, detached, reasonable, liberal or as humane as they may have believed. On the contrary, they have been blasted from many quarters and now tend to be seen as white, male, conservative, exploitative, prejudiced, western and middle class. Their history has ignored 'herstory'. It has rationalised more than reasoned. This, for many, has been enough to condemn liberal humanism entirely as incapable of providing solutions to the problems faced by humanity, or, at least, of more specific minorities within humanity. Yet no alternative grand vision presents itself. Instead there are the single-issue politics, introversion, interest groups and lobbying of many networks with many competing agendas. No wonder it is so tempting, then, to say that there is no point in looking for a new analysis, explanation or ideology because there *are* no overriding explanations, meanings or values to be found. No wonder, also, that people withdraw into the private and personal and seek individual and confidential support rather than sharing concerns, hopes and fears within a larger community.

As the twentieth century began, many believed that a new vision would sweep away the old establishment. Socialist/Communist governments would replace the liberal democracies, which were never as liberal or as democratic as they claimed. Victorian hypocrisy would unravel, as we each became more authentic and self-aware thanks to our psychoanalytic guide. As the twenty-first century begins, liberal democracy appears to have a greater hegemony of power than ever, along with an ever-declining confidence and belief in itself. It has been greatly undermined, and has undermined itself, in too many ways. It has lacked vision. It has often become overly comfortable and complacent. It has failed to understand and nurture spiritual needs and preoccupations. It has too often prostrated itself to commerce at the expense of humane values, thereby turning us all into commodities. It has, rightly, been accused of being far less liberal or democratic than it has claimed to be.

Yet no one seems to know what to put in its place. 'Left-wing' managers of the system, looking for a 'third way' between socialism and conservatism, wish to control its worst excesses, but have few powers and no plans to replace it. Postmodernists talk of endless varieties of networking and 'narrow-cast' interests but power inequalities are larger than ever. Many can engage in any number of cyber-circuses and distractions if they are in employment. A few have real power, recognise one interconnected global economy, and know who are the people that matter in running that economy.

Discussion of would-be grand narratives, where we are now, if there is a single 'we' at all, what is likely to happen next – these are not just abstract philosophical topics. Ultimately these issues are relevant to the question of why anyone should get up in the morning. Philosophy has, traditionally, had a lot to say on these subjects. Postmodern philosophy, at its worst, presumes no authority at all except to claim with authority that there are no authorities. This kind of talk has no future. But humanity deserves better than this from its philosophers:

> It is not (the masses) who have abandoned idealism, universalism, truth and justice. It is those who already enjoy these things who have denounced them on behalf of others. The two sides, of course, never meet. (O'Neill, p. 1)

? Questions

1. In a postmodern society is it any longer possible to believe in independent third-party outsiders providing dispassionate empathy and support?

2. Is objective and dispassionate care a simple absurdity or a complex possibility? Is it adequate for care workers to adopt the postmodernist line that there is no basis for making objective judgements and that clients can therefore explore their own narrative without regard for anyone else?

3. Just how sophisticated do carers need to be if they are to defend themselves against philosophical critiques of objectivity, subjectivity and personal identity?

4. Are grand narratives possible anymore? Can liberal humanism any longer sustain 'Renaissance people' who can embrace the liberal arts, science and spirituality within one integrated vision of life and its possibilities? Or must we all fragment into our own introverted and isolated specialisms, interests, networks and languages?

EXERCISES

1. Consider how counselling and other professional care programmes can best locate themselves between the two extremes of postmodern nihilism and naïve beliefs in neutrality, identity and objectivity.

2.   Consider how far training within professional care needs to stay abreast of the past, present and possible futures within philosophy.

Conclusion

If you submit the word 'postmodernism' to just one search engine (Altavista), forty three thousand articles are listed as mentioning this keyword. (This statement will, of course, be obsolete as soon as anyone else reads it!) University websites are jumbled together with individual, sometimes eccentric, musings. Who can read all this? Who, among all these voices, speaks authentically and with authority, and who decides? Can generalisations and a grand narrative be made that can draw all this material together? Or does this vast availability of insight/fact/opinion/wisdom/prejudice/comment/hypertext meta-language reinforce the postmodernist view that we can only occupy small fragments, networks and cells of existence?

There is now a computer program, with products available on the internet, that generates articles on postmodernism using all the key jargon, agendas and grammatical styles of postmodern philosophy. Are its articles superior to its human rivals? Can the question be asked? Can readers differentiate the efforts of the machine from human beings? Does it matter? In my own view, this tongue-in-cheek critique effectively demolishes the postmodern attempt to deconstruct all rationality and objectivity by demonstrating that absurdity is the inevitable consequence of taking irrationalism or anti-rationalism seriously.[1]

Note

1. *The Postmodernism Generator* was written by Andrew C. Bulhak, using the Dada Engine, a system for generating random text from recursive grammars. More detailed technical information may be found in Monash University Department of Computer Science Technical Report 96/264: 'On the simulation of postmodernism and mental debility using recursive transition networks'.

Websites

http://www.as.ua.edu/ant/murphy/pomo.html
http://private.fuller.edu/~clameter/phd/postmodern.html
http://www.cs.monash.edu.au/links/postmodern.html
http://www.geocities.com/Athens/Agora/9095/postmodernism.html
http://olympus.athens.net/~hartman/essay15.htm

http://briet.berkeley.edu/phil/postmodern.html
http://www.utm.edu/research/iep/

Bibliography

S. Brown, D. Collinson and R. Wilkinson (eds) *One Hundred Twentieth-century Philosophers*, Routledge, 1998

L. Cahoone (ed.) *From Modernism to Postmodernism, An Anthology*, Blackwell, 1996

T. Eagleton, *The Illusions of Postmodernism*, Blackwell, 1996

J.F. Lyotard, *The Postmodern Condition: A Report on Knowledge*, in L. Cahoone (ed.) *From Modernism to Postmoderism: An Anthology*, Blackwell, 1996

W. McNeill and K. Feldman (eds) *Continental Philosophy: An Anthology*, Blackwell, 1998

J. O'Neill, *The Poverty of Postmodernism*, Routledge, 1995

R. Tarnas, *The Passion of the Western Mind*, Pimlico, 1996

Conclusion

Who am I? What do I really know? Where am I going? Where should I go?
I suggested, in the Introduction, that the reader might take these four
questions with them as they worked their way through this book. They
are convenient pegs on which to hang much of its material.

As a child I remember the school textbooks with the answers at the
back. Philosophy does not work like that. The most interesting questions do not have 'final' answers, but this does not make any one explanation as good as any other. Our existence would be trite and dull if it
could be finally 'explained', and a trim conclusion to the works of over
thirty philosophers does not exist. I am certainly not going to be so
foolish as to attempt one now. It could do no justice to the questions
they have asked or to the process of questioning.

In philosophy, there is no easy consensus or a definitive lack of agree-
ment. There is no straightforward progress or a failure to make
headway. Important insights are forgotten and rediscovered. The work
of ancient Greece was lost to the west for a thousand years. 'Infidel'
Muslims preserved it. Let us remember that next time Islam is caricatured as being against the humanist tradition.

Progress *is* made in philosophy, however, but it tends to demolish the
simple explanation we thought we had. Our progress raises new questions and doubts. This is unwelcome if you prefer comfortable certainties to challenging enquiry.

Everyone is an amateur psychologist in that we all try, more or less
often, to understand and predict the behaviour of other people. Likewise,
everyone is an amateur philosopher in that we all ask, occasionally or regularly, why we are here, how to make sense of what we do, who we are, what
is important and where we are heading. Folk wisdom often draws on the
work of professionals, without knowing who, when or why. Some of
Freud's ideas have seeped into the mainstream. Some of the terminology of

contemporary counselling is doing the same. Cartesianism seems to structure many people's thinking, although few have even heard of Descartes.

The trouble with amateur psychology and philosophy is that it tends
not to keep up with the professionals. It is the same with music and
painting. Most people prefer to listen to what was impossibly new and
avant garde a century ago. Professionals, while not jettisoning the past,
seek to push harder at the boundaries of meaning and expression, and
search for new ways of exploring contemporary understanding.

We cannot all be at the 'leading edge' of everything, of course, and
there is no reason why we should even try. Clients have generally neither
the time nor the inclination to study philosophy. How much time should
carers and clients trying to take stock of their lives give to the subject?

I hope I have shown why more time should be allotted to the study of
philosophy. It is relevant within the training of anyone seeking to
provide support to others via talking and listening. Philosophy is
already there within such training but, more often than not, it is not
recognised. For example, cognitive-behavioural therapy imports huge
quantities of Stoic teaching. Humanistic therapy incorporates Rousseau
on a considerable scale. Existential approaches utilise Sartre but not
enough perhaps of Heidegger, or Nietzsche or Kierkegaard.[1]

Anyone who is talking or listening in order to help somebody take
stock of their predicament cannot avoid doing so within a framework
of values and constructs of self and society. Assumptions are made
about what is important, who we are and where we ought to be going.
These assumptions are all strongly influenced by the work of previous
philosophers. Philosophy thereby provides the foundations on which
the practice of human attention stands, the roof beneath which it shel-
ters, the walls within which it is contained and the windows through
which it looks out on the wider world.

In response to this argument, some counsellors claim that they are not
teaching clients philosophy, they are 'just listening', so they do not need
to know about these writers. We have seen that Heidegger, among others,
has made an extraordinarily powerful case to show that 'just listening' is
quite impossible both in principle and in practice. Counsellors have not
challenged or refuted Heidegger's argument because, of course, they are
generally quite unaware of it. This naïvety and ignorance is simply not
acceptable among people who claim to be providing a professional
analysis of how to heal and understand others via talking and listening.

A university administrator is said to have asked staff in the physics
department: *'What is it with you physicists? You want billions of dollars to
smash atoms, and you are always asking for more. The maths department*

manages with pencils, paper and wastepaper baskets. And the philosophers do not even ask for waste bins.'

Philosophers *do* need large waste bins, but the best philosophy can be worth revisiting however old it is. It is not thrown away, yet it is recognisable as old, early and belonging to its own place and time more so than to ours. The best philosophy is like a conversation that takes place down the centuries. Conversations may meander and get stuck. They may sometimes repeat. But you cannot simply put each contribution in any order whatsoever, unless each speaker is listening only to themselves and ignoring everyone else. Then, of course, it is not a real conversation at all. As in all conversations, it is not the case that everyone can make an equal, and important, contribution. Most philosophy is of minor significance, pedantic, trivial, confused. This is why philosophy departments need wastepaper baskets!

Sometimes, we read the older philosophers so as to measure how far we have moved on and in order to understand how a particular discussion began and grew. It is easier to understand the present state of any topic within philosophy when we know how and why it has developed. Sometimes, because progress is never smooth, we read the older philosophers in order to see that, in some respects, we are not moving on and we may even be moving backwards. For example, I have tried to show that some of our contemporary preoccupation with individual development may be naïve and unsophisticated when compared with, for example, Greek and later humanist ideas about personal identity and development.

It is immensely difficult to evolve new and important insights in philosophy. I certainly do not claim to have done so in these pages. But the thoughts developed by my 'Top 30' seem to be worthy of the attention of the counselling and other care professions. If I have succeeded at all, I will have shown you some of the interconnections, the relevance, the patterns and the attraction of these ideas. I have attempted, and I hope succeeded, in summarising some complicated concepts in accessible language without crushing too many of the subtleties.

If we do not look systematically at the underpinning philosophies available to us, then one or other of these will seep in on us, and determine the way in which we think, and do not think, about the practice of care and attention. For example in a consumerist society, market values can creep up on the way some counsellors think about people. They talk of building 'skills portfolios', developing confidence and self-esteem as though we were objects and products to be trained, groomed and promoted. Consumer values and the competitive marketplace also underlie the 'marketing' of 'counselling', 'counselling psychology' and psychotherapy, as each tries to protect its market share by promoting product differentiation. Market competition also underlies the current fetish to 'process', 'register' and 'accredit' healers. It leads almost everyone to assume blindly, despite all contrary evidence, that human interaction and our struggles to make sense of existence can be 'serviced' via a production line of training and supervision through 'levels' of competence and skill. Both Marxist and existential ideas would provide useful antidotes to this contemporary all-embracing delusion.

It is impossible to think and see independently of philosophy. The philosophy we adopt provides the building blocks, and the underlying organisation, to the very manner in which we perceive and reflect. However, the larger and more all embracing a philosophy becomes the more difficult it is to detect. When it gains hegemony in a society it can become completely invisible. It then provides the only way in which we can think about our world and ourselves. This is one reason why I have found it so important to introduce a number of strange and 'alien' thinkers within these chapters. Only by travelling in imagination to 'Martian' or 'lunar' philosophies, do you get a chance to see what is currently commonplace, overwhelming, but invisible, on earth.

Consequently, when people say that they do not know any philosophy, what is really meant is that they know only one philosophy, but they have no means of locating or assessing it. As a result, it structures everything they do and care about. It also prevents them from considering alternatives or placing immediate preoccupations into a larger perspective.

Each of these chapters has its own conclusions, so there should not be much need to labour the general points I have made here. But I will risk one very large generalisation: The (fifteenth-century) Renaissance has been defined as a revival in interest in classical learning and values after a long period of cultural stagnation. 'Renaissance man'[2] believed in himself, in his ability to learn, to take a full, rounded, integrated, intelligent view of his life and opportunities. Here was to be an end to superstition, penitence and pessimism. The (believed in) interconnections between all areas of knowledge and creative expression were to be explored and celebrated. Human beings had dignity. Progress was not guaranteed, as Sophocles made clear. But the heroic spirit sought to attempt to make progress anyway. The goodness in people deserved celebration;[3] but we also needed to deal intelligently with human duplicity.[4]

This optimistic and energetic spirit, in its seventeenth- and eighteenth-century manifestations, was described as the 'Enlightenment' by historian metanarrators. Once again the message was that we could use our own brains to make sense of existence, rather than merely searching for, and interpreting, truth in so-called 'sacred' texts. We could gain an overall picture of the workings and interconnections of nature and humanity. The world was coherent and orderly and if we took a methodical, creative and disciplined approach to it we could unravel its underlying *logos*. We could thereby learn to co-operate, become more free and live more happy and fulfilled lives.

As we have seen, subsequent critics from the nineteenth century onwards have asked whether our ideals of rationality and progress are not themselves narrow, oppressive, irrational or simply untrue. Romanticism in the arts saw many constructions of 'reason' as dead, mechanical and detached from the underlying truth of the human spirit. Rousseau, Schopenhauer, Kierkegaard, Marx, Nietzsche and Freud, have each, in different ways, shown how there is no case for naïve optimism concerning the likely success of 'reasonable', enlightened, humanist progress and co-operation.

But should we, therefore, abandon the entire humanist project altogether? The Greeks, and their Renaissance and Enlightenment admirers, were well aware that progress was not easy either to define or achieve. But they subscribed to a heroic and robust mentality that rose to, rather than shrinking before, the challenges of our ordinary, limited and fallible humanity. Any philosophy that encourages us to wallow in our own private experience, our latent despair, our pessimism concerning the difficulties of understanding and relating to ourselves and others, is not likely to be of much use to us. If such pessimism has a future it will be because we allow ourselves to slip into another 'Dark Age' of doubt, despondency and disillusion. Then, perhaps, the humanist agenda, in all its complexities, uncertainties and underlying faith and hope, will have to be rediscovered yet again. If this book serves any important purpose it will be because it provides one tiny contribution in helping to keep humanism alive and well without being complacent about its difficulties, complexities and limitations.

Another fundamental concern in many of these chapters has been the question of describing, respecting and valuing the 'spiritual' dimensions of human existence. If humanism is to have a future perhaps it needs to avoid an overtly mechanistic, narrowly rationalistic and entirely secular view of existence? Can we incorporate a vision of enchantment without becoming irrational, dogmatic or superstitious? Can we engage with the fantastic without wallowing in fantasy? Can romantic emotion and classical reason be integrated into a larger, more all-embracing apprehension of the universe? My own feeling is that they can, which may take me a long way from postmodern fragmentalism. Neither do I think that such integration requires an easy consensus, or 'final synthesis'. I persist in the felt sense that spirituality does not have to edge us towards escapism, dogmatic theology or irrationalism. Science itself, I would suggest, leads us to a sense of awe, wonder, tentative enquiry and a basic faith that 'grand narratives' are possible and that, however many perspectives we may take on it, there is one universe to be shared rather than endless incommensurable private worlds.

Classical liberal humanism, I am convinced, is much to be preferred to postmodern solipsism and, at its best, incorporates rather than rejects a romantic spirit. Sadly, such humanism can disintegrate into a disenchanting, lifeless individual and amoral consumerism. Happily, liberal humanism can be enlivened with a social and spiritual awareness that does not presuppose dogma, superstition or vague and shallow sentiment. Therefore, future 'big names' will be so precisely because they get serious about, and make a significant contribution towards, the task of putting the spirit and romance back into the classical humanist agenda.

I have assembled batteries of questions and exercises that relate a particular philosophical perspective to the everyday practice and concerns of anyone trying to help make sense of the human predicament. I hope that they provide their own explanation and justification and that sufficient links are established between chapters to at least whet readers' appetites.

Philosophy is what we all end up doing, as youngsters, when we persist in asking awkward questions about the answers we have just been given. There are too many questions about the nature, insights and limitations of professional care and empathy that have been ignored for too long. I hope that these pages will have helped readers clarify many of these questions while also suggesting a wide variety of routes along which these fundamental concerns can be usefully and constructively explored.

Of course, there are times when the process of questioning itself becomes a cowardly substitute for action. The act of repeatedly asking why can disengage us from committed involvement. Often, as Heidegger observed, the meaning is found in the doing. Therefore if we stop doing and go on and on asking what we should do and why we should do it we may, because of this very process of questioning, end up feeling that everything is pointless, arbitrary and absurd. This was the experience of Sartre's Roquetin.

After a sustained and insistent questioning of every answer, cracks may appear in the boundaries of our universe. A cold shaft of meaninglessness, emptiness, nothingness may come pouring in. In repeatedly asking why, we may disengage ourselves from the activity and discourse that provide the answer. It can be a vicious spiral, well known to those susceptible to depression. We can always step outside any system of meaning and ask why. This provides us with new opportunities and threats. Similarly our capacity to be self-aware can take us outside whatever construct of identity we previously inhabited. This 'going beyond' the self we thought we knew is well understood within varieties of oriental philosophy. This self, as being-*towards*, has also been explored within existential philosophy, as we have seen. I think is constitutes a crucial form of progress in our understanding of identity and it deserves to be more widely understood.

Meaning comes from action and commitment. The very process of questioning meaning disengages us from such action and may therefore pitch us into a felt sense of meaninglessness. But human progress, however defined, requires that meanings and understandings should be questioned if we are to find their limitations and improve on them. A balance has to be found, within any area of human activity, between questioning assumptions and acting on them. In my opinion, within the present mushrooming growth of the psychotherapies and other care programmes, there is too much attention to actions and technique, and not enough concern to examine presuppositions and their underlying philosophy.

In my efforts to explain the ideas of, and the relations between, these philosophers, I hear a symphony not a cacophony. I have sought to present something of their song. As my word ceiling looms, I hope that some of this music of the intellect has reached you. Above all, I hope it will inspire you to question and explore further some of the issues raised, for yourself.

Notes

1. Heidegger worked with Boss in applying his philosophy to psychotherapy but Sartre, without question, has been more generally influential. Heidegger's involvement with Nazism, not surprisingly, did great damage to his reputation.
2. Equal opportunities policy in fifteenth-century Europe does not appear to have paid much attention to women.
3. As, for example, Erasmus made clear in *In Praise of Folly*, 1509.
4. As we have seen, for example, in Macchiavelli's *The Prince*, 1513.

Appendix

Applied Philosophy – Organisations

This book has argued that philosophy, at its best, informs, underpins, guides and constrains all practice, in therapy as elsewhere. Words and theories that do not point to action and commitment become drained of meaning. Conversely, actions divorced from theory lack wisdom or perspective. Philosophy, then, is a foundation and framework to all therapy and not just a particular kind of therapy. The following list of contacts will, however, put you in touch with practitioners explicitly concerned with integrating philosophy within the practice of counselling and the psychotherapy.

UK

Society of Consultant Philosophers
The Old School Centre, Newport, Pembs SA42 0TS

Anglo-American Society for Philosophical Practice (AASPP)
School of Psychotherapy & Counselling
Regent's College
Inner Circle, Regent's Park
London NW1 4NS

USA

American Society for Philosophy, Counselling and Psychotherapy (ASPCP)
37 Parker Drive
Morris Plains, NJ 07950
ASPCP Web Site: http://www.aspcp.org

American Philosophical Practitioners Association (APPA)
The City College of New York
137th St. at Convent Avenue
New York, NY 10031
Website: http://www.appa.edu

Canada

Canadian Society for Philosophical Practice
473 Besserer Street
Ottawa, Ontario K1N 6C2

Germany

International Society for Philosophical Practice
Hermann-Loens-Str. 56c
D-51469 Bergisch Gladbach
Germany

Netherlands

Dutch Society for Philosophical Practice (VFP)
E. Schilderinkstraat 80
7002 JH Doetinchem
Netherlands

Norway

Norwegian Society for Philosophical Practice
Cappelens vei 19c
1162 Oslo
Norway
Website: http://home.c2i.net/aholt/e-nsfp.htm

Israel

Israel Society for Philosophical Inquiry
Horkania 23, Apt. 2
Jerusalem 93305
Website: http//www.geocities.com/Athens/Forum/5914

Index

A

a priori, 198
Adler, 301
Alexander the Great, 39
Amnesty International, 78
analytic, 198
Anglo-Saxon empiricism, 220
Anglo-Saxon philosophy, 315,
 320, 323, 357, 359
Aquinas, Thomas, St, 81, 106
Aristotle, 36, 96, 213, 294, 298
Arnold, M. 20, 21
Assagioli, R. 223
atomism, 215, 222, 293
Auden, W.H. 287
Augustine, 131, 233, 234
Auxiliary, 34

B

Bach, 6
Balkans, 116, 151
barbarian, 52
Basho, 44
Bentham, J. 238, 246
Berkeley, 136
Boadicea, 67
bodily 'humours', 13
Bosanquet, B. 217, 223
Bradley, F. 217, 223
British Association for
 Counselling, 151, 208, 210

Buddhism, 15, 76, 138, 146,
 228, 280

C

California, 68
Calvin, 110, 112
Calvinism, 241
Capitalism, 267, 268, 269, 272
Carnegie, D. 348
Carroll, L. 361
Charles V, 109
Christ, 228
Christianity, 363
Chrysippus, 66
civil service, 71
cogito ergo sum, 129
Coleridge, 145
Communism, 36, 262, 269, 270,
 271, 272, 364
'counselling psychology', 370

D

Darwin, 278
deconstructionism, 359
Democritus, 13
Derrida, J. 357, 359
Descartes, 138, 140, 144, 152,
 153, 154, 158, 164, 165, 166,
 208, 250, 292, 327, 342, 355,
 359, 369
Diogenes Laertius, 57

Disraeli, 104
duty, 71

E
education, 41
Einstein, 48, 161, 314, 322, 329
Ellis, A. 73
Empedocles, 13
empiricism, 148
Engels, 263, 273
Enlightenment, 359, 361, 371
Epictetus, 59, 63, 67, 68, 69, 71, 72
Erasmus, 111
evil, 56, 57
existentialism, 249, 257, 258, 259, 260, 328, 341, 346, 352, 354, 355, 357, 369, 371

F
false consciousness, 269, 271, 272
Faust, 279
Feynman, R. 219
Fliess, W. 289
four elements, 13, 14
Frederick of Saxony, 109
Frege, 316
Freud, S. 5, 12, 17, 18, 19, 22, 232, 233, 236, 301, 349, 352, 363, 368, 372

G
general will, 192
gnosticism, 305
Goethe, 145
Guardian, 34
Gulf War, 101

H
Handel, 311
happiness, 40
Hardy, T. 233
Hegel, 14, 136, 257, 258, 260, 315, 341

Heidegger, M. 11, 132, 136, 260, 319, 321, 341, 342, 343, 345, 349, 351, 354, 355, 369, 373
Heraclitus, 336, 343
Hinduism, 15, 138, 146, 161, 228, 234, 236
Hippocrates, 13
Hobbes, 149, 150, 294
honour, 46, 49, 53, 54, 71
Hume, 10, 154, 197, 198, 199, 200, 202, 203, 215, 221, 292, 293, 317, 357, 359

I
idealism, 222, 225
inequality, 48
Innocent I, 235
Islam, 39, 96, 368

J
Jagger, M. 210
Jesus, 112
Jung, 146, 291

K
Kant, 10, 179, 211, 226, 228, 234, 305, 336
Keynes, J.M. 315
Kierkegaard, 91, 341, 342, 354, 360, 369, 372

L
Leibniz, 136, 140, 144, 146, 148, 155, 198, 199, 225, 226
Levi-Strauss, C. 359
liberal education, 36
liberal humanism, 356, 364, 373
Locke, 10, 120, 165, 166, 167, 169, 170, 172, 174, 193, 197, 292, 299, 359
'logos', 3
Lucretius, 55
Lyotard, F. 361

M

Machiavelli, 115, 266, 282, 355
Manichaeism, 309
Mann, T. 233
Marcus Aurelius, 63, 67
market economy, 35
Marx, 191, 194, 280, 286, 360
Marxism, 346, 351, 356, 363, 371
mechanism, 215
Mercedes, 184
Methodism, 112
middle class, 51
Mill, 120, 193, 207, 211, 251,
    266, 279, 280, 281, 286, 359
monads, 158, 159, 160, 161,
    162, 163
Monk, R. 313
Morris, W. 191
Mother Courage, 69
Mount Olympus, 144
mysticism, 296

N

Napoleon, 282
Nazism, 280, 284
Nero, 67
Newton, 3, 48, 155, 161, 176, 234
Nietzsche, F. 69, 86, 233, 259,
    260, 302, 303, 304, 306, 310,
    334, 338, 341, 342, 354, 360,
    369, 372
noumena, 226

O

O'Neill, J. 365
Oedipus, 17, 18, 19, 20, 21
orient, 13, 49, 146, 303
oriental philosophy, 374

P

Pauli, W. 305
Pax Americana, 118
Pelagius, 234
phenomena, 226

Plato, 7, 39, 41, 42, 45, 46, 50,
    53, 54, 130, 183, 225, 228,
    294, 298
Pope Leo XIII, 90
post-modernism, 357
pride, 46
primary qualities, 154
Protestantism, 109
psychoanalysis, 110, 356, 363
psychodynamic therapy, 110
Pythagoras, 18

Q

quantum theory, 215
quietism, 65

R

rationalism, 145
Reformation, 93, 112, 113
relativity theory, 215
Renaissance, 112, 365, 371
Robinson Crusoe, 188
Rogers, C. 5, 12, 195
romanticism, 144, 145, 183, 279,
    285
Roquetin, Antoine, 353
Rousseau, 281, 294, 296, 369,
    372
Royalist, 116
Russell, B. 43, 162, 218, 315,
    316, 317, 318
Russia, 116, 272

S

Sarte, 369
Sartre, 136, 204, 257, 259, 260,
    356, 357, 373
scholasticism, 91
Schopenhauer, 218, 250, 278,
    280, 295, 317, 342, 360, 372
secondary qualities, 154
Seneca, 67
shopping, 360, 361
Smith, A. 268
Socialism, 268, 364

Socrates, 12, 176, 181, 209, 289, 313, 320
Soloman, 49
Sophocles, 371
space, 199
Spinoza, 136, 158
Spock, Dr 182
St Petersburg, 68
Stoicism, 180, 369
structuralism, 359
survivalism, 65
synthetic (truth), 198
synthetic a priori, 198

T
Tacitus, 67
Thatcher, M. 353
'The Apostles', 315
'third way', 364
Thrasymachus, 278
three elements, 30
time, 199
Titanic, 123
tradesmen, 34, 35
Trafalgar, 349
Turing, A. 134

U
US Constitution, 149
ubermensch, 275, 276, 284

unconditional self-acceptance, 74
universals, 41
utilitarianism, 207, 208, 209, 210, 211, 212, 285, 293

V
van Deurzen, 259
van Deurzen-Smith, 19
Vinci, L. da, 293
Voltaire, 162

W
Wagner, R. 233
Watts, A. 258
Waterloo, 349
Wayne, J. 69, 281
Whitehead, A.N. 24
Wilbur, K. 218, 223, 224

Y
yoga, 138, 296

Z
Zen, 347
Zeno, 63
Zwingli, 110